The Complete
Scribes of
Speculative Fiction

The Complete *Scribes* of Speculative Fiction

A COLLECTION OF INTERVIEWS

Conducted by

Cristopher DeRose

BearManor Media
2018

The Complete Scribes of Speculative Fiction

© 2018 Cristopher DeRose

All Rights Reserved.

No part of this book may be reproduced in any form or by any means, electronic, mechanical, digital, photocopying, or recording, except for in the inclusion of a review, without permission in writing from the publisher

For information, address:

BearManor Media
P. O. Box 71426
Albany, GA 31708

bearmanormedia.com

Typesetting and layout by John Teehan

Published in the USA by BearManor Media

ISBN—978-1-62933-318-2

With this latest (and my first hardcover) edition, I feel I should give thanks where thanks is either due, or perhaps way overdue.

I'd like to thank my Editor, Ben Ohmart, for believing in me and this project, and exhibiting patience of nearly paranormal proportions over the past… wow, several years now.

Thanks must also go to my collaborators, Michael McCarty and Ryan Grable. Their help has been more significant than represented here and they helped to make the road a bit less bumpy for this author.

Bruce S. Larson (another collaborator!) must also be thanked for his invaluably assistance in help make this come to fruition, even to the extent of submitting himself to an interview, which is above and beyond the call of duty.

Scott Edelman, for his constant support and humor during the SyFy Channel days. Scott, I owe you. I don't know what, exactly, but I do owe you.

Obviously, thanks to everyone who saw me fit enough to endure subjecting themselves to my questions over the past… sixteen or so years?

And thanks to all those who follow/friend me on Facebook or Instagram (cristopher_derose). It's nice to know you're out there.

&

I would be remiss if I did not dedicate this to my boy, Ryan, a worldly sixteen years old and an absolute wonder and blessing in my life.

I love you, Little Bear.

Table of Contents

Always Eat Dessert First 1
    Introduction by Scott Edelman

Briane Keene 3
Ben Bova 9
David Brin 15
Bruce Balfour 25
Lois McMaster Bujold 39
Jeanne Cavelos 47
Max Allan Collins 75
Christopher Golden 81
Eduardo Sanchez 89
Gregory Maguire 125
Laurell K. Hamilton 129
Jane Espenson 137
Michael McCarty 141
Orson Scott Card 145
Jerry Pournelle 153
Kristine Kathryn Rusch 177
Sephera Giron 181
Alan Dean Foster 191

Jack Vance	197
Wil McCarthy	207
Chelsea Quinn Yarbro	213
Yvonne Navarro	219
David J. Schow	225
Elaine Cunningham	229
P. N. Elrod	235
Jasper Fforde	241
Joe R. Lansdale	249
Geoffrey A. Landis	255
Mark McLaughlin	261
Eric Van Lustbader	267
Peter S. Beagle	273
Michael McCarty & Mark McLaughlin	279
Ray Manzarek	289
Piers Anthony	295
Steven Erikson	299
Raymond Benson	305
Weston Ochse	311
Jack Ketchum	317
Raymond Feist	321
Scott Leberecht, Ed Sanchez, & Matt Compton	325
Joe Schreiber	331
Caitlin R. Kiernan	335
William Nolan	341

Nancy Holder	345
Tad Williams	349
Kathe Koja	353
Tom Piccirilli	359
Kevin J. Anderson	365
Storm Constantine	371
Darrell Schweitzer	377
Brian Hodge	383
Paul Di Filippo	393
Steve Rasnic Tem	399
Norman Prentiss	409
Chet Williamson	413
Nancy Kress	419
Mike Resnick	423
Donna Burgess	429
Roger Price	433
Charles De Lint	439
Sandy DeLuca	443
Nancy Kilpatrick	447
Megan Hart	453
Bruce S. Larson	457
Jay Wilburn	467
Richard Chizmar	473
Rob E. Boley	477

Always Eat Dessert First

BY SCOTT EDELMAN

I HAVE A CONFESSION TO MAKE—as books and magazines make their way into my house, I always read the non-fiction first.

The reason I call it a confession is because, well, aren't we supposed to appreciate the art more than prose that seeks to explain, dissect, and interpret it? And I *do* value the novel and short story, I really do. But somehow, I can't resist letter columns, editorials, essays, memoirs, anything that will take me behind the scenes and let me see how the literature I love was made.

These things are both my appetizer and dessert, and though fiction will always be the main course, there's something addictive about the forms that both prepare and reward our literary palates.

And as for interviews…don't get me started on interviews.

(Actually, I do have to get started on interviews. Isn't that why we're both here?)

They say you're never supposed to see sausage or politics being made, because it will only disappoint. Or disgust. But when it comes to seeing how science fiction, fantasy and horror are made, I believe crawling into the minds of the creators can only make our experience richer.

Which brings us to Cristopher DeRose's wonderful collection of interviews, *Scribes of Speculative Fiction*, which surprised me in a way I didn't expect.

It turns out I actually know twenty-two of the people interviewed in these pages you're about to read, know them not just from their works, but as people, in the flesh, and I still learned something new about each one of them. And if that can happen to me, imagine how much more valuable this book will be to most of you, who will likely know the subjects (unless you're very lucky) only as words on a page.

For example—

I've known Geoffrey Landis for about 25 years, we've critiqued each other's stories, stayed in each other's homes, but this is the first time I've heard of the children's book that changed his life.

And I know Wil McCarthy, I've published him, he's published me, and yet I never knew that the lesson he took away from editing an anthology was, "Never edit an anthology."

As for Jeanne Cavelos, I've known equally as long, and even taught at her Odyssey Workshop, but didn't know until now what preshredded pants have to do with publishing trends (nor did I know her favorite brand of chocolate.)

During a fun and fruitful weekend with this book, I learned things I never knew before about all of these people. Cristopher managed to make strangers feel like friends, and friends feel like strangers.

Get ready to learn some things you didn't know about people who—whether you already know them of not—you'll want to know better.

And I can think of no better compliment for a collection of interviews than that.

BRIAN KEENE

READERS OF BRIAN KEENE always know when they're reading the work of the man behind such works as *Fear Of Gravity* (Delirium Books), *The Rise And Fall Of Babylon* (with John Urbancik, Earthling Publications), and *No Rest At All* (Delirium Books) because they recognize the familiar urge to pick themselves up and dust themselves off. Longtime readers of Brian's know this feeling, as they remember it well from his *Hail, Saten* column in his *Jobs In Hell*, a publication that won the Stoker in 2001.

They always come back for more.

Whether for his editing skills exhibited for horrorfind.com, or the pair of its *Best Of* collections, or his imagination that leads readers by the hand (or throat, in some cases) into stories like his latest, the zombie thriller *The Rising*. It was during a break in his promotion of which this interview took place.

Brian's website, www.briankeene.com, contains such helpful things as household decorating tips and favorite recipes.

As an outspoken voice in contemporary speculative fiction, do you feel that your opinions have had either a more negative or positive effect on the degree of your success? Or has it not mattered at all?

To some extent, I think it's been positive—but on a small scale. It's certainly got me noticed among my peers; fellow authors, editors, and publishers. But on a larger scale, I don't think it's had much of an impact. Your average horror fiction fan doesn't care what their favorite author's thoughts are on the HWA or which publisher is ripping off whom. They just want a good story—something they can lose themselves in for a while.

How do you feel about the demise of Jobs In Hell?

Truthfully? I'm ambivalent about it. I'd sold it to Kelly Laymon almost a year and a half before its demise, so I wasn't involved with it at all during the final era. Kelly did a great job, but we had different visions during our respective turns at the wheel. Her version of the newsletter was much different than mine. In many ways, it ended for me when I stepped down and turned it over to her.

How has being a parent affected the way you view the world of the horror genre, and being a writer in that genre?

I don't think you can truly know horror until you become a parent. It comes with those nights when your baby won't stop crying and you wonder if something's wrong. Or when your child is playing ball in the yard and you hear the sudden screech of tires out front. Or when they get their license and aren't home by their curfew. These are truly terrifying moments—human moments.

It's a theme that shows up a lot in my fiction. 'Lest Ye Become' and 'A Darker Shade of Winter', both from *No Rest At All*, were based on parental fears; the first was school shootings and the second was bullying. I used it to a greater extent in *The Rising*. Take away the zombies and the post-apocalyptic elements, and it becomes a novel about a divorced dad searching for his son. I've known a bit about that.

What level of success would you like to achieve?

Well, I'm writing professionally, meaning full-time. I always thought this was the level I'd be happy at. Of course, I didn't realize how little money is involved [laughs]. Seriously, I'm comfortable where I'm at. I make up stories and write them down and people seem to enjoy those stories. They write me nice letters and buy the books and help my wife and I make the mortgage payments. I don't think I can ask for anything else—except maybe an affordable health insurance plan.

It's been put that during the Universal Horror days, the appeal came from audiences wanting to escape from the real world. Are we seeing the same thing these days?

Definitely. Our daily lives are filled with very real monsters. We've got monsters flying airplanes into buildings and abducting eleven-year-old girls from behind car washes and butchering their pregnant wives and molesting little kids. These are dark times we live in, and everybody, regardless of race, creed, or religion, fells it in the air. Something's not right. Something is wrong. The center cannot hold. People are scared of everyday life, and it's good to curl up with a make believe monster, rather than the one outside your door.

As the horror genre progresses, we still can find just as many stories involving the traditional standbys such as vampires and zombies and the like, but with contemporary twists. Why do you think this is the case, rather than 'New' monsters being created with equal fervor?

Well, I do think there are new monsters being created. Take Richard Laymon's *Beast House* or some of Edward Lee's and Michael Laimo's recent creations, or the monsters from Tim Lebbon's *White*. But the old-standbys work, you know? Down through the history of the genre, each generation has put their stamp on them. Take vampires for example. Bram Stoker gave us his vision. Stephen King knocked it on its ear. Anne Rice made them cuddly and angst filled. Then Simon Clark came along and made them scary again. But each author broadened the horizons for what had come before.

Using The Rising *as an example, you use gore to great effect, but do not rely on it. Is there a point in editing when you ask 'Is this too much?'*

There's a scene in the book where a woman who was pregnant at the time of her death comes back as a zombie. Obviously, the fetus is now a zombie too. It proceeds to chew its way out of her womb. I almost balked at that scene—but it was just too much fun not to include.

You've got to remember, I came of age reading Skipp & Spector, David Schow, Ed Lee, Jack Ketchum, Richard Laymon, etc. and watching movies like *Evil Dead*, *Phantasm*, and Romero's trilogy. It's rare that I say 'This is going too far.' The important thing is that there has to be a story somewhere in all that grue. It's like the old Eddie Murphy routine: Bill Cosby takes him to task for cursing on stage, and Eddie says "It's not like I just get on stage and say 'Fuck, Shit, Bitch, Damn.' There's jokes in between the curse words."

Were you concerned with any comparisons that might have come up between The Rising *and the film* 28 Days Later *in terms of the military's involvement?*

[Laughs] Oh hell yes. The hardcover edition of *The Rising* came out about two months before the release of *28 Days Later*. Geoff Cooper and myself took our significant others to see the movie opening weekend. I loved the film, but I was mortified the whole time. Strong black female lead. Similar military plot. The zombies even had some of the same traits. Since the hardcover was a limited edition, I knew most people hadn't read it. But when the paperback came out in January of this year, the comparisons started right away. What I'm happy about is that most people seem to prefer the book over the movie—which really makes my head swell, because I thought the movie was brilliant!

Why do you use pop culture references such as Cheerios in your stories?

Because Cheerios paid me a lot of money for that product placement. No, I'm kidding of course. I guess it's to ground the story in reality. If I have a kid watching cartoons vs. a kid watching *Dragonball Z*, on a subconscious level, the reader is going to identify with the second example much quicker than the first.

What led to the decision to use a cliffhanger ending in The Rising?

The million-dollar question, and the one *everybody* is asking. First off, if you read the book carefully, it's not a cliffhanger. There are hints as to Jim and Danny's final fate from early on. It's not so much a cliffhanger as it is just fucking dark and unhappy. People don't do unhappy endings anymore. I wanted a lady or the tiger style ending. I wanted the ending to be just as bleak and unsettling as it is. Remember the ending of John Carpenter's *The Thing*? Kurt Russell and Keith David are about to freeze to death and one of them may be infected and then suddenly the credits roll! It was up to the viewer to decide what happened next. That's what I wanted to do.

But I guess I blew it. For the entire novel, I showed everything up close and personal. When it came to the end, I hinted at it instead. Some readers enjoyed that ending and some didn't. But in either case, everybody, and I mean everybody—editors, publishers, and fans—are demanding a sequel. First thing both of my editors asked me was 'What happens in the sequel?' 'What sequel?' I said.

So now I gotta write a sequel, and I'll be starting that as soon as I finish my current novel.

In the case of writers like Stephen King, we've seen the very fanbase that built him start to tear him down over the past years. Do you feel that's indicative of his success, or of the genre he writes in?

I feel it's indicative of human beings. We love to destroy our heroes. We build them up and then tear them down—especially in the media. Kennedy. Elvis. Pete Rose. Even poor old Ozzy Osbourne.

Do I think he's on top of his game? No. *Dreamcatcher* and *From A Buick Eight* are good novels, but they don't compare to *Christine* or *The Stand*. Some of that is natural. Our muses change as we get older. And some of it is his success. *Insomnia* could have been a decent book if they'd taken out about 200,000 words. But what editor in the world is going to have the balls to suggest changes to Stephen King?

Is your readership composed of more writers than 'civilians,' for want of a better word? Does such a thing matter?

When I was first starting out, it was more writers. These days, it's civilians. It definitely matters. You'll never expand as an author if it's only the same 300 fellow writers buying your work. But when you're first starting out, especially if you're in the small press, that's just how it happens. I'm grateful to both audiences though. I don't care who you are, author or steel-mill worker or goth chick working at the record store. If I wrote something and you enjoyed it, then I'm indebted to you. Because without that, there's no point.

BEN BOVA

DR. BEN BOVA'S WORK has stretched across 120 fiction and nonfiction books since 1959. In that span, he has won several prestigious awards for his work, become President Emeritus of the National Space Society and received the John W. Campbell Award for Best Novel of the Year (*Titan*, 2006). In 2008, Dr. Bova was awarded both the Robert A. Heinlein Award for his 'Outstanding body of work in the field of literature' and the First Annual Ben Bova Award 'For Outstanding Achievement in Science Fiction Literature.'

Dr. Bova has also become known as a teacher, having received his Doctorate in Education from California Coast University, a Master of Arts Degree in Communications from the State University of New York at Albany and a Bachelor's Degree in Journalism from Temple University. He has taught Science Fiction at Harvard and the Hayden Planetarium and is a regular on the lecture circuit regarding such topics as human immortality, space exploration, and the craft of writing.

He was the Editorial Director of *Analog* and *Omni* and has won the Hugo for Best Professional Editor no less than six times. His website is at benbova.com

Which came first for you, an interest in Science Fiction or one in science?

I became interested in astronomy first, after a class trip to the Fels Planetarium when I was about 10 years old. That led to an interest in astronautics (going to the Moon was considered a fantasy in 1942) and then to science fiction.

How do you feel about human cloning? Is it a case of 'Just because you can doesn't mean you should?'

I think reproductive cloning could be important to people who cannot have children any other way, which is a very tiny percentage of the human race. Therapeutic cloning, however, could become a major medical benefit for almost everyone.

With some of the research into cloning involving the use of human fetal tissue, is cloning ethical?

Yes. The fetal tissue used in such research would never develop into a viable human being.

Jerry Pournelle told me that it's difficult to write SF these days because it's harder to tell what the future is going to look like than it was when he started writing. Do you agree, and if so how do you overcome it?

I disagree. In the first place, we have much more detailed information about scientific research to use as material. For example, we've learned more about the bodies of the solar system since space exploration began than ever before. In the past ten years our concepts of the possibilities of extraterrestrial life have enlarged tremendously, thanks to the discovery of extremophile organisms on Earth. Politically and socially, we have a much more chaotic situation than we did during the decades of the Cold War, but a student of history can see parallels with earlier eras that could be helpful in creating future scenarios. Besides, if it's harder to tell what the future will be like, that gives the science fiction writer *more* scope for his imagination, not less.

Has contemporary SF films and TV had an adverse effect on SF prose and how it is viewed?

I think 'Sci-Fi' films and TV shows convince most of the public that science fiction is for kids, at best. It keeps them from looking into serious science fiction published in books and magazines. It's been this way for generations. You can count the number of serious science fiction films on your fingers.

What do you consider to be serious SF films?

The 1950 British comedy, *The Man In The White Suit*, was a true science fiction film, in that it dealt with the impact of a new scientific discovery upon the lives of the people and the society in which they lived. Kubrick's *2001: A Space Odyssey* was motion-picture making at its best, in my opinion. *Day The Earth Stood Still*. Hawks' *The Thing*. The more recent *Space Cowboys*. And *Galaxy Quest* was a hoot.

The Story Of Light is written to where a casual reader of science fact isn't lost or talked down to. How did you go about achieving that?

Practice it for a few decades. And use writers such as Isaac Asimov and L. Sprague de Camp as your models.

What was the biggest challenge in writing The Story Of Light?

The enormity of the subject matter. I had to choose which areas I would emphasize very carefully. Organization was another major challenge. Once I hit on the idea of beginning—and ending—the book with "Let there be light," the organizational problems were solved.

What led to your writing Return To Mars?

The story of Jamie Waterman was obviously not finished at the end of the novel *Mars*. It's still not finished; some day I'll write a third novel about him.

What was the inspiration behind the creation of Leviathan in Jupiter?

Big planet, big ocean, big critters. The idea of a large-sized creature being composed of a colony of semi-independent parts was my stab at creating a truly alien biology.

Will there be, for instance, a Mercury?

Although I don't intend to write a novel for each planet of the solar system, I am at this moment working on *Mercury*. Saito Yamagata is a major character in it.

What can you tell us about it?

Nothing. I don't talk about works in progress.

What led to the development of Dan Randolph?

That's a stumper. Most of the character development happens in my subconscious mind. I go around for years thinking about this character or another one. Then a story situation arises in which the character fits. When I needed a hard-driving space entrepreneur, Dan Randolph was there, ready and waiting. Incidentally, he will be the protagonist of a near-contemporary novel titled *Powersat*, which deals with Dan's start in the space industry business.

What defines a character?

Actually, a character's actions are driven by the conflicts within the character's soul. The consequences of those actions define the environment in which the character operates.

What is the basis you use for creating believable political situations in a futuristic setting?

Like Patrick Henry, I have but one lamp that guides my feet, and that is the lamp of experience. I know of no way of judging the future except by the past. History shows how humans have reacted in the past. They tend to react the same way, no matter what the era. The technology changes, but not the human spirit.

As humanity gets closer to living forever, do you think we will also gain the insight to answer the religious hurdles immortality will present?

Of course we will. Religious concepts change, slowly. Once religious believers thought it blasphemous to erect lightning rods or inoculate people against smallpox. The big thing is to avoid allowing religious fanatics to gain political power. Throughout history, when churches get their hands on political power, human freedom shrivels.

Will immortality have an effect on how people view the question as to whether to have children and when?

I should think so. If (or when) the death rate drops close to zero, we will have to lower the birth rate or suffer tremendous population growth, with all its attendant ills.

Will this be more of a social or political issue?

Yes. Different societies will deal with this problem in different ways. Authoritarian societies will write laws and enforce them. More democratic societies will probably depend on market forces and social mores.

Have private companies been a positive or a negative presence in our space program?

Private companies have been largely a neutral presence in the U.S. space program, and in the space programs of other nations. Government funding tends to drive out risk capital.

How did the end of the Cold War affect the space program?

It removed one of the political forces supporting space development. The much-publicized Space Race of the 1960s was a reflection of the deadlier race in the 1950s to develop ICBMs. The USSR's lofting of the first *Sputnik* proved to skeptics that the Russians had missiles that could drop hydrogen bombs on any city in the world. The USA rushed to catch up in the 1950s, and the 'missile gap' became a major political issue during the Presidential campaign of 1960. Kennedy's decision to go to the Moon was a political ploy, aimed at one-upping the Russians. Once it worked, there was no further political reason to push space development. It's a minor miracle that we have been able to carry out scientific explorations such as the *Voyager* and *Viking* programs. As long as space development depends on government money, the decisions will be made for political reasons, not scientific or economic reasons.

Do you think the international space station can function as well as intended?

Yes. And even better. But once again, the determining factor is the political decisions made by the governments supporting ISS.

Is there anything you'd like to add?

I think that the resources of energy and raw materials in the solar system are so abundant that each human being on Earth could become a multimillionaire if those resources were utilized properly and shared fairly. *The Grand Tour* novels are my attempt to show some of the possibilities of humankind's expansion through the solar system, and the reasons why this expansion is important to the human race's survival and prosperity.

DAVID BRIN

WITH HIS FIRST NOVEL *Sundiver*, now in its twelfth printing since 1980, and *Startide Rising*, his second, in its twenty-seventh, author/father/husband/scholar of science David Brin continues his stride through speculative fiction.

David has set his particular standard with dynamic collections and novels, not the least among them being the Nebula and Hugo-nominated *The Postman*, which went on to win the Locus award and become adapted to the big screen. Along with various other works, there would come to follow *The Uplift War* and *Earth*, both of which came away with being nominated for the Hugo Award. His latest novel, *Kiln People*, has also seen nomination for the award.

He has also touched on numerous scientific topics, among them xenology, for respected magazines such as Analog and Science Fiction Age and become a well-recognized voice in matters involving political and social concerns. Things from game design to academic papers has been visited by David at one point or another.

You can visit David at his website, www.davidbrin.com.

SF has been used to great effect by a number of authors to tell stories of human interest, and how one decision affects many, all the while making the 'Message' easier to digest. Sometimes, technology can take a backseat to this.

Only a fraction of SF authors have backgrounds in science. The topic that nearly all of us tend to read for pleasure is history. I often thought a better name for our genre might be Speculative History—extending the human saga in what Einstein called '*gedankeneksperimenten*', or collaborative thought-experiments, with the reader as an active partner. The future is one dimension for such experiments. Others may involve filling in a plausible past or an alternate present, as even Nabakov tried to do, in his novel *Ada*. In a general sense, SF is about expanding the available range of settings beyond the parochial present or familiar, freeing literature by extending the human story into realms of the possible. (Fantasy goes further, by diving into the improbable.) This happens to match what's done by the most recent and powerful portion of the human brain, the prefrontal lobes, or the 'lamps on the brow' that we use every day to explore our options, making up scenarios about tomorrow or the next day. Nothing could be more human. Yet some appear compelled to disparage SF with a caricature—that it consists solely of *Star Wars* pastiches in outer space. That's like claiming all detective films star Cheech and Chong. I have no idea why they do it.

Keeping that in mind, what is your take on cloning?

Cloning is as inevitable as flight or electricity. It needn't damn us. The key moral point is that a clone of any person will be a living, organic person, with his or her full suite of human rights. Duplicated genes won't change this, any more than we view one identical twin as a 'spare' of the other. If we make this stand, the straw-man moral quandaries—like rich people growing a fresh organs to harvest from a new self in the basement—nearly all vanish. That's not a spare. It's a child, imprisoned by a monster. *Glory Season* dealt with cloning in a far future. *Kiln People* is about something quite different—making truly disposable temporary copies of yourself. Fashioned of clay and lasting just a day, these dittos—or golems—aren't independent organic beings, but extensions of the original person, who redeposit their memories at day's end, offering people the convenience of being in two or more places at once. In other words, it's a busy person's wish-fantasy—with consequences.

Do you have a special approach to showing how people deal with change?

Well, I try to avoid putting the New Thing solely in the hands of some convenient, secretive elite—some dark cabal, government agency, corporation or mad scientist. These conventions have made for some cool stories—on their way to becoming terrible cliches. Instead, I like to imagine—what if everybody gets to share the New Thing? Bottle it. Give it to the masses. Not only is this more interesting, it's what we do.

What's on the horizon for Uplift?

Some readers want the same experience, over and over again. Fortunately, most of my fans say—'Take me somewhere I've never been before. Surprise me.' That's what they liked about *Stratide Rising* and *Earth*. Of course I love the *Uplift* Universe, and I do hope to get back to Tom & Creideiki. But there are other stories to tell along the way. Meanwhile, I've posted a few gifts for *Uplift* fans on my web site.

Did being born in Southern California have an effect on your writing?

Does the environment of your upbringing affect your writing? Science fiction flourishes under conditions like those I knew as a child—a mix of optimistic confidence and new kinds of abstract terror. One never imagined hunger or serious privation as a personal possibility, but witnessed them abundantly portrayed on TV. One saw unprecedented abundance, yet felt a daily burning in the lungs from smoggy poisons that filled the Los Angeles basin.

History books show that every other time in human history was more violent than my calm neighborhood, a safety that felt amazingly frail, balanced by an almost certain expectation that the world might, at any moment, fry in nuclear war.

These juxtapositions meant that I—and many other Californian writers—felt safe to discuss and explore flamboyantly, with total lack of personal inhibition. No threat of being burned at the stake! At the same time, we weren't calm. From a position of safety, we could stare in horror at a myriad failure modes, ten thousand ways that bright hopes can go bad. It taught the habit of always asking—'What if?'

Of course this wasn't the first time that paradox fostered exploration. In every culture, there have always been a few crazy children of the aristocracy willing to challenge convention. Only now those few numbered many, many thousands, and not just scions of the rich. Eccentricity has become the most admired personal trait—at least as portrayed in mass media. Something definitely changed, and Sci-Fi played a role.

Was being pigeonholed as a Science Fiction author ever a concern for you?

It can be mildly irksome. Those who desperately seek to build ghetto walls are often self-proclaimed literary mavens, who foster a reverence for "eternal human verities"—one of the creepiest phrases I can imagine.

It extols a belief that human nature is intrinsically static—that the same exact issues of personal angst and confusion, the same transfixing errors and terrors, must plague every generation. They even portray this as a *good* thing!

Don't get me wrong. Rich poignancy can be found in tales of tragedy and repeated-error. SF acknowledges the worth of great literature of the past, from Aristophenes to Melville, from Shakespeare to Shelley. But over the long run, *must* our children wrestle with exactly the same agonies that were portrayed by Euripides, Dostoyevsky and Fitzgerald? Isn't one purpose of a good story to convey empathy for another's pain, so well that others *don't* have to repeat it? Might children prove capable of learning from their parents' mistakes, growing larger and better as a result of our own efforts? If so, they will surely have *new* problems and face new challenges, just as we have taken on tasks our grandparents thought impossible.

Instead of 'eternal verities', science fiction is obsessed with notions of transformation and change. Exploring possibilities—good and bad—that lie ahead. What genre could be more relevant to the times we live in? But these very same notions terrify would-be arbiters of taste.

On a business-level, do you prefer dealing with publishing or filmmakers?

Hollywood has the advantage of being awash in filthy lucre—at one level or another, you can't resist. Publishing, in contrast, is relatively impoverished. The good side of this is that most of the huge egos get attracted to film. Publishing is much less avaricious and meddlesome. If you prove yourself as an author, you are left pretty much alone to create the exact story you want. Midway in-between these two is the world of graphic novels. My second—a huge, 144 page hardcover Graphic Novel titled *The Life Eaters* has been a fascinating collaboration with a great artist, Scott Hampton, plus letterer Todd Klein, as well as producers, art directors, etc. The scripting process—the give-and-take—has been very much like directing a movie. A low budget movie with gorgeous (though flat) special effects and the complex satisfactions that arise from participating in a real team effort.

I expect there will be more such intermediate art forms in years to come, till the whole notion of movie-making and storytelling will merge in really complicated ways.

How do you stay on top of current technology?

People send me stuff. I get invited to speak at scientific conferences. I'm asked to consult as a 'techno-futurist' by cutting-edge companies. In other words, I'm well paid to ask questions of the brightest minds around. (Dang, life is so unfair.) I keep recalling that, in other civilizations, they used to burn guys like me at the stake. Despite a myriad dangers and rampant stupidities, this is a bona fide renaissance.

What helps to inspire you?

The dour saga of human history. Every morning that I awaken and find that barbarians have not burned down my home and taken my children starts out a great day. Anyone who denies the palpable existence of progress knows nothing about life in the past.

But it's a frail new hope. It could crash if we are foolish or don't strive as hard as we can. I don't want my children to return to the caves. I want them flying around like gods, in a world that's been saved. Is that too much to ask?

The grouches and nihilists who carp endlessly, without seeing the progress, aren't trying to make things better. They are just enjoying the dopamine rush of resentment, without contributing anything constructive. Anyway, I had better be right. Because only a world filled with smart people will be able to handle the problems that lie ahead. Big problems, worthy earnest attention from a mighty civilization.

How much of your writing is instinct and how much is technical?

We are mixed creatures. I'm comfortable being a blending of ancient and modern. Late at night, I can pound the keys in a frenzy as vehement and emotional as Shelley, screaming at Heaven during a lightning storm. By day, the rational me then sighs, rolls up his sleeves and *edits* all that stuff. Skill and inspiration can work together. You gotta hope so.

Yes, I have written some pieces sharply critical of romanticism, with its arty emphasis on the personal, the metaphorical, the mysterious, nostalgic and feudal. I defend the maligned Enlightenment values of reason, pragmatism, open knowledge-sharing and egalitarian hope. The chief propagandists of our age—who are mostly romantics—seem bent on portraying these things as cold and sterile. But these values made a world in which the grandchildren of peasants can become billionaire movie directors while spinning fables of mind-blowing splendor.

In truth, we'll be poor creatures if we don't build lives that are rich in both sets of traits.

Did you consult with Benford and/or Bear when working on Foundation's Triumph*?*

We worked well together. More loosely than in a collaborative novel, but with attention to each others' plot concerns.

Of course we always remembered, the Foundation universe still belongs to Isaac Asimov. Isaac dropped plenty of hints, before he died. Hints that made it pretty clear, at least to Benford and Bear and me, where the next dilemma lay. Clues and 'hanging questions', using these as hooks for the next tale.

New books that take up this tradition should continue should keep asking more unanswered questions.

What matters is to stay enthralled, ready to be provoked by new thoughts. To keep pushing back the curtain a little bit, learning and discussing more about our future. Whether the topic is robots—how to keep them loyal and interesting—or almost any other dramatic device of science fiction... dramatic devices that may become tomorrow's world-wreckers, or household conveniences.

When starting out, did you mimic (for want of a better word) other writers in order to find your own voice?

One does this unconsciously, of course. I even recommend that beginners 'copy' deliberately so they can learn to recognize it, until finding their own voices.

But no, when I wrote *Sundiver* it was for the pure fun of combining science fiction with a murder mystery in which the body is dumped into the sun. When you are ready, you stand up and write what you want.

Was Foundation's Triumph *written with the intention of a book to follow, maybe between the Gaia and Foundations?*

Anything is possible. But there is so little time... and so many stories to tell. I implied that the core events of the Foundation universe fall into a certain time. I feel Isaac was heading there. Perhaps that part of the saga will be told.

Why was the history of the Interregnum between the Empires left incomplete?

To a careful reader, the story is now clear. *The First Foundation* has to prevail. Isaac's universe comes full circle, all the way back to his first love. He implied it all along.

In a different fashion, Earth *dealt with some of the same issues Le Guinn wrote about in* The Left Hand Of Darkness. *Was that intentional?*

I'd be interested in your thoughts on this. I had not seen a parallel.

Okay, at the risk of sounding like a thundering looney: Structures of government/political bodies, and the contradictions and compliments of same.

Well, I had LeGuinn more in mind when I wrote *Glory Season*. I wanted to give her—and the other pastoral-feminists—what they seem to want. Only *without* the typical and horribly-clichéd collapse of civilization that nearly always precedes most 'gender-bending' SF, a collapse that then justifies relentless anger. I wanted to see if a decent world by-of for women might be created *without* undue anger or dread, or convenient coincidence, but instead arising from calm and deliberate design by dedicated, skilled and determined radicals with a plan. I'm pleased to say that every woman scientist I know, who has read Glory Season, seems to like it. I sure appreciate and wanted that.

What made you decide to use press clippings between chapters in Earth?

Not just press clippings but also web pages! Back in 1989 mind you. (I was 'algored' a lot about that. But no, I did not invent the Web.) *Earth* was inspired by John Brunner's *Stand On Zanzibar*... and the novel USA by Dos Passos... in which the reader is offered total immersion into a world, not just a linear narrative thread. Brunner's book also did something I deeply admired. Instead of portraying yet another future in which the masses are like a throng of sheep, clueless and stupid, *Soz* suggested that we all may in fact be getting smarter and better... and then suggested it may not be enough.

I deem that possibility to be *far* more dramatic than the standard, contemptuous notion that all our fellow citizens are sheep, and that they always will be.

What is the responsibility of today's SF writer?

To be free. To explore. To be warily delighted by change and transformation and to share that wariness—and delight—with the people who will be experiencing rapid change throughout their lives.

How much of a role does social disorientation play in today's SF?

Too much, I believe. Too few authors are willing to consider the possibility that commonfolk are smarter than they think. In fact, I find it astonishing how adaptable regular people have proved to be. If they were utter fools (instead of merely foolish lots of times) we'd all be dead by now.

Then why do so many authors act as if they invented moral outrage and black leather? There is no message more common in mass media—from rock videos to movies to novels—than Suspicion of Authority (SOA). We all suckled the message from an early age. I can never get over the near infinite capacity of creative-smart people to convince themselves that they invented the very same tropes they were weaned on.

What can you tell us about your projects you have in the works?

The title of my new novel—the most original thing I've done in years—is *Kiln People*. (2nd Place Winner, 2003 Hugo Award.) Take the notion of golems—temporary clay people (not clones!)—and now imagine a near future when everybody can make them. Using a 'home copier' you ditto your memories—perhaps even a genuine imprint of your soul—and off goes the duplicate to run your errands, attend your classes, or do all the drudgery work. Then, at day's end, you download the golem's memories. This is a book with ideas for grownups... mixed into a fast-moving noir detective story that's just plain fun.

Paramount and DC-Wildstorm asked me to come up with a new hardcover graphic novel. The Life Eaters covers a much, much darker theme than anything else I've done, building dramatically from a novella called *Thor Meets Captain America* that came in second for a Hugo some years ago. This bold work asks: what might the Nazis have really been up to? Perhaps a hidden agenda that nobody knows about even to this day? The theme is explored with stirring imagery by the brilliant artist Scott Hampton, all the way to a surprising finish.

Contacting Aliens: An Illustrated Guide To David Brin's Uplift Universe (Bantam) is a fun tour of the many alien races people enjoyed in books like *Startide Rising and The Uplift War*. And from NESFA Press has just published my third story collection, *Tomorrow Happens*.

Also soon to be revised and released: the legendary *Uplift* game, GURPS Uplift! In preparation for the long-awaited publication of the new, updated edition, author-designer Stefan Jones has vastly expanded content of interest to gamers and *Uplift* fans alike.

Also in the works, a 'Heinleinian' book in which aliens kidnap 3,000 kids from a Californian high school. What a way to start a colony!

Any final advice for living in the 21st Century?

Question assumptions. Bend the expected.

My Sci-Fi author colleagues—my fellow ranting assumption-benders—are actually paid to do this. Many other cultures would have burned us. Hell, *this* culture might suddenly sour and do just that—it's nearly tipped that way lots of times.

We're lucky just to be alive. But to be appreciated, too? For having loose wires in our minds? What a deal. I'm loyal to you folks. If you keep asking for stories, I'll keep trying to come up with my share.

BRUCE BALFOUR

BRUCE BALFOUR HAS NOT ONLY MADE his name in the field of SF, but he has also been a NASA employee trained in the field of Artificial Intelligence. He sold his first piece of fiction to *Twilight Zone Magazine* in 1982, thus beginning his career as an author.

A passion for the speculative side of fiction helped fuel his game design of the bestselling games Neuromancer, Wasteland, The Dagger of Amon Roa, and Outpost. His first novel, *Star Crusader*, was followed by *The Forge of Mars*, *The Digital Dead* and *Prometheus Road*.

An amiable sort, Bruce loves to travel and lives North of San Francisco with his family and what he call 'The numerous voices in my head.'

His website can be visited at brucebalfour.com.

What did writing The Forge Of Mars *teach you that you were able to use in* The Digital Dead?

To reuse my research. For *The Forge Of Mars*, I spent about two years digging up the details of such things as possible nanotech building methods, Hohmann transfer orbits, the geology of Mars, current research in artificial intelligence, underground military installations in the former Soviet Union, the American "shadow government" that echoes the actual federal government and is activated during national emergencies, what daily life is like for the average person in Moscow these days, and so on. I was almost forced to write a sequel to get my full use out of these notebooks full of material I put together. Of course, I expect that the lead characters will reappear in a third book eventually, so that will make me feel terribly efficient, I'm sure.

What influences went into the writing of The Digital Dead *that we didn't see in* The Forge Of Mars?

Ariel, the homeless woman in San Francisco whom we first meet in *The Digital Dead*, was originally going to play a minor part in the story, essentially as an attractive puppet to lure followers into Brother Digital's high-tech cult, the Church of the Ping. She was also going to draw attention to the ongoing issue of a vast population of homeless people who have essentially built a second phantom city within the confines of San Francisco fifty years from now. As I learned more about this almost parasitical infrastructure within San Francisco, the more I was drawn to Ariel's character and how she would adapt to her environment. She's a well-educated woman forced onto the streets, so she doesn't fit the stereotype we see so often when homeless characters are used. Then she became the focal point to illustrate how someone would visit and interact with a deceased loved one using the virtual immortality technology of Elysian Fields, Inc. And then she became something even greater....

What led you to use the Navajo culture for the character Tau Wolfsinger?

Contrast between the modern, high-tech, fast-paced world of mainstream society and the traditional culture, low-tech, slow-paced world of someone raised in an environment where children are raised to place the common good above their own desires. Tau's Navajo background is based on various people I've known, and the time I spent on the Navajo Reservation in the eighties, and his traditional upbringing creates some nice conflicts with his education and experience with the rest of the world off the reservation.

A real event that I adapted for *The Forge Of Mars* had to do with a Navajo park ranger I know who was raised in the tiny community of Shonto in northern Arizona. His father was a famous medicine man, so he learned a lot about medicinal plants and curing ceremonies when he was young. He was also responsible for raising sheep. Like most children raised on the reservation at that time, he had a close-knit family, but he still had to go away to a boarding school for most of his education, and that was where he learned more about the world outside the reservation. He did well in school and eventually went off to the University of California in Berkeley. When he arrived in Berkeley, he discovered that the mutton he bought there didn't have the same flavor as the mutton back home, and he eventually realized that the sheep on the reservation eat sagebrush, and that spices the meat. So, he made a trip back to Shonto during his Christmas break, and brought two sheep back with him to Berkeley, which he slaughtered behind his apartment building. You can imagine the delight of his neighbors while this was going on, many of whom may not even have been aware that meat actually comes from live animals, and not just from a wrapped package at the grocery store. He was like an alien among the 'mainstream' white culture in Berkeley, but he learned to adapt, and he gained a whole new perspective to balance out his view of the world.

In *The Forge Of Mars*, as a contrast to this sort of behavior, I have an entire group of people, the Veggies, who have taken vegetarianism to its logical extreme. They refuse to eat animals or plants or anything else that could conceivably die to provide food or clothing for humans, so they wear synthetic fiber clothing and receive implants that allow them to photosynthesize for the cellular energy they require. This lifestyle leads to a certain amount of grumpiness, but they continue to live by their ideals, making them seem both admirable and crazy at the same time. And I wasn't poking fun at vegetarians per se—some of my best friends are plants—but at the militant, evangelistic attitudes of some of these people who want to be taken seriously where a rational person would just look at them and see they've gone 'round the bend.

How much of yourself is in Tau?

Well, he appeared out of my head and will obviously reflect some of my own attitudes and inclinations. He has no patience for inefficiency or bureaucracy, for example, because he has a constant awareness of how short his life really is, and he doesn't want to spend a third of it standing in line at the post office. Tau is a computer scientist at NASA, which I have been, but he's a genius, which I am not. He's a polymath, so he's interested in, and understands, a lot of different subjects; this is true in my own life, for better or worse. If Tau took an aptitude test, the results would be almost useless because he's what a vocational counselor would call a 'TMA'—Too Many Aptitudes. I think this is a common trait in many science fiction writers, and you often see that reflected in their careers where they easily jumped from one occupation to another to earn a living while they were trying to establish themselves as writers. Of course, this career jumping might also mean that SF writers can't hold down normal jobs, but that's for you to decide.

Tau compares himself to Don Quixote in The Digital Dead—*is he constructed to indeed be Quixotic, or is that solely how he sees himself?*

Tau does, indeed, go off to fight windmills. If they were smaller windmills, he might be able to succeed, but instead he chooses to fight shadowy international windmills that refuse to step out into the light and show themselves. Or he'll pick fights with NASA, which is in the business of making windmills. So, he can win a battle here and there, but these windmills will always go after him and gang up on him to try to teach him not to do it again. But he never learns. In other words, he's a lot like you and me.

What was the reaction from NASA co-workers to your work?

Mocking laughter, thrown garbage, burning me in effigy—the usual sort of thing.
 Actually, a lot of people work for NASA because they were introduced to this kind of speculative thinking by reading science fiction, and many of them still enjoy it, even if they have to read it in the closet so that their peers will continue to take them seriously. They understand what it means to try to do original research in a government bureaucracy, and the associated paperwork and funding problems that go along with that, so I think it amuses them to see someone poke fun at the system.
 I've actually had one or two e-mails from readers who have never worked in this type of environment, and they think I have some kind of a grudge with NASA. I don't, really. I was proud to work for them when I had the chance. The research and technology legacy of NASA, and the methods they developed to orchestrate complex projects while managing vast numbers of employees, are simply amazing. Over time, NASA developed the same issues as any other hulking organism of that size, and the old machinery is slow to adapt to new social and economic environments, but I think it will eventually overcome its difficulties. Change may come with the necessity of funding NASA projects with financial support from private industry, perhaps in the form of the commercial sponsorships I mentioned in *The Forge Of Mars*.
 As is usual with the media's interest in government organizations, we hear a lot more about the occasional failure than we do about the numerous successes, and that's unfortunate because the general public bases its opinion of NASA on the explosions they see on the television news, right before the sitcoms and quiz shows come on in the evening.

NASA forgot about how the public viewed it after the budget cutbacks in the post-Apollo era, and they've only made sporadic efforts at PR since then, when cute little vehicles roll around on the surface of Mars and so on. Of course, as its image degraded in the public mind, the reasons for its continued funding seemed to diminish as well, because the average person doesn't understand why basic research needs to be done in the first place. As long as they have a car, a television, and a place to live with electricity for the television, the average person is happy. They simply don't understand, and not enough people are trying to explain it to them, and that leaves us with science fiction and other forms of entertainment as a way to reach these people and show them other possibilities.

Okay, I feel better now. What was your question again?

There is a subtle yet quite realistic sense of humor in both your narrative as well as your dialogue; How do you manage to not undermine the plot by using humor or perhaps, satire?

As my wife keeps reminding me, I am not the reincarnation of Voltaire. However, I try not to take myself too seriously, and that spills over into what I write. If one of my characters is starting to sound too strident, I can use humor to deflate him or to get him grounded again. If only real life were like that. However, I may be typing away on a novel one night, having a great time amusing myself, then look at what I wrote the next morning and wonder whether I thought I was writing material for a television sitcom or a stand-up comedy routine. Maybe it's something in the water, or the drugs that the nice men in the white coats keep giving me—I don't know. Anyway, in the cold light of morning, I think very hard about whether I have to have a fish wearing pants in my serious science fiction novel, then I throw out all that material and start over again.

There are other times when I can't help myself, but my wife will read through my material before I send it off to my editor, and she is more than happy to point out when I've gone too far. She'll pat me on the head, tell me I'm funny, then tell me to cut entire sections out of the manuscript. And I do, because she has our best interests at heart, and I have no self-control.

On the other hand, the humor or the satirical approach may be the best way I can get a point across in a particular scene, or it may be shorthand for what would otherwise be a long and tedious character description. When I have the Vice President of the United States eating peanuts off the floor of the Oval Office, you know right away that something isn't right with the man. If I describe a cemetery that's been modernized into an amusement park built around the theme of death, then I can express my opinions about the commercialization of the funeral industry without having to write a newspaper editorial that nobody would read. If I write about yet another former film actor elected to a highly placed political position, I can comment on what I perceive as the close ties between politics and entertainment, at the expense of experienced political leadership, while efficiently making large numbers of people angry with me.

By the way, I had no idea that Arnold Schwarzenegger would run for governor of California when I wrote *The Digital Dead*, even though I referred to him as former President Schwarzenegger in the book—but life imitates art, I guess, and I'll look like a genius if he becomes governor.

Who are your literary influences outside the SF genre?

Well, let's see, I mentioned Voltaire already, so I guess that leaves an assortment of thriller writers such as Dean Koontz, Stephen King, Frederick Forsyth, Robert Ludlum, Martin Cruz Smith, and Graham Greene; humorous mystery writers such as Carl Hiaasen and Donald Westlake; Borges and other magical realists; George Bernard Shaw, Gore Vidal, Roald Dahl, Douglas Adams…okay, basically anything I've ever read, which is one of the many reasons why I'm so screwed up today.

Do you think a mission to one of Jupiter's moons, specifically Europa, would yield more conclusive results concerning life on other planets, given the theory Europa's surface floats atop flowing water?

The Galileo mission indicated a good potential for liquid water on Europa. If NASA can keep the Europa Orbiter mission funded, it would use a radar sounder to determine if there's a liquid ocean under the icy surface. Last I heard, they were talking about a launch in 2008, which would put it in orbit around Europa in 2011. If the oceans are there, and we can get hydrobots on a later mission to melt down through the ice layer, then these little submarines would certainly provide a good show while they hunt for life. We know that hostile conditions around hydrothermal vents in the deep oceans of Earth can support life, so why not something similar on Europa?

What is your opinion on the current Mars mission?

After both rovers have safely landed, I'm thinking they should poke around and look for water a little bit, finish their missions, get roaring drunk in a rover bar beneath the surface, then attack each other in a battlebots scenario that would capture the interest of the larger viewing audience.

Given the current budget limitations, these small 'follow the water' missions seem the best way to keep a Mars exploration program going in the near term while still managing to acquire new data, but it will take something on the scale of a manned mission to get people excited about exploration again. Of course, gathering the popular support required for funding such a mission is nearly impossible at the moment, so I suspect that Microsoft will be planting its corporate flag on Mars long before NASA or any international space consortiums will get there.

Do you think the next major advance in science will be genuine AI?

So far, I think AI research has either generated software algorithms that have been absorbed into common applications such as word processing and computer games, or it has led researchers into dead-ends. A lot of useful work has come out of developing strategies for searching vast quantities of information, and other approaches in cognitive science have demonstrated how complex our brains really are. Hardware capabilities continue to advance, but software lags behind due to the complexity of trying to model even the simplest tasks that a human takes for granted.

As a simple example of this software complexity, a good computer model of a real system in the physical world will often exhibit 'emergent behavior.' Emergent behavior is why freeways have traffic jams—the system should work if everything operates as planned, but then someone does the unexpected, driving too slow in the fast lane, and turbulence builds up as people try to pass the slow driver, and more people brake to avoid the slow driver or the passing drivers, and suddenly the freeway is backed up for miles as the chaos spreads.

Intel has computers that create the detailed designs for new computer chips, but we still have the limitations of human programmers to slow us down because we don't have computers that can write their own software. There are projects such as 'Cyc' that involve years of building a giant database of common sense rules such as, 'Don't wear a plaid shirt with striped pants,' or whatever, in the hope that the software will eventually be able to apply common sense reasoning to novel problems, but these are still only early attempts at AI. I expect that we'll get closer to 'real' AI once we start enhancing live organic brains with the faster processing power and memory of computer chips. Then, with the awesome computing power available a few years after that, the ultra-intelligent machines of our science fiction fantasies will start to emerge. And then we'll be enslaved by our toaster ovens.

You describe a near-future version of the Internet that is too complex for unaided humans to understand. Tau interacts with the datasphere through an AI that hunts down information. Do you think this is how the Web will evolve?

I think dealing with the vast amount of information on the Web is already too complex a task for many people. A few years ago, politicians were talking about the 'Digital Divide,' and that focused a lot of attention on getting computers and Internet access into the schools. Now, underprivileged kids are almost as likely to be familiar with the Internet as their middle-class counterparts. A lot of seniors have taken the time to learn how to use e-mail and surf the Web. But there are still a lot of carpenters and grocery store clerks who don't see any need to buy a computer or get Internet access, and a new underclass of the 'information poor' is developing. Each day, more information floods onto Web servers all over the world, but data is not knowledge, and just because the information is there doesn't mean that I can get to it just because I have an Internet connection. The search engines, like Yahoo and Google, continually hunt down that information and attempt to categorize it so that we can find it, but they only cover a small percentage of what's out there, and almost any search you do will turn up more website links than you can use, and most of those links will be garbage. Web directories with human editors, such as about.com and the Open Directory, do a better job of pruning out the garbage links and categorizing the information, but they can't cover everything either.

Is artificial intelligence the best way to handle this information glut?

Some form of AI will be the best approach for these massive tasks that are beyond human capabilities. At the Los Alamos National Laboratory, they have the Distributed Knowledge Systems project, and the idea there is to create a sort of super website that can continually rebuild the links between pages to adapt them to the needs of the users. Normally, hyperlinks between website pages are set by the website builder. The DKS project puts new hyperlinks into its website pages whenever it thinks it can open up a new path for web surfers to find information, and it closes down links that don't get used. If you think about that for a minute, you realize that the human brain operates the same way: when one neuron is activated after another, the synapse connecting the two gets stronger. The more often that link is used between those two neurons, the stronger the synapse connection grows. If those neurons rarely fire, the synapse gets weaker. On a large scale, in the rapidly paced digital world of the Web, this type of adaptive algorithm will start us down the path toward a thinking, reasoning datasphere—a global brain—that we will depend on for our information needs. Of course, this global AI will depend on us for information as well. The development of ubiquitous computing— where an individual will have a constant, wireless connection to this datasphere, possibly enhanced by an AI interface—is a logical extension of this super Internet concept. Imagine having much of the world's knowledge available on demand in your brain—you'd still be responsible for creative thought and the application of that knowledge, but think what fun you'd be at parties....

You've created websites specific to each of your books; How have the results of this worked out?

Unfortunately, I know way too much about the evolving strategies of what's required to optimize websites for search engines to make them visible in the vast digital sea, so I build multiple websites to create a wider footprint on the Web. Since I also track the keywords used in search engines that bring visitors to my websites, I'm also surprised by some of the strange things people look for that bring them to my websites, such as 'graves golf course neighbors' or 'ancient Navajo technology.' Of course, I also build a website for each book so that I can give each one an individual style and load it up with different kinds of information without being restricted by what I did the last time around. A lot of people have asked me about the tombstones used as landfill under the approaches to the Golden Gate Bridge, for example.

How has the scientific community reacted to some of the ideas you put forward in Digital?

Well, much of what I write about is already starting to appear in one form or another, so it's not a stretch for most computer science researchers, or hardware designers, to imagine these technologies being used in this way.

Microsoft has been working on a database that records almost everything in the daily life of one of its researchers, effectively creating a digital memory recording without some of the sensory input. The Max Planck Institute has developed 'neuron transistors' that can detect the firing of a nearby neuron in a brain, or switch the neuron on and off. There is two-way communication between these transistors and the neurons, and they've demonstrated it by controlling the movements of a leech from a computer. This will lead to more detailed models of neural pathways and to our understanding of how the brain does its thing.

We've already done a lot of work in virtual reality environments, and a little more hardware power to handle the graphics will make virtual worlds much more realistic. Ray Kurzweil estimates that a visit to a 'website' in 2030 will be more like a trip to a fully-immersive virtual world, complete with sensory input moderated by nanobots controlling the sensory signals in the brain.

So, when you put all of that together, recording someone's personality and memory in a biochip, then uploading this data from a deceased person to a virtual environment, then 'animating' the data with artificial intelligence and giving it an avatar that looks like the real person did in life—the things I write about don't seem all that farfetched for a story set about fifty years from now.

How do you pick the social circumstances you use as background or foreground?

More research. For example, in *The Forge Of Mars*, I mentioned rich kids forming street gangs in San Francisco. I called them 'skin gangs' because their members like to wear the expensive 'nanotattoos' that move around on a person's body, maintaining their tattoo design as they react to light and migrate in search of salt deposits on the skin. I think this kind of consumer-oriented thinking is what makes a lot of otherwise exotic or 'spooky' technologies palatable to the general public—nanotechnology, in this case.

Anyway, these gangs of rich kids formed to emulate their idea of street gangs from lower economic classes. Sociologists have noted a recent general decline in the level of violence from gangs oriented along traditional lines, although the sheer density of gangs in places like Los Angeles—where they estimate a population of 150,000 to 175,000 gang members—generates more gang conflict and more media attention. Gangs are supposed to be a response to a complex urban environment, where people are attracted to a small, organized social group with understandable rules and established pecking orders, but gangs aren't new, and this kind of random violence isn't restricted to a particular social class. In 18th century Bavaria, bored rich people routinely killed each other in duels, and this became such a problem that the Bavarian government refused burial to the victims of duels, turning their bodies over to anatomists for dissection instead.

In *The Digital Dead*, one of the main characters is a homeless woman, so I spent more time discussing homeless issues and how San Francisco would still be trying to deal with them fifty years from now. Homeless people in San Francisco currently live on the streets, in alleyways, in parks, and even underground in the massive sewer pipes and BART train tunnels beneath the city. I extended their range a bit, giving them a simple technology to hang sleeping bags off the sides of buildings, which allows them to comply with local laws by getting 'off the street.'

Is it more difficult for SF writers nowadays to write effective SF than it was when you first started?

I don't think so, but ask me again in forty years to see if I have a different answer. There is always the issue of trying to be more aware of what was written in the past so that you don't repeat a story that may have already been told better by someone else, but if you're making projections based on new technologies, there's less of a problem with that. Consider how few science fiction writers anticipated the Internet; now you can't toss a dead cat out the window without hitting someone writing about the datasphere, or the matrix, or the *Digital Dead*, or...well, you get the idea.

What's the biggest challenge in writing the contemporary SF novel?

Trying to stay ahead of rapid changes in technology and society. I can make jokes about Arnold Schwarzenegger becoming President of the United States, and then by the time *The Digital Dead* comes out a year or two later, the real Schwarzenegger announces that he's running for governor of California.

Or I can think I'm terribly clever by digging up all this old information about the vast underground military installations under the eastern United States, and then use these abandoned facilities in *The Forge Of Mars*, and then a big terrorist attack occurs and these facilities are suddenly reactivated and modernized just one month after my book comes out. A lot of that information that I dug up has now disappeared from the websites where I found it, as it has apparently become classified information once again.

In a sense, you might say the biggest challenge is in finding enough time to do all the research for a good science fiction novel, followed by the ability to write fast enough before all of your research becomes outdated.

On a more practical level, the challenge is that there aren't as many people who read science fiction now. Surrounded by high-tech marvels and the complexity of modern society, people seem more inclined to avoid thinking about the future, preferring to read books and watch movies about elves and fairies, or about how their neighbors are getting murdered, or about finding relationship fulfillment in their own back yards. I have nothing against these other genres, but I'd like to see more people buying science fiction again. Not that I have any vested interest in that....

What do you want to accomplish with your writing?

Vast wealth, worldwide fame, and the freedom to get away from these ridiculous jobs I keep taking to avoid having to move my family to a new home in the local sewer.

Okay, it would be nice if I could get a few people to open their eyes again and look at the world around them with that 'sense of wonder' that we had as children, thinking about future possibilities for human society and technology, rather than dwelling on what kind of car they're going to buy next. I always hear about scientists who got interested in their careers because they read science fiction when they were younger, so maybe I can help generate more interest in the sciences. Of course, those readers are really my target audience in the first place, but one can always hope that we'll win over a few converts from the rest of the population, eh?

Will we see Kate and Tau return in your next novel?

God, I hope not. They keep stirring up trouble and then I have to get them out of it.

Actually, my next novel, *Prometheus Road* (Ace) unless they change the title again. It's essentially a science fantasy that operates in three dimensions: an inner dream world, an advanced virtual world, and the real world. It's set primarily in the San Francisco Bay Area, which has become a wasteland due to a massive nanotechnology 'accident' prompted by a group of sinister artificial intelligences known as the Dominion.

I also have a light mystery novel floating around that's primarily set among the wind tunnels and exotic aircraft at NASA's Ames Research Center in California. I spent a lot of time flying around on the Kuiper Airborne Observatory, which was a C-141 with an infrared telescope mounted inside of it for astronomy at high altitudes, and I finally decided to use it as a closed environment for a mystery novel. Our team used the KAO for Space Shuttle intercept missions so that we could get an infrared image to show actual heating conditions on the Shuttle underbody, so I learned a lot about the eccentricities of the aircraft and the people who worked on it. They retired the KAO a couple of years ago, intending to replace it with a 747, but I don't believe it has started flying yet.

However, I do expect to see Tau and Kate again eventually.

Bruce, thank you for your time, is there anything you'd like to add?

Have I mentioned that my novels make lovely Christmas gifts, appreciated by young and old alike? And, believe it or not, the movie rights are still available....

LOIS McMASTER BUJOLD

CONDUCTED WITH RYAN TIMOTHY GRABLE

WITH MORE THAN A DOZEN titles (translated into fourteen languages) under her literary belt, winner of both the prestigious Hugo and Nebula awards (for *Falling Free, Barrayar* and *Mirror Dance* to name just a few,) and just this year the Mythopoeic Award for the recent release, *The Curse Of Chalion*, Lois McMaster Bujold is a testament to growth in the world of Science Fiction. Plucked from the veritable 'slush piles' in the mid 80's, she began her career with Baen and has since paved a formidable literary trail with her tales.

Lois began writing in junior high school, and became an English major at Ohio State before going on to work as a technician in the pharmacy of Ohio State University Hospitals, and leaving that position when she made the decision to begin a family.

Not happy to leave writing as only a hobby, Lois completed her first novel, *Shards Of Honor* in 1983 and got her first professional break with *Twilight Zone Magazine*. In 1985, her first three completed novels were picked up by Baen Books, seeing the shelves the following year. *Analog Magazine* serialized her next novel, *Falling Free* in their 1987-1988 editions.

In 1992, *The Spirit Ring* brought with it her first hardcover sale and saw the publication of *Cetaganda* serialized in *Analog*'s 1995-1996 run before it too was released in hardcover by Baen, followed by the sequel to *Mirror Dance; Memory*, which garnered a nomination of both the Hugo and Nebula. *Komarr* came in 1998, and was the winner of a Minnesota Book Award in the category of Science Fiction/Fantasy and was followed in 1999 with its own sequel, *A Civil Campaign*.

Fans of Lois's have also been treated to *The Curse Of Chalion* in 2001 published in hardcover by Eosbooks and *Diplomatic Immunity*, published, also in hardcover, in May of 2002. Her comprehensive website can be found at www.dendarii.com.

You landed your first novel sale with Baen without an agent. Would you recommend this course of action to a new writer?

Not especially. Since the mid-80's when I broke in, the slush piles have grown bigger and the number of publishers who will even look at un-agented submissions has grown smaller. Baen is one of the few publishers who still reads slush (unsolicited novel manuscripts), but even they can only 'start' perhaps one or two new writers a year. It's worth it to try every channel, but if you can land an agent who likes your stuff, so much the better. While no agent can sell a book that wouldn't sell on its own, once you have an offer, you'll want an agent anyway to do things like retain sub-rights, be sure your contract is reasonable, and market foreign sales.

Most agents do not handle short work even for their established clients, so of course new writers who can work at both lengths should send off their short tales to the magazines themselves. There isn't much to negotiate or change in most magazine contracts, and a short story sale looks good in one's cover letter when offering a novel. No, it is not *necessary* to write or sell short stories before tackling novels; different writers have different natural lengths, and it's not a bad idea to play to one's strengths in the beginning.

After you won your first Nebula, did it boost your confidence or cause you to feel more pressure in the course of your follow-up novel?

Yes. Now, first thing to note is the lead time. I wrote my fourth novel, *Falling Free*, in 1986, it spent 1987 in the publishing pipeline of both *Analog Magazine* and Baen Books, was published in book form in 1988, and won its Nebula in 1989. By the time of the actual win, the next book (*Brothers In Arms*) was already finished and published, the one after that (*Borders Of Infinity*) was finished and in the publishing pipeline, and I was at work on yet another, *The Vor Game*. So I had already passed the point of the distraction being able to affect 'my next work.' I think this probably helped keep the win from throwing me off my stride too much.

Was the Vorkosigan series written from a detailed outline spanning ten volumes or did it grow as you continued writing the series?

I've always written the Vorkosigan series one book at a time. Not only do I not know what's going to happen in the next book, I frequently don't know what's going to happen in the next chapter. I use outlines constantly in my writing, as a memory aid to capture and organize thought, but they are in no way fixed; I make them up chapter by chapter, in layers of increasing detail, and I'm continually revising and re-working them as I go. Almost all of my structural revisions and tinkerings take place at this outline stage. What's left to do after the first draft is mostly fine-tuning.

That said, it was evident to me from the time I wrote *The Warrior's Apprentice*, which was my second novel, that I had a world and a cast of characters that would support several books. Part of the fun for *me* has been in the finding out of just what those books would be, one chapter at a time.

A large portion of your work was published out of chronological order. Was this deliberate?

Because I don't have that ten-book outline, the possibility of jumping around the series timeline has always been there. It depends on where the enticing ideas take me. The next thing I'd written after *Warrior's* was the novella 'Borders of Infinity', which jumped forward several years in Miles's timeline. *The Vor Game* was therefore a fill-in story, answering the question of how did he get from *here* to *there*?

Now, in the case of *Barrayar*, a direct sequel to my first novel *Shards Of Honor*, the first part of the tale was already written. I'd cut off the last six or eight chapters of *Shards* because at the time I didn't quite know how to end a book and had rather over-shot the ending, and had to back up to find a good stopping place. I set this fragment aside in my attic for several years. So about the first third of the book was already written when I was moved to go back and explore those themes and characters. I think it was a stronger, better book for the wait and the extra writing experience I'd accumulated in between—and certainly with a somewhat different plot—than if I had gone on to write it directly instead of turning my attention to *The Warrior's Apprentice* instead. My other prequel, *Cetaganda*, had been kicking around for a while in the idea-form of 'Miles and Ivan go to the Cetagandan state funeral, and…' with no idea of what happened next. When I finally came to write the tale, it just seemed to call for younger and more naïve characters, so I set the way-back machine to their early twenties. The story might have fallen elsewhere in their timeline, but would have been a slightly different tale.

What influences your imagination when you are building the world your characters inhabit?

Strictly speaking, I usually start with the characters and their story, and make up the world around them and the story's needs as I write. The ideas are pulled from every corner of my life—everything I've done or read, everyone I've known, anecdotes people have told me, travels, personal disasters or triumphs, specific bits of research I look up.... everything goes in somewhere.

Did you study contemporary or past examples in politics as a template for that in your own world?

'Study' is perhaps too strong a term. I read lots of history, of various periods and places that catch my interest—Renaissance Europe, Japan, China, anything long ago and far away. And I'm picking up odd bits all the time from all sorts of sources. These all go into the compost heap of the imagination, ready to be drawn out when the triggering need occurs. I am actually interested in characters, not in politics; the politics just give the characters something significant to do.

The Curse Of Chalion, my recent Fantasy (which won the Mythopoeic Award in 2002) actually did have a partial source in some coursework I took. In a semi-idle moment I'd signed up for a class in Spanish medieval history at the local university, partly for fun because it was an area I'd known little about, partly to explore completing a degree, partly because it was taught at a time that fit my schedule. I was delighted with the wonderful lurid true stories of the late Spanish medieval period, and was determined to do something with this great material. But it wasn't until I came up with a fresh character who interested me that it all really came alive and I began to see how I wanted to re-work the good bits into a book.

Did you choose to write in the world of SF/F, or did they choose you?

This give me a mental picture of SF editors out knocking on the doors of random housewives, like Fuller Brush men in reverse, asking them if they would please write some stories… Of course I chose. The world does not come to you; it doesn't know you exist, till you do something to make it notice. I first became interested in SF and fantasy at the usual early age—nine, in my case—because my father read it, and so the magazines and books of the period were lying around the house. I read SF extensively in my teens (the 1960's), although in my twenties I mostly caught up with the rest of literature. But in my early thirties, when I finally sat down with the serious intent of writing something salable, it just naturally came out as SF. I have a secondary interest in mysteries, and might have gone that route instead, but since mystery incorporates easily into SF, I don't really have to leave the F&SF field to scratch that itch.

In Ethan Of Athos *you broach the subject of homosexuality. What was the inspiration for this?*

While it may once have been true that homosexuality wasn't much addressed in SF, back in 1985 when I sat down to write *Ethan*, the subject was indeed rather thinner on the ground. *Ethan Of Athos* actually explores not so much homosexuality as gender role reversal. I had read some of those dreadful Amazon-planet tales from the 50's and 60's, written by men, and wondered what would happen if one turned the trope around. I had also had the experience of being a parent by then. So, what would happen on a world where the men had to do *all* the housework…? Stir in my medical background, make my hero an obstetrician who takes on the quintessential female role of (technological) child-bearing for his woman-free planet, and the thing grew from there.

In your writing of magic usage, there is always a price to be paid for using such powers; is there a similar effect in the use of science or technology?

Yes, probably: one of the prices, certainly, is change. One must give up large pieces of the past to make room for the future. This theme is explored quite a bit in the *Barrayar* stories, a planet whose recent history I deliberately structured to echo that of our own 20th Century, wrenched from the past to the future rather faster than some of its inhabitants wanted to go.

Did you intend to integrate religious beliefs in the Vorkosigan series, or did the story come to require it?

Since the Vorkosigan universe purports to be a descendant of our own, if I wrote a tale where no such beliefs existed, I would have to have included a great deal of back-story to explain how they came to be eradicated, I should think. Miles's universe doubtless includes all the beliefs of ours plus a lot of new ones invented since. People are like that. Nonetheless, Miles's own world-view is largely secular. When I wanted to explore religious themes more directly, I went to a new universe, that of *Chalion*, and new characters.

Did you have any difficulty selling a book that took place out of the Vorkosigan world?

Back when I wrote my first fantasy, *The Spirit Ring*, my agent shopped the proposal around to yawns, so I ended up back at Baen with it after all. A decade and eight or ten genre awards later, when she took the finished manuscript of *The Curse Of Chalion* out, things went much better. Note, because Baen has the option on the next Vorkosigan universe book, I couldn't offer anything *but* something new to other publishers, at least not without first spurning Baen, which I do not care to do. They have proven themselves the right publisher for the Miles books, over time, I think. Despite the covers.

Many female authors stick to their own gender as far as main characters go, pulling from their own life experiences. However you show a tremendous insight into the internal and external actions of your male characters. How did you achieve this insight?

Men and women aren't that different from each other, in most areas of life. I think the proper question is, how do other writers *avoid* the insight into the opposite gender? Guys are all around us, all the time. We live with them— I had a father, grandfathers, brothers, a husband, a son, male colleagues, bosses, fellow students—we read books written by and about them… nowadays, we read on-line posts by them, in perhaps more startling variety than one's immediate family might offer, or so I would hope. I think some people must screen out this data, as if knowing, or at least, admitting to knowing, was somehow a violation of their own gender identity. I was on a convention panel once with a male writer who was complaining—actually, covertly bragging—that he couldn't write female characters very well, the not-so-hidden subtext being that he was so ineluctably masculine, the terrible effort at getting his mind around this alien female viewpoint was just beyond him. (As though it were a subject impossible to research!) I didn't think he was ineluctably masculine. I just thought he was a poor writer.

Is your character, Miles Vorkosigan, modeled after an individual person or several?

Miles came as real people do—from his parents. I have a catch-phrase to describe my plot-generation technique—'What's the worst possible thing I can do to *these* people?'

Miles was already a gleam in my eye even when I was still writing *Shards Of Honor*. For his parents Aral and Cordelia, living in a militaristic, patriarchal culture that prizes physical perfection and has an historically-driven horror of mutation, having a handicapped son and heir was a major life challenge, a Great Test. Miles has a number of real-life roots—models from history such as T.E. Lawrence and young Winston Churchill, a physical template in a handicapped hospital pharmacist I'd worked with, most of all his bad case of 'great man's son syndrome', which owes much to my relationship with my father. But with his first book, *The Warrior's Apprentice*, he quickly took on a life of his own; his charisma and drive, his virtues and his failings—and he has both—are now all his.

With Gregor Vorbarra married off, Miles Settling down, and his clone Mark right behind, What do you have in store for Ivan Vorpatril?

That actually has to be one of the most frequently asked questions I encounter, lately. Clearly, I'll have to think about something special for Ivan. He'll hate it, but he doesn't get a vote, heh.

Is there any expansion on the Cetagandan race in the works? Will we ever hear of the Quaddies again?

Beyond what I've shown in *Diplomatic Immunity*, I haven't set anything yet.

What was your inspiration for the Quaddies?

The Quaddies were developed for my fourth novel, *Falling Free*. I was playing with some ideas about technological obsolescence, and what it might mean in terms of bioengineering. I came up with the idea of a race of humans bioengineered to live and work in free fall, whose *raison d'être* would be knocked asunder when a practical artificial gravity was developed. As I researched what was then (1985) known about free fall physiology, it seemed to me that most of the obvious changes wouldn't necessarily leave people unable to return to a gravity environment. I came up with the notion of a second set of hands to replace legs after conversing with a NASA doctor about the dual problems the astronauts faced of leg atrophy, and their hands growing excessively tired as they took over the task of bracing oneself in place while working that on Earth is done by gravity. I decided to begin the Quaddies' tale at the beginning, came up with the main characters, and from there, just followed their actions to their logical conclusions.

JEANNE CAVELOS

JEANNE CAVELOS IS AN AUTHOR, editor, scientist and teacher who started out as an astrophysicist and mathematician teaching astronomy at Michigan State University and Cornell University and working in the Astronaut Training Division at NASA's Johnson Space Center. As an editor, she created the Abyss imprint for Dell Publishing, publishing renowned authors Poppy Z. Brite, Kathe Koja, and Tanith Lee, among many others, winning the World Fantasy Award while she was at it. She has gone on to write such acclaimed works as *The Science of the X-Files* (Berkley/Boulevard) and *The Science of Star Wars* (St. Martin's).

Somehow, she manages to find time to run Jeanne Cavelos Editorial Services as well as Odyssey, a six-week writing workshop held in New Hampshire College.

Jeanne is no stranger to the unique *Babylon 5* Universe and the stories not covered by the series. Her novel, *The Shadow Within* (Dell) covered the stories of Morden, Anna and John Sheridan and the crew of the *Icarus* when the Shadows were awakened. This time around, she covers the mysterious Techno-Mages in her new *B5* trilogy, *The Passing of the Techno-Mages* (Del Rey), beginning with the first installment *Casting Shadows*.

More information on Jeanne is on her website, www.jeannecavelos.com.

Was it difficult to follow J. Gregory Keyes' and Peter David's work on the last two trilogies?

I didn't look on it as some sort of competition, so it wasn't difficult at all. I think we each have our own styles and strengths, so we can each make our own contribution to the *B5* universe.

Their work was actually helpful to me. I referred to Greg's books to see how he'd described telepathic scans, since I have a telepath in my trilogy.

What was interesting was that he described the scans mainly from the telepath's point of view, while I describe scans from the recipient's point of view. I think the two perspectives work nicely together. Peter was writing his books at the same time that I was writing mine, so we conferred on a couple points. I told him a little about Techno-Mages so we wouldn't have any major inconsistencies, and he told me about the Drakh, so my treatment of them would mesh with his. It was great to have the opportunity to make everything consistent (I hope).

How much will be revealed about the Techno-Mage belief system?

Over the course of the trilogy, you'll find out all there is to know. The Mages have certain principles in which they all believe. Those core beliefs—their Code—hold them together. Yet there's also great diversity among them, so they disagree on many things. The trilogy covers a key period for the mages, during which their order undergoes major changes.

What was it like to work with J. Michael Straczynski?

I had a great experience working with Joe on my previous B5 novel, *The Shadow Within*, so I felt very comfortable agreeing to write the trilogy. We all understand that tie-ins need to be consistent with the spirit and the details of the series. But I think Joe, as a writer, also understands that writers need freedom to create something of their own within those parameters. Without that freedom, tie-ins become mechanical exercises rather than vital works of art. I know the idea that tie-ins could possibly be art seems ridiculous to many people, but I have a huge respect for B5 and the writing of the episodes. I feel the novels should be of that same high caliber—should be treated (by the writer) as equal in worth and potential to any other novel. That's how I approached the books, and Joe has been very supportive in allowing me the freedom to bring my own ideas and variations to the story he outlined.

The process of working with him consisted mainly of two parts. First, if I had a question about something—say a date when something happened, or a couple facts that seemed inconsistent with each other, I would e-mail Joe and Fiona Avery. They were both very helpful. They'd give me the answer if there was one, or if there wasn't, I'd propose something, and they'd give the okay.

The other thing I did was just keeping Joe informed about what I was doing, so he could let me know if he had any problem with it. After receiving Joe's outlines for the trilogy, I wanted to flesh things out, establish characters, and plot events in detail. I'd never written a trilogy before, and I wanted all three books to really work together—I wanted to set up plotlines in Book 1 that wouldn't come to fruition until Book 3, and that sort of thing. So I wrote a 200-page outline for the trilogy (okay, I'm… let's just call it 'organized'). I sent that to my editor at Del Rey, and to Joe and Fiona, so they could see what I was planning to do and raise any objections before I got into the actual writing. But Joe was fine with the outlines.

To give you one example of something I changed in Book 1, Joe's outline called for a love triangle between Galen, Isabelle, and another male Mage. This would trigger a fight between Galen and the other Mage. I felt that the fight between Galen and the other Mage (who became a character named Elizar) would tie into the overall plot better if it was not motivated by rivalry over Isabelle but by a desire for power on Elizar's part.

(Why he wants this power is something that we figure out only later…) So I cut the love triangle and added other motivations, but the fight between Galen and Elizar remains.

Is there a B5 character that you'd like to write a novel around? What might it involve?

There are so many great characters on *B5*, that's a hard question. But I feel in most cases Joe showed us the major story of each character's life right in the series. Galen, Elric, Morden, and Anna Sheridan are all exceptions to that, which is why I enjoyed writing about them so much.

I think it would be interesting to write a novel about a pre-*Shadow Within* Morden, working for Earthforce's New Technologies Division.

Considering some of the criticism Star Trek *fans have leveled at B5 in the past, can we hope to see these two fanbases peacefully co-exist?*

At this point, I think they are peacefully co-existing. At least I don't know anyone who's still fighting over which is better. We should just be happy that Science Fiction is doing fairly well on television and in the book market, so that high-quality product has some chance of getting exposure and reaching us.

Do you approach writing horror any differently than your SF?

Not really. I do a lot of research for everything I write. The subjects being researched might change, but my process is basically the same. If I write about a character's arm being burned, then I need to know how it would look, how it would feel, how it would smell, and how it could be medically treated, if that's part of the story. I think giving details that allow readers to feel like they are there is critical, no matter what genre I'm writing in. Most of what I've written recently has actually been a science fiction/horror combination (I'd put all my *B5* novels in that category).

Can we expect to see a Science Of Babylon 5*?*

I'd be happy to do something like that down the road if they wanted me to. There's certainly more science in *B5* than in a lot of other Science Fiction.

Right now I'm developing a near-future Science-Fiction novel of my own, so I'd like that to be my next book (assuming a publisher buys it). It involves some fascinating research I discovered while writing *The Science Of The X-Files*. After that, I'd love to visit the *B5* universe again, either in fiction or nonfiction.

We've seen cameos from the ancestors of B5 *characters in the past trilogies, can we expect something similar from this set?*

No. The trilogy is set during the time of the *B5* series, so you'll see many *B5* characters involved in the storyline, particularly in Books 2 and 3. John Sheridan, Anna Sheridan, Morden, Londo, Vir, Kosh, Garibaldi, Lorien, and Elric (the Techno-Mage from 'The Geometry of Shadows') all play interesting parts. Characters from Crusade are also featured—Galen, Alwyn, and Isabelle. Galen and Elric are the main characters of the trilogy.

I tried to write the trilogy, though, so that readers could understand it even without having seen *Crusade* or *B5*. If I've done my job correctly, people who have seen both series will gain extra enjoyment from seeing how events in the books relate to those in the series, and from learning more about various characters. But those who don't know *B5* backwards and forwards should still be able to become involved in the story and enjoy it.

Do the Techno-Mages have an overall role in the B5 *universe?*

That's a fascinating question. The answer is yes, more than you can imagine. You will learn their role in the last sentence of Book 3.

The writing styles of the past trilogies mesh very easily with the B5 *mythology we've come to know from the TV series. How did you continue this unique thread in* The Passing Of Techno-Mages?

Since the trilogy occurs concurrently with the series, it was very interesting to think about how the mages' story intertwines with and affects the *B5* story as we know it. I tried to be consistent with everything that's been established in the series, yet at the same time reveal that we didn't know the whole truth of certain events. You'll find the trilogy closely tied to several *B5* episodes. I don't think I'll be revealing any major secrets if I say that Book 2 includes events from 'The Geometry of Shadows'—the one episode of *B5* in which Mages appear. But you'll discover that what you *thought* happened in that episode is not what happened at all. Appearances can be deceiving, and the Mages, like any good magicians, are all about deception and manipulation.

How did your experience writing your previous B5 *novel,* The Shadow Within *prepare you for this series?*

The Shadow Within actually serves as a sort of 'prequel' to the trilogy. It's not necessary that you've read *The Shadow Within* to understand and enjoy the trilogy, but you'll get added pleasure from the trilogy if you've read it.

I really became steeped in the *B5* universe writing the earlier book, so that familiarity helped a lot in writing the trilogy. To do a good job, avoid inconsistencies, and play off of established facts, I had to know the series extremely well (and I also had a great team of *B5* fans helping me out where my memory failed). There were also certain themes that I had introduced in the earlier book that I found I could now explore in more depth, and examine from a different perspective. That was very interesting. And plot points that I had worked out involving Anna Sheridan, Morden, and the Shadows come back again in the trilogy.

Writing *The Shadow Within* in eight weeks (the amount of time given to me by the publisher) helped make writing the much more complex trilogy—where I had about six months for each book—seem manageable. I needed every minute of the six months, though. I followed a strict regimen, ingesting large quantities of Diet Coke, chocolate, and grated Romano cheese, and eliminating several hours of sleep a night.

What did you learn by writing The Passing Of The Techno-Mages?

That Brach's is my favorite type of chocolate, and Russell Stover my second favorite.

Seriously, I learned a huge amount. I believe Orson Scott Card said, 'To be a good writer, you have to know everything about everything.' I can't say I know that much, but my research has certainly taken me in some fascinating and varied directions. I learned a lot about how magicians work, the history of magic (many of the Mages in the book are named after real magicians), how to read body language, how the brain works, the damage caused by burns (which the Mages seem prone to), micro-electronic devices, and other topics I'd rather keep secret for now. I also learned a fair amount about military figures who used misdirection(one of the Mages' favorite techniques) in wartime. I love looking at history for parallels of situations in my books, because I find history to be a great resource—truth is usually stranger and more interesting than fiction, and when I've never been in a particular situation myself, I like to learn about people who were, and how they reacted. Since my husband studies history, he's great at giving me examples.

I also learned a lot about my weaknesses as a writer. It's my feeling that the journey to become the best writer I can be is a life-long one, and I'm constantly trying to identify my weaknesses and improve those areas. I have many people read various drafts of my manuscripts and rip them apart—err, I mean critique them. That feedback is invaluable in showing me where I've done what I intended and where I've failed. A few of the things I learned on these books—I tend to belabor the obvious; when I try to be subtle no one gets it; and I like to start too many sentences with 'And,' 'But,' and 'Yet.' I cut out about 800 of those in Book 3. Hopefully I'm making progress on these areas and can look for a new bunch of weaknesses to target.

Who influenced you as a writer?

So many people, I hate to name anyone, since I'm sure to leave someone out. But I'll say Frank Conroy, Ursula Le Guinn, H. P. Lovecraft, and Edgar Allan Poe, among many others.

How can writers incorporate the science *back into Science Fiction without becoming inaccessible?*

I think it's important that any science included in the story be relevant to the plot and to the theme (and it would be nice if it was also important to the character). Science shouldn't be included for the sake of proving one's knowledge or justifying oneself. An author's purpose is to tell a story, and if the science is in service to the story, and it is conveyed clearly and with only those details that contribute to the story, then I think readers will remain interested and will be able to understand. I'm not of the school that things should be explained in great scientific detail just to prove they are possible. A couple years ago, Dr. Miguel Alcubierre wrote a fascinating piece describing how warp drive might be possible. That was a scientific article in a science journal, which is where such a discussion belonged. Not in a novel.

In the trilogy, you'll find scientific concepts and information introduced only when they are important to the plot, theme, and character—at least that's what I was trying to do. Many things in the trilogy aren't explained scientifically at all, because the characters don't understand them.

How did your stint as an editor effect your writing?

Editing has improved my writing a great deal. I'm much more aware of the common pitfalls in writing, so I'm less likely to fall victim to them. I also think I've attained some degree of objectivity about my work that helps me to see some of the flaws and attempt to fix them. Editing (or critiquing) the works of others can help any writer improve his skills. That's why I stress critiquing so much at the Odyssey Fantasy Writing Workshop that I run.

Have the effects of film and television been good or bad for the SF genre?

Filmed SF is different from written SF. The expectations of the audience are different, and the techniques and tools the creator uses are different. Many developing SF writers have gained the majority of their knowledge of SF from TV and movies. That background does not serve them well as writers—you need to read to be able to write. There are many common flaws in the work of beginning writers that immediately reveal their lack of knowledge of written SF. I don't blame films and TV for that; we've had some wonderful filmed SF, and I value what those forms contribute to our genre. I do wish that written SF received more attention, because wonderful work is being done in that form as well. Speaking in very general terms, written SF allows for more sophistication, more complexity of ideas and characterization and plot. Filmed SF allows our genre to reach out to a larger audience, and offers exhilarating visuals and a more immediate, visceral experience. In a way, Joe managed to get the advantages of both forms in *B5*, because the series is in many ways a filmed novel.

Horror is an emotion; can SF be equated to an emotional response?

SF is not as focused on a particular emotion as horror is. Emotionally, it's a more diverse genre. But most SF makes us feel awe and wonder—at moments we can have an almost religious sense of our own smallness in the face of a vast universe. I'd say that a fair amount of SF also evokes horror.

How do you keep work like the 'The Science Of...' series fun instead of feeling like academics?

In the case of *The Science Of The X-Files* it was easy, because the show itself often has a great sense of fun. I can't imagine anything much more fun that researching whether humans might be genetically altered to have green blood, or whether a man whose every cell was cancerous might regrow a severed body part. I guess that tone carried over into *The Science of Star Wars*—those movies also have a great sense of fun and adventure, and if I can, I want to make the exploration of issues like hyperspace fun too (it ain't like dusting crops, you know).

How does one write, teach, edit, and still find time for an iguana?

When the iguana declares that it is mating season and you're the lucky object of his affections, it's hard to fit in anything else. But it is very flattering.

How do you approach writing a tie-in novel?

In many ways, I approach it the same way I do a regular novel. I actually believe that tie-ins have the same worth and potential as any other novel. I believe, if done well, they can be great art. I know that idea may seem ridiculous to many people, because the quality of many tie-ins has been inferior to other types of books, but I don't think it has to be. I approach these books with the goal of creating great art. Readers can decide whether I succeed to any degree.

I also try to write my tie-in novels so that people can read and enjoy them even if they don't know much about *Babylon 5*. If a story is strong enough, it should be able to carry readers along without requiring any pre-formed motivation to read. I had a number of people critique the trilogy who had *never* seen the show, and they seemed to enjoy the books just like regular novels, which is what I'd hoped for.

If I've done my job right, people familiar with the series gain extra enjoyment from seeing how events in the books relate to those on the show, and from learning more about various characters. In several cases, the events in the trilogy intertwine with events we've seen on the show, and *B5* fans learn that what they *thought* happened on the show is actually not what happened at all. A whole new layer of truth is exposed.

How did The Passing of Techno-Mages *differ from your writing* The Shadow Within?

The techno-mage trilogy is much more complex than my earlier *Babylon 5* novel, *The Shadow Within*, so it required much more planning. After I received Joe's outline, I wanted to flesh things out, develop characters and plot events in detail, so I wrote what turned out to be a 200-page outline (yes, I'm crazy). Luckily I had more time to write the trilogy. I had eight weeks to write *The Shadow Within*. For the trilogy, I took several months to do research and write the outlines, and then about six months to write each book. The additional time was necessary because these are longer and more sophisticated books, and it also allowed me to do more revisions, after receiving feedback from my many critiquers.

How has writing and editing changed since you first made the decision to pursue those kinds of work?

I don't think writing has changed much at all, but getting published certainly has. Publishers' lists are shrinking, with more slots now devoted to best-selling authors and fewer slots devoted to 'midlist' writers, meaning writers who aren't New York Times best-sellers (i.e., almost all SF/F/H writers).

Publishers are less interested in building an author over time and more interested in grabbing onto the next big thing. It's easy to get very pessimistic, but I still believe that most editors love books and want to publish good books, so good books still have a chance. Science fiction and fantasy remain strong, commercial genres.

Editing has changed in that these big conglomerate publishers don't reward, teach, or encourage actual editing any more. An editor might turn a mediocre book into a great book, but since most people at the publishing house don't read either the original version or the edited version, no one knows what the editor has done. Because of this, there's not a lot of motivation for editors to put much effort into actual editing. Quality is not valued. Sales are. Pushing for a large marketing/publicity campaign, or convincing the sales reps that a book has a good 'buzz,' can be more helpful to an editor's career.

Since editors change jobs often, they usually aren't around to reap the benefits of a long-term effort to improve a writer's skills. The appearance of success is more important than actual success.

Can you use the same writing influences for SF as you would for horror?

I don't really think of 'using' different influences. I've been influenced by many different writers of all genres, and I think all those influences sort of combine inside me and affect the various choices I make in my writing. I don't really think those influences change if I switch to a different genre.

Whatever I'm writing, I try to think of other books, TV shows, or movies with similar plots, so I can examine the common elements in those plots what made them work or not work, and how mine compares to them. Hopefully I discover a way in which my work is distinct from what's been done before, and also discover some underlying requirements of this type of plot and make sure I've fulfilled them.

I saw a few minutes of *The Dead Zone* movie on television last night. That's one of my top five favorite movies; I just love it. I realized, as I watched it, that some hints of the things that I love in that movie had made it into *The Passing of the Techno-Mages*. *The Dead Zone* is about a character who has a special power, and that power brings him mostly pain. In the trilogy, Galen has a similar problem.

Have you been able to apply science in horror?

I think most of the fiction I've written in the recent past has been a science fiction/horror combination—I would classify all my Babylon 5 novels that way, and many of my short stories. So science definitely comes into it. I found myself thinking a lot about H.P. Lovecraft while writing my first *B5* novel, *The Shadow Within*. That book has many parallels with

Lovecraft's novella 'At the Mountains of Madness,' which is one of my favorites. Lovecraft combined science and horror in that, and I did the same in *The Shadow Within*. In *The Passing of the Techno-Mages* trilogy, I'm working with characters who are part scientist, part magician. In a way, they are the perfect characters to embody a combination of science fiction and horror—they often think of things in scientific terms, yet at the same time there is an aspect of the mystical about them—a sense of mystery and the unknown that can easily lead to horror.

Is your background in astrophysics and astronomy a kind of liability in Science Fiction *as opposed to Science* Fact?

I don't think so, but that's because my science knowledge is in a different part of my brain than the writing part. I do try to set up situations that are scientifically believable, but at the same time I realize that our understanding of the universe is changing all the time. Things that scientists would have laughed off as impossible twenty years ago are now commonly accepted as truth, or at least as possible. And a lot of science fiction is about technologies far in advance of ours, technologies that create awe and wonder. I have no problem creating a technology that can do something that currently seems impossible. If I didn't do that, it would hardly seem believable as something far in advance of our technology. And if the characters in the story don't understand how it works, then I don't feel any explanation of it is appropriate or necessary.

As a writer, I'm only concerned with science when it will further the story. It should be relevant to plot, theme, and character in order to be included. The science should serve the story, not the other way around.

How have The Science of... *books been received by your colleagues in the scientific community?*

When I started working on *The Science of the X-Files*, I thought I'd have a very hard time getting experts in the various fields I discussed in the book, and to get their opinions on particular episodes. Instead, everyone I contacted agreed to be interviewed, and they even agreed to answer some of the most outlandish questions (I'd always work up to those, leaving them until last, in case the scientist would get mad and hang up on me): 'So, Dr. X, could eating human livers possibly have any effect on the aging process?' Many of them actually got excited during my interviews, because my questions led them to speculate in areas they hadn't thought of before. One scientist doing cancer research actually got an idea for a possible new cancer treatment from one of my questions!

In writing *The Science of Star Wars*, I found many scientists who were fans of the movies. One robotocist actually watched the movies on video before our interview, so she could study Artoo and Threepio. She was completely freaked out that their behavior reflected some of her own research.

Both books have gotten surprisingly positive feedback from scientists. They realize that, amidst all the fun, readers actually learn a lot, and many of them become more interested in science.

Is it more common than some may think that scientists are able to suspend disbelief?

Absolutely. They didn't particularly think these shows were scientifically accurate, but it didn't matter to them. They weren't watching the shows as research; they were watching them for entertainment. That's the same way I do it—turn off the science part of my brain and have fun. Only when a scientific goof is really prominent and critical to the plot do I have a problem.

When I'm talking a movie over with friends later, or if I'm asked to analyze the science, then I start thinking about it.

For some people, I know, looking for science nits is part of the fun, so they keep that part of their brain active all the time. I'd rather just enjoy the story, if I can.

How did you make The Science of... *books accessible to the average reader?*

I first had to have a thorough understanding of the subjects myself—some of which I was familiar with, and some of which I wasn't. So I did tons of research. For each book, I read about 100 books and about 1,000 scientific articles, then interviewed scientists. Once I felt I understood the issues involved, then I imagined I was explaining them to my mother, or my husband—intelligent people with no real science background, but with a love for *The X-Files* or *Star Wars* and curiosity about what they'd seen. I wrote the books as if I was talking to them.

Do you have a theory, or subscribe to one, about dark matter?

So many new facts about the universe are now coming to light—for example, the recent discovery that our universe is expanding at a constantly *accelerating* rate, which defies everything we've believed—I don't think we can definitely say whether dark matter even exists or not. I believe other questions have to be answered first before we can make any judgments about dark matter.

What do you think about the international space station?

I'm glad we've got *something* up there, though it's sure a far cry from the space station in *2001: A Space Odyssey*. I hope that we can send more missions to other planets, both manned and unmanned. The space station should be able to help with that, though we still have to make the commitment of money, and these days, people don't seem to have space exploration very high on their list of priorities.

What's your opinion on expenditures for the US Space Program?

I think we ought to be spending a lot more. Our understanding of the Earth is extremely limited, and one way that we can learn a lot more is by having data on other planets for comparison. We need a better understanding of Earth if we're to survive here.

Also, we should make it easier for independent companies to explore space. I have no doubt they can do it more cheaply and efficiently than the government.

Religion was given quite a bit of attention in the B5 universe... can religion and science truly co-exist?

This is actually one of the major questions explored in the trilogy. Some of the mages have strong religious beliefs; they would say that science reveals an order and design to the universe established by God. Others don't believe in any god; they feel the nature of matter itself dictates scientific principles, not any higher power.

As for myself, I'm in the former camp. I haven't held onto many of the Catholic beliefs I was raised with, but when I imagine the universe, and all the energy in it, including us, I believe there is some kind of unifying or organizing power, which you may or may not call God. What survives of my religious beliefs actually survives *because* of my attachment to science, not in spite of it.

Has Odyssey turned out the way you intended?

When I first thought of starting up a six-week summer workshop for SF/F/H writers, I had no clue how much work it was going to be. I also had no idea how much it would enrich my life. Every year there comes a time—usually just before Odyssey begins—when I ask myself why the heck I'm doing this. And then every year there comes a time—usually a couple days after Odyssey has started—when I realize how much I love running the workshop. When I left the rat race of New York publishing to focus on my own writing, I knew that I still wanted to work closely with authors, as I had as an editor. Helping an author make his manuscript the best it can be is something I really enjoy. In a way, it's sort of like solving a math problem—figuring out what's not working right in a story, and how it could work better.

The thing I didn't anticipate was the intensity of working with authors for six weeks straight, and the wonderful relationships that form. It's great working with people who share the same passions I have. I've met many extremely talented writers, and when the workshop ends they are no longer students, but colleagues and friends.

Have there been any shortcomings to Odyssey you've had to correct?

Every year I try to improve the class, adding new information and figuring out better ways to convey particular ideas about writing. I've also expanded the time spent on certain topics that tend to cause a lot of trouble for developing writers, while reducing the time spent on others. Point of view is something that I find again and again is a weakness, and if the point of view isn't working well, the story is dead in the water.

What does Odyssey offer that other programs don't?

I approach Odyssey as an editor, giving an editor's feedback on stories, letting students know how an editor would react to their work, why an editor might reject one story and buy another. As an editor, I have a somewhat different perspective on things than an author does. I've worked with many different authors, so I realize each author has his own process and his own goals. Rather than pushing students to do things my way, I try to help them improve their own process. We're the only major workshop run by an editor.

There are some other differences as well. Some workshops have a different instructor each week, which can have advantages, but also has disadvantages. At Odyssey, I am the main instructor for the six weeks. I plan out the lectures so that by the end of the workshop, we'll have covered all the major elements of fiction writing. I also work very closely with students throughout, starting with reading two stories by each student before the workshop begins to get a sense of each person's strengths and weaknesses. We have individual meetings over the course of the workshop to chart each person's progress, and I suggest individual exercises and goals. So there is a coherence and comprehensiveness to the lectures, and a continuity of feedback over the six weeks.

We also have guest lecturers who come in once a week, for about 24 hours, to lecture, answer students' questions, critique students' work, and meet individually with some students. That gives students other perspectives and techniques to use.

For the fifth week of the workshop, a writer-in-residence takes over the lecturing. This summer that will be Terry Brooks. I work closely with the writer-in-residence in advance, so his lectures will be integrated into the rest of the workshop. He and I then both critique stories submitted during this week.

How do you choose a writer-in-residence for Odyssey?

I look at the most respected and successful writers in our field, and search for those who have teaching and critiquing experience. It's important not only that a writer write well, but that he also can explain or describe what he does. Dan Simmons, whom we had last year, is not only an incredibly talented writer, he's also an award-winning teacher. In addition, I try to provide, over the years, a variety of perspectives and backgrounds.

Many publishers have questioned the legitimacy of webzines. What are your thoughts on web-publishing?

Right now, in SF/F/H, I believe there are only a handful of webzines that are maintaining standards comparable to those of a print magazine or book publisher. It's not that print is inherently 'superior' (though I will admit I prefer reading a printed page to a computer screen), but print magazines have had to prove themselves commercially in order to survive. If they don't provide quality fiction and nonfiction that pleases their readership, then people will stop buying their magazine and it will cease to exist. On the web, many people post fiction and articles, and since this costs minimal money, there's no requirement that many people read the work or enjoy it. In many cases, it's like reading the stories that would be rejected by a print magazine.

There are exceptions, however. The fiction on scifi.com is of magazine quality, due to Ellen Datlow's expert editorial direction. I just learned of *Strange Horizons* recently, when I met editor-in-chief Mary Anne Mohanraj at a symposium. I was very impressed with her understanding of the field, and when I took a look at the fiction published here, I found it to be of very high quality. So those are two, and I'd say there are maybe two or three more. In time, I think we'll have a few more high-quality webzines.

As far as whether having a story published on the web will help your career as a writer, editors are aware of those few good webzines. If you are published on one of them, it will be a useful credit. If you are published on one that they haven't heard of, then it won't hurt or help you.

Is print on demand an asset or liability?

At this point, it's useful mainly for authors who have a book go out of print. These days, the huge conglomerate publishers require a certain rate of movement for a book to remain in print; it must sell a certain number of copies each month. Few authors, particularly in SF/F/H, are able to maintain that rate of movement. Thus many books, some real classics, become difficult to find. An author could have his earlier books available through print on demand, so he could continue to make a bit of money on them, and readers could still buy them.

Launching a new, original novel through print on demand is extremely difficult, particularly if you are not a well-known author. Your friends and family may buy copies, but chances are few other people will. They just won't know that it exists.

The line between the small press and large press seems to be more distinct than ever; what can those two groups keep in mind in order for speculative fiction to continue to grow?

The growth of the small press is a good thing for SF/F/H, because it offers more outlets and more opportunities. People working at small publishing houses have to be very focused in what they publish. They have to find a successful niche and publish for that niche. Small presses can go under when they start acting like big publishing houses and try to target the mainstream. They don't have the resources or manpower to do that. Thus you'll find small presses that focus on vampire fiction, or on high-quality limited editions of works by famous writers, and so on. They've found what works and are sticking with it.

Big publishers, of course, should be monitoring the work of the small presses and feeding off it. When a niche grows and becomes big enough, major publishers need to get into that trend and start publishing works for that audience. That's really how all popular culture works. Some kid in New Hampshire decides to shred his jeans and wear them to school. Other kids do the same, and the trend spreads. Major jean companies observe the trend and start to sell pre-shredded pants. The trend gets incorporated into our culture, kids lose interest because it's no longer edgy, and they come up with something new.

How does a writer know when to stop revising?

I think you have to develop an instinct for it, just as you have to develop a sense of when something is working in your story, and when it's not. Getting feedback from others can be very helpful in identifying your weaknesses and going through a story and fixing them one by one. I always think of writing a first draft as creating a bunch of big messy problems. When I revise, I'm solving those problems. The number of weak areas decreases until at last I feel I've dealt with them all to the best of my ability.

Spotting the weak areas in your own work is the hardest thing for a writer to do. The best way to develop this ability is to do a lot of critiques on other people's stories. It's easy to see the flaws in other people's work. As you critique others' stories, you develop the editor part of your brain. You start to view stories differently than other people. You are studying them, seeing how they are put together and whether they are effective. As that editor lobe of your brain grows like a tumor, you slowly become able to apply it to your own work, and to begin to see some of the problems in your own stories.

What should be kept in mind to be the best editor one can be?

First, you need to be focused on discovering what the writer intended, and on helping the writer to better accomplished that. Your job is not to tell the writer what story *you* wish he was writing; it's to tell the writer how better to write the story *he* wants to write. Next, every piece of feedback you give the writer should be both truthful and helpful. This may seem obvious, but it's constantly violated by editors and by critiquers in writing workshops. Never say anything that's not true (don't say you liked it if you didn't), and don't say anything that won't help the author improve. Saying 'This story sucked' doesn't help the author, doesn't give the author some direction to move in to improve the story. Saying 'Your characters were flat and your plot lacked conflict' is helpful, because now the feedback is more specific, and the author has some clue about what to do to fix these problems. Being as specific as possible about the weaknesses of the story is extremely valuable. You need to identify the weakness clearly before you begin offering solutions. Once you've told the author what the problem is, you can offer various suggestions for fixing it, which the author may take, or he may find a solution of his own.

Sometimes it can be difficult to figure out exactly why a story doesn't work; the editor's job is to study the story and think about it until the answer becomes clear.

An editor, also, should have a very strong knowledge of the language and grammar, and should have an extensive knowledge of literature. Above all, do no harm to the manuscript. If you're not sure whether a change will improve the story or not, don't make the change. Making a manuscript worse than it was when you received it is the most heinous crime any editor can commit.

What can today's writers learn from the authors you worked with at Dell?

I was fortunate to work with some extremely talented writers. Studying the work of good writers can improve your own writing a huge amount. Look at the style of Kathe Koja or Dennis Etchison, the atmosphere of Tanith Lee or Poppy Z. Brite, the characters of Joan Vinge or Melanie Tem, the tone of Patrick McCabe, the rhythm of Barry Gifford, the villains of Brian Hodge, the voice of Jeanne Kalogridis or Peter Dickinson, the plotting of William F. Nolan—those are great ways of learning what is possible in fiction.

I find the best way to learn from other authors is to pick a short story of theirs that I really like, read it over and over, and really pull it apart and study it. It's in reading it over many times and looking at the details of its construction that I learn some wonderful things about writing.

As an editor, you worked closely with your writers; is that sort of relationship harder to come by these days?

There are still good editors out there who are committed to the editorial process. On the other hand, as I mentioned earlier, there are an increasing number of editors who don't really know how to edit and/or don't have much desire to do so. As an author, I've worked with four different editors on books (and many others on short fiction). Of those four, only one has attempted to give serious editorial feedback. Of the others, one changed one sentence in the entire book; the second edited only the openings of each chapter; and the third simply crossed out a number of my prepositions for no apparent reason. While I'd love to think that my books were so perfect they required minimal editing, the editor lobe of my brain prevents me from believing that.

Since editors change jobs so often, it's increasingly rare that an author works with the same editor for more than one or two books, so developing a relationship becomes more difficult.

Is it true that art is never finished, only abandoned?

I don't believe that. I believe that art is never perfect; it could always be improved. But there is a time when it is 'finished,' a time after which any changes you make will not improve the manuscript any further, and a time after which you lose the mindset you had while creating it, so that you are no longer the same person and can't make a contribution to the art that would be consistent with the rest.

Your works have featured Morden more than any of the other B5 books. Why the attraction to the character?

Morden is one of the most mysterious characters on *Babylon 5*. Since we see him only a few times in the series, that sense of mystery is never broken. In his role as a servant to the Shadows, we see him doing a lot of very interesting and awful things to the other *B5* characters, but we never really know what motivates him. In the terms JMS established, we never really discover who Morden is, and what Morden wants. He appears to believe in the Shadows' agenda, but we don't know why. At first glance he seems totally evil. Since every other character in Joe Straczynski's universe seemed to contain both good and evil, I was immediately drawn to Morden, interested in discovering whether he had any bit of good inside him. There was a lot of room there to explore and develop, which as a writer I found very exciting.

What do you know about Mr. Morden that we don't?

Most of what I learned about Morden in my exploration of him, I put in *The Passing Of The Techno-Mages* trilogy, and in my earlier *B5* novel, *The*

Shadow Within. The main thing I learned was that Morden is certainly not a good person, but he's not an evil one either.

On the critical issue of boxers or briefs, I'll keep the answer for myself.

With a tone that darkens with each installment of The Passing Of The Techno-Mages, *did you consider having a character named Bunny a liability?*

Of all the characters I created and named, from Ing-Radi toDjadjamonkh to Gali-Gali, I got the most heat from my critiquers on the name Bunny. Some of them just could not stand that name, or the fact that she had long blond hair and wore a short pink dress. People told me that science-fiction characters should wear suits, not short pink dresses, and that they shouldn't have long blond hair or be named Bunny. That, of course, only made me more determined to keep Bunny as she was. I wanted to create characters who felt like real people, not science-fiction 'types,' and I felt Bunny offered a nice contrast to all the techno-mages with their weird, fancy names, formal dialogue, and black robes. As for how she fit in with the dark tone, she is a sociopath, so I don't think she breaks the mood too much. Most villains tend to act seriously, dress seriously, and have serious names. Elizar really covers that territory, so I wanted something different from Bunny. I tend to think that giving her the sweet name of Bunny makes her a little more scary.

The level of violence in each of the B5 trilogies has been more extreme than in the TV series—is that because you work with an editor rather than a censor? Does it have more to do with the way a given author interprets the outline JMS has written?

I can't speak for the other authors, but for me, when I read Joe's outline, it seemed to me that the story of the techno-mages would have to be very dark. They're in an extremely bad situation, and trying to minimize or ignore that, I thought, would have been a horrible cop-out. I realized that would make the trilogy probably the darkest thing in the *B5* universe, but I felt that was necessary and believable.

I had a friend critique my 200-page outline for the trilogy. She said, 'You can't have a trilogy with three *Empire Strikes Back* endings!' I took that as a challenge. *Empire* is my favorite *Star Wars* movie, mainly because we learn how much more serious and dangerous everything is than we'd thought. I love the darkness of that film. But I actually don't believe Book 3 has an *Empire* ending.

As for the violence, the degree and nature of it wasn't really described in the outline. I grew up loving horror and gore, so I don't think a whole lot about it. I just put it in where it's important to the story. In the single episode of *B5* that included techno-mages, 'The Geometry of Shadows,' the mage Elric tells Vir, 'Do not try the patience of wizards, for they are subtle and quick to anger.' I pretty much took that line and ran with it. The Techno-Mages are a violent group caught in dangerous circumstances, so the fireballs are going to fly, spells of destruction will be cast, and people will be crushed. Some things I described in the books—Drakh being squeezed to a pulp, Blaylock's hands being cut open—would certainly be inappropriate for a mainstream television show. On TV, you have to think about children who may just be flipping by looking for the *Teletubbies*. In a book, nobody is going to be reading it unless they've reached a certain reading level and have an interest in the material. I tried hard to maintain the feeling of the *B5* universe in the trilogy, while at the same time I tried to take advantage of the novel format to do things that weren't possible in the series (such as going into characters' heads and giving their thoughts).

How has the fan response been to the trilogy thus far?

I've gotten just wonderful, wonderful feedback from people. E-mail is a great thing. I put my e-mail in the back of the book, and I get hundreds of messages from people telling me what they think of my work. Luckily, no one has spotted any major goofs so far. I've had people tell me I made them cry, and people curse me out because they have to wait a couple months for the next book (I love that; I love torturing people. I discovered that's the best thing about writing a trilogy). One woman told me she called in sick to work because she couldn't stop reading Book 2. A guy said he got into a hot bath and started Book 1, and found he couldn't stop reading until he was done, even though his bath had turned freezing cold. I've even gotten a lot of mail from people who don't watch *B5* but bought the books because they like my other work, and they've loved the trilogy as well. I know I'm far from a great writer, but I gave it all my effort and wrote the best books I could. I tried to write the books so that they could stand on their own and be favorably compared to 'real' novels. So many bad media tie-ins have been written; I love *B5* and I just wanted to do it justice. I know that some writers think it's ridiculous to put a lot of effort into a tie-in, because, they think, 'those readers' won't know the difference. But I'm one of 'those readers,' and I know that we do know the difference.

In The Passing Of The Techno-Mages, *we learn a great deal about what 'really' happened on an episode or two of B5—were you concerned about any backlash from fans that may have felt manipulated?*

You always take a risk when you try to add something new to an existing work that has many fans. Since the universe Joe created is so rich, every fan experiences *B5* a bit differently, and has developed his own ideas about it. For example, I've heard from many fans who've said they imagined Morden was totally evil. But when they read my account of Morden's past and motivations, they find it really interesting, and most end up incorporating this new view into their image of the character.

I could have played it safer and just reproduced the scenes from the episodes as they appeared on TV. But I felt that wasn't terribly interesting, and also that I'd be wasting an opportunity to reveal more about the characters and their situation. Since by their nature techno-mages mislead and deceive, it seemed natural that wherever the mages went, there would be hidden layers of activity, and that through their points of view, those hidden layers could be revealed.

Certainly if I was writing about some other group of people or some other episodes, that may not have been the case, and I wouldn't have 'revealed' any hidden layers. I didn't want to change things just for the sake of changing them. Book 3 has just come out, so I haven't heard much from fans about that yet, but readers seemed to find the hidden layers revealed in Book 2 really intriguing.

How is the Odyssey Writing Workshop coming along?

Great! We've just finalized our plans for the Summer 2002 workshop, and we're already getting applications.

When I was working as a senior editor at Bantam Doubleday Dell, I found that I loved working with writers, helping them make their work the best it could be. When I left publishing to focus on my own writing career, I wanted to find some way to continue working with writers, so I created Odyssey. It's a six-week workshop for fantasy, science-fiction, and horror writers held each summer at Southern New Hampshire University. Developing writers aged 17-65 come from all over the US and Canada to attend. People can find more information at www.odysseyworkshop.org.

Terry Brooks was your last writer-in-residence for Odyssey. Who will be next?

We've had great people like Terry, Harlan Ellison, Dan Simmons, Ben Bova. For 2002, our writer-in-residence will be Charles de Lint, who is an incredible writer and teacher. Our guest lecturers will include R. A. Salvatore, Elizabeth Hand, and James Patrick Kelly.

Does your experience in the field of science curb your imagination in SF or does it enhance it?

I think my science background feeds my imagination. It seems as if science and SF have always fed off each other. Writers learn about new scientific possibilities, and that triggers story ideas. Good stories often inspire scientists to steer their research into new areas.

As a scientist, I think it's important that a story be plausible, and that authors know enough so they don't break scientific laws without realizing it (to give a classic example, there shouldn't be sounds in space). As a writer, I believe story is paramount, and a writer cannot be a slave to science. So if there's something I want to happen in my story and it seems scientifically impossible, then I need to come up with a reason why it could be scientifically possible. The techno-mages do many things that seem to break current scientific laws. But the technology they use is millions of years in advance of ours, so it seems quite reasonable to me that it *would* do things that currently seem impossible. I'm very aware of all the things that science has yet to understand, and the history of science tells us that as our understanding evolves, things that previously seemed impossible become quite possible. So I think its far less believable that this extremely advanced technology would do no more than we can do today.

How has your writing SF affected your view of hard science?

As a child, I loved SF, and I loved thinking about the big questions: Where did the universe come from? What's going to happen to it? Is there alien life? What is it like? How will man react when he meets aliens? What will happen when the sun burns out? I was fascinated by these things; I remember being upset the president didn't have a policy to deal with the sun burning out. My career goal was to become an astronaut just like Charlton Heston in *The Planet Of The Apes*.

These interests led me into a career in astrophysics and a job at NASA. But I found that, for me, NASA was too constricting, concerned mainly with practical issues and not with these big cosmic questions. I realized that what I really loved about science was not the nitty gritty of research, but exploring the ideas, their implications and possibilities. That led me back to science fiction.

For a while I was kind of down on science, because NASA had been a big dream of mine and hadn't turned out to be right for me. But after a few years my fascination with all those issues returned, and I finally had the opportunity to explore all those questions in my books *The Science Of The X-Files*, *The Science Of Star Wars*, and in my science fiction.

As editor, writer, and teacher, what constitutes a good story?

Characters that the reader cares about, struggling to achieve a goal that the reader cares about, written in prose so vivid the reader is caught up in the unique world of the author. In a great story, the reader will recognize truths about life that he always knew but never articulated.

What can today's editors learn from today's authors?

I sometimes feel that in the great cycle of karma, I'm paying now as an author for all the things I did before as an editor. I once told an author I could give him only three weeks to write a book. When Dell called me and asked me to write my first *Babylon 5* novel, *The Shadow Within*, they told me I could have four weeks (I eventually talked them up to six weeks—oh, the luxury!).

Over the past 10 years or so, the role of editors has gradually changed, as publishing houses have merged into giant corporate conglomerates. In the old days, an editor's job was primarily editing—go figure. Today, editors have very little time to spend on editing, and the publishing houses do not value editing. An editor spends most of her time chasing after hot properties and trying to generate enthusiasm within the company and the industry for her books. Editors are considered good at their jobs if they buy books that have a lot of 'buzz,' and they can increase that 'buzz.' Editors still can work in-depth with authors on their manuscripts, but the editor-in-chief, in most cases, will never know or care.

Since most editors begin as editorial assistants and learn how to edit from their bosses, what's happening now is a new generation of editors is coming up, and many of them haven't been exposed to basic editing skills. In science fiction, there are still some wonderful, wonderful editors around. But an increasing proportion of those in the industry either neglect the editorial process or lack the skills for it. Those editors have a responsibility to the books and authors they publish. It's really a sacred trust, between author and editor. The editor, as Hippocrates said, should first of all do no harm. And second, should try to help the author make the book what he wants it to be, the best it can possibly be.

I don't know that authors are the ones to teach this to editors, but now being an author, I have a much greater understanding of the benefit or harm that an editor can generate.

As a fan of SF, are there any movies you're looking forward to seeing?

Well, if we're talking TV movies, I'm of course dying to see the new *B5* movie, *The Legend Of The Rangers*. I'm definitely ready for a new *B5* fix.

As for movie-theatre movies, it's fantasy, but I'm dying to see *The Fellowship Of The Ring*. I've tried not to get my hopes up, but they're way up there. To refresh my memory, I've been reading the novel out loud to my husband—rapped my way through the Tom Bombadil section—and it's just a constant wonder what a wonderful story Tolkien wrote. (And the parallels to *B5* are fascinating!) I really hope the movie will be great.

What affect from medium-sized publishers have on the larger houses?

Smaller publishers help discover new trends. The big houses don't take a lot of chances these days—or let me rephrase that, when they do take chances, they tend to take them on proven authors and proven categories. So they might spend a ton of money on Bill Clinton's memoirs, which in a sense is taking a chance because they're overpaying, but the book is in a proven category that will definitely succeed to some degree. Smaller publishers, in the last 10-20 years, have been increasing their releases in the areas neglected by the big houses. Two particularly successful categories mined by these publishers have been true historical adventure and literary historical fiction; two best-selling examples are *The Perfect Storm* and *Cold Mountain*. Big houses have seen the huge success of these books and have jumped into those categories. Books of this type then sell for higher amounts, which smaller publishers can't afford, and smaller publishers look for some new area to develop. This is the way popular culture works in general—individuals or small subcultures create innovations which are then co-opted by larger organizations and the mainstream culture.

How has promoting a book changed since your days at Dell?

Publishers are doing less publicity on fewer books. Back in my day—God, I sound ancient—in the early '90s, nearly every book that was published, hardcover or paperback—was promoted with bound galleys (early copies of a book sent to reviewers), a press release, and its own promotional mailing. Now, only the top releases receive this treatment. Other books might just have a press release sent out, and others have next to nothing done to promote them.

What this means is that you, as the author, have to be much more active in promoting your work. If you don't do it, no one will. And remember, if the book doesn't succeed and make money for the publisher, they won't realize the error of their ways and give you a bigger publicity campaign on your second book. They just won't publish your second book.

What are your five 'Must reads' for aspiring SF authors?

Well, there's so much great SF, I think you can read lots of different things and still be fairly well-read in the genre. But here's my shot at it:

> *The Time Machine* by H. G. Wells
> *I, Robot* by Isaac Asimov
> *Do Androids Dream Of Electric Sheep* by Philip K. Dick
> *The Martian Chronicles* by Ray Bradbury
> *The Left Hand Of Darkness* by Ursula K. Le Guin

What can you tell us about your upcoming projects?

I'm working now on a science thriller set in my own universe, involving cloning and genetic manipulation. It's set about twenty years from now. It explores an issue that I've been obsessed with for about the last ten years—how much control we have over the way we behave. I explored that from one angle through the techno-mages in the trilogy and Galen's struggle for control, and I'm going to explore it from another angle in this new book. I don't know about you, but I continually find myself behaving in ways that I don't like. I'll be impatient with my husband and say something cruel to him, then regret it and resolve never to do it again. Yet the next day, there I am, doing it all over again. The latest research suggests, to me at least, that a great deal of our behavior is genetically determined. Our genes determine which chemicals are released in our brain at what times, and how strong an effect those chemicals have. They can make us depressed or manic, can predispose us to alcohol or drug (or chocolate) addiction, can encourage us to seek thrills or to hide from them. So the book is going to explore how much choice we do have, and how much responsibility we carry for our actions.

How did you end up moving from a scientific career to a writing and editing career?

I wrote since I was little (won a pumpkin in second grade in a Halloween story contest, and wrote and produced a science-fiction musical when I was about ten), but I always thought I had to do something more 'important' with my life. My career goal was to become an astronaut just like Charlton Heston in *The Planet Of The Apes*. I'm not quite sure why he was my role model, since he blew up planet Earth and everyone on it in the second movie, but I loved the idea. As I studied astrophysics, and later worked in the field, though, I slowly found myself becoming dissatisfied. I loved thinking about the wild scientific ideas raised in science fiction, and I also loved thinking about the big issues—where did the universe come from? Where was it headed? These are questions of astrophysics, but not questions you could really focus on in research or at NASA, where work had to be narrowed to smaller, more practical issues. I also realized that one thing I loved about *Planet Of The Apes* and other science fiction was the freedom fiction provided—the ability to explore ideas and their consequences. And I realized that writing was what I most wanted to do, and that whether it would change the world or not, I should do what would make me happy. So I went off and wrote a novel, then earned a master of fine arts in creative writing, and got a job in publishing to support me until I made it as a writer.

How did you get the B5 *tie-in spot?*

I was a senior editor at Dell Publishing when *B5* debuted. I was very excited about the show—I thought the pilot and first few episodes were terrific, and the interviews I read with Joe Straczynski indicated that this show was going to be different from anything that had been done—a five-year story with a beginning, middle, and end, virtually an epic novel told over five years. I was really enthusiastic about that idea, and called Joe and asked if he would like Dell to do some novels based on the series. He agreed, and I talked my boss into going ahead with the line. So I got the Dell novel line started. Later, I quit publishing to focus on my own writing career. When the woman at Warner Bros. who handles book rights learned that I was leaving Dell to write, she said, 'Why don't you write a *Babylon 5* novel? You'd do a terrific job.' I said no, I had a half-finished novel I was determined to finish, and had never thought of writing a tie-in novel before.

I moved to New Hampshire, and after a few months I got a copy of a form letter that Joe had written to possible authors, giving a couple ideas for possible *B5* novels. I actually stumbled across this letter a couple days ago. There was a phrase in it—'the discovery of the Shadows by the *Icarus* and Sheridan's wife.' That's all it said about that idea. The second I read that phrase, though, I was taken with the idea. I started thinking of what that would have been like, and I wanted to figure it out.

The next thing I knew, I'd put aside my half-finished novel and written a 25-page synopsis of my proposed novel. I sent it to Dell, they liked it and sent it to Joe, and he liked it and gave his okay.

Who are a few of your favorite authors?

Ursula Le Guin, H.G. Wells, Edgar Allan Poe, H.P. Lovecraft, Philip K. Dick, Ian McEwan, J.R.R. Tolkien. Shakespeare (There are a number of Shakespearean references in the Techno-Mage Trilogy.), Aeschylus, and Frank Conroy.

MAX ALLAN COLLINS

MAX COLLINS IS NO STRANGER to lovers of the mystery, specifically the '30s-50s era of the classic detective, ranging from Eliot Ness to Nate Heller, but some may be unfamiliar with the impressive body of work in the graphic novel genre encompassing not only 'Mickey Spillane's Mike Danger and Batman, but his ambitious work, *Road to Perdition*.

Max is also conversant in the art of adapting a script into a novel, most notably *In the Line of Fire*, *Saving Private Ryan*, and a pair of *NYPD Blue* novels, *Blue Beginning*, and *Blue Blood*, and in the role of filmmaker (*Mommy* and *Mommy 2*.) as well as a writer of non-fiction such as *Stolen Away*, detailing the Lindbergh baby kidnapping.

He also took the time to talk about his musical project with *Lost in Space* and *Babylon 5* star Bill Mumy, Seduction of the Innocent.

Taking place shortly before his promotional tour for his latest work, *Regeneration*, Max took some time out to answer questions regarding not only his prose, but his work in graphic novels and his experiences with Seduction of the Innocent.

How do you prefer to be thought of; mystery writer, editor, etc.?

I'm a storyteller, which also makes me an entertainer. It's fun to see people describing me as a 'Filmmaker' now, but film is just one way to tell a story—like writing novels or short stories or comics or songs.

What is your opinion on the growing media tie-in market and what some are considering the death of the mid-list?

I've heard the mid-list is dying for decades now. I just press forward and keep at it. Doing media tie-in work is something I'm good at, so I'm perhaps less threatened than some writers. I would hate to see my real novels fall by the wayside, but if they did, I bet I could still make a living doing media-related stuff. I could get mad about this, but what good what it do?

The best thing a writer can do is create something so big it becomes 'Media.' I've recently had two comics properties sell to the movies... should one of them actually get made, I'll do my own media tie-ins! I already did that, to a degree, by writing novels out of my two movies, *Mommy* and *Mommy 2: Mommy's Day*.

What do you see for the future of speculative fiction?

I'm on the outskirts of that field. My favorite SF material tends to be classic stuff—Ray Bradbury, Harlan Ellison, the EC comics—and I've been a *Star Trek* fan for many years (classic *Trek*), and my whole family is into *The X-Files*. Fantasy seems to be much stronger, as the dream-like quality of it lends itself to fiction writing—my 16-year-old son reads reams of it, the Feist and Jordan books, for example.

Speculative fiction, on the other hand, is so well and thoroughly served by film, it's hurting the prose writers. With CGI, how can a mere mortal compete? I would have gladly taken a crack at the novelization of *The Matrix*, but it would have been hard to pull that off as effectively in prose as it was on screen. I preferred *The 13th Floor*, by the way, a movie nobody seems to have liked—maybe it was the noir-ish quality of it, and that it actually had a story.

Which do you prefer; writing or editing?

Editing is a small sideline. I'm working with Jeff Gelb right now on a new anthology series, designed to follow his horror Hot Blood series with a *noir* variation.

What process do you follow when adapting a screenplay to novel form?

I read the screenplay (which is about all I'm given) several times, breaking it down into chapters, Imagining it as a movie, but also imposing novel structure onto it... figuring out which sections could be written from which character's point-of-view, for example... looking for chapter cliffhangers...

that kind of thing. I have the script broken down into chapters before I begin writing.

Are you still able to surprise yourself in your plotlines?

Sure. Good stories are organic. You set stuff in motion, and the characters take over. Even in historical novels, which are bound by the reality of events, surprises take place. They better.

Touching on Seduction of the Innocent for a few moments, do you have any particular musical influences?

I am strictly garage-band all the way. I grew up on British Invasion and the likes of Question Mark and the Mysterians, the Kingsmen, and Paul Revere and the Raiders. I particularly like the Animals, Them, The Zombies, obviously The Beatles; my '60s band opened for acts like the Rascals, Buckinghams, Turtles. We were heavy metal in its earliest form, doing Vanilla Fudge and Deep Purple and Zeppelin and Hendrix.

My own musical tastes are pretty eclectic. My favorite singer is Bobby Darin—from his swing stuff to his rock and every stop in between, which was a lot of stops—and I was a huge New Wave fan. The bands I currently listen to are the likes of Garbage and the Cardigans. Just picked up an incredible CD by Mike Viola and the Candy Butchers.

With your schedule, how do you, and the other members of the band, for that matter, find time to practice as a group and as singular musicians?

Seduction of the Innocent only plays now and then, whenever a comics convention has the good sense to hire us. We rehearse when we get to the location of the gig. In between we all have our own musical interests—Bill Mumy is really a full-time musician; he's always either gigging or in the studio, as far as I can tell; he's the real deal. So is Chris Christensen. I'm not sure how much Steve Leialoha plays in real-life, but he's very experienced, and Miguel is a world-class drummer—he played for both Bing Crosby and Keith Moon... how many drummers can make that claim?

How did the band form?

We were standing around at a San Diego Con dance, listening to a mediocre local band butchering cover material, and looked around at each other and said, 'We could do better than that.' I barely knew Miguel and Bill (who were and are tight) or Steve, either, for that matter. We just were casually discussing how all of us were in bands and that our bands were better than this one. So we offered to play the next year, and they took us up on it!

Chris joined later. His little record company, Beat Brothers, put out our *Golden Age* CD. He came aboard as a pick-up guy... somebody who could cover for anybody on any instrument, if, say, Bill or Miguel or I went out in front to sing. He's terrific, so we asked him in as a full member. He switches from guitar to drums.

What has been your musical experience outside of SOTI?

My band, the Daybreakers, was formed in 1966. We had a national record out in '67, 'Psychedelic Siren' (it's on lots of garage-band/psyche anthologies), opened for lots of big acts, as I mentioned. We shut down in '72, and started back up in '75 under the name Crusin'. We were one of the first classic-rock acts in the midwest. The band has been active, off and on, ever since. Most recently, we recorded the songs for my two movies. A limited-edition CD, on Chris' Beat Brothers label, has just come out: Cruisin' AKA Daybreakers *Thirty-Year Plan*. 22 songs spanning 30 years.

> *Originally published in 1999 with the following information:*
> *It's $15.00 postpaid from M.A.C. Productions, 301*
> *Fairview Ave., Muscatine, IA 52761. Former teen idol*
> *Paul Peterson (one of the stars of Mommy 2), sings a song with us.*
> *Only 200 copies will be pressed.*

What motivates you to take on such a variety of projects?

I don't know. I work hard, but it's all stuff I enjoy. Everything I do that amounts to making a living is some hobby or other that got out of hand.

Is there a particular work of yours that stands out as being the one you'd like to be remembered for?

The Nathan Heller historical detective novels. If I have a posterity, they are it. The new one, *Majic Man*, is about Roswell. *Flying Blind*, the Amelia Earhart one, is just out in paperback, and the Lindbergh novel, *Stolen Away*. will be out in paperback for the first time since '91, next year. Heller is a traditional Marlowe/Hammer P.I. whose cases are all famous unsolved mysteries of the '30's/40's/'50's, meticulously researched. Bill Mumy wrote a song based on the first novel, 'True Detective.' It's on the *Golden Age.* CD.

Is there a book or movie you wished you'd written?

I wish I had written *The Maltese Falcon*. I wish I had directed *Kiss Me Deadly*.

Which book or author motivated you to become a writer?

Mickey Spillane.

What do you think of the Internet's growing presence in the world of publishing?

This is hard to tell. It's great for communications purposes, but how it can be turned into something that will allow writers to make a living, I haven't the slightest idea.

You've written tales concerning some of the most famous detectives—from Batman to Eliot Ness—do you have a favorite character/universe?

Nate Heller, in the criminal reality of the '30s, '40s and '50.

What made you pursue writing for comic books?

I was actually hired to write the *Dick Tracy* comic strip prior to writing comic books. The comic book publishers sought me out, but I was eager, having been a comics fan since childhood.

Road to Perdition *is almost 300 pages long, quite a difference to the traditional comic book length of less than 30 pages. Did you approach this project any differently because of this?*

That novel was many years in the making. The artist, Richard Piers Raynor, is a genius, but not a speed demon. I would write 15 or 20 pages of script, completely forget about it, then months later get a phone call from the editor saying, 'We need more!' I would do another 15 or 20 pages, but always after re-reading everything that had gone before—because I invariably forgot it! Seriously, it took from 1993 to 1998 to complete that work.

Your body of work goes through several genres and mediums. What's next for Max Collins?

I am writing the second draft of a low-budget feature I'm going to direct myself, early next year. Then a novel about Eliot Ness, after which the next Heller awaits.

CHRISTOPHER GOLDEN

BORN AND RAISED IN MASSACHUSETTS, this best-selling author of *The Ferryman*, *Myth Hunters*, and *Strangewood*, to name a few, has also made his mark in the world of fiction for teens and young adults with works like *Body of Evidence*, and *Poison Ink*.

Christopher is also a skilled collaborator, working with Tim Lebbon for *The Secret Journeys of Jack London* and alongside Thomas E. Sniegoski for *The Menagerie*, *OutCast*, and *The Sisterhood*. He also collaborated with actress Amber Benson for their *Ghosts of Albion*, an online animated series of the supernatural.

In the field of nonfiction, Christopher has kept busy by producing both *The Stephen King Universe*, and *Buffy the Vampire Slayer: The Watcher's Guide*

Christopher's website can be found at christophergolden.com

As an author of books expanding on Buffy, The Vampire Slayer, *how do you feel about the series finale, both as a fan and as a writer?*

On a basic level, I enjoyed both Seasons Six and Seven of *Buffy*. As a writer, I thought that season seven was poorly constructed, with the bulk of the season given over to re-treading the same speeches and postures again and again, and the really important character and relationship bits jammed into an hour finale that probably should have been stretched over three episodes. Two, at least. As a fan, I felt that season seven in particular lacked any of the intimacy of the character relationships we had come to expect. These people aren't even friends anymore, just people who used to know one another. That's a shame. Certainly the characters from the first five seasons would not have gone on and on with the events of Season Seven and not confronted one another with their feelings and concerns. They just didn't behave like friends anymore. There were moments of brilliance in the season, and in the finale particularly, but unfortunately they were a reminder of what we weren't getting the rest of the time. Though I think the cast-Sarah Michelle Gellar and James Marsters in particular-did an excellent job. And Tom Lenk was the surprise standout of the season.

Is there a particular character in the Buffyverse that you'd like to focus on that you haven't had the chance to yet?

Not really. I like them all, some more than others. I wanted to do a Faith novel, but Fox shot it down. I'd also like to have done a full-length Willow and Tara novel, young witches in love kind of thing. But with Tara dead, it seems morbid. So I've pretty much said my piece, where Buffy's concerned. That isn't to say I wouldn't ever write another Buffy novel, but I'm fortunate enough to be busy writing original novels at the moment, so if there are other Buffy works to come from me, they wouldn't be for quite some time.

How did Ghosts Of Albion *come about? How did you come to collaborate with Amber Benson?*

I had written several Willow and Tara comics with Amber, who is a fantastic writer in her own right. She had written a couple of plays, one of which I had read, and that led to our doing comics together. She'd also written, directed, produced, starred in and edited her own film, *Chance* (www.chancemovie.com). A fellow at the BBC, Rob Francis, whom we both knew and who had enjoyed our comics work, approached us with the idea that the BBC had a concept they were interested in having us expand upon to create an online animated serial drama. Supernatural, of course. The short version is, for various reasons we didn't want to go with their idea, so we pitched them one of our own. *Ghosts Of Albion* was born. It's a period piece featuring siblings Tamara and William Swift. It's 1838 and the Swifts have just discovered that they've inherited both an enormous amount of magical power and the responsibility to protect England from malign supernatural forces. It's a classic set up, in many ways. The Swifts are aided in their duties by the spirits of various figures from English history. In 'Legacy', the first hour long episode, the ghosts include Queen

Bodicea, Admiral Lord Nelson and Lord Byron. We've got Emma Samms, Anthony Daniels, LesliePhillips and a lot of other wonderful actors in it. And Amber directed. She is a fantastic director.

Was there any thought of making Albion *live-action early on?*

That simply isn't how it came to life. Now, however, we're thinking about a lot of things. We've just written a novella for the BBC to serialize online and we hope to get that into print as an actual book soon. A verbal deal's in place but I don't want to comment until we have paperwork. We're also talking to publishers about doing a series of full length novels based upon *Ghosts Of Albion*. We'll likely do a second hourlong webisode, but there's no confirmation on that yet. And of course we're looking into live-action film and television opportunities. We're at the beginning of all of this, and hoping *GoA* will be around for a long time. We'll have to see what happens.

Did you read comics, and if so, what were the ones you read when you were younger, whether they influenced your writing or not?

As a kid, my brother's favorites were *Spider-Man* and *The Hulk*. Mine were *Daredevil* and *The X-Men*. We both loved *Tomb Of Dracula*, *Werewolf By Night* and *The Avengers*. I don't think there's any question that comics have influenced my writing. If you read my work and you're familiar with comics, it'd be hard to miss. But at the same time I always try to ground my characters enough so that the reader can identify with them. That way no matter what insanity may lie ahead, the reader will hopefully be willing to go along for the ride. As an adult, I still read all kinds of comics. I highly recommend: *The Wretch* (collections now available!), *Strangers In Paradise, Herobear And The Kid, Powers, Hammer Of The Gods, The Goon, Hellboy, Liberty Meadows*, and almost anything written by Geoff Johns, Brian Michael Bendis, and Mark Millar. That's just scratching the surface.

Also, I've written a five issue *Doctor Fate* miniseries for DC that's due to start coming out in August and Mike Avon Oeming and I are doing a creator owned series called *Nevermore* that should debut from Image this fall or winter.

Was the romance in Strangewood *planned before you began the book, or did it come out as you wrote the story?*

What an odd question. Do you ask it because you liked the romance, or because you hated it? Heh. In any case, it was planned. *Strangewood* was written the way almost all of my original, adult books are. I have the idea, the basic concept, I write the first half of the book from my head and then vaguely sketch out what has to happen in each chapter of the second half to make sure that I don't leave any threads dangling. The romance was part of my concept of what the 'status quo' is at the beginning of the story for this fractured family. It's damned inconvenient and it gets in the way of these two divorced parents as they're trying to deal with what's happening to their son. At a time when they should be able to lean on one another in spite of their divorce, when they should be speaking each other's language again at least for their child's sake, this other man's presence interferes with that. That's life.

Strangewood seemed styled after English fairy-tales. Is this an accurate observation, and was it intentional?

There is an element of that and it certainly was part of my consciousness while I was writing it, but I wouldn't call it intentional. *Strangewood* came out of two things. First, a conversation I was having with my friend Hank Wagner, during which I was explaining that my toddler son and I had watched about seventy million hours of *Winnie The Pooh* videos. I said I loved Pooh, but that after a while I got to the point where I would have loved to see armed warriors ride into the Hundred Acre Wood, skin the little fuckers and nail their pelts to trees. The second was a talk Clive Barker gave at DragonCon, where his advice to other writers was not to second-guess yourself, not to handicap your own imagination. If it seemed insane, that only meant it was different from what everyone else had done. I took that to heart. That conversation with Hank was when I got the idea. But listening to Clive was what gave me the confidence to just say, 'screw it, yes it's nuts, but just write it down.'

Many strong characters met their end in Of Masques And Martyrs. *What motivated your decision to kill them off?*

I have a sort of reputation now for killing off characters. The woman who runs my web site tells people 'Don't tell Chris your favorite character or he'll kill them.' This isn't precisely true, but it isn't totally off base either. I wholeheartedly believe that when you're writing about the world being in danger, or anything of similarly high stakes, that a victory without loss, without cost, does not feel very triumphant at all. If you're going to win, it's got to cost you something. Some have accused me of being capricious, gratuitous and sadistic in the way the body count goes up in my books. While all of those things are probably true, none of them is the real reason you see this sort of thing so much in my work. It's just the price of victory.

What led you to write The Shadow Saga?

I'm not particularly fond of vampires. At least, not any more so than other monsters. And, frankly, there's a certain stigma attached to vampire novels. Even so, I had been thinking about how stupid the "Rules" of vampirism were. If you could become a wolf or a bat or a rat or mist, it seemed more than a little silly that that was *all* you could become. You can change your body on a sub-atomic level, but you can only choose from these few things to change it to. That was lame. So, with that in mind, I sort of reverse-engineered vampires but in a world where everyone still believes those ridiculous rules and hasn't quite realized they're ridiculous yet. Until they start to unravel. At the same time, though I am Catholic, I'm also a skeptic. If the Pope is infallible, what about when there were *three* Popes at once? They couldn't all be infallible. What about the Crusades? Definitely some fallibility there. The Inquisition?

I wanted to challenge the hypocrisy of the Catholic church. That's become fashionable in the last couple of years because the church has been operating more like the Mafia than a religious group, trying to cover up hundreds of cases of priests abusing children instead of shedding light on it, taking care of the victims, and doing everything they can to see it doesn't happen again. They're more concerned with their reputation and their damnable, hypocritical, evil secrecy than they are with the people that have been scarred forever, even destroyed. I guess I was ahead of my time.

Is there a particular character of yours that you identify with the most? Which one?

No question in my mind that it's Jenna Blake. She's the protagonist of my *Body Of Evidence* mystery series for teens. Guess I'm just a nineteen year old girl at heart. Heh. But in the way she thinks, the way she behaves, the way she treats the people around her, and the way she hurts as well, Jenna's without question the one I identify with the most.

Who are some of your earliest influences?

Stephen King, of course. *Night Gallery, Tomb Of Dracula comics, Twilight Zone*, Doc Savage novels. Jack London. *X-Men*. Poe. All sorts of movies, good and bad. Mostly bad. *Kolchak The Night Stalker*. Short story anthologies edited by Charles L. Grant. Oh, and did I mention Stephen King?

What are your thoughts on why people read (as well as write) horror?

I've always said I think horror is cathartic. That if you can frighten or excite someone to a level of true anxiety, and then relieve that anxiety, you've done them a service. They'll feel elated afterward, on a natural high. But more than that. If reading one of these novels or stories can make you believe, even for just a moment, that ghosts or demons or monsters are real, then for that moment you have to believe there could be angels, that there could be an afterlife, that there is a God. Even if you never think about it that way, you've opened up your mind to it. I want to believe in ghosts. I really do. Mainly because I hope that after I've lived to a hundred or so that I get to be one.

What would you like to accomplish as a writer that you haven't yet?

Make a billion dollars. Win a Pulitzer. Heh. In the immortal words of Foghorn Leghorn, 'That's a joke, son.' I want to make a film, but that may well happen soon. I want to keep doing more of what I've been doing. But specific to your question, two things: I would like to have just one shot at readership on a ridiculously massive scale, just to have them give me a shot and judge the work based upon its merits. If they come back for the next one, great. If they don't, well, I had my shot. I think that's all we can hope for. The problem is, most books are never seen by 99.9% of their potential audience. People can't express an interest in it if they don't know it exists. So that's the first thing… one shot at that huge readership base. It would be nice if it happened with the novel I just wrote under my new contract with Bantam, *The Boys Are Back In Town*, which comes out in April. I think it's the best thing I've done and the one with the broadest appeal.

The second thing, though, is that I've got an historical mystery novel I'm planning to write. Everyone I tell about it loves it but I have to write at least the first four chapters or so to get anyone to look at it seriously, and I just haven't had time to do that. Little things like work, paying the bills, keeping up with deadlines and seeing my children get in the way. I have to do the work I'm being paid for, and it hasn't left a lot of time for developing this other thing. So I'd like to get a bundle of money from someone in Hollywood or from a book publisher that would buy me a few months to work on this historical mystery so I can finally get it out there in front of people. It's the best idea I've ever had.

Is writing more instinctual or learned?

That depends on if you think you can develop instincts. I was fortunate enough to be born with a natural facility with things like spelling and grammar. They came easily for me. But rhythm, plot structure, character, dialogue… all of those things are learned either through hard work or through some strange osmosis where you pick it up simply by experiencing it while doing your own reading and film viewing. The interesting thing is that you can learn the basic skills, the grammar, the spelling, the traditional plot structure, but in order to do rhythm, character and dialogue, you really just have to have a knack for it.

What advice would you give aspiring writers?

What I always say is very simple advice: read as much as you can, write as much as you can, go to conventions where you can meet other writers and editors, and try to find an agent who'll champion your work. But I'll add a sort of paraphrase of the advice Clive gave once upon a time. Don't put chains on your imagination. Don't assume because it's wild and different and strange that you should tone it down. Run with it.

I'd also like to remind everyone that my new novel *The Gathering Dark* just hit stores. It's the latest in *The Shadow Saga*, but it's also a completely new direction and can stand alone. It's another one of those insane bits of story that years ago I would have thought was too crazy. When something starts stealing entire cities and leaving demons behind in their place… well, you'll see what I mean.

EDUARDO SANCHEZ

With co-director Daniel Myrick, Cuban-born Eduardo Sanchez was responsible for one of the most popular, and widely debated, films to come to the horror genre in recent memory. The film was *The Blair Witch Project*, a movie that featured camera work and ad-lib dialogue supplied by the actors, who portrayed film students that had gone missing while researching the mythology of the Blair Witch.

Rich with background information and clips from the movie, blairwitch.com became a standard by which movie makers within the studio system re-evaluated the Internet's power to promote a movie as the film, and its offshoots, *Sticks And Stones, The Blair Witch: A Dossier*, and *The Curse Of The Blair Witch* showed the filmmaker's stock-in-trade with creating mythology.

Despite the fact its sequel, *Book Of Shadows* did nothing to further the initial ripple effect, the original stands on its own, a sign that you don't need an unspeakable amount of money and an A-list cast to pull off a smash hit.

My meeting with Ed came on the heels of the early January *Newsweek* article on the five-year anniversary of *The Blair Witch Project*'s premiere at the Sundance Film Festival, an article that, while not containing the most positive of slants on the effects the film had on the careers of the actors, was one that Sanchez was able to take in stride while he was in Southern California to talk to Lion's Gate Films about the possibility of a prequel to the smash hit *Blair* with Dan Myrick.

As tall as a tree, and very friendly, Ed was very open about talking about everything from his passion for filmmaking to love of quality movies.

Whatever became of Heart of Love*?*

It was a real low-budget movie, so we were literally doing everything for three years on this movie. And we were just done with the horror thing. We didn't want to put our heads in that horror mode. So we did a one eighty, and we tried to do this totally ridiculous, goofy comedy called *Heart of Love*, which is the stupidest frickin' title to come up with for a movie, I mean, *Heart of Love*? What the hell does that mean? And we came up with the title before we had the script! [Chuckles] and we just built this script—which I think it's great script—I mean, people… you either get it or you don't get it, and I think if you know Dan and me, if you know our sense of humor, if you've hung out with us a lot, the movie makes a lot more sense because you get an idea of how it's going to be executed. But if you don't know us, it's kind of a hard sell, and a lot of the feedback we were getting was like, 'It's either a masterpiece, or the biggest piece of shit I've ever seen in my life.' [Chuckles]. And we wanted to make this comedy the likes of which nobody had ever seen before… so it was kind of a mixture of Monty Python and Saturday Night Live, and some of the Farrelly's first movies and a lot of *Airplane!* humor, and just kind of mixed everything, and when you thought the movie was going in one direction, it would kind of flip over and go this direction, and it was kind of stupid and kind of politically incorrect and childish and crazy.

The basic story is that this young guy in his thirties throughout the course of the film, discovers he is God. And he's the master of this thing called the *Heart of Love*, which is calling out to him. It's been calling out to him his whole life, and at the end of the movie, it's a stupid comedy, so you kind of have to visualize it's literally this guy, and this winged heart comes crashing through the ceiling of this place he's at, and it picks this guy up and he floats up into the heavens and he becomes… I don't know what the hell he becomes, I guess that's the sequel. But it's just like this thing where we wanted to be as ridiculous [with] the most spectacular ridiculousness you've ever seen in your whole life, and the whole movie is like that.

So we wrote the script and we had a distribution agreement with Artisan. It was a verbal agreement, and we were working on the contracts, and this and that, and we went to Cannes and we raised a bunch of foreign money to do it, and we had most of the money, but then we had some legal problems with Artisan as far as *Blair Witch* is concerned, and kind of held up *Heart of Love*. It held up Artisan becoming fully committed to *Heart of Love*, and by the time all that legal stuff was out of the way, and we were able to make the movie, the foreign money was starting to go away, and then 9/11 happened, and the whole bottom dropped out of all of us because it was last thing any of us wanted to do, and we were hemorrhaging more and more money every frickin' day, and it just got to the point where we were like, 'well, you know, we don't have enough money to make this movie,' and had to call everything off. But then, we still talk about *Heart of Love*, and a week doesn't pass where I don't chuckle to myself about one of the scenes or something. We were going to do it for eight million bucks.

I still think there was no way it was going to lose money. There was plenty of stuff we could have put in the trailer. There's a lot of midgets ad a lot of ridiculous sexual situations. A lot of scatological humor. A lot of good stuff to put in the trailer. I think you put enough of that stuff in the trailer, and you put 'From the Creators of *The Blair Witch Project*' and it's an eight million dollar movie, and you open it up on fifteen hundred or two thousand screens, you're going to get your money back. So it was real disappointing for all of us at Haxan for that to fall apart, and ever since then, we've just been trying to get other things out there. We've written a bunch of scripts and tried to do low-budget, big-concept movies, and we just haven't been able to get going on anything, unfortunately. And last year, when I came up with *Manabal'wak*, it's the first horror script I've completed since *BW*. It's like the first new horror idea since *Blair Witch*, so it took me years back into the horror genre and get excited again about doing a horror movie, and the problem was that once *Heart of Love* fell apart, I think Dan and I were still very resistant on making another horror movie. And we were kind of thinking, 'Well, do we want to do another horror movie?' and like I said, it took a long time to get *Blair Witch* out of our systems. But now I think all the Haxan guys are just kind of ready to get back and do another movie. As a matter of fact, my partner Gregg Hale just finished a movie, totally not horror. He's entering it into festivals right now. So it took a while for me and Dan to get back into this horror mode. In fact, I'm going LA next week, and we're going to have a meeting with Lion's Gate, who bought Artisan, about possibly doing another *Blair* movie.

Is that the prequel that we've been hearing about for a long time?

We're not sure what it's going to be yet. We have three or four pretty good ideas of what the movie can be and we just kind of have to sit down and figure out which ones excite us the most, but we're not sure what it's going to be yet.

From Blair *to now, what has that experience taught you?*

As far as like the business, you learn a lot. What I learned is that none of us are studio filmmakers. At least now. Who the hell knows, maybe in twenty years, we'll be doing the stupidest frickin' movies just for paychecks. But we all learned that we just weren't going to fit into the studio system like a lot of indy filmmakers; they make they're big hit, their indy movie, then they move right into the studio system, and it doesn't seem to phase them. But for us, we kind of just… real resistant to get into that and make a studio movie.

I think that after a while, the studios became resistant to what we were doing, because they didn't understand what we were doing, and also the didn't understand *Blair*. I think there are a lot of people out there who don't know if Dan and I can make a normal movie. So it just becomes this situation where neither side trusts the other side [chuckles] and it's frustrating. But at the same time, we made a lot of money on *Blair Witch*, and we're all comfortable, we're all fine. There's no hurry to do anything, but at this point, it's like, 'We've got to make another movie.' Just for artistic reasons. I'm gonna go crazy if I don't make a movie soon. So I guess what I learned is that we still have to make something whether we're the guys who made *Blair Witch* or before we were the guys who made *Blair Witch*.

We still have to make movies. The same way. From the heart, and with good people around you, and with as minimal interference from the outside as possible. And we all feared it after *Blair*; we all got sent a lot of horror scripts and we just had to tell our agent, 'Look, we aren't going to do another horror movie for now.' And he just kind of stopped sending us scripts, and we realized if we get into the situation with a big studio… we got sent *The Exorcist* prequel scripts, which I think in itself is cursed [chuckles] we read that in early '99, and I know that they've shot some stuff, and another director had to take over… the script just wasn't there. It was like twenty percent there, and they wanted to get moving immediately. They wanted to get shooting immediately.

And we realized, 'Man, we just did a movie for thirty thousand bucks, they're going to kick our asses, and we're going to make a horrible film.' And that's not what we wanted to do. That's one of the things our agents always talks about.

Do you keep in touch with the cast members?

Heather and I just don't keep in touch. Actually, I haven't talked to either Mike or Josh in a while. But they've just been so busy. Mike moved back to New York, and Josh is still in Los Angeles, but he's always doing something, he's always traveling or has some crazy thing going, and he's directing music videos now, so he's doing pretty good. The thing about it is that they're all so talented, and I think that when you have such a huge thing like *Blair Witch*, like what our agents tried to do to us, just because it makes sense, like, 'They did a horror movie, now they're going to do *another* horror movie.' And I think their agents tried to do the natural thing and tried to mold them into something that could be popular and could be sold to teenagers or college kids or wherever they thought they could fit into. And I think that for the most part, so did Heather's. It's like they tried to market her wrong. Like she's a really intelligent woman, but she's kind of a geek, which is cool. I'm a geek, and most of our frickin' friends are geeks. And they tried to make her into this Jennifer Love-Hewitt, hot actress, and she *is* beautiful, and she's kind of moving into that now, with *Taken*.

This one time, we went out with the producers of one of the *Star Trek* franchises, and she was like, 'I'd *love* to be on a *Star Trek*, but my agent doesn't want me to do it.' And it's like if you want to do it, you think it could be cool, and you could do a good job, then you should do it... and I think maybe now she's figured it out or whatever... when you come from nothing like we did; we were making movies in Orlando, and these actors were just struggling actors in New York... I always say if I hadn't gone through this with four other guys, it would have been a much different story. And you would be writing about something completely different right now. I would have made more movies, I may have been more successful, but probably would have been a disaster by now doing it just by myself.

So, as for *Blair Witch*, we knew what we wanted to do, but if we had taken our agent's advice, then we would have done *Exorcist 4*, there would have been the re-write on *Freddy Vs. Jason*, things that would have probably led to some really bad movies. And we haven't made another movie, and it's bad thing, but it's a good thing, because we haven't had a terrible second film coming out. As far as *BW*, you could put us in that column, but there's still some people who still really dig *Blair*, they dig the idea, and they dig us... I couldn't stand the thought of one of the fans going to our movies and saying 'God-*damn*, they just completely sold out!' who knows what'll happen in ten years; I may be doing two studio movies a year and doing just schlocky movies for money or whatever, but at least for now, I'm still young, I still *can* do it, and financially I can afford to say no to some things. And all of us at Haxan are just like, 'we want to do some good stuff from the heart. Quality stuff.' And even if it doesn't hit, at least fans can say, 'Well, at least they weren't selling out, they just tried doing something that was kind of too weird for this reason or whatever reason.' Our thing is just try to nurture the fans, and give them something that we can be proud of, and be proud to put our name on. What happened to the actors of *Blair Witch*, and what happened to us, it's part of this explosion that happened, and nobody expected it. And even now we don't have the answers. Nobody had the answers, you just kind of have to find your own journey, and for us, we were all on the same path, and for me personally, it's taken me about four years to get to a place where I can come up with another horror movie idea, and I can get excited about doing another horror movie, and I'm in a place with my family, too, where I've been here enough, just doing the family thing, and now I can go and do movies, and bring the family along, but not need the hundred percent dedication, I can fit a little bit of my career into this big family pie.

Before, I just wasn't ready to do that, to go away and not see my daughter for months at a time, and even now, I can't do it. Now it's like, wherever I go, I'm going to bring them along. You have a little boy, so you know how all of a sudden, it just becomes the most important thing in your life, and no matter what the hell anybody else says, I wouldn't trade the last four or five years of *Blair Witch* for anything. I think it's gone perfectly. I'm happier than I've ever been. And I'm still excited about making movies.

And even when you're part of the club, you don't get to do what you want to do, a lot of the time. Even the big directors who have been making movies for twenty, twenty-five years still complain about the studio getting in the way, so I think for us, and for all filmmakers, the whole digital revolution is really exciting, and the Web is really exciting, too. The reason the movie and television studios have so much power is because they control distribution, so you have to go through them to show your movie, and the studios financing these films are so expensive that I think the Web becomes a real viable option to distribute films and TV shows, and eventually, it will be; the way that computers are being designed now, as multimedia centers, where you can watch things off your hard drive. When you're watching TiVo, you're basically watching TV off a computer. I don't think it's as far away as people think.

It's certainly geared that way, with so many software application just for media.

Exactly, man! It probably turned the corner on audio. I think there's finally people making the minimal amount… 99 cents a download, or whatever. They're all doing pretty well right now, and I think that video is not far behind at all. This whole thing about networks losing young males in their demographic. They're wondering where they're going; they're going to videogames and to the Internet for their shit. So I think there's a huge market of people out there who will click on something and watch something for half an hour in front of their computer, and if you have a high-speed connection, which a lot of people do now, you're not going to be waiting there three hours to download the freaking thing; you wait maybe five or ten minutes and you have it.

There are no excuses anymore. If you charge just enough to stay in business but not too much where people are going to go, 'I'm not going to pay that much to watch this thing!' it can work, and that's kind of what we're trying to do right now.

What did you think about the results of the second movie?

[Pause] I didn't like pretty much anything about the second movie. I think Joe Berlinger, the guy that directed it is a really talented filmmaker, but I think that he put himself into a situation where it was very difficult for him to make a good movie, and *his* movie, period, and we knew that, not that we're fortune-tellers or anything, but they had this accelerated schedule. They had a release date before they had a script. And it was like, less than a year, so… they tried to get us to do it, they were going to give us a bunch of money, they were arguing with us about what kind of movie we wanted to make, and they finally told us, 'Do whatever you want to do, but we've got to be shooting in two months.' Man… you're taking about writing a script, and casting, and finding locations, and building sets, and we were all like, 'Nah, we can't do that. There's no way. It'll be disastrous.' And we knew it was going to happen. So, they signed us on as executive producers, just to have our names, and at first, I think they wanted our input, but we told them we though the script wasn't scary, and it didn't excite us at all, the conference calls just stopped.

We kind of just left each other alone, and we were still executive producers, so they sent us footage, and mock-ups of the poster design, but I think they were just trying to keep us in the loop, but kind of take it where they wanted to take it, so it was kind of disappointing, and then the movie came out, they made a big deal about us not saying anything bad about it; we were executive producers, so they didn't want us out there saying, 'Oh, it's a terrible movie.' But we didn't do any interviews, like their whole thing was they came down and tried to convince us to do some interviews, at least with *Premiere*, and *Entertainment Weekly*, and we were like, 'Well, we'll do the interviews, but when it comes down to it, when they ask us if we thought it was a good movie, we have to tell them the truth; we're not going to lie to them.' And they were asking, 'Well, what's *positive* about it, is the cinematography... or this, or that...?' and we were 'Yeah, it's a good-looking film, but they're going to ask me, 'Did you like it?' What am I going to say?' Dan Myrick and I were like, 'we're not going to lie for you guys.' It's a really disappointing thing for Artisan and us and everybody involved. You want to distance yourself from the movie, but you don't want to distance yourself *too* much, because it's based on the original movie. And at the time, we were still going to do *Heart of Love* with Artisan.

It was kind of tough. It was disappointing with the way it came out and the way it was slammed... we didn't want to become enemies of Joe, and I think he's a good filmmaker, but it's just weird to see him go through these things that we knew were going to happen.

It was hard for me as a fan, and somebody who was writing about this kind of stuff to hear about all these horror stories from the production, and this guy who was just trying to do his best and kept getting the rug pulled out from under him.

It got to the point where he had to do an explanation for the beginning of the DVD, about what happened... that's really bad, man. But he's doing well. I read an interview with him and he's done that Metallica documentary *Some Kind of Monster* he obviously learned some stuff.

It's more to you having control over your own things.

Yeah, or like getting into a situation where you're going through studio projects, there's many studio projects. But they're very low-budget horror movies, and my thing about those is, care enough about the movie to believe in the idea and to nurture the script and make it as good as possible and to have moments to build characters. In the end, fight as hard as you can to keep control of it, but realize you're going to lose a little bit along the way, and my thing is at least right now, I have this illusion that they're going to leave me alone for the most part as long as involve myself with the right people. I think I've met some cool people who I'd like to work with. But that's the big scary thing, man… early *BW2* meeting were the five of us Haxan guys around a table with a conference phone with seven or eight Artisan executives from all the different branches chiming in on the story, and sometimes we would mute the call and say, 'are you guys as repulsed by this as I am?' We were making a movie by committee! The whole time, we were like, 'Man this is a train we don't want to get on. There's something so frickin' train wreck about to happen.' It scared all of us. Dan came out here and wrote a really good script and tried to get it out there, and they were like, 'No, we don't want to do that.' I've sent scripts here and there and done meeting, but haven't been able to get anything going. I think for the most part, that's kind of good, because you're so afraid of the frickin' mutation that happens to most projects. I just hear horror stories from everybody, even from the beginning.

I remember one time I was at a party, and I met the director of *The Avengers* [Jeremiah S. Chechik] and he was telling me the studio wouldn't let him make the movie he wanted to make, it was like a fifty-fifty movie, and it just came out terrible, and it's like 'I can see that.' And then you see something else from a director that's great, and it's like, 'What happened?' Like what happened to Danny Boyle; he did *Trainspotting* and then he came to the United States and did *A Life Less Ordinary*. I know a guy who was on that production, and he said it was a nightmare. And now Danny's back to doing his own stuff in the UK. He made *28 Days Later*. You could see the difference, because he was controlling it, and whoever gave him the money let him control it.

You would never see that in a major studio.

And that's what's frustrating, man. We have the *Blair Witch* magic, and it's no different. The major studios would never done something like *Blair Witch*.

Certainly not the way it was done and the way it ended.

Absolutely. And then they hire you, and they're all excited, for like the *freakylinks* TV show. They tell you 'we want you to make it different, to get a young audience…' and all along the way, they're telling us 'You've got to make this more like this, you've got to make this more like *X-Files*, you've got to hire this guy...' and at the end, they took it to a point to where the co-creator of the show took his name off the show. He just picked a name and put it on there, because it wasn't a show that they had originally thought of and it went for eleven episodes and they cancelled it, and it's like 'Yeah, *you* cancelled it because *you* created it. You put our names on it, but you created it. You guys who did it, are going to keep making shitty shows.' And that's what's been happening with a lot of the stuff that we've been submitting. If we were to submit *Blair Witch* to a studio, their reaction would be 'This is never going to work, what are you, crazy?' We've got things that aren't as out there as *Blair Witch*, but it's like 'I don't understand this.'

Manabal'wak is more character-driver than monster-driven. They're like, 'Well, why do you have top make it a period piece?' You can't create that situation in modern times. It's isolation. You'd have helicopters going over the crash site, you have cell phones now... people don't get it, and they don't trust us enough to say, 'All right, do it.' I think eventually I'll get to do *Manabal'wak*, whether I do it, or somebody else does it, but if nobody picks it up by the time I make my next film, or maybe two films, so I can show a progression, 'Look, I've done a one-million dollar movie, and now I've done a seven-million dollar movie, why can I do a thirty-dollar movie?' I think I'll eventually get to do it. I think the comic book might help, laying the foundation down to direct that movie. There's no guide, you just sort of bump down a dead end until you figure out how to do it, send shit out, get people sending you notes that you absolutely know they did not get the script; 'why don't you set it in the Seventies, instead of a train, make it a bus....' the most important thing about the movie is not even the Sasquatch, the most important thing about the movie is the characters. It's a disaster movie, it's of coming together; the blacks and the whites, the hunters, that's what it's about. And they don't get it. Some people have gotten it, but the right person hasn't gotten it yet. The right person is the person who has the power to say, 'I live this, let's do this exactly the way you want to do it.' So the meantime, you stay busy doing other things, building a foundation for *Manabal'wak*.

Is that the push project for you?

If you looked at all the projects I have, and I had to pick one, then yeah, that'd be the one. I think it's a cool movie; it's something that's different enough where people will like it. If I get financing for any of the things I'm working on, I would be very happy. I have an alien abduction script, it's not really, but that's really the only way I can describe it. It's around the seven-million dollar range I can maybe make with a studio. By this summer, I should have two other scripts that I can push into the studio system in the seven-to-ten million dollar range. And then I have this other movie, called *Faceless*, and it has thriller elements, I want to do a lot of experimenting with camera moves, weird in-camera stuff, cool set design, a lot of surreal stuff, real gritty. It's going to be cool. It's about a kid that witnesses his mom's murder, a really violent murder, but in the process, gets attacked, and gets knocked in the head really hard, and he develops this very rare condition I can't even pronounce, where you can't recognize faces, but you can see people's eyes, nose, and mouth, but you can't put them together to say, 'that's Joe, or that's Cristopher.' So now he has to deal with the fact that his mom's dead, he's fourteen years old, and the killer of his mom is out there, and he's seen him, but he doesn't know who the killer is. It could be the guy he's talking to… but this condition is a real condition. And I'm enjoying the collaboration process with everybody I'm working with. I feel so lucky I've found these people. They're all unknowns, but they're really talented.

So you're trying to keep in the spirit on what you originally based your success on?

Well, you know what, I'm controlling it. If I want to hire people no one else wants to work with, I can do that. But I can guarantee you that a lot of the people I'm working with now are going to be huge writers or directors or whatever they want to be. Maybe not because of me, but because of something that I'm doing. They're really good people.

There's this recurring theme of isolation in your material. Why is that?

Isolation is the heart of every good horror movie. Because it just makes sense. The character can be mentally isolated, or physically isolated. *The Shining*, *Jaws*, even *The Sixth Sense*. The kid was completely alone in a creepy world. So it's just basic. A lot of thrillers have that, too. That's the mode I'm in right now. Not only am I completely comfortable with producing that kind of movie, but also, injecting it with stuff they might not expect. Like with *Manabal'wak*, with *Faceless*, a lot of other stuff. You can make a movie like *Manabal'wak* that turns out to be a social commentary or with *Faceless* where we examine the whole megacorporation and how this kid just becomes another number without a face. Now you can buy things from Wal-Mart without ever seeing another person, and we're isolating ourselves even as we speak. The Internet has brought people together, but you're not really *meeting* anybody. So I liked to examine that, in a subtle aspect. Sort of like 1984…

Do you know when Manabal'wak *is to be released as a graphic novel?*

I have plans to have it finished in March. And what I'm going to do, is I'm building a website now at manabalwak.com, and we're just going to put the comic book up as a Flash presentation, with some audio. Not really sound effects or dialogue, but just kinda maybe some moody music and this and that, so when you go through each issue, things'll pop up here and there, and I think it'll be a pretty cool presentation. And I'm going to sell it for pretty cheap, you know, a couple bucks to see the whole Flash presentation. And then later, what I'm hoping to do is also based on how much time I have if I get into pre-production on a movie or get into serious development on any of these projects, I'm going to have to drop pretty much everything. But I at least want to get it onto the Internet, onto the Web, so people can start checking it out. And then I think if there is interest in publishing it, I'll probably end up shopping it around to see if someone wants to publish it based on the numbers I get from the website, but my dream would be that we get a lot of interest on the website, and it gives either the studios or a producer or a production company just a litte better idea what this movie's about and what it could look like, and also the fact that I think it's a story that not only young people can get into, but kind of an older crowd that doesn't usually go to see horror movies can get into. And I think that's the key I'm trying to start with *Manabal'wak*; that it's a really intelligent—at least I think—it's an intelligent monster movie. And I think it's something that can do something kind of like what *Jaws* did, or like M. Night Shyamalan's *The Sixth Sense* or *Signs*. To do that kind of box office, obviously tapped into an older market, and that's good. At least *The Sixth Sense*, and I liked *Signs*, too. I thought it was a little wacky at times. It didn't make sense to me sometimes, but still, he makes intelligent monster movies or horror movies. And I think *Manabal'wak* has the potential to do those numbers to bring about people that don't usually go see *Texas Chainsaw Massacre* or *Freddy Vs. Jason* into a theatre.

It's an entirely different market

Yeah, I think so. And also, I think that's kind of just a mis-step that my agent made with *Manabal'wak*, because we originally sent it to horror movie producers, producers who are making *Texas Chainsaw Massacre*, and *The Ring* and we sent it to Sam Raimi's company. We're trying to make these 10-15 million dollar horror movies for the teenage and early twenties market. So this movie's absolutely wrong for that, and my whole thing is we should send it out to producers who don't normally do horror movies, because the way I see it, this movie's like *Cold Mountain* meets *Alien*. And I think my agent was just kind of looking at it as a horror movie from the *Blair Witch* guy, for the teenage audience, and it's not really like that.

Both Blair Witch *and* Mananal'wak *use the theme of mythology. One manufactured by you, and the other already sort of in place for you. Why do you draw inspiration from that? Is this intentional?*

I think using mythology, using some kind of evil… in *Manabal'wak*, it's not really evil, but it's just an animal. But having something like *Blair Witch* that was just old, that's been there for a long time and has been happening to a lot of people just makes it seems like it makes it more hopeless. For me it makes it scarier. Because there's this force like with *The Exorcist*. Dealing with this force. Not only do you have to deal with *this*, but you have to deal with this thing that has been around for a long time. I think what made *The Exorcist* a very scary film… the whole villain which is Satan, and he's this malevolent force that's been around for so long. The same thing happened with *Blair Witch*, something that's just so old… it just seems like so many people have tried to deal with it and nobody has been able to figure it out and now you're stuck in this, so it makes everything just helpless. And as far as *Manabal'wak*, this kind of mythology just makes for a creepier adversary as far as the people are concerned, like I said, helpless, this feeling of like, the Indians have been dealing with these creatures for at least hundreds of years, and now they're here, and it's like well, the Indians kind of learned to co-exist with them, what are *we* going to do with them? I gives it this old feeling that it's not something new you can figure out right away and get rid of, it's something that a lot of people before you have tried to figure out and nobody has really been able to do it, so for me it just makes it just a little creepier and also gives more depth to the story, to the background of the story, which is always good.

Why did you choose to set Manabal'wak *in 1872 instead of modern times? What preparation went into the story?*

I came up with the idea around January '04, and all of us at Haxan have wanted to do a Bigfoot for a long time, but nobody had come up with a really unique idea... a unique premise to put the Sasquatch in so I came up with this idea of a stream train derailing in the middle of the night in1872 Utah a train, and I thought of the setting immediately; somewhere in the middle of the woods around the Reconstruction. It's just a real interesting time in history, you know what I mean?

And then as far as preparing, you know, I did some research into trains and the railroad and me and co-writer Mark Eaton tried to figure out where this was going to be, what's the best place for this to take place, geographically. And as far as the train stations were concerned, like how far apart the stations were at that time and what lines and this and that. And then a little bit about history, a little bit about the Indians in that area and then I pitched the idea to Mark Eaton, and a couple weeks later, Mark sends me a draft of the script, it's like sixty pages long, and I had already written the beginning, I had already written the crash, I had written maybe seven or eight pages at that time. And he sent me this things, and it kind of close to what I wanted, but story-wise, it was completely different. But tone... he nailed the tone of it, and that's really what's important.

You can kind of work on story and stuff, but if the writer can't nail the tone, it makes it a lot harder to collaborate, and the fact that he nailed the tone, I was like, 'Well, you know what, let's sit down and really think about this and talk about it and I'll give you the whole story, I'll give you all the details I have worked out.' And he kept writing, and we came up with the script. I think it took about three or four months, maybe.

How has raising two kids affected the way you write or appreciate horror?

Well, obviously... after you have kid, everything changes. You think differently, and it's almost like you appreciate different movies, and this and that, and the big thing with me and horror is that now more than ever, I'm always thinking... this sense of dread that the kids are going to watch this movie. Unfortunately, kids watch horror movies. You know what I mean? I mean, maybe not your kids, and maybe not my kids, but a lot of people's kids watch horror movies who shouldn't be watching horror movies, there are a lot of people who don't understand. So it's kind of that fear, but it doesn't stop you [from] making art because who's going to see it, but to a certain extent, you… think about it more and also everything, you know.

Sometimes I see films and something happens in the movie that's child-related, and you immediately realize, 'Okay, the person who wrote that script doesn't have any kids.' It's a person thing you start noticing about certain things. For me, it gives me a drive not really to make horror movies, because I think that Dan and I were never horror movie makers, and we're not really huge horror movie fans. We just love movies. I love all kinds of movies. I even like stupid romantic comedies. A good movie is a good movie.

Having kids makes me think 'You know, I've got to get out there and make these *other* movies, and also with *Manabal'wak*; I'm going to do a monster movie, but I'm going to say something in it that is important.' For me, it's given me that extra sense of responsibility that if I'm going to do a horror movie, people are going to like it because of the creatures, but other people are going to like it, because it deals with racism, it deals with social issues… things that are usually not looked at in horror movies… I want to at least put something in there that you're hoping can make a difference, even if that's just making somebody think about it just a little bit as they leave the theatre. Its not a total sense of 'I've got to do this on every frickin' movie.' You know how it is with kids… when you have kids, you see what's going to happen to the world when you die, like all of a sudden, you have a personal tie to what the world's going to be like when you die, and I think before you have kids, you don't really… care. You don't fully understand it. And obviously, having kids that are going to hopefully live after you die, you look at it like… [chuckles self-consciously] and this may sound so stupid… 'I've got to try to make the world better for my kids.' And it happens to everybody. Some people get more politically aware and become more politically active, and start reading stuff or start looking at history, or whatever it is. I think as a filmmaker, I'm just… the first thing is to entertain, that's what movies are for, but also it's if I can put something that means something to me I think it'll mean something to at least one other person, then I'll make that connection, and in my own little stupid way, I'll make the world a little bit nicer than it was before. [Laughs]

You want to pick and choose your projects.

Exactly, and that's the way the media is with everything, especially with entertainers; if you have something big like a hit album, and you don't do something right away, they're like, 'Well, what happened to you? Are you a one-hit wonder?' It has nothing to do with that. If you're a real artist, you have to be inspired by the work you're doing. You need to be inspired *to* do the work you're doing. And sometimes life gets in the way, I'm sorry. Sometimes you have to take this journey so you can create more unique art at the end of this journey, and you have to take this journey; you can't just go from one project to the next and not experience what it is you're putting into your movie. I think you're right; it's about choosing your projects wisely, and also for me, it was having control of my projects.

Is that what you were talking about earlier, the film on the web kind of thing?

Yeah. I think distributing things on the web is a viable option right now and it's not this massive paycheck at the end of the road with that, but I think there is enough interest and enough people out there where you can make a living doing a show, as long as you keep the shows relatively cheap; you can't spend a million and a half dollars on a show. But our plan is to build a whole season of a show for like a million, a million and a half dollars; a whole season; thirteen shows, or twenty shows, or whatever it ends up going, and then self-distribute it on the web, and we answer to nobody. We can do whatever we want with the shows, we can have nudity, we can have cussing, we can have exploding clowns, whatever we want to put in there, we can put in there, as long as people are willing to download it. So for us, if the idea works, it's really exciting, because it's all of a sudden, it's a way to put stuff out there without anybody's approval. And it's so hard getting approval from LA and New York, and these people who can green light things, you've gotta be part of this club.

Right now I'm just doing the family thing, and now I can go and do movies, and bring the family along, but not need the hundred percent dedication, I can fit a little bit of my career into this big family pie. Before, I just wasn't ready to do that, to go away and not see my daughter for months at a time, and even now, I can't do it. Now it's like, wherever I go, I'm going to bring them along. You have a little boy, so you know how all of a sudden, it just becomes the most important thing in your life, and no matter what hell anybody else says, I wouldn't trade the last four or five years of *BW* for anything. I think it's gone perfectly. I'm happier than I've ever been. And I'm still excited about making movies.

You're adapting your period story regarding the Sasquatch myth, entitled Manabal'wak, *for publication online as a Flash presentation. What can you tell us about that?*

I thought that if I tried to go out to a publisher, it might be hard to control the movie rights once you agree to publish it, because I think a lot of, especially now, a lot of graphic novels… that's part of the plan; 'We'll do this graphic novel, and then we'll see if somebody wants to make this into a movie.' It's a real popular stepping-off point right now. So for me, it was more like… first of all, I don't have the money to pay an established artist. I don't know any established artists personally. And I thought I'd gotten really lucky with people like [*Manabal'wak* co-writer] Mark Eaton and other people who are not 'True professionals', but are really talented, and will soon be professionals. So I got really lucky; I've done a lot of things with people who are really talented yet unknown. So I decided to figure out if I could find a good unknown artist, and I found one. I actually went back to the Professor I knew at Montgomery College, who runs an art school in Maryland. He said 'I think I know the perfect guy,' and I found this guy named Alex Fine, and he's working on the comic book right now.

Has he done anything previously?

He actually still in school. He's graduating next year. But he's this guy who's a really multifaceted talent he is in a band, and he illustrates, and he does some commercial work, and he's in school, and he does a bunch of different things. But he showed me some of his stuff and I thought it was really amazing. I had him do a couple sketches to see if his style was going to work with what I was thinking, and the sketches were working, then and then he came to me at one of our last meetings, he said, 'Look, I like the style, but what do you think of *this*?' and he showed me some charcoal drawings and he's like, 'I'm actually a lot better at charcoal than I am at ink.' And the stuff he showed me was really great, so we decided to go that way. The comic book thing is going to have a real unique look because he's going to do it all in charcoal. It should be pretty cool and I think the charcoal lends itself better to the darkness of the movie. Shadowy and also seeing the breath of the people, the cold. I think it would have been really difficult with ink, and I think obviously with charcoal, it becomes a little easier to bring about visually, you know?

Did you send it out to studios first?

I think that's kind of a mis-step that my agent made with it, because we originally sent it to horror movie producers, producers who are making *Chainsaw Massacre*, and *The Ring*… and we sent it to Sam Raimi's company.

They're trying to make these 10-15 million dollar horror movies for the teenage and early twenties market. So this movie's absolutely wrong for that, and my whole thing is we should send it out to producers who don't normally do horror movies, because the way I see it, this movie's like *Cold Mountain* meets *Alien*. And I think my agent was just kind of looking at it as a horror movie from the *Blair Witch* guy, for the teenage audience, and it's not really like that.

I didn't think The Blair Witch Project *was for the teenage audience.*

You know, I don't think so, either, but you know what? That's generally what people in the industry think about horror movies; that's their audience. So when something breaks out of that, I don't think they really understand what happened. And the thing of it is is that they don't understand older people like to be scared just as much as young people, they just don't want to sit through a bunch of crap; they don't want to be tricked into wasting their time just to be scared. I think they want something that has real characters and real situations, and they want real drama, and I think that's what a lot of horror movies just don't have. They're just made for a young audience, and they kind of lose something.

It goes for more spectacle than substance these days.

Yeah, and that's fine for that audience. But I think obviously, *Manabal'wak* needs to be nurtured by somebody who doesn't feel that way, and that's kind of what we're looking for right now.

We've talked about M. Night Shyamalan both in this interview and off the record. Aside from Sixth Sense, what are your thoughts about his work?

I liked *Unbreakable* more than I liked *Signs*. I thought *Signs* was really cool, but I didn't appreciate that he left these huge holes in logic that I couldn't fill with anything. The problem with all alien invasion movies is that *War Of The Worlds* worked because it was the first to do it. But now, things are so sophisticated, you couldn't do that the audience would say 'Well, can't the aliens sense things in Earth's air?' We can see what compositions planets have, so the aliens would say, 'Hey, there's something that's gonna kills us down there; let's send in some robots.' And that's the thing that *Signs* had, there's these huge mothships over all the cities, and when it comes down to it, they send naked soldiers with no weapons to attack with. I just couldn't get over that. But the thing about Night is that he creates these really cool moments in his films, and not many people can do that. But it's interesting, because his next movie takes place I think in the same year that *Manabal'wak* takes place in.

Who are your contemporaries?

Oh… I don't know, man. I can't really compare myself to anybody… I think Kevin Smith, really talented writer, a funny guy and he makes good movies. I'm not as good as he is at a lot of things. Filmmakers my age… the thing is, I bring up a name just for comparative reasons. I can't get this going… and it gives me motivation for me to get out and do it. Because I don't have any track record. I never compare myself. Like M. Night; people will come up to me like 'I saw M. Night on the cover of *Time* or *Newsweek*…' I think you have to have a certain something. The most difficult part is what we had for four years leading up to *Blair Witch*, is how do you develop that talent, and how do you make a living at it. All these filmmakers around me have different talent; some people are just super talented, I can compare myself to them; M. Night, Spielberg… I think I can make certain films that are just as good as theirs, in different ways. Like I think when I'm at the end of my career, and I've made ten or fifteen or five films, people can say hopefully 'You never know what he's going to do, or what style he's going to bring in.' I think Stephen Soderberg does that really great, and he was saying something in an interview about *Full Frontal* about which filmmaker he needs to be to make this film.

Yeah, he's got a style, but it's different from film to film

Exactly. Not that I'm as talented as him. That's why I don't like to compare myself. Spielberg I think is the most talented director out there right now. He's made his mistakes, like everybody else, but his body of work… nobody comes close to that. Just the way he personalizes things. Like with *Blair Witch*, I remember Dan Myrick and I were walking back from dropping something off at the camp, and I was like, 'This friggin' movie might be a complete disaster, it might not do anything, but Stephen Spielberg could not make this movie the way we're making it.' There's certain things I can do better than anybody, but I just don't know what those things are yet. I think all filmmakers are like that. You don't know what you can do until you do it. Like who knew what Peter Jackson was going to do.

It's a lot of money. There are people who do things better than me, but in that certain little niche of whatever the hell it is, I'm as good as anybody else I think. And I think Dan's as good as anybody else. It's a matter of finding that; I think that's the problem with a lot of filmmakers, where they can't find that. The budget's too high, people are telling they to do this and that, they don't trust the filmmakers, and my whole thing is just to make films that I'd want to see. if the question is who do I admire, I admire a lot of people; Kevin Smith, Robert Rodriguez, Tarantino's a super-talented dude. Scorsese's great. Even George Lucas, man… he's built this empire that nobody else has. And what I admire about him is that he found a way to make money off of ninety-nine percent of the movies that Hollywood makes, either THX, ILM… you look at all the big summer movies have something to do with putting some kind of money into George Lucas' pockets, and it's a business thing, but it's a business thing that he built so that he could make whatever the hell he wanted to make, so he could take the criticism he took on *Episode I* and still make and *Episode III* for whatever the hell money he ended up doing it for, and write it himself. Whatever you say about the moves, they're definitely not as good as the original ones. Obviously, the visuals are better.

Yeah, but they're not as organic-looking.

No, they're not. They're different movies, but for me, it's still that *Star Wars* universe, and I looked forward to *Episode I*, but I'm also looking forward to what else is going to come up, because they're not going to stop doing *Star Wars* stuff, I met with Jim Ward, the head of marketing a couple of months ago, he's a real good guy, and he's going to keep doing *Star Wars* stuff after the last movie, and he's not talking about movies yet, but he's doing TV shows and cartoons and novels and video games, and I'm a huge *Star Wars* fan, and to me, that's exiting. Really, I hope to work in that world sometime.

My dream would be to direct another *Star Wars* movie, or *Star Wars* TV show, or something in that world, because I know it. I admire just about anybody. I don't want to say any names, but I think there are some horribly overrated filmmakers out there, and I don't go to see their movies anymore, I just think it's a waste of frickin' time and money and I come out of the theatre mad. When you have a family, and I know you know this, it becomes about making a living. I've got to make a living for the rest of my life for my family. It's not like you can say, 'Well, I'll just quit and live at my Mom's house.' There are no options like that, there's no safety net. And a lot of times when I go to the movies now, I think 'I can at *least* do this. I can at least do what I just saw, with my eyes closed, and I just want to get a shot to do it right, because I don't want to fail because they wouldn't let me direct this scene the way I wanted to direct it, or let me put in Harvey Keitel instead of somebody else. I don't want to go through what Joe Berlinger went through, like 'My name's on this movie, and I didn't even control fifty percent of what's in it.'

When word gets out before it's even edited, about dailies being complete messes, no one likes it, and the studio's going to shelve it…

And the studio re-shoots a bunch of stuff without your approval.

There have been times that after reading a book or watching a movie that was just absolute trash that I've had to take a step back before writing a review of it and ask myself, 'Wait, am I going to slam this because it's a bad movie, or because I could have done it better… can I write this without being biased?' and sometimes the answer has been no.

Unfortunately, that's not how all critics feel.

Well, no. But then, a lot of critics are writers who failed in what they wanted to do.

Yeah, but you can see it sometimes… I would rather fail doing something I really believe in than something that I thought had potential, but just didn't get there, either my fault or somebody else's fault. I'd rather it be my fault. If I make the mistake, I'm learning. If somebody else makes the mistake, I'm not learning anything; all I'm going to do next time is try to avoid a given problem, but I'm not learning to be a good or better filmmaker… right now, we're trying to do things at Haxan that *we* control. If the *Manalba'wak* comic book doesn't work, or if the movie doesn't work, it's my fault. It's so much easier, because you can't make excuses. You can't say 'Oh, I should have done this.' Well okay, go and do it and fix it. For me and the Haxan guys, there *is* a happy place where we can make stuff we like.

With Blair Witch, *there was a gigantic amount of background information you provided… there was the website, and the* Dossier… *do you see yourself marketing another like that?*

I think you can market just about any film a million different ways, but the thing about *Blair Witch*, was that it was a perfect thing to do that to. And the marketing just grew from us having to have a backstory with Heather, who's our main character, to study. Then we had to build this mythology. Then when we started editing the movie, I had some time, so I started building a website and we had to decide what we were going to put up there… it was nothing like 'Oh, this is gonna be huge!' It was our only way for thirty dollars a month to be able to spread the word… we had no money. And as far as everything else, Artisan came in and pushed us, and took a bunch of our ideas and ran with them, and we had the *Curse Of The Blair Witch* TV special. The original idea for *Blair Witch* was more like *Curse*, more like a documentary, with more footage. Did you ever see *The Last Broadcast*?

Yeah, actually, I wanted to talk to you about that.

Well, *Blair Witch* was supposed to be a lot more like *The Last Broadcast*. But it didn't turn out that way. We actually saw *The Last Broadcast* in August of '98… right before we had the Sundance Festival… and we had heard about it months before, and we were freaking out, we were like, 'We had the same idea!' and Dan and I went to their website and we saw the whole trailer, and we were like, 'Oh, my God…' we came up with the idea in '92, and Dan and I were like, 'If we had gotten to this idea two year earlier…' but after awhile, we didn't hear much about *The Last Broadcast*, and we were really nervous, that it was going to blow *Blair Witch* out of the water. Then we watched the movie, and it was a completely different movie.

It really was. On the face of it, it sounded the same…

It sounds exactly the same, but it's very different. And I personally think it was a cool movie; it was a cool concept, but their execution wasn't authentic enough for me. That's the whole thing that what Dan and I wanted… the prime directive on *Blair Witch* was to make it look real, and in every decision we made in making the movie was aimed towards that; getting the most realistic performances, getting the most realistic look, everything… even the mythology… the investigation… we would argue, would the local authorities handle the case, would the FBI be brought in? Just logically trying to work everything in. and even wit the casting, I think with *The Last Broadcast* as a filmmaker, you could tell there's a lot of fake stuff in there. Like with out newscasts in the *Curse Of The Blair*

Witch were *awesome!* Obviously, there's no Channel 11 or whatever if you lived in that area but other than that, you can't tell that *isn't* a real local newscast. Because we cast it right, and we made the bugs look right. And I remember the only detail there was in the last broadcast that looked fake, that indicated a different sensibility than we had with *Blair Witch* was that there was an interview in front of a house, and there was no bug on the microphone, the reporter was like, nineteen years old, and the bug in the corner was almost a quarter of the frame, I'm like… 'People don't do that. There's no bugs in the corner of the frames that big.' They were just trying to draw attention to the fact that they had built a bug, instead of trying to make it authentic, and make it *small*, where you're not going to notice it. And I remember that detail because we had such a freaking nightmare building those freaking bugs… we had to jerry-rig this boom holder with little rubber bands, and we had to make the logos… we paid a lot of attention to these stupid little details…

But that's what pays off.

But that's what pays off. I think it pays off for people like you, and like people who are really into the details. And I think that's what people loved about *Blair Witch*, is that you had to dig really deep to realize it was fake. There wasn't anything where you saw something, and you were like, 'Oh, that's Tom Cruise!' There was no *technical* reason to not make it real.

The stuff that was the flashbacks to Lucan Johnson in the Seventies, that I was just awestruck by the way that was done, because I was like, 'I'm watching a 1975 documentary on witches, because of little touches like his glasses, and even the grain of the film.'

Yeah, we nailed it. The producer, Greg [Rebis] had five-year-old film in his freezer, and I was like, 'Okay, we'll use that.' We tinted it a little bit orange, and the guy who played the character was this perfect dude, who was actually a real witch, and we put him in front of this Seventies fireplace made of rock… I mean, even the cutaways… there were a lot of stuff we didn't use.

How much footage did you not *use?*

Of them in the woods, we had about twenty-two hours.

Total, or usable?

No, no, not usable. We had about maybe six hours of usable stock. Maybe five, six hours of stock. If somebody had said, do twelve half-hour shows, we could have done that... it was filmed in ten days.

Did you intentionally overshoot?

It just came out. We just told them to videotape everything. We constantly kept giving them tapes, and batteries... and then for *The Curse Of The Blair Witch*, we didn't shoot that much. A couple hours, maybe.

Did you shoot extra stuff for that?

We shot most of the interviews, but we already had the Lucan Johnson *Mystic Occurrances* documentary, and the Rustin Parr newsreel.

That was brilliant... I mean, I know I sound like a geeky fanboy for saying stuff like that, but the Rustin Parr stuff was just insane.

No, you know what, man? Me and Dan think that even if we hadn't had anything to do with *Blair Witch*, we definitely would have dug the *idea*, because of the attention to detail that we could do. That's what I think the big difference is between *Blair Witch* and *The Last Broadcast*, and I hate when they're compared, and I hate the whole thing of people saying like we ripped them off, it's just absolutely not true. And there's so many ways to verify that.

They are two very different films.

They are. And the whole thing for us was that we wanted people to go into the theatre or pop the movie in the VCR, and for those 90 minutes or whatever, think it was real... have no clues in the movie at all that this is not real, so you'd have to do some research to realize it's not real. All I wanted to do for those 90 minutes of watching that movie you're thinking it's real, even if somebody's told you it's fake, you're so convinced by the style of it that you're thinking this is really happening. There's nothing in *Blair Witch* that you can say, 'Oh, that wouldn't happen!' We didn't want people to say, 'There's a dude floating in the woods... that's not gonna happen, you can tell that's a guy on a rope...' none of that. And we were tempted to do that… And it came down to, 'How are we gonna end this? How are we not going to sell out? How are we not going to have the frickin' witch's *arm* in the shot or something?'

Did you have to fight for the ending?

We fought with Artisan, but it wasn't hard. Artisan before *Blair Witch* was released was the coolest company to be in business with. We have no complaints about them. Prior to the release of the movie. They gave us final cut on *Curse Of The Blair Witch*, we wrote and directed it and edited it at our production house at our little Media 100. It was a collaboration. They would send us the trailers, we'd be like, 'This is really cool… what about doing this?' And they would take our ideas and suggestions, and the same thing with the ending. The let us do exactly what we wanted with the sound mix. We re-did the sound mix, and we added a few more things here and there, and they made us go back and shoot some new endings.

What were they?

They were like the same kind of thing; Heather coming down, and Mike in different scary positions… like in one, he's levitating, in another one, he's on a stickman cross. In another one, he's bleeding and he has his shirt off… another had her where she comes down, and there's nothing there, and she turns, and Mike's there hanging all out of focus [Chuckles]. We talked to Bill [Block], who was the President of Artisan back then, and we told him we wanted to go with the original ending, and he said, 'It's gonna cost us millions at the box office, but we'll go with your ending.' But Artisan was really cool, man. Then after *Blair Witch*, they just were like, 'Okay, we need to make more money… we need to make more money… we need to make more money no matter who the fuck we piss off, no matter what the fuck we do, we need to make money,' and after that, they just ruined themselves.

But with the attention to detail, we would have arguments over things for people like you, man. The people who were like, 'I don't want to have to pretend that this is real, I want whatever the hell's coming at me to try to convince me that it's real *constantly*.' Even when I go to the website, and I check out the photos, and I look at the Rustin Parr newsreel, that's what newsreels in the Forties looked like. That's what 1970's frickin' documentaries looked like… that looks like real news studio… that's the angle they would use, that's the language that they would use, that's the graphic they would use...

I remember we got into an argument during filming of *Curse* where the cops are looking at the evidence... there's a CP16, and there's all these film cans and the guy who's videotaping is describing them, and I got into this big argument with Dan and Greg about would he pick up the camera and know what a 16mm camera look like? I don't think a cop in 1995 would know. I didn't know what a CP16 was before I went to film school. And the cop said, 'Hi-8 video camera'. But the camera didn't say Hi-8 on it anywhere on it, because it had been rubbed it was so dirty, and Hi-8 in 1995 was a really new format, and this is a cop in a small town... he'd say 'This is a video camera.' Later in their investigation, they'd recognize the specifics, but little things like that... we wanted to be authentic, and for me, that was the best part of the movie; making all these little things.

I was researching the impact that this particular movie had on contemporary culture, and there were people on the internet insisting *that this thing happened, or there were people going on bulletin boards asking, 'Did this* happen?' *There was even a point right before the release when my Mom saw the second trailer for the movie with Heather screaming her lungs out and asked if it were real based solely on Heather's scream because it sounds so genuine.*

Yeah, it's not 'Movie acting.' Like if you were really scared.

It's not something you see in your usual horror movie when someone screams. What she Heather had was such a primal thing.

And they all had it. There's that scene when Mike is calling out to Josh in the woods... they completely captured that... This guy was here this morning, and now he's in the woods being tortured... for us, we knew that we got the right actors, and we put them in the right situations, and we controlled the world around them, we knew we were gonna get something special, but we didn't have any idea we were going to get this kind of performance from these people, like Heather's pointing the camera at herself during her 'Confession' because you never see it in a normal movie. That scene ran for like fifteen minutes in the original version, and Dan and I were like awestruck.

The first time I knew *Blair Witch* was gonna work was when were watching the dailies... we were still shooting it... we had like a fifteen page outline of everything that was gonna happen to them, and we nailed just about everything, mostly through notes we would pass on to the actors… they did everything we wanted in the outline, but the scene where Mike admits to kicking the map in the river was *not* in the outline. The map was just supposed to become this obsolete thing during the trip…. That's another thing that pissed me off about the critical notes about the movie like 'They should have just followed the creek.' But it was kinda obvious that there was some kind of supernatural thing happening there… they were like in the Bermuda Triangle or something, and the cell phone argument really pisses me off, too. You can explain that *not* supernaturally; first of all, it's 1994, what college kid had a cell phone in 1994? Plus, when we were shooting the movie in 1997, in those woods, which was a two-square mile area and it's surrounded by house ands streets… we were constantly trying to take out the plane noise… they weren't isolated at all, but there was no cell phone coverage out there. We had to drive out to the edge of the park to call… just things that piss me off sometimes… what the hell was I talking about before?

The notes.

So when we saw that Mike kicked the frickin' map into the creek, and we saw the whole reaction from Heather and Josh, and his reaction, it was working for *us*. He kicked the map into the creek like a couple of hours before that, and he was just waiting for the right moment to tell them. And the thing about them, is that they're really talented actors, and also they were so tired and hungry… we started diminishing their rations as the days went on, so for them, I think it was very easy to switch into this thing of being tired and uncomfortable.

They looked miserable as hell.

They were. [Pause] I don't feel bad about [the fallout covered by *Newsweek*], because I think eventually they'll get to the point where all of them will they want to be… just because they don't have the success of Julia Roberts doesn't mean they're unhappy. Or they're not doing what they want to do or whatever… I thought they deserved a lot more credit than they got.

They got a lot of credit as a unit, but not individually. Heather got the most attention. But it was an ensemble cast, which was something I noticed about the Manabal'wak *script.*

It's how life is, man. In *Altered*, I have a part for Mike. I haven't told him about it yet. I'd like to include Josh… but I think that putting them together again wouldn't work. I wouldn't mind working with Heather again, either. I don't dislike Heather at all. I think she's a great actress. But reforming the cast would just be too much. Mike lives in New York, and he has a kid now, and he's just a real good guy, and I definitely am going to put him in my next movie somehow, and I see a lot of roles in films that Josh would be great at. Like *Cold Mountain*… there's this albino guy that I though Josh could have done a great job at. The actor did a great job, too. But I think Josh could have done just as good a job. I think there's a place for all three of them. They're just great actors, man, with amazing ability. I think everything will be all right, if it isn't all right now, for some reason.

Assembling the same cast can be suicide. If it works, it needs to be The Sting.

Well, the reason that worked was it was kind of the same movie… these two likable people who have this cool relationship with each other. I mean, it's Paul Newman and Robert Redford, but you're right; sometimes it just doesn't make sense to do it. For horror, if you do something with two or three of the *Blair Witch* cast members, it's not going to work. If you do something else, like a comedy, it might be different. It might not work. But I'd love to work with them again, just maybe not together.

Is there anything that would make you try it?

Well, The *Blair* movie that we're talking to Lion's Gate about will probably have opportunities to use them. Whether they'll do it or not, I don't know. I'm pretty sure that they'll do it, if the original production staff are involved, and the story's right; and that's *our* thing, that if we get involved, then we're gonna make sure that at least *we* believe in the frickin' story. And we have some cool stuff already. Actually, we're kind of surprising ourselves about how much stuff we have that we're excited about.

Are you going back into the mythology and finding inspiration in stuff you may have forgotten about?

Yeah, definitely. And we're also trying to take the mythology that we've created and like, re-invent it. Y'know, the Rustin Parr thing; he killed seven kids… well, maybe he didn't. Maybe it was something else. Maybe he's innocent. I think Dan described it well when we were discussing this with a couple people about it. We want to do a movie where we answer a lot of questions, but by the end of the movie, you're wanting just as many answers as you were the first one. But maybe you're more satisfied because we've touched on these little moments, and the fans are gonna love it. Even to *Blair Witch*, because we're planning on doing some stuff to that, too. We'd like to do some new stuff to *Blair Witch*, to sort of lead you into the next movie.

You mean, you're going to tweak the original?

Tweak it, add some stuff on an alternate disk. The plan would be to do some kind of Special Edition DVD.

With some new footage?

With a *lot* of new footage.

Are you expecting any backlash like Lucas got?

No, I don't think so, because the thing about the alternate footage, is that it's not really deleted scenes, it's just more evidence.

Are you going to put it in the body of the original?

We don't know yet. We'll probably leave the original the way it is. But who knows? The first thing is do they want to make another movie, and thing is how much of our marketing do they want... do they want us to be involved in marketing, which to us, is very important. We know what people want, and it's not an egotistical thing, but we know what we would want out of another *Blair Witch* movie, and that's what we did with the first one; we did a movie that we would have wanted to see, and that's what we're gonna do with the second one, and that's what we're going to do with the Special Edition DVD. But the DVD is kind of a long shot... there's so much production costs to do that that they might look at the numbers and say, 'Well, we're not going to get enough people to buy this.' Who knows? I think the numbers would work out, but you don't want to do a Special Edition DVD that has five minutes of new footage.

We've always wanted to do the entire Rustin Parr newsreel, which you've only seen in clips. We shot tons of stuff for it, the voice-over, the music, the logo in the beginning... we want to show the entire Lucien

Johnson *Mystic Occurrances* documentary… show the whole half-hour show, with the commercial break fade-outs, that kind of stuff. We even had an opening for it that my cousin wrote the music for, totally Seventies… it sounds perfect, like an *In Search Of…* and we did this thing where the logo comes at you, but it's like one of those optical logos, we skipped three of four frames so it looks like they lost some frames in the film chain… all those thing pre-tape were all just on film… in the Eileen Treacle story, with the hand coming out of the water, we were going to cover that in the *Mystic Occurrances* episode, we took this mannequin arm and we were in the creek in Maryland, and I got underwater—and it was *cold*—and I had to tie something to myself so I could sink down [laughing] and Dan would roll the camera, and I would just pop the arm up, and we were gonna do it like those cheesy re-enactments those shows would have with the snap-zooms and dramatic music, and we had a reenactment of the legend is that the water was filled with oily bundles of sticks floating down the river, and that the water was undrinkable, and we put these stickmen in the water, and just these cheeseball cutaways… for the Coffin Rock, we did some 16mm stuff where we had sections of rope and we bloodied them all up and had Kool-Aid running down the rocks [imitates dramatic music] where Lucien could be talking about it, and there would be these cutaways… we'd like to do a new commentary track, and maybe get an actor commentary track.

We think it would be cool, and this has to be off the record, but what we want to do, is that we'd like to get Josh, Heather, and Mike back and put them in the original clothes and shoot more stuff in the woods on Hi-8 just like we did *Blair Witch*, like almost do a mini-shoot and I think it'd work. Obviously, they've changed, but I think it would work, because 95% of *Blair Witch* is Heather talking, and shots of their backs…

The woods…

Trees… Mike is our marketing monster, and he thought about doing the first DVD with *Blair Witch*, not the film version, because what they did is they transferred it off the negative… so it's got this kind of weird look… we wanted to go back to the digital beta master and have just a straight video copy that looks like Hi-8, there's no film look at all, we thought would kind of be a cool look to the movie that people hadn't seen, just a full-frame of video.

We could put *Curse Of The Blair Witch* on there, with maybe some commentary, then the Rustin Parr documentary and *Mystic Occurances*, and we have like a full *Making-Of* documentary that's never been seen before. And have another disk that says *Evidence: Black Hills Disappearance*. And you pop this DVD, and it has no graphics, it looks like something somebody burned themselves and all it has is number files, where you go in, and all it is is raw footage with time code at the bottom, just hours of this, different reels, all the film footage, all the 16mm footage that they shot, which is just a lot of pretty shots… sun through the trees and stuff there's a lot of cool stuff… and most of this is MLS [no sound], so it'd be kinda creepy, so our whole thing is that this stuff is evidence, of stuff you've never seen before, but in no sequential order… you actually have to go through it, and there's hidden things in there, and what the plan is in the mythology in the proposed prequel is to go back and shoot some stuff with Heather, Josh, and Mike… imagine the scene where they're running out of the tent, but looking a it from an outside point of view, in 35mm, and either someone's watching them, or someone's having a hallucination and is imagining it. Same thing with going back and doing something with Elly Kedward, her tied to a tree freezing to death… sort of like a *Jacob's Ladder* ride through the *Blair Witch* world and on the second disk, we want to put things in there that we add ourselves that we've actually re-shot and inserted it into the original video, nobody's going to be able to tell when we shot it, but we want to put those in there to kind of give clues to what's happening in the prequel movie we're planning, so you'd see the movie and if you had watched the disk before, going 'I *saw* that!' Imagine if there was a shot of them *after* they got to the house, or what happened to the when they were hiding in the woods, and the camera wasn't running… just little things that actually happened to these kids, but you could never have seen by watching the movie, but adding stuff that gives you a kind of bridge between the first movie and the prequel.

Would you solve anything in the prequel?

No, but we'd give clues, and we're gonna add American Indian mythology… we're going to go back even further, like *Blair Witch* existed to the Indian hundreds of years before white men even got to that area. In the original version of *Blair Witch*, it was going to an in-depth documentary, like I told you and we were going to have the documentary filmmaker analyzing the film frame-by-frame, like when Heather goes, 'What the hell is *that*?' we were planning, and we shot it this way, but it didn't come out because we didn't do enough tests, but we had a dude all in white, like long johns, and socks over his shoes, and a ski-mask, twenty feet in the woods running next to them, so that when she says that, she's seeing this white figure in the woods, that probably looks goofy in person, but in the camera, that jiggling, we wanted to capture glimpses of this humanoid figure like a ghost, and we wanted to do that all throughout the movie, so that's what we want to do to the footage that hasn't been seen, and that all of a sudden, you catch a glimpse, and you're like, 'Holy shit!', and with DVD, you can go frame-by-frame, and say, 'Look at that shit! It looks like a woman in the woods.'

And what we want to do is create something with a discussion board, so that people can post stuff like, 'Dude, check out Reel 10, timecode whatever, frame 22. What is it?' And so we'd like to create a puzzle in that footage where the only people who are gonna see it are the people who are going to sit there and watch everything and hyper-dwell on this footage, just like they've been on the original website, so we'd like to create something where the DVD comes out, and people are like, 'Aw, it's just another Special Edition DVD.' But then, people start realizing clues that are gonna be in the next movie, like 'Did you see what they were talking about in this scene?' and then maybe put some stuff in the trailers, because you need to market it to everybody, but if you put inside jokes, or information, that only the geeks are gonna get, the geeks are gonna go nuts. And that's how I'd react. So we're hoping that it'll create a kind of excitement so that people'll go on the boards and telling their friends, kind of like what *Blair Witch* did.

Obviously, it's not going to do the same thing that *Blair Witch* did, but if we're going to go back and do another *Blair Witch* movie, we need to go in running on all cylinders, it has to be like a bombardment of cool shit, just like the first one, where you have to *really* pay attention to it, and do a Special Edition DVD, do stuff that hasn't been done before, and what we want to do on the website is… Lion's Gate went back to the website and eliminated all the *Book Of Shadows* stuff, which was a great thing, so we'd like to take the website, and without any kind of updates or anything, just start inserting more mythology, so that the average person who goes there will go, 'Did you notice that they added a new date? And they added this new picture of this book or this journal that they found from one of the Blair residents?' Start filling it in, and even going back to the Indian time, and all that is is setup for the next movie, just give people more backstory. Obviously, you can't print any of that, but as one fan to another, that's what we want to do. I think it'll be cool, man.

Lion's Gate thing is that they want to do a low-budget movie, like $7-10 million dollars, which is totally doable for a *Jacob's Ladder*-type thing, and what we want to do with the movie, is just make it this frickin' wild ride into like, *Blair Witch* hell, not violent or anything, but just creepy as hell, and touch on as much of the original mythology as possible.

That's what the first movie was, it wasn't about the gore.

No, it wasn't. It was just straight fear, man. Just primal fear. So now, it's like, what's the end result of the prequel? Not that it's going to tie itself up at the end, *Blair* movies aren't supposed to do that. In my opinion. What's going to be the danger, what's going to be the fear? But we're coming up with some cool ideas, man. and this is off the record, but Greg came up with something where... you know how the Rustin Parr house fell down from the hurricane that came through? So, Greg was thinking like near the end of the movie, the protagonist, who we don't know who it is yet, we're thinking it might be the Professor who helped Heather with the project... like it's ten years later, and he's pretty much lost his mind, not to where he's living in an asylum, but he's like real eccentric, teaches at this small college, but just a real weird dude, and you go into his house, and he just has evidence everywhere from Heather's disappearance, trying to figure out what's going on with this *Blair Witch* thing.

We're thinking he goes back into the house, and he pulls open some of the wood, and he ends up going back to where Mike was standing in the corner, and as he's doing this, maybe we'll do it with an optical effect or may be a cool set design, but you start going back in time, and seeing all the different things that have happened, like the house built up, the camera turns around, and you see Rustin Parr in the background killing one of the kids, and more of the mythology that's going on around you, then at the end of the camera move, you see where Mike was standing was where Elly Kedward was tied up and left for dead in that same position in the woods. It's a lot of stuff that goes back. You're like... reinventing the mythology, but I think Blair fans would be like '*That's* why he was standing there.' I mean, part of the reason was the whole Rustin Parr thing, but that's something we came up with afterwards, too. For us, it was like, 'How do we end this movie?' And we came up with that like, two days before we shot it, and for us, there's nothing more creepy than these people who have been together for so long, and for some reason, Mike's just standing there, not... *responding*... to... her! I mean, what could be happening that Mike wouldn't respond to Heather yelling and screaming behind him?

So we're having a lot of fun figuring all this stuff out, like what a stickman means, and I think we're going to find a lot about it through the Indian stuff, we'd like to build this whole Indian mythology where the

Indians realizes early on not to fuck around with those woods... there's something there. If you go back even further, like real basic mythology of *The Blair Witch Project*, like one of the ideas we've had about it was like, whatever created the planet left these entities on the planet that were part of building the animals. kind of like architects or construction workers... not very scary, but some of these things stayed behind, either they were criminals or outcasts... but that's what the *Blair Witch* is. This completely foreign thing that lives on the earth, and is attracted to turmoil. I like the theory of like when bad things happen, like the Civil War battlefields, and where I live, there are Civil War battlefields all over the place, and people say that there's this energy there, like you can hear the guns going off at night... and when I go there. there's this battlefield named Monocacy like five minutes from my house... I haven't been to Gettysburg, but I've been to Antietam, and you go to Antietam, and you're walking on this field, and there like this *energy* there, so I love the whole idea... even animals, like the mass slaughter where the Indians used to scare the buffalo off a cliff... that kind of like turmoil... I love the idea of an energy staying behind after that, and an energy being attracted to it, the energy that humans give off; feeding off your fear and that's what I think the latest thing in *Blair Witch* is that he saw this happen to Elly Kedward, and he saw the fear in the village, and he or she or *it*, was feeding off this, and manipulating things, and every once in a while, it wants to go back ands to the same thing in that area... you never understand what it is.

I got the idea that there was something else going on besides Elly Kedward. She was the catalyst... there was something else.

Yeah, it's definitely not her. We had an idea... like the Horse Lady that Mary Brown talks about in *Blair Witch*... about a woman covered in horse hair... like the opening for the prequel would have... it's snowing... no sound except the sound of this wagon going through this woods, and it's freezing... everybody's wear hoods... there's a woman in the wagon—Elly—she has a hood on her head, and there's a couple of guys holding her, and they go as far as they can into the woods. They end up on foot, and this woman can barely walk... you can see their breath... and they tie her to this tree, and one dude ties her really tight, and the other one kinds of loosens things up, and he says 'God bless you.' You can tell he doesn't think this is right, but he's going along with it. So they leave her, and you can just see her breath, and you haven't seen her face yet, and you cut to dusk, and you can barely see anything, and the sky is like dark blue and the trees are casting shadows, and the camera's going around, and you can tell she's dying; she's more limp, she's gasping for breath, she's freezing to death, and all of a sudden, the camera stops with this side shot of her face, and she just looks up with this ridiculous energy, and you can see her face, now she's this old lady, like late sixties, and she's just like totally aware and conscious, and then you cut to what she sees, and it's the woods just before night completely falls, you can barely see the trees, and you can just make out the outline of a man, and you can tell he's a little too high to be standing up… he's floating… something's watching her, and this huge full-rack deer comes out of nowhere and sits there next to her, and lays down on the snow, and she looks down, and her wrists are untied, and she goes over to the deer, and I haven't really worked it out, but she either with her hands, she tears open the deer… she does a sort of Han Solo/Tauntaun thing, and warms herself, and then later on, when the people from the village go to see if she's dead, her body's gone, there's blood all over the ground, and there's marks like something's been dragged across the snow. And the whole thing about the Horse Lady is that Elly wore this deer carcass, with the hair and the blood… and that's part of the mythology and kind of what we want to do, just little things like that that are cool… I came up with that years ago, then I was like, 'That's the Horse Lady! It makes perfect sense!' Obviously, I think the *Blair* fans are going to dig it, and we hope Lion's Gate gets into it, and gets into it enough to let us do what we want to do with it. My thing about the meeting is that I want to be enthusiastic about it.

It's going to have to carry the creator's names on it so they don't think about the second movie… not to slam it too hard, but it was radically different from the first.

What really pissed me off about the second one… I think if they had kept the *Blair Witch* name off of it, it would have done a lot better, because the expectations wouldn't have been so high, and it really had *nothing* to do with frickin' *Blair Witch*, y'know? It's like starting *The Empire Strikes Back*, by saying, 'Boy, *Star Wars: A New Hope* was a great movie, wasn't it? Okay, let's start.'

A sequel to a movie can't start by commenting on the first movie… Joe was trying to experiment, but they should have just called it *Book Of Shadows* and had some *Blair* references in it, and it would have been like 'Oh, this is a separate movie; it has nothing to do with the *Blair* mythology.' Because *Book Of Shadows* doesn't leave you with anywhere to go. You just destroyed the franchise because the first part of the second movie destroys the franchise… it just goes through and destroys it… it tells you it's bullshit. It does nothing except say that the movie wasn't real, and I thought what he was trying to do was cool, like about the whole thing about perception, but it had nothing to do with *Blair Witch*, that's my problem with it… [shakes head] anyway, enough talk about the second one… we'd like to forget it, and not treat it as part of the franchise, and Lion's Gate wants to do the same thing. But we'll see what happens, man. I don't think they're thinking about re-visiting *Blair* without us, and I think they're still probably trying to figure out what the hell to do with Artisan assets, but hopefully, they'll believe in it enough to move forward with it. I think it'll be a cool movie to do, and we *know* it, I think that's the thing that makes us most confident; we know we can do it.

GREGORY MAGUIRE

GREGORY MAGUIRE HAS MADE A NAME for himself with his tilted slant on the mythology of fairy tales like *Confessions of an Ugly Stepsister* and *Mirror Mirror*, but also of the Land of Oz, as works like *Wicked*, perhaps his most famous work, prove.

Wicked would also become a presence in the world of musical theatre, introducing audiences (and new readers) to his quirky take on stories they thought they knew well.

With a Ph.D. in English and American Literature from Tufts University, Gregory has worked as a consultant in creative writing and a public speaker worldwide. He founded Children's Literature New England, Incorporated in 1987 and is a voice in children's literature with works like *Three Rotten Eggs*, and *Four Stupid Cupids*.

What would you like to tell us about your upcoming book, Mirror, Mirror?

Mirror Mirror is dressed up with another one of those gorgeous dust jackets by Douglas Smith, in which the dust jacket features one piece of art and a peek-through dye-cut hole, and the actual book binding is printed with a separate piece of art that changes the mood, reveals more, and rings a change on the central image glimpsed through the hole.

This is a pretty good metaphor for any novel. A novel is intended to start with a set of givens and then work a process of revelation upon them, cue by cue and clue by clue. My novels, in that the givens are drawn from the common culture of childhood lore, provide a more established starting point than some. ('Snow White is offered a poison apple and falls into a coma'—for *Mirror Mirror*—is a more concise description than 'A woman plans and hosts a party'—for *Mrs Dalloway*.)

So *Mirror Mirror*, as the title suggests, takes aspects of the Snow story, the irreducible elements of poisoned apple, magic mirror, dwarves, and wicked stepmother, and sets the tale in a distant Tuscan farmhouse during the High Renaissance. Nothing is quite what it seems. Lucrezia Borgia, the fabled beauty and noblewoman notorious for her political cunning and amorous exploits, is a central figure, here imagined as the guardian and assaulter of my Snow White, Bianca de Nevada.

What has your body of work taught you that you have been able to apply in Mirror Mirror?

I wrote children's books for many years—17 in fact—before publishing my first adult novel, *Wicked: The Life And Times Of The Wicked Witch Of The West*. I began that novel ten years ago, in my late 30's, when I felt old enough to do research reliably. Research on Oz, you might ask: what did that require? It required having a mature enough view of the world to be able to ask questions—and imagine answers—about all aspects of a culture—religion, art, education, social policy, history, geography, etc. I needed a set of anthropologist's tools if I was going to make Oz come alive.

Since then, research has provided the backbone (and helped reveal the story) of the other adult novels *Confessions Of An Ugly Stepsister*, set in Harlem in 1627 or so, was derived in part from an informal survey of the paintings of the Northern Renaissance. *Lost*, a contemporary ghost story, required me to travel to London and Mont St. Michel in France, and read much on Dickens and Jack the Ripper. For *Mirror Mirror* I got to travel to Venice(for the first time) and, several times, to Tuscany and Umbria. And I read much about Italian politics, especially the corrupt papacy of Alexander VI, Lucrezia Borgia's father.

What was the deciding factor in letting Stephen Schwartz and Winnie Holzman take Wicked *to the stage as a musical?*

I was not hard persuaded to give the project a green light. Stephen Schwartz pitched it as invevitable: in musical theater, singers channel the high emotions of the characters directly at the audience through spectacle and song. *Wicked* is a book of fierce emotions, and the muted acting of high-resolution movie cameras would have been harder to carry off, and perhaps less authentic. I suspected that the book would be transposed into a different key—perhaps a lighter key—and in that, I think I was right. But I don't disapprove.

Are you familiar with Neil Gaiman's work Snow, Glass, Apples, *itself a reworking of the Snow White story? What was your opinion of it?*

I know Neil Gaiman's work only through *Neverland*. I've just checked the dust jacket to see if *Snow, Glass, Apples* is mentioned—did I see it and borrow the thought subconsciously? It isn't listed there (nor in the 'other books by' page preceding the title page). I've never read it, clearly, but till you asked I had never heard of it either.

What is the status of The Dream Stealer *coming back into print?*

The Dream Stealer came back into print in hardcover last year from Clarion Books, with a great new cover in blood red and black paper silhouette cutouts.

Are you happy with the results of Confessions Of An Ugly Stepsister *as a miniseries? What did you get from the experience?*

I was most pleased with the look and integrity of the set, and greatly charmed by the actresses. I found the script a bit lacking, though I suspect that that had something to do with the Disney/ABC people ironing out the wrinkles of ambiguity about character and motivation. I try hard, in fiction, to supply a number of different reasons for why a character behaves as he or she does, without settling it for the reader. A TV script can't often be that tolerant of subtlety.

How are you able to bring, for want of a better term, a certain harshness to the well-established world of fairy tales while retaining the keen sense of awe found in their original counterparts?

I would argue that my novels are merely more detailed, not in any way more harsh than the original tales, especially those that were recorded by the Brothers Grimm. In the original Snow White by Grimm, the stepmother was made to dance in red-hot iron shoes at the girl's wedding to the prince until she fell down dead. In *Mirror Mirror*, while I bring the stepmother figure to her deathbed, I think in fact I am slightly more tender than that—at least at first.

Admittedly, there are some crude details in *Mirror Mirror*. At one point Lucrezia Borgia scares Bianca de Nevada by appearing at the cottage wearing a carnival masque made to look like a set of flopping, semi-erect male genitalia. I hasten to remark that I wouldn't (I think) be capable of inventing a detail like this, though I am capable of presenting it once I have read, in a biography of Lucrezia Borgia, that there was some house party she gave on New Year's Eve in which masques of that sort were featured.

What made you use present tense for Confessions?

I wrote *Confessions* originally in the traditional past tense of the fairy tale—of the told tale. Perhaps because I was also trying to evoke archaic language (not to imitate it, just to imply an otherness of diction) the book seemed too distant to be easily readable. I tried one or two chapters in the present tense, and the thing slapped itself to life, and made the hoary old story urgent and even, perhaps, mysterious again.

Gregory, thank you very much for your time. Is there anything you'd like to add?

For some reason or another I had to spend an hour recently hunting through my novel *Lost* the other evening. Understandably enough, though it sold pretty well, *Lost* got little press attention when it was published in October 2001. The papers had little room for book reviews that sorry autumn. I think the book suffers from an unfortunate cover, ghoulish and a bit silly. Had the book been published with a plain, restrained cover, under my working title *Revenant*, I think it might have had an entirely different reception and might be much more read. I'm very proud of it—perhaps proudest of it—and I draw it to the attention of your readers.

LAURELL K. HAMILTON

IN THE WORK OF LAURELL K.HAMILTON, momentum both of popularity and page-turning drive lends itself not only to her series of books involving fan favorite Anita Blake, Vampire Hunter, but also in her works outside of Anita's world with the likes of the Merry Gentry Series, populating her character's surroundings with supporting characters as memorable as those in the lead.

Strong female protagonists confident in their sexuality and abilities may seem to be almost a cookie-cutter order, but Laurell sidesteps this pitfall in her works, and provides the reader with a satisfying read time after time in her early appearances in *Marion Zimmer Bradley's Fantasy Magazine* to such books as *Nightseer, Guilty Pleasures, Caress Of Twilight,* and, *Cerulean Sins.*

What preparation went into creating the world around Anita Blake? (In other words, did you research the paranormal and/or reread Dracula *and the like?)*

I cannot say how strongly I object to people using other people's writing as research. Research is non-fiction, especially for horror, fantasy, science fiction. Do not take your research from other people's fiction. Just don't. They may be wrong. I, like most people, who set down to write have been reading something in the area of what they end up writing for years. We've done all the fictional background we'll ever need before we come close to the computer. I'd read nonfiction for years about folklore, mythology, and monsters for years. Just a hobby. Probably the old Hammer vampire films were as a great an early influence as any book. I watched them at quite a tender age, and they are very sensual, very lush, pretty evil. But by the time I sat down to write Anita, I hadn't seen a Hammer film in years. I had almost stopped reading other people's horror. I'd actually just begun to read mysteries.

Anita would be very different if I'd never picked up a hard boiled detective mystery. I actually knew more about vampires and werewolves than I was able to put in the first book. But I knew almost nothing about voodoo. That was the biggest paranormal research I had to do. Guns and police procedure were the other area I had to research. I didn't know nearly enough about either.

Anita Blake has come to understand the world is not simply black and white, but has shades of gray in it as well, and its happened in a very natural progression. Was this something planned from book one or did it happen as the characters matured?

When I first researched Anita's world I talked to policemen for the first time in depth about their job. I learned something of the cost of the job. I watched my brother-in-law, go from bright and shiny to tired. As I continued to research for Anita, I talked to combat veterans, and was privileged to have them share some of their experiences with me. Because Anita really has a violence level that is far above most police work. I use to joke she lived in a combat zone until I did one book where she visited what amounted to a real combat zone, and she was out of her depth. Book nine, *Obsidian Butterfly*, we visited Edward's world, and saw something closer to real soldiering.

It was frightening. But as I talked to the men, and some women, about their lives, I realized that to keep Anita at the level of violence that she was, would have a price. Part of that price is innocence, and the knowledge that the world is not black and white, and answers are not as simple as they seem.

Anita had to go through this process, or it would have felt like a betrayal of those people who spoke with me, and shared their experiences.

Do you see yourself going back into the world you created for Nightseer *for a follow-up to that novel?*

Maybe someday I'll go back to *Nightseer*'s world, but not soon. I'm doing two series at once now. I couldn't possibly do three.

Was breaking away from the Anita Blake series a conscious act of starting something different or was is more a matter of natural progression?

I'd written five Anita books in a row. I needed a breather. Merry was that breather.

Did you sell either series from an outline or did it come from a completed manuscript?

Guilty Pleasures was a complete manuscript. A beginning writer needs to finish a book before they try and sell it. But by the time Merry came up, I had a track record, and I was able to sell the series from an outline.

The line between what is sensual and what is pornographic is thin, and varies from eye to eye. Is there a point when you write a love scene that you consciously won't go past?

I haven't found a point in love scenes that I feel is off-limits, yet. I do avoid medical terms, clinical phrases.

Merry's attitude towards sex is very matter-of-fact and positive. Was this something dictated by the character?

I wanted someone with an easier attitude about sex. Someone I wouldn't have to argue with all the time the way I do with Anita. Merry was that person. Truthfully, sometimes she's beyond my comfort zone, but that's my up-bringing, not hers. Be true to your characters and they'll be true to you.

How did you come to help the American Society for the Prevention of Cruelty to Animals?

I feel that if you are blessed, or lucky enough, to be doing well, you should help others. I love animals, always have, and it seemed natural to help the ASPCA. Animals have no voice of their own, so we have to be that voice. It was my assistant Darla Cook, who first brought Granite City to my attention. She was made aware of them through a news article. We visited them, liked what we saw, and the rest, as they say, is history. I also support Pug rescue, but that is personal, and not something I raise money for.

Do you write about things that scare you personally, or things you think will scare your readers?

I don't write about scary things. I write about what comes to me. The only time I've ever consciously tried to be scary was in *Obsidian Butterfly*. I had to come up with something that would scare Edward. The scene in the hospital when they first see the survivors is still the most frightening scene I've ever written. At least to me. I realized that anything that would be bad enough to frighten Edward would scare the heck out of Anita, and me. It's the one scene that no matter how many times I read it, it just gets creepier.

Can we expect any more short stories from you any time soon?

I just don't have the time for short stories anymore. Sad but true.

What prompted you to post the first two chapters on your website?

The third chapter is in the back of *Narcissus In Chains* in paperback. It seemed cruel to have the third chapter out there without the first two chapters. So if you've got web access you can at least read the first few chapters without having to wait for *Cerlean Sins* to hit the stands in April.

As an admitted technophobe, what led to your decision to have your own website?

You can blame my husband, and Darla (my assistant). They both had websites up long before I even knew what one was. This was back when my husband was just my friend, and it had never occurred to us to date. Though I am a little overwhelmed by technology, I see its uses, and its advantages. I have never written a book that wasn't on computer.

Your grandmother told you horror tales taken from the hills of Arkansas, leaving you with the thought 'Rawhide and bloody bones will get you if you aren't good.' Do you ever think back to those stories for influence or inspiration?

I don't really think back to my grandmother's stories for inspiration, but I think that I have absorbed those stories into the pores of my being.

It was simply an accepted fact that ghosts were real, that the dead didn't always rest easy, that things could move by themselves, and that simple things could be frightening. I used to blame my families penchant for macabre true stories, and other real life tragedies for my dark turn of mind. Recently, I've had to rethink that. My daughter is eight, and she loves mummies. Her favorite book for ages was *Cinderella Skeleton*, where all the characters are ghouls and such, and the main character looses a lot more than just her slipper running down the stairs. It's made me remember that long before my mother's death, when I played cowboys and cowgirls, it wasn't enough for the chairs to be tall cliffs. No, we had to have a pit of rattlesnakes at the bottom of the cliff, so we'd be bitten to death. A fall, just wasn't horrible enough. My daughter's childhood is making me rethink my own. Apparently, it wasn't early tragedies that made me this way, maybe, just maybe, it was the way I came.

How important is it for a writer or reader of horror to know why they enjoy such dark topics?

It's not. Soul-searching is fine, and good therapy is a many-splendored thing, but don't spend too much time wondering why you think the way you do. Just accept your muse, the way she comes, and move on.

Is networking conventions and other places writers gather essential to long-term success these days?

Yes, and no. At the beginning of your career. Very yes. First, dress for success. Dress nice. You can be dramatic, by all means be yourself, but don't show up in jeans and a t-shirt, unless you look really good in jeans and a t-shirt. Be clean, neat, presentable. This is a business, treat it that way. I highly recommend dressing nice, so you don't look hungry. By that, I mean, if you look and act like you need this job, need this contract, need to sell a book, people will run from you, or treat you badly. If you act businesslike, and not like the fate of the world, or at least your sanity, rides on this editors opinion, you'll do better. Trust me. I speak from experience. Act confident, no matter how you feel inside. Have business cards made, but make sure they look good, not cheap. You can do some pretty nice ones on most computer printers these days. But they must not look cheap.

You can be the best writer in the world, but at a convention no one is reading your writing, they're just seeing you. Remember that. If you present yourself badly, you hurt yourself. You don't have to be brilliant, just professional. I had breakfast meetings, lunch meetings, dinner meetings, snack meetings, every-kind of meeting, over the years. I think of all those meetings that I sold one short story, and no books. Was it wasted time? No. Some of my fellow writers, (members of my writing group) Deborah Millitello, and Mark Sumner, to name two, sold more short stories than I did, at the same meetings. It led to a book contract for Mark. So it wasn't wasted. You never know what contact will pay off. I met my first agent at a convention. Though that is highly unusual. But be wary, some people that go to conventions are not always as good as they seem. Anyone can claim to be editing an anthology, or be an agent. Get the agent's client list. Find out who they represent.

If they are legitimate, then they will have people you can call, that will tell you what kind of job they're doing as an agent. Though bear in mind that the agent isn't going to give you names of people that think they suck.

With the proliferation of things horror in TV and film, like Buffy The Vampire Slayer, Angel, *and any given number of vampire movies, are you concerned with oversaturation effecting the enthusiasm of yourself or your readers?*

Nearly twelve years ago when I was first trying to sell *Guilty Pleasures*, I had one publishing house reject the book on the grounds that the market couldn't bear another vampire book, and the week they were going to make the decision another vampire novel came out from another publisher. They used that as a reason to reject me, and Anita. They said that the vampire market was dying out, and no one wanted to read about vampires anymore.

As you say, interest in vampires and thinks that go bump in the night seems at a high point, so I don't think I'll worry about people growing tired of it all.

Are there specific problems you've faced as a female author or as a woman writing what some might call 'erotic mysteries'?

I was told by a prominent mystery editor that if my Anita Blake mysteries had been straight mystery, no horror elements, or fantastic elements at all, that I'd have never gotten published. Because I am a woman writing from a first person woman's point of view, that no one would have touched it.

Maybe that's true. Maybe it was one of the things that sent Anita around to nearly every publisher before it found a home. I don't know. No one complained about the sexual content of the first book, but then, there wasn't any. I don't know if I'd have had more trouble if the first few books had had a higher content or not. I do know that by using the tropisms of several different genres, I get to play exactly the way I want to play. I get the tough as nails attitude of a hard-boiled-mystery; the monsters and gore level of horror; the sex and sensuality of romance; the shear wonderment of fantasy; and the feeling of reality that the best science fiction gives to amazingly odd facts. If I hadn't chosen to mix genres I might have had a harder time.

Though most people told me that mixing genres this badly would doom me.

Just goes to prove that you have to believe in yourself and your vision.

What can you tell us about Cerulean Sins?

I am really bad at spoilers. I always give away too much. So about *Cerulean Sins* what can I say? Anita gets to raise the dead on stage, which we hadn't done in books. We get to have the police on stage a lot more, so Dolph and Zerbrowski and the gang are back on stage. We learn a lot more about Jean-Claude and Ashe's background, and about Belle Morte herself. Because it's almost impossible to learn about the two men, and not have Belle Morte in the story somewhere. She is what brought them together, after all.

Jason is very much on stage. We get to see Damian, Nathaniel, Micah, and Richard. There are others, but those are sort of the highlights. If Darla doesn't think I've given too much away, I'll stop.

JANE ESPENSON

FANS OF SPECULATIVE FICTION will know Jane's work from Joss Whedon's *Buffy the Vampire Slayer* television series with her classic episode, 'Band Candy' along with many others. She was recognized along with fellow Mutant Enemy staff writer Drew Goddard for their episode, 'Conversations With Dead People,' winning the Hugo for Best Short Dramatic Presentation in 2003, shortly after this interview.

Jane would go on not only to pen the 'Shindig' episode of the short-lived *Firefly*, and worked of *Tru Calling* and *The Batman*, but also showed her prowess with non-genre hits such as *The OC* and *Gilmore Girls*.

She has acted as Editor for the non-fiction collection *Finding Serenity: Anti-Heroes, Lost Shepherds and Space Hookers in Joss Whedon's Firefly* and will join the *Battlestar: Galactica* spinoff, *Caprica* in 2009.

Given that months have now passed since Buffy *ended, what are your thoughts on the finale?*

I loved it. I think Joss did an amazing job of bringing it to an apocalyptic and yet redeeming ending for our characters—tying up the past and looking forward to the future. You know, for those who survived it.

You wrote some of the funniest episodes for the show; how much leeway did Joss give you in writing a given episode like 'Superstar' and your first, 'Band Candy?'

I had leeway where I wanted it and support when I needed it. Pretty much every beat of every story on Buffy came from Joss. I sat down to write those scripts knowing all the actions and attitudes and turns. But the words, the jokes… that's where Joss allowed us each tremendous freedom. I feel very fortunate that so much of what I wrote found its way to the finished product—this is not always the case in television. Joss was very good at sending writers back in to do additional drafts until the script was ready to be filmed, ensuring that the writers' words were what would be ultimately filmed.

In 'Pangs', Spike provides a kind of voice for America regarding the conquering of the natives and Willow does, as well. Did that come from a need for conflict amongst the characters or a more personal place for you?

'Pangs', as I recall, came from Joss' interest in having a dead Indian on a Thanksgiving dining table—the irony of our annual celebration striking him, I think, in both a tragic and a darkly comic way. I liked the conflict between Willow and Spike in this episode because her impulses came from goodness and kindness, but his had the dark edge of reality to them—and no one was entirely wrong—it was both horrific to have to kill the avenging spirits and also inevitable and necessary.

Did you have any ideas for a story on the show that were rejected? Can you tell us a bit about them?

Early on, I tried suggesting story ideas often, but I soon realized that the majority of the stories for the show came from Joss's own wonderful brain. I recall pitching a story in which Xander's job made him older—turning him into 40-year-old Xander. And I remember one I pitched a number of times in which time slowed down during a class at school.

What sort of effect, if any, did the Internet and the chat rooms and spoiler sites have on the creative direction of the show?

A number of the writers, including me, enjoyed reading about what the viewers thought was going to happen. But these were much more likely to make us avoid a path than follow it—we wanted to confound expectation. But usually these sites had no effect one way or the other… it's hard enough to forge a story arc that satisfies without trying to add even more constraints or even suggestions.

Who are some of your influences your fans may not expect from you?

Hmm... well I've talked a lot about Jane Austen elsewhere, and about the TV shows of my youth. How about this: Weird Al Yankovic's 'The Saga Begins'—he takes the story of *Star Wars Episode One*, and turns it into a song that is funny, skillful, and, get this, emotionally involving. It works better than the movie. If there's any lesson that I have to learn over and over in this business it's that I need to constantly try to find that real emotional core even amidst the funny.

Do you feel the end result is better when writing solo or with a partner to bounce ideas off of?

Well, in TV there's really no such thing as 'solo'—the story of every episode is worked out by the entire writing staff. That's really the bouncy idea phase. Once the actual writing begins, though, I prefer to work alone. Even when two writers are credited with an episode of Buffy it usually means they split the work, or possibly that they alternated rewriting each other—it did not mean that they sat down together to write the same scene at the same time—I find that to be a difficult task.

Who are your comedic influences, and what led to your leanings toward comedy rather than drama?

I love oddball 'thinky' comedy like Stephen Wright and Steve Martin and early George Carlin... stuff about words just tickles me. As a kid, the first movie I loved all beyond reason was Mel Brooks' *Silent Movie*—strangely, a movie not about words. I have never cared for mean comedy or gross comedy. Even classic stuff like *Don Quixote* just leaves me cold when I feel that it's laughing at someone. As for comedy vs. drama, that's easy... some people like a good cry, but everyone likes a good laugh.

You've called yourself a 'TV Person' rather than a 'Movie Person'; what are the programs currently on your must-see list?

Hmm... I love the *Law and Order* series... great twisty little stories that feel like a good Ann Rule 'True crime' book. I would never be able to write them, but I love watching them—possibly in part because they are so different from what I do that they don't feel like homework. I like lots of stuff on the History channel and I have a shameful affection for some of the reality stuff—*The Amazing Race* is riveting for some reason.

Which TV show (past or present) would you like to write a script for?

Oh my goodness…. *MASH, Northern Exposure, Twin Peaks, Mary Tyler Moore, Star Trek* (!!!), *Soap*…. too many to name.

What made you decide to The Gilmore Girls *rather than another show?*

Gilmore seems to me to be the best fit for my skills—it's a hilarious show that nonetheless is about more than the sum of its jokes. It's established and shares a lot of overlap audience with *Buffy*. And it has been very welcoming to me. The writers here are wonderful and I'm having a great time.

What can you tell us about what you're planning to do following Gilmore Girls?

I hope to write pilots and create shows of my own. I'd love to work also on more projects with Joss and Doug Petrie and Tim Minear… all the *Buffy* alums!

Can we expect a commentary from you with the Firefly *DVDs?*

Yes… I recently completed a joint commentary on 'Shindig'—loads of fun!

Gotta know—did Dawn really kill Miss Kitty Fantastico in a freak crossbow accident?

Personally, I think she winged her.

MICHAEL McCARTY

HE HAS TALKED WITH SUCH LEGENDS as Dean Koontz and Ray Bradbury, still receives Christmas cards from the likes of Charlee Jacob and Frederik Pohl, and has talked shop with Peter Straub over donuts… Michael McCarty, going from his roots in his first published work in his school paper interviewing his teacher to taking time out with legends and soon-to-be's.

By the time he graduated college, he was already a writer for *Starlog, Science Fiction Chronicle,* and *Sci- Fi Weekly.*

His books, which come out at an almost alarming rate, include *Giants of the Genre, More Giants of the Genre, Dark Duets, Ghostly Tales* with Connie Corcoran-Wilson, *Monster Behind the Wheel* with Mark McLaughlin and the upcoming *Liquid Diet.*

You can catch up with him at http://www.geocities.com/mccartyzone/

What criteria do you use when selecting a subject to interview?

The most important thing for me is if this is a person whose work I'm familiar with. I usually don't worry about getting interviews, I have the luck of the Irish on my side for that.

My first interview for a national publication was with Frederik Pohl for *Starlog*, I read over 20 of his novels, so I had no problem generating questions for him.

How did you choose which interviews to appear in Giants Of The Genre *and which to leave out?*

The concept behind *Giants* is that is my Top 20 interviews with some of the masters of the fantastic. I had a wealth of material to choose from—Ray Bradbury, Dean Koontz, Neil Gaiman, Peter Straub, Poppy Z. Brite, etc. etc.

Giants represents 10 years worth of work that I put together in 10 days. There were a handful of interviews that didn't make the cut for *Giants*. But I'm nearing completion of the sequel with the working title *More Giants Of The Genre* and that should be out in 2004 from Wildside Press and will include even more interview subjects.

There are a few collaborations in Giants Of The Genre, *and you have worked with many others—do you use any different techniques to ensure a successful collaboration?*

Patience and being open to new ideas. I really enjoy collaborating with the writers in non-fiction and fiction because my collaborators always take me to brand new worlds I never thought to explore.

Who is currently pushing the boundaries of the horror genre?

The interview subjects of *Giants* are really pushing horror and sci-fi. Outside of those 20, I would add the established Stephen King, Richard Matheson, Clive Barker and Anne Rice. There is a new crop of up-and-coming writers to keep an eye on Gerard Houarner, Brian Hopkins, Brian Keene, Mark McLaughlin, Jeffrey Thomas, Tina Jens, Tim Lebbon, Simon Clark, John Wooley who has a great new vampire book *Awash In the Blood* and Teri Jacobs.

Does a writer need to be a successful author in the given field if he/she wishes to be a valid critic of it?

Not really. One only needs a good working knowledge of the genre and an open mind to be a successful critic. I was the book critic for *Indigenous Fiction* and I had a blast while it lasted.

Do you have a preference to writing fiction to non?

I enjoy both. I'm always writing, be it an interview, a short story or on my two novels.

When writing fiction, you are able to use humor in your horror to great effect—how do you avoid it becoming parody?

I use to be a stand up comedian so humor comes naturally to me. I tend to use it more for effect, to break up the darkness.

What was the first horror or SF story that had an impact on you?

For horror, Anne Rice's *Interview With A Vampire*, I read that novel when I was a teenager and it made me want to do interviews and write vampire books (laughs).

For science fiction, *Gateway* by Frederik Pohl and *Logan's Run* by William Nolan. They both had a big impact: making me a Sci Fi fan for life.

As a kid, which comics did you read more—horror or hero?

Horror. I loved *The Occult Files Of Doctor Spektor* a bi-monthly comic book that ran bi-monthly in the 1970's from Gold Key. *Doctor Spektor* was a predecessor to *The X-Files*. I also would read *Creepy* and *Eerie* too.

What are your top five Halloween movie rentals?

1) *Night Of The Living Dead* (1968)
2) *The Brood*
3) *Halloween*
4) *Carnival Of Souls* (the 1962 film, not Wes Craven's)
5) *Beetlejuice*

What can you tell us about the projects you have in the works?

Wildside Press will be publishing two books of mine next year *More Giants Of The Genre* and a collection of short story collaborations named *Dark Duets*.

I have a vampire novel I'm currently shopping around called *Liquid Diet*. I'm also working on two novels with Mark McLaughlin.

ORSON SCOTT CARD

CONDUCTED WITH RYAN TIMOTHY GRABLE

IT WOULD BE EASY TO SAY that Orson Scott Card is one of the greatest contemporary Sci-fi writers around; From his short stories up to the epics; His religious dramatizations to his glimpses of modern day fears.

With his soon to be released novel, *The Crystal City* (the sixth in the Alvin Maker series) and the pre-production of his first novel-to-film translation (*Ender's Game*, the work he is most widely known for) Mr. Card likes to stay busy, but always has time to keep up on his weekly website updates, and even has time to do some interviews.

His first published work, *Listen, Mom and Dad* was a children's book. His first step into Sci-fi was 'Capitol,' most of which can be found in *The Worthing Saga*. Though several of his works were put out to critical praise, it wasn't until 1985, when *Ender's Game* (the full novel, it was based on the 1977 novella of the same name) was published that he struck gold. *Ender* brought in the Nebula Award in 85, and the Hugo, Hamilton-Brackett, and the SF Chronicle Readers Poll Award in 86. He followed *Ender* up with three sequels, each earning critical acclaim. Other works of note are two epics, *The Tales of Alvin Maker* and *Homecoming*. His work has been translated into several languages Including (but not limited to) Catalan, Danish, Dutch, Finnish, French, German, Hebrew, Italian, Japanese, Polish, Portuguese, Romanian, Russian, Slovakian, Spanish, and Swedish.

Card is a devoted husband and loving father of five, Each of which are named after famous literary figures, Geoffrey, Emily, Charles, Zina Margaret, and Erin Louisa (named for Chaucer, Bronte and Dickinson, Dickens, Mitchell, and Alcott.) He has degrees from both Brigham Young University and the University of Utah, and worked in the mission field in Brazil for two years with the Mormon church. He currently resides in Greensboro, North Carolina. His website can be found at hatrack.com.

*Some of your earlier work (*Folk of the Fringe, Worthing Saga*) was published as similarly themed short stories. Do you anticipate doing more in the future?*

That's the sort of thing that just comes up sometimes—I find a milieu that I like well enough to explore it from different angles. Now, though, I tend to do it at novel length—hence the Alvin Maker stories and the Shadow books.

I may be dating myself, but what was your inspiration for Treason?

Treason is still in print—I'd like to think people can still discover it as a 'new' book even now [grins]. Like most of my books, it came from two unrelated ideas. One was the idea of people growing body parts the way we do piercings and tattoos today—so you show up at the party with an extra breast or an arm or a nose. But I had no story to go with that. I also doodle maps, and had drawn one where, on a whim, I started naming the countries with surnames of different nationalities. And then wondered, how could a world get nations with such names? Combining the two gave me the idea of a world where people have developed different skills, knacks, or traits, and where each nation is descended from a founder from our universe.

When do you expect the next chapter in the Tales of Alvin Maker *out?*

I just finished writing *The Crystal City*, the sixth novel, which will be published in November. There will be one more after it, called *Master Alvin*. I have also written a couple of standalone Alvin stories for the Legends anthologies. The first one, 'Grinning Man,' in which Alvin meets Davy Crockett, was in Legends I, and the new one, 'Yazoo Queen,' in which Alvin meets both Jim Bowie and Abe Lincoln on a trip down the Mizzippy River, will be in *Legends II* (both edited by Robert Silverberg).

Regarding the Tales of Alvin Maker, *What was your inspiration for taking a part of history and showing how thing could have been so different?*

This isn't really 'alternate history' in the sense that if someone had made a different choice, all of history might really have been changed. Here, the 'change' is that the magic people believed in actually works—so it's a fantasy rather than an alternate history. Still, I'm having a great deal of fun twisting up American history and yet trying to be true to the great themes and ideals that gave shape to our country.

You have an obvious love for both history and religion. What do you do to study up?

Now and then I have to do research on a particular place or time—for instance, for *Crystal City* I had to research what was going on in New Orleans in 1825. Not so I could duplicate history, but so I'd know the kind of thing that would be available in such a polyglot city. But most of my 'research' comes naturally—I read history constantly and voraciously and have all my life. In fact, I tell my writing students that they shouldn't major in English in college—they should just read all the books and poems and stories and form their own opinions. What they should major in is history, because that's where you learn not only all the varieties of human society and human behavior, but also how negotiable the issue of causality is, and how many different plausible reasons for things to happen can be advanced from the same set of evidence. It's the best training there is for a fiction writer in any genre, but is especially essential for writers of science fiction, so they can know enough to step outside the bounds of their own culture, at least a little bit.

You make no mystery of your personal religious beliefs. How do you choose whether or not to inject them into a story?

I never consciously inject my own beliefs into a story. Rather I let my characters express what they believe. People keep thinking that I'm preaching my own religion when I have a character speak about his or her beliefs, but it just ain't so. Instead, I trust that my own deepest beliefs will emerge in my fiction without my being aware of it at the time. Sometimes I find out what I really think by rereading what I wrote and seeing how a story took shape and realizing what was important to me, unconsciously, while I was writing it. I think when a writer consciously inserts his own ideology—about religion or politics—into a story, then it will be consciously received by the reader, and probably limit his readership only to those who already agree with him. Whereas a writer who trusts his own unconscious mind to express his deepest beliefs will end up with stories where the belief system is only subtly interwoven ... and thus has a much greater chance of influencing readers. However, of course, the writer runs the risk of having his books influence people toward what he really believes rather than toward what he believes that he believes—and trust me, there is usually a wide gap between those two things in most people.

The majority of your work deals with an alternate past or a distant future, not a whole lot touching down on the current time frame. What inspired you to write a story like Lost Boys *that takes place in the (relatively in comparison) modern world?*

Lost Boys, Treasure Box, Homebody, and Enchantment are all set in contemporary America. Strange lands and cultures are wonderful to invent or visit in my fiction, but sometimes I have stories to tell in my own time and place. I'm just glad when a publisher is willing to take a chance on a writer who is moving 'out of genre.'

Were any of those characters based on you and people in your life?

Lost Boys is intensely autobiographical. So much so that it became too emotional and I will never do it again. While the climactic events never happened in our family, most of the lesser details did, and the oldest son was based on my oldest son, Geoffrey (who is very much alive and designing electronic games in Seattle). Imagining his death was too painful; it was only bearable because at the time I had not yet lost a child. Now I could never write that book. So I guess I'm glad it's already written...

As with both Homebody *and* Lost Boys, *Do you plan on doing any more work based in the present world?*

I have two books under contract with Del Rey. One of them is set in a black middle class neighborhood in LA, where magic breaks out into the world and the people in this neighborhood have to get it back under control without much outside help. The other is based on a story I wrote for an anthology of modern dragon stories, in which dragons have taken up residence in the electrical current in modern houses. This story turned out way cooler than I had ever hoped, and I love the characters, and it just cried out to be made into a book that carries the story much farther along.

Similar as to what you have done with Bean, are there any plans for the individual stories of other character's from the Ender Saga? *Can we expect also a prequel (if I may be so bold) about Mazer Rackham?*

I had thought of doing separate books on other characters, but it turns out they're weaving themselves into the *Shadow* books already. There might be room for books about what happens to many of them after they go off to colony worlds (after Peter succeeds in becoming hegemon), but I can't see writing any others that follow the pattern I followed with Bean—a parallel story interweaving with the previous books. By now, the Shadow books belong as much to Petra and Alai and others as to Bean.

As for a prequel about Mazer Rackham, I've been toying with that off and on for years. We'll just have to see if there's a book in his life. I have done some prequel stories—one about where Ender's father gets recruited for Battle School but gets out of it, and one where Ender's father and mother meet. They're in the slim collection *First Meetings*, which is coming out this year from TOR. Graff shows up in those. But Mazer Rackham is his own set of problems. One real problem is, in the book he's half-Maori; in the film, he probably won't look that way at all, since the actor will be chosen for box office clout, not apparent ancestry. That would complicate people's acceptance of a prequel about a character who is nothing like the image they'll be familiar with from the film.

With Sarah, *you wrote from a women's perspective. What motivated you to choose a woman's POV, and what research did you do to be as convincing as possible?*

Women are human. I write about humans by studying history, knowing the people around me, and imagining as thoroughly as possible the bits that I haven't experienced myself. I have always written about female characters as readily as males. *Sarah* isn't my first book with a female protagonist, either. *Wyrms* is centered on a woman named Patience. And I use female characters' viewpoints constantly in the *Homecoming* series —about as much as male viewpoints—and quite often also in the Alvin Maker books. I have always felt free to get inside any character's viewpoint if it's necessary for the telling of the tale. Nobody asks Ann Tyler if she does special research to write about her male characters [grins], and so it should be no surprise when a male writer can create convincing female characters.

The truth is, however, I've always fit in well with women, and so have a lot of experience to draw on. My real problem is trying to write convincingly about macho males who fish and drink beer and watch sports on TV. That takes real imagination on my part, because I've never hung out with those guys.

How did the creation and actual writing of Sarah *influence* Rebekah?

I planned it as a series from the start. The only connections are that they're both drawn from *Genesis*, the same research helped with both, and the same writer wrote them. *Sarah* and *Rebekah* are very different women who led very different lives.

What is your overall opinion of the publishing world these days?

It's following the same cycles as always—big corporate mergers reduce the competence of the editorial staff as they become overworked and are constantly second-guessed by marketing types, who are always looking for last year's bestseller. Therefore there's always room for new startups or for small publishers to make a move for the big time. Then, of course, there's the fads. E-books ... books on demand ... each of these has a niche, but they aren't going to replace the regularly published book for the simple reason that they aren't as convenient and don't give the same sense of pride-of-possession that a physical book, well printed, can give. E-books, however, are the perfect way to get scholarly monographs cheaply into "print" and widely available. I foresee a day when all college and community libraries will have copies of all scholarly books just a few clicks away from the scholars who need them, without having any publisher risk more than the cost of editing and putting it out online.

Apart from that, the publishing world is just the normal collection of heroes and rascals. But the spectacularly bold ones, and the spectacularly wicked ones, left for the movie business long ago ...

Do you feel the Internet is a good place for beginning writers to get their start?

For now, at least, publishing in print is still the big time, and any story you put out electronically doesn't feel as if it had been truly published. That may change, but I don't see it yet—most attempts at online fiction publishing fail. But online is a great way to establish writing workshops that remain about the writing instead of about the personalities in the group. I run writing workshops for free (supervised by Kathleen Woodbury, may her name be blessed), and there are many other writers who get together electronically to critique or collaborate. And when you're a real beginner and your stuff isn't publishable anyway, why not put it up online to get a response that might help you understand what you're doing wrong? Though in truth, writers learn far more from reading other people's failed manuscripts than from any critiques they might get of their own flawed work.

You wrote the musical, Barefoot to Zion, *with your brother Arlen. What music do you enjoy listening to, and do you use it to inspire your writing?*

I listen to music constantly when I write—all kinds. It's hard for me to write in silence. But I'm quite eclectic—few genre boundaries keep me out. I have collections of country, classical, Brazilian MPB, vocal jazz, folk, lots of rock and pop from the 60s on forward, Broadway, film, even some opera, though that's a taste I've come to only lately and with misgivings. Rap, unfortunately, doesn't function as music for me—it demands attention like shouted poetry, only as poetry it rarely scans well and the topics are usually boring. Anyway, I can't write with rap on—too distracting. But I cycle through many other kinds of music.

Some writers have said that they've had difficulty getting their works published unless it takes place in a particular world they created previously with success. Have you come across any of this with say, the Ender Series?

My *Ender* books sell better than my other books, so naturally my publisher is happy to see a book that he can put the name 'Ender' on. But I have a great publisher in Tom Doherty, who is willing to go with me into risky off-brand ventures. I also have found some other publishers willing to take a chance on non-genre books, like the Women of Genesis published by Shadow Mountain and my contemporary fantasies now published by Del Rey. I have some mainstream literary novels in my head, too—but those will probably be published under a pseudonym, because in li-fi the fear of writers who have done well in other genres is so paranoid that unless you find a way to be 'cool,' like the cyberpunks (li-fi people are absolute suckers for coolness, as if they were still in junior high), it's almost impossible to break in without some kind of disguise. In other words, when I do write li-fi, I won't announce it's me until after I win the Pulitzer.

    That was a joke, by the way.

You've noted that your favorite book is The Lord Of The Rings. *As someone who has written an epic yourself, and one that is becoming a movie, how do you feel about the film adaptation of Tolkien's world?*

Ender's Game isn't an epic. It's just a novel. *Alvin Maker* might be an epic, and Homecoming certainly is—but nobody's making movies out of those.

I think the adaptation of *LOTR* is superb so far—faithful without being tedious—and it is matched in recent memory only by the adaptation of the brilliant novel *Holes*. Both achieved their greatness, as movies, because they were written and directed by people who didn't believe all that screen-writing class crap, or at least didn't allow it to destroy stories that didn't have to rely on such pathetic crutches for their structure.

Is religion portrayed as well as it could be in Science Fiction?

Science fiction, by and large, is religious fiction, precisely because it takes place outside of any one particular religion. So when religion is dealt with overtly in sci-fi, it is usually dealt with only culturally rather than as a possible source of truth. For instance, my Folk of the Fringe is a series of stories set in a future Mormon culture—but it never, not for a second, asks the reader to decide whether or not Mormon religion is somehow 'true.' However, most sci-fi that doesn't consciously use a particular religion as cultural background is in fact deeply concerned with the great religious questions. Sometimes it becomes extremely obvious, as in the movie *The Matrix*, which is the most piously religious film since *The Robe* or *Ben-Hur*. Most of the time it's more subtle. But it's almost always there.

What's your writing regimen?

When my wife tells me we're about out of money, I finish something. Otherwise, I avoid writing the way any sensible person avoids work when nobody's making you do it.

Is there something as a writer you'd like to accomplish that you haven't already?

I'd like to write stories I haven't thought of yet. But that's what I've always wanted, and so far I've been able to keep thinking them up and writing them down. As long as I can keep doing that, and people still want to read them, I'll be happy with my career.

JERRY POURNELLE

LOUISIANA-BORN JERRY POURNELLE served in the U.S. Army during the Korean War before going on to received several degrees, including a Ph.D. in psychology and political science from the University of Washington. Dr. Pournelle would collaborate with Stefan T. Possony to publish *The Strategy of Technology*, which would be used at both the United States Military Academy and the United States Air Force Academy.

He has also made his name in the field of aerospace technology and operations research for Boeing, and North American Rockwell. He was also the Founding President of the Pepperdine Research Institute.

In early 2008, Dr. Pournelle began a battle with a brain tumor. As of August 28th of that year, he reported he is cancer-free.

Jerry's published fiction is a veritable must-read list, among them *Janissaries,* and his collaborative efforts with Larry Niven, *The Mote in God's Eye, Inferno, Lucifer's Hammer, The Gripping Hand,* and *The Burning Tower.* His website is located at jerrypournelle.com.

What has changed the most in the field of SF during the last few years because of advances in science?

The advances in science? I don't think there *has* been anything. Well, in one sense... okay, you no longer have much in the way of knowing what to do in a big, epic novel about the future because nobody knows what the hell is going to happen. The last attempt at that I think was Clarke's *Imperial Earth,* and it stunk. I mean, Arthur's one of the most wonderful people I know. Now I wrote *Mote*... Niven and I did, but I wrote most of the technology and I had set it a long way in the future because I had intelligent computers. Now it doesn't seem like it's going to be that long before that happens. But I had *pocket* computers; Literally I had this [picks up a notebook computer from his desk] in *Mote*. You could talk to it, you could dictate to it, you could record conversations with it. But in 1971, nobody in the world believed that would live to see such devices. So, I guess the answer to your question is very few people can bring off a novel of the future because it's just so damn hard to make it look like the future. Bova tries. Like me, he's an old aerospace guy and he does what he can to project it. Heinlein pretty well gave up, you'll notice his last books really had very little of the old Heinlein technology flavor they look more like … what do they look more like… romance or fantasy.

Let me ask you, what you think the next breakthrough in science will be, or where it would come from? If that's a fair question.

Antimatter? (Pause) [Dr. K] Eric Drexler keeps talking about his nanotechnology… I think it's not going to be mechanical, I think it's going to be biological. I think Greg Bear is probably the guy who's closest to following this stuff more than anybody else. Organic chemistry and genetic developments and all of that sort of stuff. I thought I was for a while with the computer SF. Computers, I think have a finite end. I don't mean they haven't had a big impact, but I don't think they've made their fundamental change, basically. And now, machines that are far more powerful than anything I do with them and nobody seems to be able to think of something to do with the next generation of computing. But getting them smart turned out to have a plateau to it, I think. Maybe, maybe not. Maybe I'm just wrong. But on the other hand, nanotechnology, that sort of thing, I mean, don't think the future's in tiny mechanical bugs. Think of what an intelligent white blood cell could do.

I don't know. I mean, I can write stories on that. When I was in psychology fifty years ago, you take personnel psychology… You have two different tests, and they're classification and there's assignment. Assignment; you've got a certain number of jobs to fill and I've got a certain number of people applying for them and all I've got to do and take the best qualified people and put them over there and that's that, right? What if I have to use them *all*? You see what I mean? That's an entirely different problem. Mathematically it translates into the traveling salesman problem, which says it's assignment. But you've got to think to do… something… with… the… people… you've… got… in… your… country. And if you export their jobs because that's cheaper, then you make this guy feel like he's a valuable member of the society and if he doesn't feel like one, well then, what the hell does he have a reason to be loyal to? Perfectly good right-wing politics, it seems to me, but or… maybe it's left wing, or maybe… I don't know. It's *beyond* left and right. It just seems to me, common sense. And nobody seems to act that way. People don't talk like that. Ands you pick up the telephone and you call tech support for your computer, and you're very likely to get somebody in Bombay now.

Right, I've noticed that a lot lately.

Well, tell me exactly what does the guy who was obviously smart enough to do that before and has been fired in this country, what is he going to do now? Become the Unabomber? What's his motivation for not? I spent ten years in tech support, and you fire me one day because you sent my job to Bombay. Well, here's twenty-six weeks of unemployment. I'm not stupid, and I know how your system works. And maybe there's ten thousand of us, and two of us are *mad*. The classic disgruntled employee. I would worry if I were a computer company or internet company and so forth. When you piss off enough smart people, who know how your system works… I could write *that* novel.

Insulting the people who cook your food.

Yeah! Uh-huh. Spit on the cook! Why don't you do that? You know? He's got access to the toilets, to a typhoid well, and your food. So let's go be contemptuous.

For your writing, does the story come first, or the world it operates in?

You create the world, but it depends on what you mean… Let me give you an example. *Mote*'s a perfect example. *Mote In God's Eye* started with my empire, which was designed to allow me to write Hornblower type stories. I wanted a technological reason to be able to have naval battles. Space is *big*, and in the age of sail, every battle took place within sight of land with almost no exceptions and most of the navy battles happened only either by accident or by because of narrow channels, like the English Channel or Gibraltar… you see what I'm getting at; they're natural channels, and you can guard them. Well, space is big, space doesn't have anything like that, so I went to some JPL guys and we sat down and tried to design an interstellar flight system that would create natural choke points so you could have blockades and battles, otherwise you're over here [indicates a far distance] and he's over there [indicates another distance opposite] and you approach each other at two million miles an hour and you know, the battle's over before it starts, so that ain't going to work. So I designed it that way and Niven had come up with this notion of an alien and all he had was a picture. He had no idea how it had come about so I said 'Well, let's see if we can't design a sociology and a histyory for this critter so that you have an assymetric critter with species and make it obvious that they had worked on genetic alteration; they couldn't possibly have evolved naturally, not in any Darwinian path.

So we put that together, we built this Motie society and I already had my empire with the narrow choke point battles and such. You put them together, and bygumgollies, it makes quite an interesting story because how was it that they didn't know the Moties were there? Well, that's part of the story, you know, how did they get there? And they've been doing they're thing for a million years over here and nobody knows about them why hadn't they ever gotten out of their little quarter of the universe well, we came up with that, and it worked. And that set a pattern, and from then on, Niven and I at least, designed things with enough detail that the internal consistencies… we've got a story in mind, but we want to have a background for it, right? But if you do it that way, after a while you will run into a difficultly in your storyline that you are not anticipating, that in a detailed world, if the world is determined enough, it's going to generate certain structures, including social structures, and they're gonna be there, and they're there, whether you like them or not and your characters run into that, and now you have a problem you didn't have before.

The difference between real hard science and science fiction and fantasy in my judgment is precisely at that point. Some writers will just go back and change the premises so the problem goes away before you have to have it. But if you have done everything just right, if you look into your world hard enough, you will find the solution is in there, too, and you didn't anticipate either the problem or the solution and they're both in there if you've done it right. So the story line comes first in the sense that we intend a certain climax to the story but we pretty well invented the world first. So to say it again, if you've done it *right*, then the solutions to the problems you've created will also be in there.

What responsibility does a SF writer have, and has such a thing changed since you first started writing?

Good question. Responsibility. Well. I'll give you *Heinlein's* answer; We're basically after Joe's beer money and Joe likes his beer, so you *better* make sure that what you give him is at least as pleasurable to him as having his six-pack of beer would be. Now, Stanislaw Lem found that so intolerable that he almost went insane… you know, but then, Stanislaw Lem is a literateer, and he is the only man I know of to have had a novel [*Solaris*] made twice into movies that nobody could understand. The same novel. And nobody understood it *either time*. And it didn't sell very well, either. So, he's a literary writer. I guess the obligations are different for literary writers, and I'm not a literary writer, I'm an entertainer. I wrote the science fiction article for the Encyclopedia Britannica and basically I said in it that as far as I'm concerned, we are not any different from the old storytellers, the old bards back in Bronze Age time who would go from campfire to campfire and they'd see a warrior sitting there and say 'You fill my cup up with that wine you've got there and chop me a piece of that boar you're roasting and I'll tell you a story about a virgin and a bull that you just wouldn't believe!' We sing for our supper. If that's what you're after, then the song ought to be good enough to be worth the supper. I didn't have to go kill the damn boar! Or make the wine, I don't do any of that stuff. I live pretty good off of selling words. I didn't build this house… You see what I'm getting at. So my obligation is to the people who buy my books is to make sure they get their money's worth. Now, literary writers I guess have different stories and different answers to those questions, but I'm not one of them, so I don't know.

What do you do to unwind?

I like online games. I like *Everquest* and *Dark Age Of Camelot*.

Do you see the Internet and e-publishing as blessing or curse in the field of publishing?

I dunno. I really do not know. Jim Baen believes that— Jim Baen puts up all these books, full text, the whole business, because he thinks that most people would rather buy the book than start reading it and like it they'd actually go buy it and he has some data to show that the book sales are effected positively by just putting them online and just giving them away. He has this subscription deal, although I'm sure he's making money off of it and it's my guess that he's probably got ten thousand subscribers at ten dollars a year and a hundred thousand dollars is not much money in publishing. That's a guess—you'd have to ask him. He might tell you, he might not. But my guess is that he'd be fortunate to have ten thousand subscribers at ten or twenty bucks a year, and while that may be significant money for an individual running a website, it isn't for a publishing company. So basically he thinks that electronic publication of books is a big plus, that it's free advertising.

And do you agree with that?

I have no evidence to the contrary. Intuitively, every online son of a bitch that has stolen my books and has put them online. And I've had people *proudly* send me email saying 'I noticed one of your books was not online, so I scanned it and posted it.

They're proud of it. They think 'I'm making it available to your readers'. And I try to tell them 'It was out of print for a reason. Basically, we're incorporating it and two other books into a bigger and thicker book, we're going to be putting it out shortly, so I let it go out of print because I *wanted* it out of print. And you haven't really done me any great favor.' But I never sued anybody, and I've never given them anything that looks like permission. I really have no idea whether it's a blessing or not. I think that my guess is that you give it five years, this [holds up a notebook computer] will be the way most people read books. It's just so bloody convenient. There it is, the screen is bright, I can read it in bed without waking my wife up, the text is big and clear. This'll run about four hours before it needs to be recharged. It's a little heavier than a hardbound book right now, but on the other hand, there are probably in this one right now, twenty books, in addition to reference books. And most of my manuscripts. I don't see why when these things are ubiquitous and selling for a hundred dollars people would pay twenty-five dollars for a hardbound book when they could buy *one* of these and read as many books as they want. I don't know what's going to happen with publishing, but I don't think it's all that bright. I was the science editor for *Galaxy*, and I wrote a whole bunch of columns that got put together into a non-fiction book called *A Step Farther Out* which stayed in print for many years, they're printing another edition of it now which just tells you that it's a lot easier to predict the future in the Seventies than it is in 2003. And a lot of things I said were about to happen are happening and one of the things I said we'd end up with was I could put a book up on the web, and you read it and send me the money and where's the need for that bloodsucking publisher? Well, of course, publishers do a lot more than just take the money. But there was something in it, and that's happening more and more.

How did your work with Larry Niven affect your collaboration with SM Stirling?

Not much. Larry and I are peers. Steve has *become,* perhaps, a peer. But when we were doing those stories, he was very much the junior writer. And I would throw whole chunks of his stuff away. It was pretty good, but it just didn't happen to go where I wanted the story to go. Steve has become a pretty good writer in his own right, although I notice he's worked with a lot of other people. There was a lot more tension between me and Steve in the stuff. We don't understand each other as well. Steve writes villains extremely well. Much better than I do. For reasons I do not understand, he can tell what villains think and do better than I ever could, and that makes them a lot more realistic and it makes for a better story. The troubles is he wants them to win. And you can't have a story in which the villain wins, at least you can't have a story that people will pay you for. I mean, try writing a novel in which Hitler wins and see how many copies you sell. Isn't that what the theme of *The Producers* is about? There're going to try to write the worst play that they can imagine so that'll it'll definitely flop, so let's do 'Springtime for Hitler.'

You can't have the villains win and you can't make them too powerful. People may read that kind of story, but they won't read it very often. I mean 1984, you wouldn't keep reading many of those, would you? But then on the other hand, Orwell wouldn't have written many of them. He did write *Animal Farm* and then topped it off with *1984*. But you notice he didn't do it often even then, and he was not really an entertainer and wasn't intending to be an entertainer.

Would you consider him to be on the literary side of the field?

Yeah, well. You know, I mean he was an essayist who put an essay into a damn good novel form is what it amounted to. Aldous Huxley's a little that way. Very few people read Aldous Huxley in the same way they read other novels. You do not read an Aldous Huxley novel, whether it's *Point Counterpoint,* or... you might read *Antic Hay* as a kind of an entertainment, but even then it grates after a while. And you certainly don't read *Brave New World* as an entertainment.

Now, I don't mean entertainments can't have messages, but in my judgment, as I used to say about *Burning City,* 'Yeah, it is a sort of a novel of social commentary, but fortunately, the characters don't know it.' As long as the characters don't know they're in a social drama, you can get away with a lot of stuff. As soon as the characters realize that they are in fact archetypes… And I don't write that. Very few people can bring that off. How many copies did *1984* sell when it first came out? *1984* is one of those weird books that kept selling a few more every year, you know? And it's always stayed in print, it didn't become a bestseller until maybe recently. Unlike Joseph Conrad, who when he sold stuff, he told stories, and people bought them but for stories, and only later did they realize there was more to *Lord Jim* than just a pretty good adventure story in the South Seas.

Do you think his characters knew they were archetypes?

No. But then, Conrad wasn't trying to… Conrad was storytelling. Like me. If you want to compare me to somebody, Robert Louis Stevenson comes close. I don't think of him as a lightweight, but he would never have called himself a literary writer. He was a storyteller, an adventurer, and that's what I think I do. I try to be Sir Walter Scott, there's another one. Scott wanted to make a living at writing, did for a long time. And yeah, he had stories to tell, he had messages in his stories I have messages in mine, for God's sake, but the characters don't know that. Falkenburg knows he's a messenger, but he's got a different purpose in life. He's not *just* a messenger, he's also a teacher. He's got to teach his junior officers *why* they're killing people in addition to how. So I can get away with Falkenburg, but I couldn't have when I first started it, you see what I mean. He had to establish his reputation as being a guy whose advice was worth taking before I could let him give advice. The closest I ever came to preaching was in that scene in *Prince Of Mercenaries* in the helicopter when Falkenburg is lecturing to the young prince who says 'I don't do this very often, but then you don't very often get a future king as a captive audience, either.'

What sort of impact would you like to make, both in the genre you write in as well as in, for want of a better term, 'civilian life?'

Well. I don't know. [Mischieviously] I want to make money.

[Interviewer laughs]

Well, money's a good scorecard. Niven wants to make money, and he doesn't need it. Niven chose the right grandparents, so he doesn't need to make money at writing. I started in this racket in the early seventies and when I was president of the SFWA, of which I was like the sixth president, I was the first one nobody ever heard of. The organization was really in bad shape. Silverberg was the closest one. We sat down, Norman [Spinrad] and I tried to make a list of how many people made a living at SF. We couldn't come up with more than twenty. And in that, you would've had to count Niven and Asimov, and Asimov hadn't written a science fiction novel in ten years in 1971, 1972. And Niven didn't need the money. Niven could probably have lived on his sales, not the way he would have liked, but he could've lived on it. In a boarding house somewhere. Asimov hadn't written any fiction in ten years. *The Gods Themselves* came out in about '76 or so. Asimov was the reason why we changed some rules in the SFWA, and I'm not convinced we changed it for the best. Isaac pointed out we used to have this prequalification you had to continue to publish something every now and again and he said 'Any Science Fiction organization that thinks I'm not a professional science fiction writer...' And he was right. Just because he hadn't written anything lately didn't mean he was not a professional Science Fiction writer. So we changed the rules, I think not for the best. But anyway, there were probably what, three hundred science fiction members in the SFWA whom probably a hundred were active members in the sense that they were selling something every year, or every couple years. Maybe twenty of them made a living at it.

That was in the Seventies. And of those twenty, there were no best sellers. *Lucifer's Hammer* was the first Science Fiction novel to break a hundred thousand dollars for an advance. It was the first best seller in Science Fiction. Arthur Clarke had done a three-book deal for a hundred thousand dollars, but we got two-hundred and thirty-six thousand, five hundred dollars, that's pretty good.

We got a lot of money for *Lucifer's Hammer*, and it was fourteen weeks on the New York Times Best Seller List at number two. It would've been Number One except that goddamn *Thorn Birds*. Then that woman [Colleen McCullough] had the nerve to go off and write these wonderful historical novels after she finished doing that… There weren't any best sellers. There were people well-known, of whom Asimov, Bradbury, and Clarke and Heinlein who had done well. You probably didn't have any book that sold under a hundred-fifty, two-hundred thousand copies, which is pretty good. Heinlein never had a best-seller. Even, I think, with *Stranger In A Strange Land*, I don't think it was actually on the New York Times Best Seller List, I don't remember. If it was… I mean, I don't claim to be the first one. But we hit it big, and to some extent, I think *Lucifer's Hammer* probably changed the field. We didn't make any secret it was SF, we were SF writers. It made enough money. I mean it earned out. And now I would guess that there are fifty, seventy-five people who a living at SF? I don't know, on the other hand, I think that's shrinking, because the mid-list writer who can eke out a living in genteel poverty go into litereary-tese in order to eat and uh, y'know, wearing out jackets with suede leather patches on the elbows and so forth was a standard literary figure not in SF so much as in just the world, and *he's* vanishing.

Do you think that'll change, or continue on that level?

I don't know. You see, the problem is, and I think the dot-com bust helps, for two reasons; Entertainment usually does better in downtimes than up. And we are in a counter business. And in downtimes it shakes a lot of the bad SF out a lot the stuff that was bought *for* literary reasons, which is neither entertaining nor great literature. And I won't name the stories, but you can think of them. That are touted as 'Big Literature,' but aren't and aren't very entertaining, either. And they usually give SF a *terrible* name, somebody buys one of these things and tries reading it and thinks, 'Jeez, if that's what SF is, I'm not interested in reading that.' And meanwhile, the publisher is saying what good SF writers are. Saying good from the point of view where a girl with a Masters in Fine Arts and Literature who spend four years as an apprentice in a publishing house is now finally an Editor and able to buy books, and her view of what is good SF is not that of Joe Six-Pack. And she says 'Good SF writers are publishing and starving, so clearly what the public wants is junk.' And her editorial committee meeting says 'Good! Because we don't pay much for junk. So go buy us some junk.' And lots of junk gets published and the field collapses even further because good entertainment isn't junk. I mean just because it isn't literature doesn't mean it's going to do well. It doesn't mean it's entertaining.

And meanwhile, the storytellers like me and Anderson, I could name a few others… Silverberg… we tell stories. People like them. They want to know how it comes out, they want to know what the ending is. SF has been like this all my life. Every time there's a bust, it never goes back to down quite as far as the previous one. It's more of a scalloping. One the other hand, the publishing trend is ghastly, isn't it? Two hundred and something distributors are now down to ten or twelve and every time a big bookstore opens, one in a mall closes. And what's the recruiting drive? You see, I used to do a certain amount of market research by going to the local drugstore and seeing what the truck-drivers would put up. Now it's all just copies from the latest bestseller list and damn little of anything else. Every now and again, they're will be a little variety, but not much. Louis L'Amour famously got rich by going to truck drivers so whenever they'd come to a Louis L'Amour book, they'd always put that out, and before you knew it, Louis L'Amour was just selling everywhere! Well, that wouldn't work now. Because the supermarkets aren't that way, so where are you recruiting new readers?

Would you say the Internet?

Maybe. That's what Baen thinks. He sure as hell not getting them from somebody casually buying a book on his way out of the grocery store and he's still got his six-pack money. And I don't know where we get them. Paperbacks aren't making much money, hardbacks are the only lucrative part of the publishing business, and the anomaly is that the bestsellers don't make any money, either. Because everybody has to discount the goddamn things just to get you into the store that the bestsellers aren't making much profit for anybody. There are few exceptions, I mean Hilary Clinton got a lot of people into the bookstores.

Harlan Ellison calls those 'non-books.' Is the influx of celebrity books recruiting new readers?

Harlan's got his views, I have mine. Mine are that anything that gets people reading is good. I think that often the best thing that's happened to SF in the last twenty years is Harry Potter.

Is that because it's getting children as well as adults interested in reading?

Both. It's getting people reading and buying books. And they're discovering that 'My God, you can have as much fun from reading a book as you can from a six-pack.'

Does the term 'Hard Science Fiction' accurately describe your work, and do those sort of titles matter?

Pretty well. Niven and I are doing what you'd call a 'Hard Fantasy' series with *The Burning City*, and the next nook is *The Burning Tower*. I don't know what the title of the third book will be, but it's part of the *Golden Road Series*. It takes place 14,000 years ago, just after Atlantis sank. And basically what we did was assume that all the old myths are true. But because the mana's getting used up the gods don't exist anymore. But they *did*. And we got a bunch of Aztec one. The Aztecs believe they started up in what's now New Mexico, and wandered for ten thousand years before they got down into where they are now, in Mexico City. That's a weird legend. And they followed a *hummingbird*. For *ten thousand years*. Why? What was there about the hummingbird? Why is a hummingbird a god? Well, we tell that story. And we're trying to do it very consistently with our theory that the magic is vanishing, that the mana's being used up; that's from one of Niven's early stories.

We do fantasy the same way you do Science Fiction; Once you create the rules, you stick with them, whether you like them or not. And once again, if you've done it right, you'll run into problems that you think 'Oh jeez, there's no way around this!' But if you work it just right, there IS a way around it, and it's already in your mind. So in a sense, we do a Hard Fantasy as well as Hard Science Fiction, and I think I probably single-handedly recreated Military Science Fiction. It was dead before I started working in it.

Does the reader without a strong background in science still able to enjoy your work as much as it has been intended?

You'd have to ask one of them. I don't know. I have lots of friends who seem to like my stories and whom I don't think know what I'm talking about. I know that an awful lot of people who are never going be in the military… hell, they've been using some of my military novels in the war colleges lately and it's textbooks on low-intensity conflicts. How to fight guerilla war. Tell me a better source. And I mean that as a serious question; tell me a better source that is real, and in fact I think I did a pretty good job.

But I sold a hell of a lot of them in PXs. We know that every nuclear submarine takes a bunch of my stories out when they're out there for months. I know that quite well now; been on one of them and found dog-eared copies of my book at various corners in the submarine.

Were you concerned about possibly alienating a potential audience by writing with a science *angle rather than one of* fiction?

Well, I wrote a couple of detective stories, they sold reasonably well and my first published work, which was *Red Herouin*, (as Reed Curtis) but that was because the characters seduced each other and I didn't think a Christian College would particularly like their political science department head on record as having published novels in which people have sex before marriage. Remember, this is 1968. I have since put them out under my own name. But the detective genre wasn't as interesting and it wasn't as lucrative. And of course, my background was science to begin with. During the 70s, I made a good living writing science non-fiction in addition to writing fiction. I was the Science Editor at *Galaxy*, I was the Science Correspondent for National Catholic Press, which was a lot money, and attending science conferences, so naturally I was spending a lot of time looking at science, so you'd think you'd probably write about Science Fiction. And in politics, I was a Cold Warrior, so it all kind of fits together. We wrote Niven's SDI speech [used by President Regan in 1983] in Niven's living room, for God's sake, so Regan's whole SDI Program grew out of a series of meetings I chaired. SDI was all ours, and acccording to Gorbechev, that's what brought the Soviet Union down, so... obviously, you add them all together and I'm doing science fact and I'm doing real military strategy, it's going to show in your work. I mean, you look around this room, about half the books are on science or military strategy.

Why was there a long delay in writing the sequel to The Mote In God's Eye, *and what motivated you and Larry to do it?*

It took twenty some-odd years before there was any sequel to it was because we couldn't think of a sequel to it. Then one day, Niven came in and said, '*The Gripping Hand!* Mr. Niven says '*The Gripping Hand!*' And I said, 'What?', and he started telling me the novella that begins that thing, and that sounded like such a good story that we decided to sit down and write it and when we did, it went on from there and I think it's a good storey. And again, there is one that illustrates exactly what I'm talking about. It turns out that the society we constructed for the Moties in the first book had nothing to do whatsoever to do with anything we saw in the second book coming. It looked a lot like Arabia before the prophet. And we had an Arab nationalist in the first book who fit in just beautifully in the second one, and it would be one guy in the world who actually have understood the Motie society because it did look just like Arabia before the prophet.

Has the business of publishing improved since you started your career?

Just the opposite. It's *worse*. By a lot. One of the factors during the dot-com boom, particularly, publishing historically has never made more than about four and a half to five percent return on investment. And part of the reason it makes even that much is because you have a lot of eager people, mostly girls, some men, with really good educations willing to work their hearts out for nothing and live four to a room in a fifth-floor walk-up in order to do it. And y'know, so there's this unending supply of well-educated apprentices to be editors in the book business. And they don't pay them *anything*. It's the old story; if the author gets to town, the junior editors fight like hell for the privilege of taking him to lunch because that's the only time they'll get an expense account! And that's another piece of advice I'll give junior writers; when you get the point where they take you to lunch, let the editor suggest where to go. She usually has in mind a place she can't afford to go and she wants to be there and if you insist on your own [chuckles], you'll get what you wanted, but you won't make your editor happy, and the world is a much better place if your editor's happy.

So anyway, historically, publishing has never made a very high return on investment. When there was a little venture capital floating around, you would get people to think, 'Hell, we efficiency experts. We'll buy that stupid publishing company that's making four and a half percent on investment and we'll just go through there and clean it up and do what we do with clothing mills and everything else and that support a lot of the jobs that let the copy editors work in Ireland and all of this other stuff,' and they come in and do it, and of course, it doesn't work. Because Tom Daugherty and people like that are not stupid. If they could have streamlined their operation more to make more… to get more money out of it, they would have done it. It's not like they're a bunch of idiots. Dick Snyder, for God's sakes, at Simon and Schuster was the meanest son of a bitch in the history of mankind, you know? He was the most ruthless bastard we've ever heard of! And he couldn't get more than four and a half to five percent out of Simon and Schuster. So you figure, if people like him can't do it, who can?

But these people come to them, the publishing houses. And it collapses. So that you now have Harcourt Brace, Jovanivich, and seventeen others all… y'know, that have been collapsed into one publishing firm. It's much worse for authors. That and the collapse of the distribution business. You no longer have the books out there in the drugstores… oh, it's much worse. Now it doesn't hurt *me*. My books tend to get into airports and places. But I don't know how the hell I'd break into this racket if I was just starting. And I think it can be done, because people are doing it, but

I don't… it used to be a lot easier to get on these coffeepot radio shows and talk shows and things. When I first started with *Mote*, there wasn't a week when I wasn't doing a telephone interview with some radio show. I'd drive up to Bakersfield to be on the afternoon talk show. The talk shows in those days all had guests and they were desperate to find the guests, and I was a good one because I could talk about things other than fiction, being in the aerospace business, and having a fairly, you know, a science background. And that probably helped the holy hell out of *Mote* and out early books. But that doesn't happen much anymore. I never hear authors on radio talk shows anymore.

I used to go up to San Francisco to be on those them morning shows up there probably every month. And there was Long John Nebel and Candy Jones, an all-night radio show in New York City and it was worth going to be on it. And you'd go there and you'd sit there from eleven o'clock 'til five in the morning just talking about your books and everything. I asked my agent the first time he asked me to do it, and he said, 'A lot of insomniacs read books, Jerry.' I don't know how you do it today. I don't know where you get publicity from today. Again, I'm well enough known, I get invited to be keynote speaker at conventions and things, but… how do you get there? And I don't know.

What are your thoughts on the state of Speculative Fiction as it stands today?

I'm not really qualified to say. I don't read very much any more. I attempt to read a copy of *Analog* every now and then. And I don't really find much. Now that's maybe me on my part, but I'd rather read an issue of *Discover* or even *Scientific American*, complete with its political biases at least it's gonna be something… I just don't find *Analog* all that interesting anymore and of course, I was originally an *Analog* author. I was offered the Editorship of it when John Campbell died. They offered it first to Poul Anderson. In fact, Campbell had in his will that they should offer him the job. Poul wouldn't take it for the same reason I wouldn't—I wouldn't want to move to the East Coast for $14,000.00 a year in 1972. We both made more than that as writers and you knew damn well you weren't going to get very much writing done. And I don't think Poul could've lived there. We both had houses here at a time when the real estate market was not like it is now. It wasn't like you could sell out and take your million. I paid $30,000.00 for this house which you wouldn't believe nowadays. That was a lot of money in 1968 and I couldn't have gotten much more out pf it in '73-4. Now, I was offered the Editorship of it.

Ben Bova ended up with it, which is not surprising, his career and mine are very parallel. He could afford it because he didn't have to move to New York City, he had a house in Connecticut.

What is the hardest part of writing SF for a living?

The hard part of writing at all is sitting your ass down in a chair and *writing* it. There's always something better to do, like I've got an interview, sharpening the pencils, trimming the roses. There's always something better to do. Randall Garrett used to have a rule, and he said no professional writer he knew ever got anything by taking classes? And I know of no exceptions to that rule to this day. Larry Niven took the famous Writer's Course, but he never passed it and in the middle of it, he started selling, so he just dropped it. You know damn well he would have sold anyway. He didn't learn anything from it. Maybe he got enough confidence to keep going. If that's what it takes to keep you finishing stuff, maybe that's what it takes, but most of these writer's support groups and writer's clubs and workshops and the rest of it… it's just lazy. Making you *feel* like a writer without having to write anything. There are a few of them that are worth something but they almost all have to do with business. Somebody's always getting me to come lecture to their writing class, and I don't talk about writing at all, I talk about the business of making a living at this racket. That's what I do, I make a living at it. A lot of kids don't have the foggiest notion as to how to do that, and as Heinlein said, you almost always have to give your first book to a publisher, what you have to do is make sure that's the *only* one you give them. And the rules change, in Robert's day, the only audiences he would talk to would be librarians. Boy, he'd go all over the country to talk to them. That's because most hardbound books in those days were bought by libraries. That's probably not true anymore.

What sort of goals should the beginning SF writer have in mind?

I'll tell any beginning writer: Write a lot. And finish what you write. Don't join writer's clubs and go sit in around having coffee reading pieces of your manuscript to people. Write it. Finish it. I set those rules up years ago and nothing's changed. Send it to somebody who'll buy it. It's pointless to send it to me. I can't buy it if I like it. Now, you know, there's people who ask, 'How do you get an agent?' Well, that's a pretty good question, and I don't have an answer to it, I must say. I never had a problem, because I was sufficiently useful to Mr. Heinlein as a science fact source that when I wrote fiction, I could call in a favor and ask him 'will you read it?' which is a *big* favor. A lot of junior writers don't understand how big a favor that is. And Robert read mine and he liked it enough that he sent it to his agent, and I've had the same agent ever since. I didn't have any struggles breaking into the field, but you've got to remember, I had probably written a million words of non-fiction before some of that was of government reports and intelligence appreciations and strategy evaluations and technical proposals, but I had written a lot, so I knew how to write a sentence. I think it takes about a million words to make a writer. I mean that you're going to throw away. That are not going to get sold. I noticed that they just auctioned off Mr. Heinlein's first novel; they're going to bring it out. Robert had suppressed it. It supposedly was lost, but I think it was lost in the sense that he'd stuffed it into a file cabinet and he never wanted to see it again and his literary estate found it. I'm not sure whether [Heinlein's wife] Ginny ever saw it. I am dead sure Robert would not have wanted it published. Because if he wanted it published, he *would* have. He did haul out *Take Back Your Government*, which he couldn't sell in 1946. And Baen republished it, so it wasn't that he had any hesitation about works that were written a long time ago and were partly obsolete. I have never seen this manuscript, but it's my guess that it ain't going to read a helluva a lot like Heinlein.

I think it takes about a million words to make a writer, and most of those words aren't going to be seen… you're going to send them to people, you're going to try to sell them, but when they come back, my advice to new writers is two: First, finish what you write, like Robert said, and start on the next one, and finish it and keep doing it until one of them starts selling. When it starts selling, do your readers a favor, burn your trunk. *Just burn it.* Otherwise, your heirs will find it, and they'll sell the pieces one at a time. There are a number of major adventure and so-called mainstream writers who made their reputations, and now you see stories that they wrote that were unsellable twenty years ago. The more you see on the market, you can tell why, can't you? They wouldn't have sold if it wasn't by Big Name So-and-So, and I don't think you're doing the reader any favor by getting them—by bullying them into reading something that you couldn't when nobody knew who you were.

There's a lot of money in these things, and more and more all the time. When you get to be my age, I mean hell, I *did* burn my trunk. Because I had the old unsold novels, and I could probably try to haul them out and refurbish them, there's a good bit of money in it, and I'm seventy years old, and it's a lot of work writing a novel, if I had a whole novel I could probably get a hundred and fifty—two hundred thousand dollars for it, even a old, beat-up piece of nothing nowadays. Or turn it into a movie script.

Any interest in going back and doing something like that?

I couldn't if I wanted to; I threw them all out. I thought at the time that if these things don't sell now, I don't see any reason why it would in the future, and I'd see why it wouldn't sell. Writing takes a lot of work, and there are no secrets to it and going to writer's clubs don't do you a bit of good, in my opinion.

What's your opinion on how SF is being represented in the worlds of TV and film?

Most of it's dreadful, but here and there are exceptions.

What are your exceptions?

I'm trying to think of them... I thought they did *The Puppet Masters* quite well. It was pretty faithful to Heinlein's... the first *Matrix* was both fast enough and new enough that you didn't tear it apart while you were watching it. The second movie's just dreadful, because there are no two frames that are logically connected anymore. They just threw in everything: 'Well, we can get away that much inconsistency in the first one, let's see if we can't *really* do it to them now.' I came away from it with the conclusion that boy, computers must really like Kung-Fu! Exactly why is it that they like it?

What did you think of The Lord Of The Rings?

Oh, all right. *Lord of the Rings* is wonderful. I thought they did *Harry Potter* pretty good. The trouble is that the *Harry Potter* stories are sufficiently detailed that it makes it almost impossible to make a movie. But then you know, a real novel can't be made into a movie, anyway.

They said that about Lord of the Rings *for the longest time.*

Yeah, but well, look at how long it's taking them to do it, too [As of July '03]. I mean, they are *huge*! How long did it take you to read the latest Harry Potter novel? You're a fast reader.

I haven't read it.

Well, the last one you read.

Oh, just in the course of a week.

Several hours, right?

Yeah.

Now, tell me how to make a movie that's that long.

Yeah, I can't.

You know, that's been the problem with *Mote*. They're now talking about making it a mini-series on the SciFi Channel, and you've got some pretty good people involved, and maybe they will, but as a miniseries; you couldn't possibly make that into a single episode.

What about what SciFi did with Dune?

[Dryly] Well, it certainly hasn't done well, has it? Frank Herbert told me before he died that he liked the four-hour version… the really long one, which they cut down to about two hours to actually show, and if you hadn't read the book, you didn't understand a bit of it. And if you hadn't read the book *recently*, you didn't understand much of it, and if you *had* read it, then you got mad because they left out parts of the book that you liked. So it satisfied very few people. Frank though they had done a good job with the big movie, but that was… The last time I saw Frank, he was talking to me about that. And he had just had a bunch of tests done because he was having digestive problems and he was sure it was just some… I hadn't seen him again after he found out [Frank Herbert died of a pulmonary embolism following surgery for pancreatic cancer]. I must say, the old son of a bitch fought hard. He went to the Mayo Clinic, and they did everything they could… Frank Herbert thought he liked the four hour version. I haven't found anybody else who said that. Maybe. I haven't seen the four-hour version, so I don't know.

Dune was a delicate story in some respects and it depended entirely on getting you to believe a bunch of things that are pretty close to unbelievable. Its space travel is limited to a bunch of fishlike creature that can navigate across space and humans can't do it. You see what I mean? You can't just build a rocket ship and go from here to there and weapons technology has got to the point where smart bombs don't work and we end up fighting with knives. Now, he can make you believe it, while you're reading it. But even there, the story, a first novel, turned on an inconsistency in his book; it was absolutely established that mentats could never be disloyal, but of course the whole key to the book is that one was. That's violating the rule… Oddly enough, one that wasn't very popular I thought that Kurt Russell's *Soldier* wasn't that bad.

You really think so?

Yeah, at least I could believe in the characters. There are a lot of Fantasies; *Spirited Away*… wonderful. I'm not sure that movies are not a better Fantasy medium than SF medium, anyway. But the only problem with movies in SF is the SF has got all these problems—we don't know where we're going anymore.

In that respect, Fantasy is easier…

Fantasy's easier because you've got a self-contained world. You don't know what the hell what the rules are in SF. I don't know what the rules are in science anymore, do you?
 I then try to… I mean, we like interstellar travel for storytelling purposes, the fact is that's Fantasy, too. Put in everything we know about science. So, I have tried to work in some higher education. Charlie Sheffield and I did *Higher Education*, that was an attempt to be realistic and I guess it has done that. And it doesn't have any faster-than-light or anything that's… you know, it didn't have anything that is inconsistent with science as we knew it when we wrote it. They're not too many stories like that. People don't want to read them. They all are Mars stories, they're all Fantasy. Most every one of them is Fantasy. Some worse than others. [Grinning] That's probably not very good news for the Sci-Fi Channel, is it?
 The Sci-Fi Channel is doing a reasonable job, I guess of doing entertainments, and trying to find the old entertainment stories, but… I don't know, what does Harlan like?
 Harlan and I are old friends. I've known him for thirty years, and are fairly close friends, although most people don't know that, but we don't have much in common politically.

Harlan's much more of a literary writer. And he is *much* less interested in consistency with the laws of nature. And he's really a Fantasy writer. Gargoyles that suddenly come to life, computers that keep you alive without any bones. They're wonderful stories, but they have little to do with anything that could happen.

Are you able to read for entertainment's sake, or does the thought process of a writer creep in to interrupt?

Oh, a little bit, yeah. It's one of the problems. Also, a lot of the stuff I see nowadays I don't like as much. The trouble is, I like the kind of stuff I write, and I don't like to read the kind of stuff I write because I'm afraid I'll end up stealing other people's ideas.

What can you tell us about your projects in the works?

Well, I'm trying to clean up. I'm finishing *Burning Tower*, which I've got to go work on this afternoon, in fact, which is the second volume in this big... what do you want to call it? It's a Heroic Fantasy the character's don't even think they're in a Heroic Fantasy, the characters are just trying to stay alive and put together the trade routes. They're not set off on any great quest to liberate the Earth. We don't have any of that. I don't know if you've read *The Burning City*.

I have.

Well, Whandall is not setting to free his people, or do anything else, he's just trying to get the hell out of a place he doesn't like living in. but it *is* a social commentary. Like I said, as long as the characters don't know it, you can get away with it. I'm doing that, finishing the second book in that series, I've got another book in the Janissaries Series I want to do, and everybody in the world wants me to do a sequel to *Starswarm*, and I may do that, but I don't know... I told the story.

You don't think you can go any further with it?

I don't know. No, I can easily exploit that story. I'm not sure that's what I want to do. Right now, my present plans are to finish a couple works that have been hanging around too long and get them done. Then I'll sit down and start thinking of what I want to do next.

Birds Of Fire has been optioned for quite a lot of money they paid enough money in the option that I'm pretty sure they're going to go on and actually make the story. I don't want anything to do with it.

What about Mote?

Same thing; I don't want anything to do with it; I'm not in the movie business. I am perfectly willing to executive produce. I'll tell you something that's probably not going to ring too well with your readers, or maybe it will; a few years ago, my agent got a whole bunch of interviews with TV and movie people, none SF Channel, a whole bunch of people at various studios that were interested in SF. And Larry and I and our agent would go in and talk to these people and we came out of one of them, and I looked at Niven, and I said, 'You realize, that if we do everything just right, we'll get to spend a lot of time with people like that, and I don't know about you, but I can't stand *any* of them.' And Larry looked at me and he said, 'You're right.' And we told our agent [chuckles] 'You don't need to do this anymore.' [Steven] Barnes apparently likes going around and pitching story ideas and working with the movie industry and the TV industry and writing scripts. I can't imagine… I would rather go back to journalism. I don't like most of those people. Met a few of them. Joss Whedon is *very* sharp. And he and I and Niven very nearly came up with a Fantasy series, which I would have loved to have worked on it, based on the notion that… suppose the magic came back. We live in this world right now, and all of a sudden, the manna is coming back, and nobody knows how to use it, because we haven't studied it in fifteen thousand years. But some people have natural talent, and it will turn out, and we had this storyline that there have been some wizards all along for thousands of years. They mostly make their living doing prestidigitation. Stage magicians. [Grinning] Every now and then, they get it right, and they feel so damn good when it works, you know. But if it doesn't work, you still have to entertain the audience… and that was going to be one of our major characters, this thirty-something year old witch who learned to be a stage magician but has far more talent than her mother did, so she gets it right more often and meanwhile, the magic's coming back; we're pumping oil out of the ground, we're bringing up ores from deep under the Earth, you know, moist of those things have manna attached to it. We very nearly made a deal with Joss on that one, and that would have been fun. *That* one I would like to have done.

What happened?

I think he just got interested in something else, or didn't have the financing, I don't know. The trouble is I really wouldn't want to work with very many people on something like that, because well, we actually came up with a story treatment for it, at least a background for some characters. The general in charge of Fort Knox… gold has an awful lot of manna in it, and suppose his daughter turns out to have a little bit of talent. [Chuckles] And he's the general of Fort Knox, you see, with all these soldiers… that was going to be the pilot. You're trying to steal the man, but of course, nobody knows there's anything to steal, so… 'Go after the gold. I don't give a shit about the gold. I don't want the damn gold, I want the *manna*.' [Laughs]. So… But in general, we just have a contempt for working with the movie industry. I make a comfortable living. I could've made more if I had really gone out and whacked at it harder and maybe if I'd pitched more stories and got into the movie business. I keep remembering that Fitzgerald did that and drank himself to death as a result of it, so…

There's that 'Inner happiness' thing…

Psychic is the one damn thing they can't take away from you in taxes, and I have deductible built myself a fairly comfortable place to live, so… it's all deductible, too. Been audited, even.

Really?

Sure, but you know, every bit of this, I can prove is somehow relevant to the way I make a living. [Laughs] And it's forty-five percent of the house in square feet. [Chuckles]. So forty-five percent of my house is deductible. So that's what I do.

Well, thank you for your time.

You're welcome!

KRISTINE KATHRYN RUSCH

KRISTINE HAS HAD THE HONOR of winning the award for Best Mystery Novel (writing as Kris Nelscott) not once, but twice. Not surprising coming from a best-selling author whose body of work has spanned not only Mystery, but Romance and Science Fiction.

She is the only author in the history of SF to win a Hugo award for both editing and writing. Kristine teamed with Dean Wesley Smith to form Pulphouse Publishing, before her stint as the editor of the legendary *Magazine of Fantasy and Science Fiction* .

She lives on the Oregon Coast, and you can visit her website at kriswrites.com

Is it easier to write using someone else's characters and universe?

No. It's harder. You don't have freedom of choice. You must follow the dictates set up by the owner of the universe—and by the fans' expectations. If you're not a fan of that universe, don't even try to write in it. It doesn't work.

How have media tie-ins affected publishing?

Media tie-ins in this form have been around for nearly 100 years. Our local antiquarian bookstore has cartoon and movie tie-ins from the 1920s—independent, original stories and novelizations.

So that's a long way of saying that tie-ins have always been with us and haven't affected publishing at all. For a while, they're more successful, and then they fade. (There was a big spate of tie-ins in the early 1970s, then it dropped off, only to resurge in the 1990s.) The fact that tie-ins have hurt 'regular' books is a complete and total myth.

When writing tie-ins such as Section 31: Shadow, *are you concerned about the reaction of the fan base will be?*

A tie-in writer must always be concerned about the fans. The books are for the fans. Of course, if the writer is a fan herself (as I am), it's not a problem. Just please yourself, usually, and you've pleased most of the fans.

You can't please all the fans because, well, you can't please all of the people all of the time.

What are the pitfalls publishers should be trying to avoid?

Well, it depends on what point of view you're asking from. If you're asking me as a former owner of a publishing house, I'd have a different answer than if you asked me as a former editor. And of course as a writer, I have a completely different opinion.

Right now, I think publishing is the most difficult for short-fiction magazine publishers. The distribution system has changed and getting to the newsstand is difficult. Once there, it's hard to attract attention. Publishers have to look to new venues to find subscribers—not just the net, but places like an independent bookstore (put the digests on the racks by the paperbacks), comic books, etc. I think publishers must expect to spend some money advertising in new venues.

Trek and the Dell magazines have a co-advertising deal going. I hope it works for them because I'd like to see the magazines advertise in games like *Tomb Raider* (maybe insert a subscription card) and in other areas that teenagers pay attention to. The readership of the short story magazine is getting older, and that's a bad thing. We need to appeal to more readers—and we're not because of business constraints.

Horror and Science Fiction have seen peaks and valleys over the years, have you seen the same for Fantasy?

No. Fantasy has been a mainstay for hundreds of years (think Shakespeare).
It will always appeal.

Is the small press producing authors the larger publishers can become interested in?

It always has and always will. Right now, there's an excellent collection of short fiction out by Ray Vukcevich from Small Beer Press. Ray is one of the best short story writers around—and no mainstream publisher would touch his short fiction because he's not a bestseller—yet.

In your collaborations, are there any unique problems because you're working with your husband?

We fight when we brainstorm. And I mean *fight*. So we don't brainstorm. He comes up with the idea and plot and I do the 'coloring'—i.e. the characters and setting. Much easier—and safer—that way.

Who are the new authors you enjoy?

Dale Bailey. Sarah Hoyt. Laurel Winter. I could go on and on, but won't except to say read and support the short fiction magazines. That's where the new writers in SF come from.

What motivates you to continue writing?

I adore it. I'm addicted to it. I can't do anything else.

Is there a subject or genre you haven't written about that you'd like to?

Historical romance intrigues me. I imagine I'll get to that someday. I'm moving into the genres that I've always wanted to write in—historical mysteries and mystery in general; stand-alone SF (for NAL); and just something I think of as Kris stories, which are very hard to define. You find a lot of those in *Enchanted Afternoon*, I think.

If you could change anything in your career, would you?

Honestly, I would have stopped editing much earlier than I did. I should have been more aggressive in asking for pay equal to my ability when it came to editing. (My husband gets paid as much for one anthology as I did for a year's work at *F&SF*.) I should have written more short stories in the mid-90s.
    But, oh, well...

What's next for you?

I'm finishing my next Kris Nelscott book and I'm also working on SF/Mysteries for NAL. Then I'll do a stand-alone thriller that's been in the works for years. Not to mention more short stories....

SEPHERA GIRON

SEPHERA ATTENDED YORK UNIVERSITY, where she obtained her Bachelor of Arts Degree in Fine Arts Studies.

A mother to two teenage boys, Sephera finds time not only to write, but to work as a horoscope columnist, a teacher for the online course available at coursebridge.com and a tarot counselor. Her body of work spans no less than twelve books and she has been certified in Reiki, and metaphysical counseling.

Those who have experienced a tarot reading from her or have read books like *House Witch* may know her as Ariana. If you wish a reading, you can find Ontario Canada's Sephera at keen.com/details/Sephera-Giron/Tarot-Reader/2425378.

I know you must get this all the time, but I have to know the origin of your name!

My parents saw the movie *The Ten Commandments* by Cecile B DeMille when mom was pregnant. Moses' wife's name was Sephora. She was played by beautiful Yvonne DeCarlo, who we all know went on to become Lily Munster. They loved the name but couldn't quite remember how to spell it from the credits.

I like the two e's better. People already say my name a hundred different ways, I can't imagine how they'd pronounce it if it had an o! For the record it's pronounced SEF-er-ah. I put an accent over the first e as a teenager in hopes that people would say the first syllable the strongest. My last name is Spanish. My father Arsenio Giron was born in Spain.

What's your opinion of TV programs like Buffy *and* Charmed *that portray the occult more as power rather than a belief system?*

I have to admit, I don't watch much TV except for shows like Dateline, *The Daily Show, Elimidate* and the music stations. I haven't seen many episodes of *Buffy* or *Charmed*, but I can certainly understand why the screenwriters would use power as a device as opposed to the belief system. I do the same thing in my fiction work. People tune in to shows or pick up a novel to be entertained.

Certainly belief systems are entertaining but not in the same way that power and the corruption of it can be! Fiction is fiction. If you want reality, watch National Geographic *Taboo* documentaries on the Discovery Channel and shows like that. I've had scathing letters from people for *House Of Pain* because of how I use the occult, saying I'm betraying witches and all that. Wait 'til they read *Curse!* How I conduct my personal life or what my personal belief system is has nothing to do with what I write. I write fiction to entertain and that's what the writers in TV do too.

Your exploration of characters is reminiscent of King and/or Bradbury. Are they 'Intentional' influences or more from the sub-conscious?

I don't think that I ever do anything consciously, but certainly I have always enjoyed the 'everyman' aspect of King and Bradbury's work. To me, a story is more interesting if the characters are accessible to the average person. Stephen King has always been one of my favourite authors so it's inevitable that he would rub off on me.

What can you tell us about Curse?

Curse is a story about a forty-year-old witch who has eternal life. Basically, even though Vanessa has magic powers and can live forever, that doesn't mean that life is easy for her, hence the title. Every now and again, her body falls apart, because of some of the things she has been through, so she has to put it back together again, with the help of virgins. Since she foolishly cast the spell for eternal life as a young woman, she had no real plans with what she was going to do if she lived forever.

She finds herself lonely and though she has the ability to cast a spell on anyone to make them fall in love with her, she wants someone to love her for her. In the meantime, she reads tarot for the locals, mostly women, and discovers that most of her clients have one thing in common. Their husbands are having affairs and disappearing. We get to know a couple of the women, Betty and Cheryl. We also get to know a young rapper girl named Ashley who is obsessed with Eminem and searching for her missing friend.

Your style entails taking very real characters, complete with faults and insecurities, and turning their world upside-down. Do you use any kind of personal experience as a point of reference for this?

Sometimes I'll base characters very loosely on people that I know something interesting about, or that I've read about or seen on TV or something I've been through myself. Even Vanessa, who is supposedly an all-powerful witch, is still consumed with human frailties that often hobble her ability to conduct herself as a witch in a more fantastical story might behave. I like to read stories where the characters are real people and then things start to unravel. So it makes sense that most of the time, I would write that way too. I have found now that I'm older, have a teenager and a preteen and have been through a divorce, that it can be easy to suddenly find your world turned topsy-turvy.

Did you have any particular difficulties in placing your work with a publisher because of its sexual content?

I have never had a publisher say they didn't want my work because of sexual content that I can recall. I tend to really study the market reports and try to make sure I'm sending my more erotic stories to the proper markets.

Do you agree with the saying 'One person's erotica is another man's pornography?'

Sure. I've been on lots of panels where people try to define the difference between erotica and porn. It's all so subjective. I guess to me, erotica has more story and flowery language, whereas porn is just the straight hump and bump. I do stress to friends and colleagues that my work isn't for everyone and I never encourage anyone under 18 to read certain works.

Sex has found a home more and more within the horror genre. Any thoughts as to why this is?

There has always been a lot of sex/erotic elements in horror novels. Certainly even more so in movies because it's such a visual medium. I think that we are more blatant about it now instead of using a lot of innuendo. Both horror and sex invoke extreme emotion and sensation. It makes sense to marry the two.

There isn't much in the world scarier then sex when you think about it, if you aren't in a committed loving relationship. I know for me, anyway. (I guess Freud would have a field day with me!) The whole idea of dating, how far to go, can he get it up, can I relax enough with him, will I get pregnant, will I get a disease, will I lose control…All that stuff, is frightening, yet we are animal and sex drives us, even those who are repressed or celibate. The power of lust can drive people to do things that they logically wouldn't do. You don't have to look further then the White House to see that and it sure as hell wasn't just Clinton. It is an animal side of us that we constantly have to keep on top of or society would self-destruct which is why there are so many rules and religions advocating denial/control. It's easy to see where the idea of werewolves and Jekyll and Hyde came about. One minute, we're normal people, following the rules and then suddenly, somehow, one person, whether it's their pheromones or hot body or brilliant mind, will attract us and we can nearly destroy our lives just for a chance to slip between the sheets. Why is that? That is a very scary thing to me. How compelling it is to betray someone, to throw away years of security, because you body is urging you do to something your brain knows logically is not the wisest choice.

Obviously, everyone is different, but if we didn't have that basic sex drive, the human race would die out. Since it's something everyone does and needs, whether they are actively participating in it or not, I tend to write about it. I may push the envelope more then some people, because I am a blunt person and say things like they are. If we all do it, why is sex so taboo to talk about, to write about even in 2003? Every single person exists because someone had sex.

I also find that when I'm writing about sex and horror, I can get to the raw emotion easier. Then there's the idea of who are we really? Is the person you're sharing your body with in that most intimate of acts, really the person you think they are? If you dare to fall in love with this person, will they still be there tomorrow? Will they die and you'll be alone? Will you be so horrible in bed they'll leave you? Will you inadvertently kill them with desire 'cause you haven't been with someone in a year? Are they lying to you? Are you as good as their last lover?

Then there's the rage aspect of it. Like in my story in *Hot Blood*, 'Wrench' where the woman is trying to find the perfect lover. When she finds a potential mate, he doesn't desire her as she desires him, so she takes the part of him she *can* have.

In 'Lying Eyes' in *Asylum 2*, a woman is obsessed with beautiful eyes, and she feeds her obsession by killing cheating husbands in the sex act. What wonderful revenge. To kill someone while they are in the act of cheating.

The Birds And The Bees seems obvious to me. I have killer birds and killer bees but then there's the whole idea of life being about 'the birds and the bees'. Nothing is more complicated and horrific in my mind then finding a life partner, trusting them with your soul and then finding out they have betrayed you. Or they become someone else. Or they fall out of love. Or *you* fall out of love. Human beings are so complex and I think some of the societal conventions we have created for ourselves go directly against our primal instincts. We have to find what works for us individually and try to be true to our beliefs. People are always hurting each other and it's one of man's basic flaws. Yet if everyone was perfect and behaved, I guess we'd be in heaven or really, really bored.

I think because of the way society is now, we are able to express ourselves more overtly about sex more then ever before. So it might seem like there is more sex in horror now then before, but it's always been there. It's just more graphic.

What was the inspiration behind Eternal Sunset?

I was at University when I wrote the first draft. I wanted to write a novel that had lots of monsters and explored all sorts of topics. Witch, vampire, werewolf, phoenix, mermaid, secret cults, celebrity obsession, the power of music and so on. I wanted a witch that didn't know what she was doing, that was just fooling around and pissing people off instead of one trying for world domination or casting spells on men to love them or something. When I workshopped part of it in my creative writing classes, people didn't like it 'cause it was 'Horror' and not literary. I've never strived to be a literary writer, I've always wanted to write Horror and Fantasy and have people read my work and say, 'Wow, that was a good ride.' as opposed to, 'It was so dense I didn't know what she was talking about but her use of language was good.' So I ended up not majoring in Creative Writing, I just got a General Honours BA. I rewrote that book for years. Even now I want to rewrite it again. It wasn't the first novel I ever wrote, but I considered it my first Horror/Dark Fantasy novel. And it turned out to be the first published.

Vanessa was a character who I wanted to be like. She was powerful and beautiful and took no shit from anyone. I identified with the Sophie character more though because she couldn't do anything right, she had a weight problem, and I always wanted to learn how to paint, though I can't.

Obviously these characters continue to haunt me, which is why I'm writing *Curse*, twenty years later.

Eternal Sunset *pulls in elements from different genres, but is it still accurate to refer to it as a 'Horror novel?'*

I often refer to it as Dark Fantasy, since it seems to be fantastical. It's one of those books that doesn't really fit into any real genre slot. The sequel, *Eternal Nightmare* has a similar issue. I'm hoping to find a house that will publish both of them. If anyone has any suggestions for who might want them, I'd love to hear from them.

What made you visit the theme of the haunted house for House Of Pain?

Here in Canada there was a notorious serial killer, Paul Bernardo and his wife, Karla Homolka who tortured and murdered young women, including Karla's own sister. It happened in St Catharine's, a small town by Niagara Falls. I followed what I could of the case, who didn't? A lot of the coverage was blacked out. Eventually the town was so distraught, they bulldozed the house where they had lived. I wondered what would happen if someone built a house on that land. Would they become like them? Was there something more sinister involved, like a cycle that had to be continued? I didn't want to really do it on Paul and Karla because I didn't want to give them more celebrity then they had already. So I changed the idea of it quite a bit. I originally wrote it as a screenplay, hoping to shop it to a low-budget movie company, but I didn't really know who to go to for it. However, now that it's been a novel, I have had a couple of filmmakers read the screenplay. I can't say more then that right now about it but I'm very excited about one possibility that might happen in the next year or so.

What made you write House Magic *under a pseudonym?*

The name Ariana is my tarot counselor name. I originally thought that if I wrote it under the same name as my horror, that people looking for happy household tips might be put off if they read some of my more extreme work. In hindsight, I should have used my real name because it's hard trying to be two people forging writing careers!

Can the uninitiated glean as much from it as those more familiar with the practice?

Certainly. *House Magic* is a book for everyone, even kids. I think that people who are more into energy work will get a lot more out of it. I would like to write *House Magic 2* one day, if my publisher is interested, where I could get more in-depth. I teach a House Magic course on coursebridge.com where we get more in-depth into some of the concepts.

Will we be seeing any more non-fiction from you in the near future?

I'm not sure at this point. I have been waiting to get the go ahead on *Office Magic,* but so far it hasn't happened. I will be working on a film book with Edo Van Belkom over the next year.

How much effect has networking, schmoozing, etc. have on your career thus far?

It has certainly made me less lonely and I've made a ton of friends. I think there may have been a couple of times recently that I was able to get in on a project by being visible, but I still had to write something worth reading.
    I think in the end, it's just a matter of sending out work and being tenacious. I didn't know Don at all before I got the Leisure deal. I was sitting in the slush like everyone else. It was almost the same with Darktales. I sort of knew publisher Dave Nordhaus from conventions and so I heard about them starting up the company, but I didn't meet the editor at all until after *Eternal Sunset* came out.

What prompted you to have an online journal on your website?

I've always had journals and then I got out of it when I discovered email and messaging! I think a lot of writers like to express themselves in a variety of mediums. Also with the journal, it saves me the hassle of trying to update my webpage all the time. Since I'm nosey, I like to read other people's journals, so I figured I might as well have one of my own. I try not to get too personal on it, though I certainly have at times. http://sepheragiron.blogspot.com

How much editing do you do before turning in a story?

Lots and lots!

It's hard to say. Every story is different. Some I constantly rewrite as I go along, especially novels. Others I just write it out rough and then go back over and over again until it feels right. Computers make it so easy to edit constantly. Sometimes I feel like that's a curse, because you can get caught up in constant rewrites. I've never not edited a story, though I can't say the same for some of my emails!

As a new voice in the horror genre, what would you say is the biggest liability to it?

It's tough breaking in. Just 'cause I'm on my third mass-market book, that doesn't mean anyone knows who I am, or what I'm trying to do. I really value fans that take the time to write to me, it means so much to me. I know my books aren't for everyone, and I'm still growing and learning as an author. I just hope that editors like Don D'Auria continue to take chances on me and let me grow. I guess too, I don't really have a 'thing' like vampire, or monsters, or voodoo or even witches. Everything I do is different. I even write stories with *no sex* in them, like 'Ah…Chicken' in *Tooth And Claw 2!* I just do my best and hope that I give my readers a good ride.

What are the differences between Canadian and American horror authors and their audiences?

There are less Canadians than Americans? Seriously, I don't know if there is one. I've been on some panels about that very issue and people try to make a case for a difference. I don't know if there is one, since most Canadians are published by US houses anyway. I know I never think about using guns in my work, 'cause it just isn't part of our culture. It just never occurs to me. Yet beer, hockey and as of today apparently, pot is part of our culture, though it never occurs to me to write about hockey either 'cause that isn't my thing. Being more willing to 'see what happens' and giving the benefit of the doubt is part of our culture. We're more like 'hippies' over here, more willing to live and let live instead of trying to conquer the world.

That of course is a very general statement and there are always exceptions. Getting my books into the Canadian chain of bookstores seems to be very difficult yet it is at Wal-Mart and various drugstore chains. I'm going to be working on a book with Edo Van Belkom about the Canadian horror movie industry and there are certainly differences in that medium between the countries.

What can we expect from your current works-in-progress?

I'm going to keep exploring under the rocks and see what is there. I recently wrote a gender-bending story that I'm not sure I'll ever see published 'cause it's weird. I have a couple of anthologies I'd like to get into, such as the next *Hot Blood* so the erotic horror will continue to flow. As I get older, I am more into the psyche and why people do what they do and age gives you different perspectives on that. My characters will probably be older as that is where my headspace is, though I certainly like to explore teenagers as well. I'm trying to get a series of Young Adult novels off the ground. I'm playing with a few ideas for another Leisure book too.

ALAN DEAN FOSTER

SINCE HIS FIRST BOOK (*The Tar-Aiym Krang*) was published in 1972, Alan Dean Foster has consistent provided stories to his readers that provide wonderful, easy to explore worlds. Some of these have been novelizations of popular films and television shows such as *Star Wars, Alien Nation, Aliens,* and *Terminator: Salvation.*

Now with his works numbering over one hundred books, Alan proves to be a voice not only of classic and contemporary SF, but also Mystery and Horror. He has received the Faust, the IAMTW Lifetime Achievement Award.

While he lives in Prescott Arizona (in a home constructed from brick recovered from a miner's brothel, no less), Alan has explored the reaches of the real world, have traveled to Europe, and the roads of Tanzania. He has spent time in the Southern Peruvian jungle, photographing fire ants and experiencing the fine dining of pan-fried piranha, to name but a few of the adventures he has enjoyed.

Alandeanfoster.com is where he can be found online.

What things are you seeing in speculative fiction today?

No one is entirely certain. Some say that *Star Wars, Star Trek,* gaming novels, and so on occupy shelf space that would otherwise be occupied by fresh new novels of F&SF and reprints of deserved classics. On the other hand, it is argued that people who would never pick up an SF novel in their lives *do* read *SW, ST,* etc., and then go on to buy Clarke, Asimov, and more contemporary writers. What cannot be argued is that more SF is published than ever before.

Which writers have you been reading lately?

Tim Flannery, Peter Tyson, William Tenn (complete works).

Is there anything that aggravates you about the current state of SF?

It wouldn't be SF if there wasn't. Fractiousness is an integral part of the field. I think there's too much fondness for dystopian subjects...but then, my own work is rarely downbeat, so it's probably a matter of personal preference on my part.

Is there a particular direction you'd like to see SF go in?

SF doesn't, and shouldn't, have a direction. SF is the literary equivalent of fireworks...half the fun is not knowing what direction it's going, and finding out as you read

How did Splinter Of The Mind's Eye *happen? Was it a proposal you came up with?*

I was contracted to do an original SW novel and the novelization of *Star Wars* at the same time. I was left alone to come up with a sequel novel, which I did. George made only two small changes in the finished manuscript...otherwise it's exactly as I wrote it. Further information is available from numerous *Star Wars* sources, so it would be repetitious for me to go into detail here.

Splinter *was darker in tone than* Star Wars. *Was that intentional?*

Actually, it was. After all, Luke, Leia, and the rebel alliance were essentially engaged in the interstellar equivalent of guerilla warfare at this point, something that doesn't lend itself to much comedy and lightness. And Mimban itself was a dark, shrouded world.

Do you think Splinter Of The Mind's Eye *would have translated well to the screen?*

I think it would have made a classic movie-for-tv, or short miniseries, ala the Ewok movie, but the plot was not designed to support a big-budget spectacular. With some minor story adjustments, it still fits rather nicely between *Star Wars* and *Empire*...something that was not a concern when it was written.

In the Commonwealth series, did you intend on creating the universe it's in, or did you decide to tie them in after the fact.

When I wrote my first book, *The Tar-Aiym Krang*, I was just looking to establish a believable background universe for the story and characters. I had no intention of doing a single follow-up, much less expanding to include series within series. It just turned out to be an easy thing to do. And doggone it...it's fun!

Why did you decide to chronicle the history of the Commonwealth?

I believe in having series follow a realistic chronology. From that, it was natural to place all the Commonwealth books in a continuous, linked chronology. And again, it's fun. A lot of the credit should go to two fans, Michael Goodwin [the artist] and Robert Teague, who put together the first rough chronology.

Why did it take so long between Flinx novels?

It's very flattering to be asked to write sequels, because it means that readers particularly enjoy a certain setting or characters. But as a writer, I think if you repeat yourself too frequently with either, you get stale. And there are many, many other stories I like to tell that don't involve Flinx. I also think it's interesting to have Flinx develop and mature with his own timeline while all these other stories are taking place around him.

Flinx (and his dragon) seem to be the only characters that have a thread through several novels, as opposed your stand-alone works or the larger universe that encapsulate many characters in detail. Is this by design?

Not so. Remember the three *Journeys of the Catechist* books. Also the *Icerigger* trilogy. Then you have a character like Skua September, who appears in the *Icerigger* books but also in *The End Of The Matter*, a Flinx book. There will be more of this...again, it's fun.

Can you tell us more about the secrets in Flinx's world, such as the Meloirare Society?

It wouldn't be any fun (there's that word again) if I had everything worked out ahead of time, before I sit down to write a book. As to the Meliorare Society specifically, I envisioned them as a kind of benign but misguided eugenics society, trying to better mankind. Their precursors are doing stem-cell research right now, I suppose.

Do you have a particular way you approach world building?

I go there. When it comes to world-building, I'm just an interstellar travel agent. I put myself in the environment, and simply describe what I see around me. I sincerely wish we had the kind of cerebral plug-in so often described in SF stories, where I could just plug everybody into what I'm seeing and take them along with me. Instead, I'm stuck with using words...a limited palette at best. But I do the best I can. When I'm describing a bit of alien vegetation, for example, in my mind's eye I'm not just seeing that particular bush, or flower, or tree. I'm seeing it surrounded by the entire alien forest, complete with fauna, dirt, sky and clouds, weather, etc.

What can you tell us about your upcoming releases like Impossible Places *and* The Big Wet?

Impossible Places is a new collection of short stories gathered from magazines and anthologies. It will contain an original Flinx & Pip short story set on Moth ('Sideshow'). This will be my sixth collection of short fiction to be published.

The Big Wet is a Commonwealth novel set on a world called Fluva (you can find it on the Commonwealth map on my website). It's different from any world/ecology I've done so far, and was inspired/is based on my visit to the Mamiraua reserve in Brazil (where the Amazon and Jaipura rivers meet).

Who do you consider your contemporaries?

Funny...that's a question I've never been asked before. I guess the writers my own age, yes? More importantly to me, I consider myself something of a bridging writer between the golden age of SF and today's younger writers.

Outside of other author's works, what has influenced your style most?

Travel, mostly. Immersing myself in other environments and ecologies, meeting other people, experiencing other cultures. Also classical music.

What has been the most significant change in the publishing world since you started writing?

The consolidation of numerous publishers under the umbrella of vast multinational entertainment companies, for whom publishing is only one component of their business. Think Time-Warner and Bertelsmann.

Was writing always a career move for you or did it grow into one?

I was going to be a lawyer. I had been admitted to USC Law School and then somehow slipped into the graduate film writing program at UCLA. I opted for the latter, figuring I could always go to law school at a later date. And then I got saved.

What advice would you give new writers as well as those still plugging away for your level of success?

Write what pleases you instead of trying to imitate someone else, and write a little bit of something every day.

What was your worst publishing experience?

I'm quite proud of the work I did on *Alien* and *Aliens*. When *Alien 3* came my way, I was very unhappy with the script, but I threw myself into it and produced what I thought was a pretty good job. The film people decided to throw out nearly all my changes (giving the convicts real backgrounds, for example, to explain how they came to be on that prison world, keeping Newt alive...stuff like that). That's why I turned down the offer to do the book version of *Alien Resurrection*.

JACK VANCE

Jack's *Blue World* is one of the first SF novels I can remember reading, and probably shaped me as a writer more than I know, and for whatever reason, the phone interview we started became a conversation about everything from our kids to jazz (in the Seventies, Jack played the ukulele and kazoo simultaneously) and the occasional note regarding what I was calling about in the first place.

Jack Vance, born in 1916, has had a lifelong passion for the outdoors and reading, so it's no surprise his career in the written word spanned such wonderful works as *Planet of Adventure,* The Demon Prince Series, The Lyonesse Trilogy, and the *Compleat Dying Earth*. The Vance Integral Edition, a limited edition of forty-five hardcover books (the last covering his work writing as Ellery Queen) was collected from 1999 to 2006.

He won the Hugo, in 1963 for *The Dragon Masters* and in 1967 for *The Last Castle*. He snagged a Nebula in 1966, also for *The Last Castle*, a World Fantasy Award in 1984 for Life Achievement and in 1990 for *Lyonesse: Madouc;* an Edgar for the Best First Mystery Novel in 1961 for *The Man in the Cage*. In 1997, the SFWA named him a Grand Master.

In 2009, Subterreanean Press will publish his autobiography, *This Is Me, Jack Vance!*

I must thank his son John and (posthumously) his wife, Norma for their help in making this interview, which became more of a conversation and an invitation to come over and 'Pour a little Scotch for ourselves' rather than anything else.

How do real-life events affect the SF field?

First of all, I hate the word Science Fiction as far as it applies to myself.

Okay, what would you prefer?

It's a terrible thing, when somebody asks me what I write, I hate the term Science Fiction because I equate Science Fiction as *Star Trek* and all this politically correct stuff… Hollywood, and a lot of foolishness. The stuff I write… I hate the word Science Fiction, and yet when people ask me what I write, I can't think of anything better to do than say SF even though I hate it. Also, I don't consider myself part of the SF field in that I can speak for the industry at all. I'm totally isolated from it. So when you ask me about space shuttles and moon landings, things like that and how it applies to the SF industry, all I can say is 'I don't know.' [Laughs]. I don't have a clue. It doesn't apply at all to me. Wouldn't even think of it.

Would it a fairer thing to say towards more speculative *fiction?*

Yeah, something like that. Yes, indeed. I kind of like to think of a… I had a word for it once, I've forgotten. I may think of it a little later. But yes, speculative fiction is better, even though that's kind of pompous, too.

I think your dialogue has a melodic sense of timing and flavor; is this influenced by your love of jazz?

No, it's purposeful. I think it's important that the writing doesn't have awkward lapses of… I don't want to use the word rhythm… Things that block the reader's attention. When you read a sentence, the language should flow so that the reader can read it easily and it has a necessary rhythm to it. And you use this rhythm to get your point across sometimes. I don't do it consciously; I don't say 'I've got to write this sentence with rhythm,' but when I re-read anything, I can… if it's got a nice swing to it, then I say, 'Good,' you know? If it doesn't, then I maybe change a word or two so that it does have a swing.

Is there a particular story that you can look back on and say at that point I found my own voice as a writer?

No, not really. It was just development… a slow development from the first stories I ever wrote, every story was better than the one before, and I think probably the story that was renamed by Betty Ballantine, *Who*

Lives Forever, that's probably the first... well, I won't even say that... the first serious story one where way I found I found my voice. That wasn't the best story but it was better than some. In other words, I just think of my style or myself as just developing, getting better with every story, that's my personal feeling. I never thought about it, to tell you the truth, I just write and...

Would you say an evolution?

An evolution is right.

What drew you to jazz music?

Well, I think I've had a tendency all my life. When I was eight or nine years old, I lived up in the ranch, out in central California, and there was always a haven there for people to... it was during the Depression... we always had a bunch strange people... not strange people, that's not the right word, but people that came in and stayed with us for a while, they were down on their luck, friends of one art of the family or another, and I remember whole rafts of different people that came and stayed with us for several weeks, months, and *picturesque* people, and one of them was a piano player name of George Gould at the time he was past middle age, and he and a liver disease or something of the sort. Even as a kid, I could see he was ill. But he was a marvelous piano player. And my mother played, but she could read, and they used to have parties, and after, they'd have dances. When George was there, she'd get him to come up and play, and what a difference; George would play, and these people would start swingin' (chuckles) and I knew at the time George was... he wrote rags: 'Whoa, Nelly'; 'The Arabian Rag'; other rags. And I subsequently learned that in the decade between 1910 and 1920, George Gould had an orchestra in San Francisco that was the most prestigious orchestra in town. Paul Whiteman was there at the time, and George Gould's orchestra was a far better orchestra than Paul Whiteman's. But it... I don't know what happened... when 1920 came, or something like that, Paul Whiteman went ahead and became more important than George's, but something happened; he didn't have his orchestra anymore, but when George played, I responded to it, but I also all at the same time, I just think I had it in me. I'd listened to the radio; listened to Red Nichols and the whole... I just loved it. And I just think there was something about the music that resonated with me or something of that sort and it's never gone the other way. In fact, right now, it's probably more profound than ever. I'm organizing the music and putting it all onto CDs and the more I get into it the more I see what a large, deep, profound music it is, so much to it, yet is so poorly known that the general public at large doesn't realize what a magnificent musical resource is there, lying fallow except to a certain group of people like myself. What about you, do you like jazz?

I really love jazz. I do.

Well then, you know what I'm talking about.

I know what it means. I'm a musician, so I know what it means that something that resonates within you, that draws you to…

What do you play?

Guitar and bass. I started out on drums, then I went to guitar and bass.

Well, I played coronet. I started playing harmonica when I was a little kid; still play. Pretty good at it. Pretty good harmonica player. Then I began playing coronet so I could play not well, but I played with some bands, then when I hung that up, I took up the banjo.

How'd that go for you?

About the same degree… not good. [Chuckles] My fingers… I don't have flexible, good fingers. Anyway, I can't get around on the either the coronet or the banjo the way a musician gets around. So, I'm a frustrated musician, but I love the music to pieces. So you don't play anymore yourself, huh?

Not really. Not to speak of. But I spent a long time doing it, so I can appreciate what you're saying in terms of enjoying on both ends of the side of the coin, because you've got the listening side, and then you've got the actual playing it, and it's… the same thing draws from one to the other.

But anyway, you didn't call me to hear my views on jazz.

The Blue World was my first book I read of yours, and is probably my favorite book of your work. Was there a particular inspiration behind it?

No. It's not *my* favorite, by any means. I don't *dis*like it, but I just think it's just another work in the development… in my story development. I think it's kind of… for a time I was trying to write these gadget stories, which would sell to John Campbell [Editor of *Astounding*]. And this *Blue World* was a kind of gadget story in the idea of taking iron out of human blood, which is an asinine idea, but it was a gadget, and anyway, right now, I wouldn't use that device, I just used it there because it had some dramatic angles to it. But anyway, I think it's… there's a lot of good things in the story, but it's not my favorite. I don't hate it, but I just think of it as a stage in the development.

Do you have a favorite work of yours?

Well… no I don't, except some of the things I like better than others. I like *Cadwell Chronicles*, and I like the *Cugel* stories; there's two, and I love those, and *Rialto* I like pretty well.

What prompted you to sell the Vance Integral Edition by subscription rather through the usual channels of distribution?

I have nothing to do with that. This is some people… Paul Rhodes who lives in France was the original guy who got it started and most of the volunteers are back East and [Jack's wife] Norma and [Jack's son] John have been helping in getting the thing together. Me, I know nothing about it. I completely was aloof from the whole business. Naturally, I'm pleased it's being done. They've got half their books delivered. Apparently they're beautiful books. From what I hear. As you know, I can't see. So I haven't seen the damn things, but apparently, they're something to be proud of.

What sort of impact would you like to make, both in the genre you write in as well as in, for want of a better term, 'civilian life?'

None. I don't have any ambitions that way at all. Maybe because I never made any so far…

What motivated you to become a writer?

Because I didn't want to work for anybody; I wanted to be independent. I just didn't want to be subject to an employer. I wanted to be my own boss.

You mentioned earlier that you hadn't had any movies made or anything like that; do you have any interest in that; in any of your stories being made into movies?

[Chuckles] I'm interested in making a lot of money. But aside from that, I don't care.

Which of your stories would you most like to have made into a movie?

Well, I always thought this *Lyonesse Trilogy* that Disney might be interested in that. But as far as I know, they've never even looked twice at it. Yet I think it would be a natural for Disney.

Is there anything you'd like people to learn from your writing?

Yeah. Let me think… is there anything? Maybe in a devious or subtle way, I suppose I'm advocating my own personal philosophy but only in a half-assed way; I'm not really serious about it. It's my personal philosophies; it's nothing outrageous or extreme. I consider it just straightforward, logical, anti-superstition, anti-foolishess. You can call me anything you like. I vote Republican, although I don't call myself a Republican, but I wouldn't vote Democrat if I was paid to [laughs]. Anything to avoid being a Democrat.

What's the biggest challenge you've faced in making a living as a writer?

Well, the same thing every writer has, I guess. Except Stephen King. In other words, selling. It's hard work and wondering whether you're going to get paid or not.

What do you do to unwind?

Well, before I lost my eyes, first of all, my son and I… this is twenty years ago. We were going deep-sea cruising in the Pacific. I got a 45-foot catch that we got ready to sail down in the South Pacific. In the end, I had to sell it, so that was the end of that particular dream, but that's still a daydream. Another thing I was always interested in was pottery, making objects out of clay and firing them and so just before… about ten years ago, I built a studio with a kiln and Johnny and I began producing stuff. I could go on talking about ceramics the same way I could talk about jazz music. But anyway, when my eyes went, I couldn't do that anymore… I like to cook.

I can't cook anymore, but I used to. I was a pretty good cook, but now all can do is *eat*, and try to avoid gaining a lot of weight, but I think of myself as not a real gourmet or anything of that sort, but I like good food, good wine, good Scotch whisky, good company. In other words, all the pleasures of a jolly dinner table [laughs]. It's almost an art form in itself is that jolly dinner occasions especially when you have people over you like and something special and good on the table and so you sit around and laugh and joke and drink and we have a room in our house… Johnny and I have built it ourselves, and there's one room in it that house that we love especially; the dining room, which is a beautiful room, if I say so myself. One stone wall… but it's a beautiful room with a fireplace in it and we've had so many wonderful dinner parties in that room with the fire going clinking and the fork and knives clanking on the… it's kind of an art form [laughs].

It's kind of a lost art.

Yeah, but nobody ever calls it that, except now I can see that you have the same general tendencies I do.

You can have a passion for that just as you can for jazz or anything else; it's good food and good company. The conversation is a lost art.

Yeah. True. It's more than conversation, though. It's kind of generating a mood having the circumstances on hand to generate the occasions. But these occasions; each one of them has it's own flavor, that is composed of the people present, the cuisine, circumstances, whether there are any fistfights or not, and ect…

You don't seem especially interested in receiving awards and the like; what sort of thing matters to you as a writer?

If I get an award, that's great. But I'm not going to bust my ass running out and soliciting for them or agitate for them, no way. I've had… It's anti-self –respect or dignity or pride or something of that sort. No, if it comes, it comes, if not, well, okay.

Which comes first when you're plotting a story; the characters or the world they interact in?

I don't know. No idea. Whatever works. [Laughs]. A story usually comes into being from a general mood or something, thinking about something and a mood comes on and then the mood kind of develops and the characters appear. That's about the size of it, no, I don't start any particular, definite way at all.

With regards to your short story writing, what are the demands of writing the short story that don't come with writing the novel?

Oh, I don't know, I don't know much about literary theories, in fact, I don't know anything about them at all. If I have an idea, I just write it, and if it turns out to be short story. If it turns out to be a novel, it's a novel.

What do you have planned for the future projects?

Well, right now, I'm putting the last licks on what was really the ending of *Ports Of Call*. I wrote *Ports Of Call* and found out I had too much material there [chuckles] at the end of it. In fact, I think I told the reader there, "Jesus Christ, if I continue, I'm going to have a book fifteen hundred pages long, so I'm just plain going to stop here and continue on another book." I forget what I wrote, but it was to that effect, so the second half of that *Ports Of Call* is now being finished; it's called *Lurulu*, and I just talked to Beth Meacham (TOR Books), the editor. She's got it on her fall list for next year. And that'll be in the second half of the *VIE* set. And then, the trouble is, I don't feel much like writing anymore. It's too slow, not being able to see and also I just don't seem to have the quickness or the adroitness or whatever it is that I used to have or maybe I'm just too fussy that I don't want to write anything that's worse than what I wrote before so I'm ultra fastidious and as a result, I'm just to damn slow. I do have another story started, but I don't think I'll ever finish it. But who knows?

Can you tell us anything about it?

I don't want to talk about it.

That's okay.

In fact, what I did, there was material left over from *Lurulu*, so I thought I'd use some of that and use it in another story, which I've got it more or less plotted, all I have to do is write it, but… most of my time is being taken up organizing these records. I've got a machine which copies one CD to another, and I've got a lot of cassettes and records, and then I record from the radio every week. There's KCSM… the Jim Cullum Band and a fellow named Dick Hadlock that has an hour of his choice of records. Hadlock, he plays soprano sax. Quite well, actually, although I've known him a long time. Sometimes he plays records I record, but he's one of these fellows whose tastes are so eclectic I don't think he has any taste at all. He'll start playing stuff from 1928 then he'll start playing stuff from the most advanced, abstract, so-called jazz from 1970, which I don't regard as jazz at all. They call it jazz, but it's not jazz. It's a lot of abstract noise. But then at eleven o' clock, this fellow Ray Smith, from South Carolina. He's a lovely guy. He used to be a drummer and played in this great band, The Yankee Rhythm Kings ten, fifteen years ago. Great band. He must be in his seventies. He's a wonderful guy, though, I just love him. And he plays music out of the twenties and the thirties. And he plays a lot of good stuff. And that's what I do Sunday evenings from six 'til midnight is sit at the radio and record music. That's what keeps me busy. It's kind of a foolish, futile occupation. [Chuckles]

Do you do any conventions at all?

Yeah. I do. I used to not go to the conventions, but then three or four years ago just on impulse, I went up to Seattle on a convention. I had a pretty good time up there. So then, a year or two ago, I was invited to a convention in Columbus, Ohio. And I went there, and it was not as much fun as the one in Seattle, but it was okay. So I'm inclined to go if just to break the monotony, not because I particularly like the convention, but if I go to the convention, I can explore the restaurants of that particular area. Columbus had a lot of beautiful restaurants and as does Seattle, and they're all paid for; I don't pay or them. I get expenses, so that's kind of fun, and I don't have to do much, except sign a few autographs and say intelligent things… try to and so I'm not [currently] invited now to anything that I know of, probably won't be, but in short, if I'm invited to a convention, in a place… I would not go to one in say, San Jose or Reno or anything like that, but if I were invited to a convention in let's say Boston or let's say Atlanta, North Carolina or England, I'd go. Just something that sounds kind of romantic. So that's the answer.

WIL McCARTHY

THE NAME OF WIL MCCARTHY will be familiar with the readers of *Sci Fi Weekly* for several reasons, not the least of which is Wil's science column, *Lab Notes*. Wil is able to make things like nanotech comprehensible to us folk who are more often than not left scratching their heads when trying to get their thoughts around such things.

A husband and father, Wil has a background in the hard sciences, among them, astrodynamics. While he has found success in the world of freelance writing, he can still be found at work for the Lockheed Martin Corporation In Denver, Colorado, where he designs satellite orbits for Flight Systems.

Wil is also the respected author of such novels as *Aggressor Six, The Collapsium, The Wellstone* and the upcoming *Lost in Transmisson* (Spectra Books, 2004) and the comprehensive non-fiction work Hacking Matter and the anthology, *Once Upon A Galaxy*. His numerous non-fiction columns have been seen in the pages of *Analog* and *Wired*.

Wil lives in Colorado, where he continues to write and explore the worlds around us. His website is wilmccarthy.com.

I thought there was an undercurrent of Lord Of The Flies *in* The Wellstone. *Is that an accurate observation? Was it intentional?*

Also *Huckleberry Finn*, and a bunch of other 'boys' adventure' novels. But it certainly wasn't deliberate; what I had in mind was something more along the lines of the Greek epics, particularly *Argonautica*. These are young men banished by a fearful monarchy, and they're on a perilous journey they may not survive, for the sake of their honor and the future of their nation. It's interesting that to American ears, these two different story types would sound so similar, but under enough stress, I suppose there isn't much difference between young men and adolescent boys. Fundamentally, the Greek epics *are* boys' adventure novels.

In your research for Hacking Matter, *did any one item provide more fascination than the others?*

The idea of 'quantum dots' and 'artificial atoms'—designer electron bundles formed in tiny electronic traps—captivated me right away. The thing that really amazed me, though, was that the obvious application—programmable matter or 'wellstone'—seemed to have been overlooked by everyone involved in the actual research.

I tried to squeeze some of these speculations out of the physicists at MIT and Harvard and Sun Microsystems, but finally I gave up and just described, in my own words and images, how such a technology would work.

The results have been amusing: a pending U.S. patent and several strong expressions of interest from government agencies and venture capitalists, and conference organizers eager to fly me out to explain the idea. My business partner and I are forming a new company around the technology, which we hope to begin marketing in actual products by the end of the decade. I find it deeply ironic that the invention came out of a science fiction novel, *The Collapsium*, and only later found its way into *Hacking Matter*, a nonfiction book, and later still into the real world.

In which field do you think the next big advance in science will be—organic or mechanical?

On the nanoscale, the lines between chemistry and physics, mechanics and biology and electronics start to get really blurry. The big advances will probably be in devices which straddle these boundaries. Naturally I'm biased toward my own inventions, which bridge the gap between chemistry and nanoelectronics. I can't promise great things there, but I'm hopeful.

Was Bloom *written as a kind of 'Cautionary tale?'*

Sure, but also as a tale of wonder. Technology presents us with the possibility of terrifying new disasters—like an artificial life form which devours the entire inner solar system—but if we use it right it can also make our lives more rewarding, by shrinking large problems like chaos theory down to human scale. It's that interplay of risk and benefit that interests me most: a world of splendid dangers. Isn't that what we really want?

Was there concern on anyone's part that the use of Calculus integrals in Flies From The Amber *might alienate parts of the audience?*

I used calculus integrals in *Flies From The Amber*, as part of a machine-to-machine conversation on the mathematics of black holes, but although they're accurate, the equations are just there as visual dressing. The reader doesn't have to understand them, or even look at them, to follow the story. Anyway, the broader answer to your question is yes, there are things I do which will alienate some of the audience. I think this is inherent in any art form. Either you're a populist, speaking to the general public and breaking very little new ground, or you're an 'elitist' speaking to some smaller group about more difficult, more interesting and novel concepts. Not everyone gets these, or wants to, and that's fine. Science fiction isn't for everyone. But there are people out there with hungry minds, who want a story that's exciting and outlandish but that could actually happen. They want a story that challenges their assumptions and brings new ideas into the world. These are the true science fiction readers.

Bloom *seemed to use elements of both the SF and mystery genres, which books/authors influenced the mystery aspect?*

This is another comment I get a lot, not just about *Bloom* but about all of my writing. I do read and enjoy mysteries, yes, and I've even written a couple. But I don't see any favorite authors or strong influences there, unless you broaden the category to include political thrillers like Martin Cruz Smith's *Gorky Park*.

I guess the answer is that like any scientist, I see mysteries everywhere, embedded in the world around us. I find this exciting—a challenge from nature itself—and I also like to dwell on the human implications, whether political or social or philosophical. So I think my work has a lot in common with thrillers, which do the same thing in a more here-and-now sort of way.

Was there someone or something in particular that inspired the 'Tickle capacitor?'

Heh. You want me to name names? Humorlessness is one of the most crippling human disorders, because it sucks all the joy out of life and also tends to be very isolating. Nobody likes a killjoy! But it occurred to me one day, in reading about the neurology of humor, that it's a curable condition. Probably right now, with technology we've got lying around to treat other disorders. It's simply a matter of recognizing the problem and stimulating a bit of neural tissue.

Does technology dictate what story you'll tell, or does the story come first and you use the tech as needed?

I wouldn't use the word 'technology' by itself in this way. I start with ideas, not just technology but a lot of things, from physics and politics to religion and food and sex. The world-building accretes around these ideas, and the characters form in the context of their world. Once I've done all this—assuming I've done it properly—the story really does seem to write itself. Proper world-building and character-building suggest an optimal plot, which seems by the end to have a sort of inevitability. Given the initial conditions, how else could things possibly turn out? I like that feeling. A lot of the science fiction out there feels very flimsy to me, lightly constructed and not well thought-out. I'd rather build a steamroller than a dinky little economy car.

What did you learn by editing Once Upon A Galaxy?

Never edit an anthology.

Were you concerned about including one of your own stories in it?

Nope. I have faith in my own work, and a good sense of when I've screwed up and when I've done well. The story was appropriate, and my co-editors agreed.

Aggressor Six *is one of my favorite novels of yours—will it be coming back into print?*

You ask at a delicate time, since this is currently under discussion. I can't disclose the details, but yes, I think we'll be hearing from that book again.

What other genre outside SF do you like to write?

I once wrote a mystery novel called *Third Time's The Charm*, which was set in the year 2000 and involved no advanced technology. Unfortunately, for some reason the mystery publishers all felt that it was a science fiction novel, and several science fiction publishers felt that it was really a mystery novel. By the time I got an offer on the book I was sick of the whole thing, and stuck it in a trunk. I figure if it's that confusing, it's probably better not to set it loose in the world. But I'm doing a lot of nonfiction writing these days, and I have to say I love it. It's much easier than science fiction.

Who are your contemporaries?

When I first started writing professionally, there was a whole gang of twentysomething SF/Fantasy/Horror writers in the Denver area. Sadly, I don't know what's happened to most of them. This is an industry which eats its young; very few survive those early years. But the successful writers of my generation include Linda Nagata, Sean Stewart, Maureen McHugh and Alastair Reynolds.

What can you tell us about Lost in Transmission?

I can say, with confidence, that everyone reading this should reserve a copy right now. *Lost in Transmission* will be my eighth published novel, and the third in the *Queendom of Sol* series after *The Collapsium* and *The Wellstone*. In very broad terms, I'll say that immortality means having to live—possibly forever—in the mess you've created with your own actions. The results are both sad and funny, which from a storytelling perspective is a wonderful combination. And of course there's cool technology.

Will we be seeing a collection of your Lab Notes *column?*

Another question I can't address this month, alas. But it's under consideration. *Lab Notes* is a real kick in the pants because it's come out every four weeks—that's 13 times a year—for over four years now. This gives me a chance to explore a *lot* of different ideas —more than I could comfortably wrap into novels or short stories. It's a conduit running straight from my brain to the audience, with no buffering.

Do you consider human cloning ethical?

Sure, why not? Or rather, it's no more or less ethical than filling up the world with random children conceived in the irresponsibility of nature. In some sense, we're polluting the world with human beings, and sooner or later we've got to get that under control. But if it's unethical or arrogant to skew the genetics of your offspring, we had better start arranging marriages by lottery. The quest for the best possible children is a deeply personal thing for most people.

In your Lab Notes *column 'Claiming Space', you wrote that for many years, 'Space has been mind-numbingly dull.' What could happen to change this for you?*

Send *me* there.

CHELSEA QUINN YARBRO

CHELSEA QUINN YARBRO HAS BEEN a professional writer for more than thirty years, delivering to her readers the rich, complex, and dark worlds her characters inhabit, not the least of these being the vampire that has set the standard for the three-dimensional vampire, St. Germain, who first saw publication in 1978's *Hotel Transylvania*.

A prolific author, Yarbro has sold over seventy books, (*Writ In Blood, Taji's Syndrome, Night Blooming,* and her most recent work, *Midnight Harvest* are nut a few titles) and sixty works of short fiction, all the while constantly pushing not only the boundaries of the vampire genre, but those of mystery, historical and science fiction, as well as mixing any other number of genres to her liking in order to create a fascinating read for both author and reader.

Averaging an astonishing three or four books per year, Chelsea still manages to produce quality, well-respected work that continues to be as enjoyable as it had been at the start of her body of work in print.

She lives in her hometown —Berkeley, California—with two autocratic cats. Her website can be found at www.chelseaquinnyarbro.com.

How important is networking at conventions like WHC, for both the beginning writer as well as the seasoned pro?

I think it is probably more important to attend specialized conventions for a journeyman writer than any other, but it's useful at all stages of a career, if for nothing else, to find out how the industry is working at any given time. Also, it often helps to see editors away from their New York offices and to have a little more flexibility in dealing with them, but New York visits are also important once you start selling. Providing a Writer isn't put off by conventions—and some are—attending them can be a nice break from the necessary isolation of writing.

How did your collaboration with Bill Fawcett start?

Bill called and asked me if I'd be interested in working on a project with him. We were going to do it as a true collaboration, but the publisher in question decided that collaborations don't sell, and so wanted a penname—we came up with Quinn Fawcett, with the addendum that we didn't think it would fool anyone. Whether it does or it doesn't, it goes on.

Do you have a particular technique to achieve a successful collaboration?

I'm not a good collaborator in general. In Bill's case Bill and I agree on a story outline, then he leaves me alone to write the first draft. I send it off to him with requests for inserts and additions, then, when he's finished with it, I smoodge the style in a third draft. Much more collaborator participation is, in fact, way too much for me.

In picking a time period for Saint-Germain, does the setting come first, or the plot?

Availability of women in the culture comes first, so long as the period is part of his history. The setting, including the culture, counts as a tertiary character, and, like all characters, shapes the story line. It doesn't shape the plot, of course: there are only seven of those and they apply across the boards to all manner of interpretations. Story lines are how characters create the plots involved in their stories.

Saint-Germain's drinking of blood leans more towards the need for intimacy rather than the simple need for food. What motivated your decision to go in that direction?

It's a matter of what the blood is a metaphor for; since one of my intentions with the character was to push the paradigm of vampire as far to the positive as I could, I decided that few things are more intimately individual than blood, and voila!

Keeping in mind that Saint-Germain does not lie, per se, but rather leaves certain things out, does this keep him from being the honorable person he otherwise seems to be?

You mean he's good at half-truths, which is true of most of us. He's had a long time to turn it into high art, and I tend to point it out in narration, as well. I don't think that's in the least dishonorable, I think it's intelligent.

When delving into vampire mythology and deciding what you were going to keep and what you were not, was the a concern on your part or an editor's regarding what readers would consider a kind of revision on mythology?

Saint-Germain's first editor knew very little about vampire lore but what little she had seen in the movies—and it wasn't much, so she had no concerns about it to speak of. Very few editors worry about heresy—their goals are much too commercial, thank goodness. Long before Joanie saw *Hotel Transylvania*, back in 1971 when I was doing my first work on the book, I literally made a chart of world-wide vampire beliefs. Anything that 80% of cultures believed, I kept. The other 20%, if I liked it, I kept it, otherwise I threw it out. What Joanie thought about was the problem of consistency, and so far that hasn't been compromised, and I've had a bunch of editors since then: Lisa, Marcia, Hilary, Beth, Greg, Bryan, Melissa, Betsy, Larissa, and Jaime so far.

What was the inspiration for Gynethe Mehaut's manifesting elements of the stigmata in Night Blooming*?*

I haven't the faintest idea. She showed up that way. Incidentally, Gynethe Mehaut is a compound first name, not a first and last name—like Jeanne-Marie but without the hyphen. Common folk didn't have last names in the 8th and 9th centuries.

It seemed that because Saint-Germain affected Gynethe so deeply that when she was tortured, it was made all the more unbearable for her. Is that a valid observation?

Certainly.

Stealth Press hasn't published their editions of your work quite in the sequence they first appeared in. Was that their decision or yours, and what led to it?

It was Stealth's decision and I have no idea why they made it.

Does e-publishing need to establish itself more as a 'legitimate' publishing venue? If so, what can it do?

The answer depends on how e-publishing sees itself: does it intend to compete with print? Does it want to go to a more variable format? What is the market it's seeking? Until an e-publisher decides where it wants to go, it hasn't a prayer of getting there. And if e-publishing wants to receive commensurate attention for what's being e-published as print publishing receives, it must establish real literary standards and adhere to them, so that what is offered can compete with the quality of print. Hidden Knowledge, the e-publisher I work with, has very specific literary and academic standards for its works, and Mike Ward, who runs the company, is a prudent and sensitive professional who treats his e-books with care, getting reviews in publications usually reserved for print, and who seeks out booksellers whose regular customers are inclined to be interested in e-publishing. For the time being, it seems to be a workable approach.

How much outlining goes into your work, and has the amount of it changed since you started writing?

I outline fairly extensively because I'm usually dealing with real events. I don't need to give myself as much information as I used to, but I still like to have two pages of outline for every projected 100 pages of manuscript.

Some authors have had difficulty finding publishers interested in works that take place outside whichever given universe they've become known for. Have you met with any of that kind of adversity?

Oodles of it. And I still do. It's like an actor being type-cast. I work hard to avoid it as much as possible, but it is a problem all writers encounter, and it's getting worse over time.

In regards to the saying 'History is written by the victors', do you agree with that, and how much does it affect the way you research?

Generally yes, I do agree with that. Which is why it is always important to research the period immediately before the period I'm writing about. It gives a greater sense of context and often, a sense not only of why the history is told the way it is, but why the winning side won—and strength of arms is usually the least of it.

Who do you consider to be your contemporaries?

Anyone born in or around 1942. Charlie Grant is my most contemporary contemporary in the field that I know of—he's three days older than I am.

What do you do to relax?

I ride horseback (arthritic knees permitting) or listen to opera. Sometimes I cook. I used to do needlework but it's hard on my hands now, so I only do it occasionally, but I like it. And, of course, I read.

How many projects are you working on now, and what can you tell us about them?

I'm working on three proposals while my agent is looking for a new home for StG, and I'm finishing up one of my once-a-week novels, on which I work, literally, one day a week, the other five working days going over to contracted work. I'm also making my way through a pair of non-fiction, pseudonymous books for Tor, but they're going more slowly than I intended, since they're about battles and I've been going through an 18 month patch of dying relatives and friends, which makes writing about carnage difficult.

YVONNE NAVARRO

YVONNE NAVARRO BROUGHT HER UNIQUE brand of writing to the public eye after her mother read a book Yvonne had given her and told Yvonne, 'You could do this.'

Starting her novel-writing career with the Bram Stoker finalist *After Age*, and following it up with *deadrush* (and another finalist nod for the Stoker), Yvonne's writing took her readers from one extreme to another, whether in one of her own worlds like that found in *DeadTimes*, or *That's Not My Name* or that of some else's such as her superlative work in the universe of *Buffy the Vampire Slayer*, *Paleo* and *Tempted Champions* (among many others, among them a trilogy regarding the fan-favorite, Willow Rosenberg.)

Your grasp of the characters of Buffy the Vampire Slayer *is particularly strong. Is there a particular character you connect with?*

I like them all pretty equally and for different reasons. I have a soft spot in my heart for Willow, since the first book I ever did for the series was a Willow book and I'm the only author who's done Willow novelizations.

How did you come to be involved with writing expansion novels and film novelizations?

I started quite some time ago with the science fiction film Species, the script for which was written by Dennis Feldman. It was something worked out by my agent and the editor at Bantam, and it was a great thing for a starting out author. They were looking for (probably) an 'affordable' author to novelize the movie, and based on the quality of *After Age*, they offered it to me. Later on I did an *Aliens* novelization (which people still look for today, even though it's out of print), the novelization for the Species sequel, and eventually moved into Buffy stuff after being recommended to the editor by Nancy Holder and Chris Golden.

Is it a job you'd recommend to other writers trying to gain a higher profile?

I guess that depends on what you're novelizing. The *Buffy* novels give me good visibility with the *Buffy* fans, but I'm not sure it carries over into mass market and other fiction.

In Tempted Champions, *there's a good amount of time on each character from the series; Were you concerned that Buffy may be overshadowed by the other plotlines?*

No. I guess you could say I write how I write. In other words, I'm writing what the story demands I write, and if you look at any *Buffy* novel, there's always a parallel plot involving a lesson learned which generally focuses on one of the other characters. We like to get every one of the characters involved in every book.

Do you have an interest in writing a teleplay for Buffy? *Have you been approached to do one?*

No, and no. I just don't have the feel or affinity for scriptwork, and haven't been approached... which is probably just as well.

How did your novel After Age *influence your approach to the* Buffy *novels?*

It didn't. *After Age* is a world apart from *Buffy*—a lot of different rules and a different world setting altogether. Those who've read might realize afterward that not a single stake is drive through a vampire in that novel, nor is a cross ever pointed at one. Holy water *is* used, but only as a method to an end.

In Final Impact, *you combined elements of SF, mystery, and the supernatural. Did you know you would have these genres represented when you started, or did they evolve as the novel went on?*

Final Impact is the only book I ever started and wrote most of the way through without an outline. In a way, I did a lot of it blind, just writing what I felt and to heck with the consequences. I don't recommend that method—at one point I found myself stuck, with no idea where to go or what to write next. Outlining is your friend. [Grin] But back to the question, I think I ended up with those things because really, I just love a good horror and/or scary story, and adding those elements to the characters made the story more fun to me.

Do characters come first, or does the story?

Characters, always. The story builds itself around the life (or unlife) of the characters.

What do you have waiting in your books-to-be-read pile?

Speaks the Nightbird by Robert McCammon, a couple of Stephen King books, several F. Paul Wilson and Steve Spruill books, a Gary Brandner book, *Welcome Back to the Night* by Elizabeth Massie, dozens of anthologies including *The Lottery* by Shirley Jackson, and about 125 more. This is why I refuse to accept novels and stories that other people want to send me. Yikes.

What's the biggest liability to genre writers today?

The failure of the publishing industry to recognize good work enough to devote decent marketing to it. Unfortunately this is death waiting to happen for 299 out of 300 writers.

What do you think of writer's groups? Do they actually help the aspiring writer?

I've never been in one, but they can—provided you find good people who can give and take criticism without becoming jealous or overly controlling.

Are there any negatives for lesser-known writers being published on the Internet?

Bad editing, no editing, and frankly, giving their work away without being paid for it. Being published without pay isn't anything to write home about,

I'm afraid. Websites are cheap and anyone can put up a webzine now. Most people don't know what they're doing, a lot publish their pals and anyone else they think might be a big name. There's hardly any editing, almost no proof reading, and few people know how to spell or properly use apostrophes. I know I'm going to get a lot of backlash on this, but if you don't get paid for your efforts, what's to be proud about? At least in real print form you get a few contributor copies, but don't get carried away there, either. Writing for free is supposed to be a learning experience, but I believe it should be a *short* one. Continuing to do it just because you want to see your name in print (or on a website) hurts yourself and every other writer. Bottom line: Why should they pay you pro rates when you'll work for free?

Is your writing influenced more by your real life or your imagination?

I think that's a mixture of both—you can't have one without the other.

What do you do to unwind?

Try to catch up on my TV viewing—I seldom watch TV real time, and I'm always about 12 or 16 hours behind in my favorite shows. I also still like martial arts.

What upcoming projects are you excited about?

The release of *After Age* as a limited hardcover (yes, it *is* going to eventually come out). Mirror Me is finished but still being offered, although slowly—my agent and I parted ways a couple of months ago. I did, however, just pitch a concept to Pocket Books for a Willow trilogy related to Buffy and have gotten preliminary approval, i.e., the go-ahead to develop a full outline for each book in the trilogy.

More on that later, when I have the outlines done and know for sure whether or not it's going to fly. In the meantime, I'm about 2/3rds finished with a novella for the third *Tales of the Slayer* anthology, and I also have another story for a different anthology, very dark and horrific, to get done after that.

What are your thoughts on being the Guest of Honor at TusCon 30? Are you nervous, excited?

I'm very excited and flattered. It's a wonderful welcome to Arizona and I'm really looking forward to it. Also, since I really don't like flying, it's great to be able to drive there!

Your latest Buffy *novels (a trilogy) are called* Wicked Willow. *What can you tell us about the storyline?*

The trilogy is based on that marvelously dark question 'What if Willow went bad?' It takes place under the premise of a parallel universe pathway which branches off when, after flaying Warren alive, Willow decides to pause to answer Buffy's question rather than continue her hunt for Jonathan and Andrew. Things spiral on from there. The titles are *Wicked Willow, Book 1: The Darkening, Book 2: Shattered Twilight,* and *Book 3: Broken Sunrise.*

What has the creative process for that trilogy thus far entailed?

Well, that would be yours truly coming up with the pitch for the idea, getting the go-ahead to submit outlines for each book, and then doing that. It's a hurry up and wait thing, but in the meantime, even though we didn't have the approval for the trilogy from Fox, the series was written in the publication schedule. I didn't want to write anything without approval, so when it did come in, it was hand-in-hand with a brutal deadline—all three books have to be completed and turned in by February 1, 2004. That's even tougher than expected; I thought I had nine months, but I only have eight.

How do you manage to work a full-time job and still find time to write novels, especially on a deadline like yours?

I have no idea. I'm not kidding.

Anything else you'd like to add?

I know it's out of date, but stop by my website now and then: yvonnenavarro.com.
    Also check out my little bookstore dustystacks.com which helps me to keep the bills at bay so I can keep on writing.

DAVID J. SCHOW

WHILE POSSIBLY BEST KNOWN to the world at large as one of the writers behind the bring of James O'Barr's *The Crow* to the screen, David J. Schow's work has also shone its glare not only in the form of novels (*The Kill Riff, The Shaft*) but also in the form of a variety of collections such as *Black Leather Required, Crypt Orchids* and *Zombie Jam* (with illustrations by Bernie Wrightson)—if you have not yet treated yourself to those last volumes in particular, seek them out, I'll be accepting notes of thanks at your leisure.

His nonfiction has included the wonderful *Outer Limits Companion*.

Screenwork from David has included teleplays for *The Outer Limits* and *Masters Of Horror* and scripts for the feature films *Leatherface, Texas Chainsaw Massacre: The Beginning*, and *Critters 3* and *4*. Sharp eyes can catch a glimpse of Schow the actor in the 1997 version of *The Shining*, and in the 'Big Moby' gunfight in *The Crow*.

David also has an eye (perhaps literally) for the documentary, most lately for *The Chronicles of Narnia: The Lion, the Witch, and the Wardrobe*.

David currently lives in Southern California. He writes where his work takes him. His official website, Black Leather Required, can be found at davidjschow.com.

You mentioned in an interview for Doomed *that you wanted to use Alice In Chains 'Down in a Hole' for the movie* The Crow. *As a fan of the movie and the band, I'd love to know during which sequence you pictured the song in?*

No specific sequence. This was during shooting and I just wanted to try to get the song into the movie somewhere. I failed. Incidentally, I just did another interview (for *Doomed* Magazine) answering the same general question and *I got the answer wrong!* I mentioned one of the soundtrack cuts that absolutely 'summed up' the film in my mind. It wasn't the Jesus and Mary Chain song (although that's a cool tune). The correct answer is 'Golgotha Tenement Blues' by the Machines of Loving Grace. Jesus, how's that for meaningless trivia?

Were you happy with The Crow *as it appeared?*

Yeah. Now that a decade has passed it seems to have withstood the whole 'test of time' thing. It seems to show on STARZ every half hour or so.

Are you comfortable with the term 'Splatterpunk' in reference to your work?

Somebody just used it in a write-up of the *Masters Of Horror* episode that broadcast (on Showtime) 20 January 2006, so I guess I'm stuck with it.

What do you think of horror genre on television such as Supernatural *or the 'newly reenvisioned'* Night Stalker? *Does it serve a purpose or cater to an audience without a sense of history of the genre?*

Well, those series usually vanish like a fart in a high wind. It's just as important for the audience to have a sense of history of the genre, which they usually do not. But the 'horror genre on television' now also includes *Masters Of Horror,* which (despite the fact that I did one) is quite well done. No 22-hour-long plot 'arcs,' no cheesy cliffhangers, no artificially-cobbled 'season finales' that never pay off worth a damn. *Masters* is a return to anthological television, and for that alone it merits consideration.

What will the writers of the future have to do in order to stand out in the genre they've chosen? We've seen various kinds of sub-genres of horror come and go (or stay) such as 'quiet' horror or 'splatter'. What do you see as the next step in horror prose?

I'll combine those two questions into one general answer: the quality of the prose desperately needs to improve. I have very little interest in pattern plots, formulaic cloning, or windy, obese overwriting. Most 'imprint-style' current horror novels are either wasting time trying to reinvent the wheel, or wasting space by bloating short story ideas to novel length, in a sort of illiterary 'roid rage. As always, there are more people writing than there are writers of talent, insight or even simple grammatical competence. In a way it's good that so much egregiously stinky prose exists in horror, because it makes the good stuff stand out more brilliantly, and bad because it tends to bury the good stuff; make it harder to dig out. You want to stand out and ride the "next step?" Then put more thought into your writing than the lazy bottom line required to scoot you onto some webzine.

You've written The Outer Limits Companion *and written a teleplay for the show; where does your passion for* The Outer Limits *come from?*

I hate to say this but it really is true: You just have to read the book to get an idea of why it remains endlessly fascinating to me after all this time. I had to think long and hard about such reasons or I never could have done the book, if you follow, and they don't fit into a soundbyte.

With some of your work rooted in music, are you musically inclined?

Nope—the only musical instrument I can play is the stereo.

What music are you listening to these days?

To answer that would date me at lightspeed, so I'm just going to sit here quietly, grinning.

What did you learn documenting the making of The Chronicles Of Narnia?

To take proper boots when you're stranded in the middle of a sheep farm in New Zealand in the freezing rain. Also that huge corporations, notorious themselves for taking credit for every-damned thing, will blithely prohibit DVD producers from listing even elementary credits, like who shot all the doco footage for the inevitably overpriced DVD special edition.

How is the prequel to The Texas Chainsaw Massacre *coming along?*

Working with elements of New Line and Platinum Dunes, we got the script into a comfortable form. Since shooting started I've heard it's been reworked again, but I've been out of the loop since August 1st.

What other kinds of projects are you working on?

The standard sort of answer would be: 'New script, new teleplay, new novel, new short stories.' But in this case, this week, it's actually true, and I hate divulging stuff about yet-to-be-formed work-in-progress, because I've found that's the best way to kill it dead before it has a chance to emerge. But I have so far this year completed another episode for *Masters*, this one an adaptation of a Joe Farris story I unashamedly pushed on them.

And this has nothing to do with anything, but since the end of July '05 I've started massive renovations on my house, a 'project' that now threatens to swallow everything. It's almost as hard as producing a film.

ELAINE CUNNINGHAM

WHILE ELAINE ORIGINALLY WANTED to illustrate books, she pursued degrees in music education and history before studying toward an MBA.

Many readers will be familiar with Elaine's work in the Forgotten Realms (*Elfsong, Daughter of the Drow*, and the *Starlight and Shadow* books to name but a few) set in the world of Dungeons and Dragons, but she's admittedly not much of a gamer, happy to leave that to her two sons, Andrew and Sean, although the family has constructed Warhammer armies.

She's been known to dabble in the field of paranormal romance with works like *Beyond Magic* and the expanding world of Star Wars novels, most notably *Dark Journey* and the upcoming *Blood Oath*.

Elaine lives in New England with her family. Her official website, elainecunningham.com, also contains links to her other interests like Elflore, Ren Faires and Arthurian literature.

How did writing Dark Journey *differ from the works regarding worlds you've built yourself?*

Most of my work takes place in one 'shared world' setting or another, so in many ways *Dark Journey* was not much of a departure. It's like writing historical fiction, except for the fact that the 'history' is imaginary. *Star Wars* has a much more detailed history than many shared worlds. The source materials include dozens of novels, reference books, game accessories, short stories, comic books, and, of course, movies. There was an enormous amount of reading involved, but even so, I was grateful for the eagle eyes of the LucasFilm continuity team.

What made you pick Jaina Solo as the primary character for the story?

I didn't, actually. Jaina was assigned to me. The folks at Del Rey wanted a smaller scale, personal story focusing on a difficult moment in Jaina's life. I've written about several conflicted female heroes, and apparently the publisher felt that Jaina and I were a good match.

How do you feel about the loss of Anakin (Han and Leia's son) in Star By Star*?*

Devastated! I haven't wept over a book since Beth bought the farm in *Little Women.* After reading Greg Keyes' two books, which really brought Anakin to life and made him an incredibly appealing hero, I reread *Star By Star* and felt even worse. In fact, for a while I had a hard time writing. As I told my son, 'Anakin is gone. There doesn't seem to be much point in going on.' He smirked, being under the misapprehension that I was kidding around!

Did it affect the way you approached Jaina?

I think so, yes. Anakin was special, and his loss made an impact on readers. It seemed to me that his sister would suffer a profound blow, first because of the family tie and their shared Jedi perspective on life, but also because she had some understanding of his importance and his potential. This, coupled with the severing of her twin-bond with Jacen, was simply was too much for her. She went into emotional overload, and responded by sublimating her grief.

You worked as a music teacher for some time. Is listening to music while you write part of your regimen? If so, who/what do you listen to?

Actually, I can't listen to music while I work. It's like trying to carry on two conversations at once.

Is writing more an instinctual or a learned thing?

In other words, what's more important: talent or hard work? They're both important, and what's more, they're co-dependent. I've had diligent music student who never progressed, and talented students who never practiced. Writing, like music, requires a certain inherent talent, but it also involves a set of skills that can be learned through practice and study.

When writing Dark Journey, *did you talk to any of the other past* Star Wars *authors for continuity?*

Absolutely. *Dark Journey* followed directly after *Star By Star*, and it was one of several books that took place at roughly the same time. This required a considerable amount of coordination. Troy Denning was particularly helpful. We spoke by phone several times and exchanged lots of email. I've got a huge file of email conversations with several other authors. We batted around ideas in ongoing discussions that made the rounds, not only among the authors, but with the Del Rey editors and LucasFilm people.

As both a Star Wars *fan and one who has worked in the George Lucas universe, can you compare the experience with the work you've done in* Forgotten Realms?

The Forgotten Realms has been around for about twenty years, and it's a setting for role playing and computer games as well as novels. Many readers and gamers invest a great deal of time and creative energy in this world and its continuing characters. Their devotion to 'their' setting helped prepare me for the passionate and occasionally vehement reaction of *Star Wars* fans to any new story or novel. *Star Wars* fans span three generations, and they're a diverse and highly partisan group. Anyone working in a shared-world setting needs to understand this and be prepared to ride out the highs and lows.

Do you go into a different mode of thinking when writing SF than you would use for Fantasy?

This question presupposes that *Star Wars* is SF. This might be opening a very large and recalcitrant can of worms, but I consider Star Wars to have more in common with Fantasy than SW, cool gizmos and space travel notwithstanding. SF is based on ideas. Fantasy involves magic (in this case, the Force,) fantastic creatures, and most importantly, a struggle between good and evil. If I had to characterize *Star Wars*, I'd say it's primarily an adventure story with a fantasy heart and an SF wardrobe.

The Wizardwar *brings the* Counselors And Kings *trilogy to an end. Was it difficult to be done with Halruaa and its people?*

In a way, yes. Both of the protagonists answered important personal questions, but these answers left them poised on the threshold of new adventures. I think that Matteo and Tzigone are in a good place, but the story ended at a time when changes are sweeping the Realms, things that will have a profound effect upon the magic-rich kingdom of Halruaa. It's not easy to walk away from that!

There's been some debate in regards to publishing being motivated more by politics rather than new writers. How do you feel about that?

I'm not sure that 'politics' is quite the right word. 'Economics' hits the mark more directly. When businesses consolidate—and many publishing houses and book chains have done so in the past few years—they find themselves with brand new debt and the need to maximize profit. Emphasizing best-selling books and celebrity authors is one way to do this. Some of the trends that help create bestsellers, such as Oprah's book club, support this strategy. Does this have a negative impact? In some ways, yes. A lot of mid-list authors are getting squeezed out. It's possible that good books are being overlooked in favor of potentially 'big books.' On the other hand, the media attention given to certain books has prompted a lot of people to read that otherwise might not have done so. I'm all for anything that introduces people to the joy of reading, be it Oprah, movie adoptions, or Harry Potter.

As for new writers, what could be more exciting to an editor than 'discovering' a talented new author? Perhaps newcomers are laboring in the shade of publishing giants, but is breaking in really more difficult today than it was a few years ago? When you factor in all the possibilities, such as e-publishing, Internet promotion, print on demand, and online bookstores, it might even be possible that opportunities are more plentiful now than they have been.

Which one of your books would you like to see made into a movie?

I seldom think in these terms. To me, a book is not raw material for a movie, but a thing worthwhile in and of itself. I love movies, and I'll readily acknowledge that some wonderful adaptations have been made, but I seldom read a book and wonder who should play the various characters. But what the heck—I'll play. If I could adapt one of my books into a screenplay, I'd pick *Elfshadow*.

What projects in the works can you tell us about?

My next book is *Windwalker*, the third book in the *Starlight & Shadows* trilogy and the continuing story of dark elf 'princess' Liriel Baenre. It'll be out in April 2003. The first two books, *Daughter Of The Drow* and *Tangled Webs*, will be re-released just before. I'm very excited about the redesign—the new cover art by Todd Lockman is worth the price of the books!

What do you attribute to the success you've had in two, some may say very different, genres?

I have to thank Bob Salvatore for the opportunity to write a *Star Wars* book. When the *New Jedi Order* series was in the planning stage, the folks at Del Rey asked Bob to recommend two or three authors. I was one of the people he mentioned. Without that endorsement, I definitely would have been lost in the crowd of aspiring *Star Wars* authors! And yes, I'll be naming my first grandchild 'Robert.' My future daughters-in-law will just have to adapt.

How important is it for authors, both new and established, to have their own websites as you do?

I'm not sure how you could quantify the importance. It's expected—let's put it that way. A lot of authors don't have web sites and do just fine, but readers today expect a certain level of accessibility. The Internet is an important way to connect with readers, to promote upcoming work, and to introduce your work to new readers. Sometimes the oddest things can pull in new readers. I have on my website several 'reference centers,' collections of links on related subjects. After the *Lord Of The Rings* movie, a surprising number of people found my site through a search on Elf languages! (And to those who are thinking about asking, no, I do not know of a book along the lines of *High Elvish for Dummies*. It's not a bad idea, though. Someone ought to schedule a meeting with Tolkien's heirs and get to work on it!) For those of us who write in a shared world, web sites, email and message boards provide opportunities to 'share.' To me, that's an important and enjoyable part of the job.

P.N. ELROD

P.N. 'PAT' ELROD BEGAN her publishing career in 1990 with *Bloodlist*, which kicked off her eleven (thus far) book series set 1930s Chicago, The Vampire Files which introduced the world to her famous Private Investigator, Jack Fleming.

Pat moved on to another series that proved quite popular, Jonathan Barrett, Gentleman Vampire, set during the American Revolution from the British point of view.

Continuing her stint in the vampire world, Pat also wrote books for the Dungeons and Dragons Ravenloft world; *I, Strahd: Memoirs of a Vampire* and *I, Strahd: The War With Azalin*, showing her continued prowess as an author at the reins of what may very well be the most popular monster in horror, but her obvious enjoyment in unusual settings.

Her novel, *My Big Fat Supernatural Wedding* made it onto the *USA Today* Bestseller List. Pat topped this by her sequel, *My Big Fat Supernatural Honeymoon*, hitting the *New York Times* Bestseller List.

Pat's website is vampwriter.com.

You've noted that Bloodlist *started out in third person, but switched to first, which has become a kind of trademark of yours. Do you write your first drafts in first person from the start, or do you fluctuate styles from draft to draft?*

The first draft of my first book began in third person, but after 20 pages it just wasn't working for me. I had to get inside this guy's skin and sweat with him to be able to fully tell his story. Once I switched to first person—which some people have told me is supposed to be a difficult point of view to write, but I've never found it so—it all came together. I've done many third-person stories and novels, but the Jack Fleming, Jonathan Barrett, and Quincey books are in first person. Strahd had to be in first person because it was a memoir. That was the best point of view to tell their stories. I don't fluctuate; the characters tell me whether they want to be first or third person before I ever begin.

When combining horror with noir, are you influenced more by noir *books or movies? Which ones?*

Just about all of them, equally. I love the old Universal monster films and the Bogart films and anything by Hammett, Chandler, and the other *noir* writers of the Golden Age. And I'm a *Dark Shadows* geek. 'Nuff said!

Is vampire feeding a metaphor for sex, a particular sex act, or unrelated to sex?

In my universe the vamps engage in blood-drinking during orgasm to draw out the climax for both (consenting) partners. It's pretty intense for them—and very nice!—but they do not rely on that small amount of blood for the totality of their nourishment needs. They could—but it would damage or kill their partner and they aren't that inconsiderate! When they really chow down, livestock is their prime food, and it's about as sexy as brushing your teeth. You try biting a stinky, hairy cow in the leg and see if it's a turn-on. If it is, get therapy. Fast.

Horror as a genre has had its ups and downs, but through it all, the vampire seems to be a staple of the monster community more than any other. Any thoughts as to why?

They're sexy, have the coolest clothes, the best lines, live forever, and are at the top of the food chain. What's not to like?

Has the vampire reached/will it reach a point of over-saturation in modern culture?

Only if it's picked up and endlessly repeated on CNN and other related news venues. I doubt that will happen while there are still real monsters roaming the world.

Were The Vampire Files *originally meant to be as long-lived as it has been?*

You can thank my publisher for offering a new writer a 6-book contract right from the start. It got addictive, so I keep writing them, watching the characters grow and change and people keep buying them. I'm delighted about it.

What were the conscious decisions you made in order to keep your vampires from being cliché?

Keeping them human and their actions and reactions realistic. Just because they've had a change in diet doesn't mean they automatically come out all over in cliché-cooties. They are the product of their past the same as the rest of us. Like Jack for example—he wouldn't be caught undead in an opera cape, preferring his double-breasted suit with a fedora. Quincey's more comfortable in his riding clothes, etc. neither of them in present times would be much interested in the Goth scene; their personalities aren't wired to that sub-culture.

Then there's the 'big bad' factor. Sure, they can kill people and maybe get away with it, but they're basically decent fellas. They can get conflicted when the temptation arises to do something bad for a good reason, *but* they get into *big* trouble when they take a dark path. I always have consequences. Mindless killing machines, angsty drama queens or ego-driven power junkies who are just devices for a tired plot and the like bore me as a reader and a writer so I avoid such characters.

What prompted you to provide an 'Alternate' viewpoint on the actions of Van Helsing in Quincey Morris, Vampire?

I loved what Fred Saberhagen did with him in *The Dracula Tape* and wholly agree. I was careful in Quincey to write something that was consistent with Fred's very perceptive view. I *so* respect that man! He accomplished something truly different with the genre when he wrote that one, so my hat is off to him. When you read the original *Dracula* with a neutral eye on Van Helsing you'll find he is not a very nice man at all.

Was Charles Escott based at all on Sherlock Holmes?

If you read the clues I've dropped throughout the books you'll work out that Escott is Holmes's son from a liaison that took place during the

'Adventure of Charles Augustus Milverton.' I did detailed research to get his date of birth correct and made logical projections on his upbringing. I'm a Sherlockian, and love putting in-jokes in for my friends in that fandom.

Example: His full name is Charles William Escott. Obviously his mother Agatha named her blessed event after her employer (Milverton) and the father: William Escott—which was the alias Holmes used on that case. I get such a kick doing stuff like that!

Did you have a say in your co-author Nigel Bennett reading the Keeper Of The King *audiobook?*

I had no say. No writer does. The producer for the tape hired Nigel to read the script, and it was a logical as well as brilliant decision for him to perform his own words.

What did you think of his performance?

Outstanding. As always. He is a hell of a fine actor, always delivers above and beyond and on exactly the right note. I have a tremendous respect for his talent, focus, concentration, and instincts.

When editing Dracula In London, *were you concerned that each writer's unique voice would make certain stories difficult for a lover of Stoker to buy into?*

Not at all. I knew that each writer would offer a unique take on the character, and they delivered as I knew they would. I'm still tickled over the collection. The anthology has a good variety of levels from silly to sublime, so there's something for everyone. It helps for a Stoker fan to have a sense of humor, because I sure do!

You mention on your website, you note that while you probably won't be writing any more I, Strahd *books, that 'Bits of him' might make it into other novels under a different name. Has this come to pass?*

Some of his attitude is bound to pop up again in my writing simply because it is me doing the writing. It certainly did in *Quincey Morris*. Much of the Dracula in that one was like Strahd, since Strahd was much like Dracula.

When you're not writing, what do you like to do to relax?

I watch *Stargate SG-1*. Richard Dean Anderson. Woof. [Elrod faints here. Totally relaxed.]

What can you tell us about the projects you have in the works?

That I'm working on them as *fast* as I can!!!!! You want updates, just check my website. We keep it current.

JASPER FFORDE

FOLLOWING HIS CHILDHOOD IN MID-WALES, Jasper Fforde began with a career as a focus-puller for such films as *Goldeneye* and *Quills* before going on to pursue his dream of full-time author. His first work, *The Eyre Affair*, is a kind of cockeyed SF/slipstream story taking place within an alternate history take on Great Britain, where the Crimean War is still going on and cloning dodos for house pets is the order of the day.

Other topics include the heroine and literary detective Thursday Next rescuing Jane Eyre from those who have kidnapped her from her own book.

When not writing, reading, or spending time with family, Jasper can be found flying his biplane somewhere over Wales. His website is located at: jasperfforde.com.

Were you concerned that The Eyre Affair *would be difficult to market because its eclectic nature?*

I had no market strategy at all. My first four novels were written for me and no-one else. I wrote because I enjoyed it and although I thought they might have broader appeal, I was met with earth shattering indifference every time I approached an agent/publisher. I wrote five books before someone expressed an interest—my second book was even a sequel to my first book which I couldn't get a publisher for, so perhaps that gives you some idea of the lack of intelligent strategy!

What motivated you to pick first-person narrative?

TN1 was third person up until about a month before the first draft was finished. Thursday seemed a bit cardboardy and distant to me so I thought I would go into her head and find out what she thought at close quarters. I converted the whole book from third to first. Small errors and idiosyncrasies still survive like flies in amber—most notably the flashback format for the chapter in which she meets Hades for the first time—as originally drafted the action moves between Snood and Thursday and Buckett and Styx with a good pace, but once first person she can't know what's going on so flashback seemed the best way to tell it. The chapter with Mycroft sending Polly into Daffodils was also a problem—Thursday doesn't appear at all. Solution: the old Mycroft was to tell me later... ploy. Once I had moved to first person she had a lot more warmth—I don't think she would be half as likeable without it—from other people's point of view I'd think she'd appear hard as nails and pretty cold.

Your work reminds me a bit of Grant Morrison's. Are you a reader of his work?

Not at all. I'd never be so rude as to suggest I'd never heard of him, but then he's not heard of me, either. I tend to sit in a bit of a contemporary fiction hermitage, really—my modern SF read list pretty much composes of *The Sentinel, Slaughterhouse 5, Tiger, Tiger,*—and all of *Wyndham*—is he contemporary or classic? Anyway, I'm more a Wells and Verne man—I just love the Gothic appeal, the low technology and passionate plot-lines, superb characterisation, high drama. I've attempted two pure SF books written in the last decade but couldn't get beyond page eight. Dense, very dense. (Me, not the book—or perhaps both). In fantasy the list is even smaller. *Wizard of Earthsea* is the only one I can think of, apart from the *Narnia* series (required reading for my generation!) and Mervyn Peake, TH White.

Did the plot of The Eyre Affair *come first, or the character of Thursday Next?*

About neck and neck. The plot was vaguely there but Thursday was equally as important. Without someone you care about to guide you through the bizarre world, then it's just a huge heap of wacky ideas cobbled together. I've always been at pains to make the odd world in which she resides nothing more than wallpaper to what is important to her: Truth, justice and Landen, although not necessarily in that order.

Do you write from an outline or just let the story unspool as it will?

I used to just let the story unspool but now I have to write a book a year I take more care over outlines; that's not to say I follow them, but at least I know the main thrust of the story and the two major subplots; I like to improvise and ideas, I find, beget new ideas as I write them, so I like to keep my plans fairly loose. I think it counts for the complexity of the plots and subplots; if I have an idea I tend to lay it over the top of the others and just stitch it in. It's misdirection, really—keep the pace and action tight and all the errors are glossed over—like rocks beneath a fresh fall of snow.

Did you originally intend the world(s) of Thursday Next as ongoing, or did Thursday's universe end up demanding it?

The existence of this world came about through absolute necessity. I wanted Thursday Next to be the person she is and do the things she does but she didn't really fit into the way we did things in our world. Instead of modifying her to fit in with us I thought I would modify our world to fit in with her. It started simply enough with everyone having an increased interest in things literary but her world grew even weirder every day and before I knew it I had thirty different SpecOps divisions policing everything from recapturing werewolves to looking after ripples in Spacetime. I had the Crimean war still raging, an all-powerful Goliath Corporation, Czarist Russia, reverse engineered pet dodos and Wales a Socialist Republic. It's a bit like eating Pringles—difficult once started to be able to stop.

What makes a cinematographer want to become a writer?

I think it's the other way round. From an early age I knew I wanted to work in *story* but saw movies as the only way to do it—writing was something that intelligent people do—not for the likes of me. By the time I was in my late twenties I realized that I could write for fun and no-one could stop me, but carried on working in the film industry to pay the bills. I wrote for ten years as a hobby; staying in the grade of Focus Puller for far to long to enable me to do it. In the perverse way that the universe works, I had decided to slow down the writing and concentrate on lighting—when I get published. Funny how things turn out.

When writing, do you miss the excitement of a movie set?

I miss the people, yes—and a movie set is an exciting place to be—but in my own little way I've got a huge movie set of my own, right in font of me—and I get to design sets, cast who I want and can do as many retakes as I want—within reason!

The Eyre Affair has multiple levels in its storytelling—how did you know when to stop the story from expanding where it did?

The multiple levels are there through an accident, really. I started with the original story which was only with Jane Eyre, then added subplots as I tinkered with the plot. The Crimean war and the plasma rifle came first, then Landen, then Goliath, then Hades in bed with Goliath and finally the Spike Interlude and her father dealing with the French Revisionists and the Shakespeare authorship. It looks a bit like a strata in rock—you can tell the oldest subplot by the proximity to the end—the closer it is, the older it is—TN has about four endings, I think!

Were you concerned at all about how your work would be received by American audiences?

Of course—nervous as hell—who wouldn't be? I had no idea whether they would love it or hate it. But my US publisher thought it would so I was kept buoyant by their enthusiasm. I didn't think it would sell beyond the UK and now—quite apart from the deal in the States—Thursday will be translated into Japanese, Korean, Hebrew, Chinese, French, German, Dutch and Croatian. I have a healthy following in Australia and New Zealand, too—and recently went on a tour in Singapore. Books, I have found, are a very global thing—but they would be—*story* is one of the human fundamentals.

In works like The Eyre Affair, *where the plotting is especially complex, dialogue can become a casualty, with lines between characters becoming interchangeable. How did you manage to retain the unique voices of your characters?*

You mean I got away with it? [big sigh of relief] All my characters by definition have to be different versions of me, and I suppose that's the trick although dialogue itself is only half the game. When I set up a character (I hope) I set them up so the reader fills in the blanks—to be honest, most of the hard work is done by the reader; I just throw up a few flags to guide them down the course.

Can someone who has not read Jane Eyre *still enjoy* The Eyre Affair?

I hope so—I considerately put in a précis of Charlotte's work for anyone who hasn't read it. Thursday explains it to Bowden on a car journey—hopeless exposition, I admit, but for the different ending plot device to work, the reader had to know what was going on.

How did you know you had a passion for writing rather than more a love of reading?

Difficult to say. How do you know that you enjoy anything? Writing, despite the great deal of fun I have with it, is still very much agony and ecstasy—agony when things don't work out well, but ecstasy when the pieces start to interlock; it's an odd experience—and the fact that you do it on your own is even odder. Painters and sculptors must go through a similar thing, I should imagine.

Your first book started as a script, went to short stories, then became a novel—will readers see any of your short fiction in print?

Eventually, I hope. The early ones were a bit ropey but they can be de-roped and served up as a cold buffet in between main courses.

Why did you make Acheron Hades the third most evil person in the world? Why not higher or lower in the rankings of evildom?

What is the fun of having a character who is the most evil man on the planet? It's a cliché. But Acheron being the third points not only to him being a bit crap as an evil genius, but also to a larger world outside the boundaries of the book. Who, given Hades obvious homicidal tendencies, is the first and second? And what do they do to achieve such a ranking? And who keeps the rankings? Do they have a self-help group with people like Blofeld and Moriarty?

Do you have any plans for stories outside Thursday's world?

Plenty. Thursday is one facet of a writing style that I hope to develop over the years. I've been only doing this two years. I am a fledgling author. I have much to learn.

Has there been any interest by filmmakers to bring Thursday to the big screen?

Plenty. But it's like selling your house with all the furniture, books and knick-knacks that you've accumulated over the years, handing the keys to someone who can burn it down if they want and never turning back. I've been in the film industry for a long time and know what a hopeless mess even well intentioned filmmakers can make out of even half decent material. That's my job. No-one is going to screw it up except me. Besides, if I make it and it turns into a hopeless piece of crap, I can always claim that this was the effect I was looking for—and who can argue?

You've said that when all was said and done with The Eyre Affair, *you managed to get your 'Own mammal out of the fish at the very end—even if it is a duck-billed platypus.' What sort of animal would* Lost In A Good Book *be?*

An echidna. Lays eggs and suckles it's young. Weird. Must have been a genetic resequencing experiment in a parallel universe.

You steered away from Jane Eyre having too much dialogue in The Eyre Affair, *but in* Lost In A Good Book, *you take more liberties with Miss Havisham of* Great Expectations *and the Cheshire Cat. Were you apprehensive of how you would go about this?*

Not really—the Cheshire Cat is such a very clear-cut character that he is relatively easy to appropriate—his non-sequiturs are wonderful and it is a joy to carry them on. Miss Havisham I wanted to add a bit more to—take the cranky, sad old man-hater and give her a new direction—hunting down bad guys or schooling the impetuous new girl, Thursday Next. Thursday is quite tough and I wanted someone who bullies and browbeats her in almost every line of dialogue—but even Havisham has a weakness—anything with an engine. I liked that. Feisty old girl, really.

What other literary figures will you cover in the next two Thursday Next novels?

I'm not sure. TN3 features a lot from Wuthering Heights but quite a few others. There is a limit to how many new people I can introduce; many characters carry on from one book to the next—and new characters always have to be introduced for a good reason—they have to be actually part of the plot or the joke wears thin very quickly. I have a problem using anything in copyright, too—so when I want to pastiche contemporary novels I tend to make up writers and novels—Daphne Farquitt is a terrible romantic fiction writer, for instance.

*Ron Hogan asked you if you could step into any book, which would it be? You answered him (*The Little Prince*) but said you'd have to think about it in case someone asks. I'm asking.*

Ideally, I'd like to travel around in books like Thursday does, but doubt I'd find them as I had expected—perhaps it would be better to stay away. How many people have you looked forward to meeting and then been disappointed? Anything created by a human will always have our frailties and faults inbuilt into it—although The Little Prince looks fantastic from the outside, perhaps inside it's not all it seems. Mind you, that's probably only the story-teller in me saying that!

JOE R. LANSDALE

Joe R. Lansdale has long made a mark on various genres, including, but not limited to, the worlds of horror and suspense, giving way to the term 'Mojo Storytelling', in other words, his unique stamp of Texas settings, believable characters finding themselves in unbelievable situations.

In addition to Joe's trademark storytelling, he's also been practicing martial arts for over thirty years, and is an inductee of the International Martial Arts Hall of Fame and owns Lansdale's Self Defense Systems. He also holds several belts in a variety of martial arts, including American Combat Kempo and Aikido.

With the latest of Joe's film projects, *Bubba Ho-Tep* (starring Bruce Campbell, Ossie Davis and Reggie Bannister and directed by Don Coscarelli) garnering rave reviews, Joe continues to show the enthusiasm and dynamics that fans first saw in his debut novel, *Act Of Love*.

Joe lives in Nacogdoches, Texas, with his wife, Karen, writer and editor. His website can be found at joerlansdale.com.

How has living in Nacogdoches influenced your writing?

I love it here. The place is pretty and it's got a lot of character. There is a dark side to any place, and as a crime writer, I tap into that kind of feel, but, I could certainly write totally different types of novels about the same place. And I think that's true of most places.

You haven't been confined to one particular genre: you're just as well known in horror, western, and thrillers. How do you manage to maintain this variety with the whims of the market and/or publishers?

I've really just tried to pursue what I want to write. I've also done a few jobs for hire, but mostly, anything under my name, I wanted to do.

Have you been told by a publisher or editor to only write within a given genre?

When I first started it came up, but I never really paid it any attention.

On the subject of the Bubba Ho-Tep *film, how has your overall experience with this project been?*

Wonderful. Don has really worked close with me and he tried to make it as much like the novella as possible, and I think he did a wonderful job.

Has it been picked up for distribution?

There's interest right now, so we'll see. This is all up to Don, and what he decides to do, but the interest is there.

The film, like the story it's based on, has roots in the elderly and some of the less appealing things that can go along with age—were you concerned this might be overshadowed by the humor in the film?

That's a lot of what I do. Not every time out, but much of the time. In the story I wasn't overly concerned with it since it's close to my own nature, but I feared the film might not be able to do this. It did. And in spades. It's a fine piece of work.

Are you pleased with Bruce Campbell's performance in the film?

More than pleased. I think it's his finest performance.

How was the Bubba *experience different from the adaptation of your short stories 'Drive-In Date' and 'The Job'?*

Well, it was a much bigger film, known actors. I really didn't have much to do with the others, besides providing a script for *Drive-In Date*. They are both pretty close adaptations, however, and aren't bad at all.

At a screening of Bubba Ho-Tep *at the Egyptian in Hollywood, Bruce (along with Sam Raimi) put a vote to the crowd regarding a possible sequel to* Bubba Ho-Tep: Bubba Nosferatu *or* Bubba Sasquatch. *The former won out. Your thoughts?*

No sequels.

How has your achievements in the martial arts helped with your writing?

Confidence. Economy of motion. Discipline.

In a story introduction in High Cotton, *you mention 'there's humor in horror'. Why do you think that, and is this a liability to horror being taken seriously as a genre?*

Fall on a banana peel, that can be funny. It can also be deadly. That pretty much explains it. It has two sides.

Can we expect any more alternate history stories from you?

I wouldn't be surprised.

Do you have anything in the works right now?

Nothing right now, but I like alternate histories.

Do you find yourself second-guessing your decisions while editing from one draft to another?

Sometimes. But I only do one draft, then a correction. I don't do multiple drafts, with a few exceptions. I also make editorial changes when necessary and correct.

In 'A Hard-On For Horror: Low-Budget Excitement', you mention 'the Sunday-School terrors of the Bible' as one of your first exposures to horror. Did this kind of influence stick with you into your professional writing career?

Without a doubt. I see it in a lot of my work. Most.

Is there any example in particular?

It's full of murder and disease and incest and horrid punishments for little to nothing. God is such a bully in the Old Testament. Even Abraham seems to be less caffeine impaired when the discussion of Sodom and Gomorrah comes up. Abraham has to calm God down, talk him into sending in angels and Lot. And, of course, to save the angels, who can't be hurt, Lot offers his daughters to the crowd that wants to have sex with the angels. You know, 'Hey, take my daughters instead.'

Did you find your own voice by (for want of a better word) imitating writers you admired?

I started out imitating, but found myself drifting more and more toward writers who had a voice similar to my own, then I found my own.

Is this a route you'd suggest to beginning writers?

I don't know what route to take. Most of us start out copying writers we love. Too many writers stay there, or never find a voice. It's been all important for me.

Is there a book you wish you'd written?

Well, I'm still young enough to have a couple books I want to write that I've yet to write, but I can't say there's anything I wish I had written. I'm still granting my own wishes at this stage.

How is the book of memoirs going?

Slowly. Too many things more immediate. I hope to get serious about it in the next couple years.

Some of your work, like Magic Wagon *and* The Drive-In *are difficult to put in one particular genre. In these cases, did you market them differently to their publishers than you usually would? If so, how?*

I was asked to do both of them. An editor named Pat LoBrutto, who I believe to be one of the most important editors of the early Eighties was at Doubleday, and he liked a short story of mine he'd read, asked me for a proposal. I gave him one for *The Magic Wagon*. He liked it. I wrote it. It sold out immediately after a rave review in *The New York Times* and elsewhere, and, of course, they never reprinted it. He read an article

I wrote for *Twilight Zone Magazine* on drive-in theaters, and there was one part of it that had a fantasy element, he asked me if I thought it would make a novel. I did, and it became one. Really no problem with them. Only problem was *The Drive-In* got chopped little more than a couple, three weeks out the door. By this time it was getting great reviews and people wanted it. Not available. But the reputation led to another *Drive-In* book.

How do you maintain your enthusiasm for the Hap and Leonard stories?

I just like those guys and that they try to be good men under extraordinary circumstances. I do take breaks from them, and there is some possibility that it'll be awhile before another Hap and Leonard, and some small possibility there won't be anymore. I have one partially written, and would love to get back to it someday.

A Fine Dark Line is told from a thirteen year-old boy's point of view; was it influenced by your own at that age?

Much of it was. We weren't quite as well off at that family, but many things were similar, though I stress most of it was not.

Some of your work can be consider noir. Did the classic 'noir movies' influence this more, or was it the novels of that era?

Both. I really like the early and middle period Gold Medal novels, and the flavor was there in many of them, even into the Seventies.

What can you tell us about the projects you have in the works?

I'm working some short stories right now, have a novel for Knopf, a few things of mine are being adapted to comics and film.

Just finished a long short story called 'Bill, The Little Steam Shovel.' Has steam shovel angst, love, sex, and heroics, as well as happy decimation of the environment, but, ultimately, a happy ending. Sort of. Working on other stories for a collection, and then back to work on novels.

In the words of Michael McCarty; Any last words?

Happy reading.

GEOFFREY A. LANDIS

GEOFFREY A. LANDIS HAS SEEN HIS WORK receive the honors of both the Nebula ('Ripples on the Dirac Sea,' 1990), and the Hugo not once, but twice ('A Walk in the Sun'; 1992, and 'Falling Onto Mars'; 2003)and the respect of SF readers, writers and editors everywhere. More than sixty short stories and novelettes of Geoffrey's have been published, with his first novel, *Mars Crossing* coming from Tor Books in 2000 and his short story collection, *Impact Parameter* being published in 2001.

He is also busy in the field of science, working for NASA as a researcher and as a poet, with more than twenty of his works appearing in print. In 2001, he returned to Clarion as an instructor along with his wife, Mary Turzillo (Mary's short story 'Mars Is No Place For Children' won the Nebula in 2001).

Geoffrey has published over 250 scientific papers in the field of and astronautics, among others, and is a member of a mysterious organization known as the Cajun Sushi Hamsters, also known as the Cleveland Science Fiction Writers Workshop (http://critters.critique.org/hamsters/)

Geoffrey's website can be found at www.geoffreylandis.com.

How have events like the moon landing and the current exploration of Mars changed the face of SF as we know it?

The easy answer is that the moon landing and robotic missions to Mars have changed SF by taking away the settings of we knew from old science fiction—the elder races of Mars, the swamps of Venus—and replaced them with worlds that are less interesting, or at least less swarming with life. It forced the science fiction of the Seventies and Eighties to either move outward, away from the solar system, and toward interstellar space, or toward the near-future thrillers on our own planet. But lately there's been a renaissance of stories set in our own solar system, where I think science fiction writers have been beginning to realize that the solar system is still, in its own way, weird and wonderful, and that there are still stories you can set here.

Do you support the idea of a manned mission to Mars?

Yes, of course, I think we need frontiers, and we need humans to explore them. Robots are great, but it's like sending a robot on vacation to send back picture postcards—it's nice, but it's not the same as going yourself. Let's go!

Your work features the element of the human condition within the world of 'Hard' SF, an element sometimes missing in the genre. How do you manage to maintain it in your stories?

Well, good stories are always stories about people. And I love science.

What was the inspiration that led you to write your first novel, Mars Crossing?

Actually, it was sort of an accident. My agent, Ashley Grayson, suggested that I should write about Mars. This was not too long after the Pathfinder mission, and he suggested I should write an outline to pitch to the movies, or for a television mini-series. I wasn't sure I had anything to say, but the more I thought about it the more ideas I had, so I wrote an outline, and then turned it into a novel. Looks like he was right about the idea of a Mars movie, but probably a little late—three of them came out the year after *Mars Crossing* did.

You wrote a Sherlock Holmes pastiche, The Singular Habits Of Wasps. *What is your opinion of other author's work in that area; Michael Dibdin's* The Last Sherlock Holmes Story, *for instance?*

Have to admit that I haven't read that one. What I like about the Sherlock Holmes stories is the characters, and I'd say I like about any story that gets the characters right.

'Ripples on the Dirac Sea' is one of my favorite stories of yours. What can you tell us about the writing of it?

I wrote 'Ripples' when I was in grad school. I plotted it out while I was daydreaming in an advanced quantum mechanics class (maybe if I'd paid attention, instead of daydreaming about science fiction, I'd have a better understanding of quantum field theory.) I wanted to write a story where the physics was real physics, a little past the usual simplifications you get in science fiction, although I do have to admit that I put together a bunch of ideas in a way that they're not really meant to fit together. And then, I entered high school right at about the peak of the hippy era. Things went weird from there, I'd guess—who would have predicted the seventies? The San Francisco summer of Love was a real place and time, vanished now, a different world.

You have not only written novel-length and short stories, but also comprehensive papers on science. Have you had any difficulty in shifting from one to the other?

I like writing science papers—it's like science fiction, but without the characters.

Can you tell us something about yourself that your readers don't know?

Sometimes when I walk by, people spontaneously explode. Oh, wait, you wanted something truthful?

With the writing outside of fiction that you've done, what is special for you about the genre of SF?

Well, I love science fiction—there's just a thrill from writing science fiction that doesn't come from anything else, it's participating in a community of people that like to think, like to be exposed to outrageous concepts and have their imaginations stretched. I guess in some ways I'm still trying to write something that would recapture the feelings I had when I was 13, when everything I was reading was new, and all the concepts were new and all were mind expanding. I really want to impress myself.

What first sparked your interest in science?

I've been interested in science for as long as I can remember. One of the first books I can remember reading, other than Dick and Jane and Doctor Seuss books, was a little children's book called *You Will Go To The Moon*. I didn't realize it at the time, but it was quite an odd book—written in second person future tense. At age 4 or 5, I had no notion that this was something unusual...

You've said that there have been some characters that you have written that you haven't liked. Who is the character you like the least, and was that a liability to telling the story?

Did I say that? No, I love all my characters—it's a occupational hazard with writers, I think. But then, sometimes I do write stories with villains in them—not very often—but sometimes. I had a story 'Meetings of the Secret World Masters,' in a volume called *Saving the World* edited by Charles Sheffield, that had some villains that I found quite slimy. (That story really was a novel, but I realized when I tried to start it that I didn't have the time to learn the biology I needed to write it the way I wanted to.)

What's it's like to live with another author in a two award-winning household. (He's married to Mary Turzillo, both have won Nebulas, Mary's short story in 2000, 'Mars Is No Place For Children.')

The great advantage with living with another writer is that when I want to ignore everything and go up into my study and write, she understands and doesn't interrupt. With the Mars mission and other things recently, though, I haven't had much time to do that—Mary keeps telling me she's going to lock me in the office and not let me out until I can show a thousand words...

You have also written humor; what are the particular difficulties in approaching a humorous slant in SF?

Science fiction has always been rather friendly to humor—Robert Sheckley and William Tenn, for example, were both writers I used to enjoy a lot of when I was a kid. A lot of the humorous stuff I've written are actually pieces that I wrote with no other intent than to amuse myself, and maybe a couple of friends, and then only later decided, hey, that's not bad, maybe I'll send it out.

Given what we now know about Mars, are the older SF stories still relevant?

Well, not as stories about Mars, perhaps, but they can still be good stories. Zalazney's 'A Rose for Ecclesiastes,' for example, still packs a punch even though the Mars he wrote about never existed. Even Wells—*War Of The Worlds* is a landmark story that still works for me.

Who (other than your wife) do you think you could survive being locked up with on the way to Mars?

Wow, that's a tough one. Somebody who knows how to fix the life support system when it breaks down, I'd say! Just give me a pile of good books, a porthole to gaze out of, and some earplugs.

What makes you laugh?

One time I was at the Nebula awards, and I sat at the bar between Karen Joy Fowler and Tim Powers. That was probably the funniest experience I've ever had—they just played off each other, Karen with her sly humor and Tim topping everything she said with something even more outrageous. I just sat there and tried not to explode.

MARK McLAUGHLIN

MARK MCLAUGHLIN'S FICTION, nonfiction and poetry have appeared in more than 600 magazines, newspapers, anthologies and websites, including *Horror Garage, Black October, The Black Gate, Galaxy, The Book Of All Flesh* and its companion anthologies, and two volumes each of *The Best Of The Rest, The Best Of HorrorFind,* and *The Year's Best Horror Stories.* Past collections of his work include *ZOM BEE MOO VEE* (fiction and poetry, Fairwood Press), *Hell Is Where The Heart Is* (fiction, Medium Rare Books), *Motivational Shrieker* (fiction, Delirium Books), *Professor LaGungo's Exotic Artifacts & Assorted Mystic Collectibles* (poetry, Flesh & Blood Press), *Men Are From Hell, Women Are From the Galaxy Of Death* (poetry, Kelp Queen Press), and new hardcover collections of his fiction include *Slime After Slime* (Delirium Books) and *At The Foothills Of Frenzy And Other Freakish Forays* (written with Shane Ryan Staley and Brian Knight, Solitude Publications).

Also, he is the co-author, with Rain Graves and David Niall Wilson, of the poetry collection *The Gossamer Eye*, which won a Bram Stoker Award for Superior Achievement in Poetry. Ellen Datlow, horror editor for The Year's Best Fantasy & Horror, has called him 'The Clown Prince of Horror.' His work with Michael McCarty (a frequent collaborator) has included co-writing the novel *Monster Behind the Wheel*, which became a Bram Stoker Finalist.

Visit Mark on the web at either horrorgarage.com or geocities.com/mcmonstrous.

You are able to use humor to great effect in your work. How do you decide when it's too much?

For me, adding humor to any horror or other story I might write is like shaking salt over a steak. I know how much to put on while I'm doing the shaking. If I get a little shake-happy, I can always scrape some off. But I'm more likely to salt every bite.

I should add, I'm using salt as a metaphor and do not actually condone the use of excess salt.

With such an eclectic body of work, how do you view yourself in the genre? Where if at all do you fit?

I sometimes worry about fitting into my slacks, especially if I've had a few too many desserts that week, but other than that, I don't care. I view myself as Mark McLaughlin and that's it. The late Karl Edward Wagner, editor of those great old *DAW Year's Best Horror books*, reprinted some of my work in that last two volumes of that series, and he once gave me the best advice of my life. He said, just be yourself.

I do find myself evolving a little bit every now and then into a slighter different, perhaps wiser Mark McLaughlin, but I don't, and never will, do it to fit in anywhere. I do it because I'm a living thing, and living things are meant to change.

As a writer who is also known as an artist, who are some of the artists you like in the horror genre?

Sandra DeLuca and Jeffrey Thomas are both artists/writers, like me, I and I really like their work. The work of the artist GAK has a fun, cartoony, bizarre quality that I enjoy. Chad Savage does wonderfully Gothic work.

What can you tell us about the chapbook Right House On The Left *and the story collection,* At The Foothills Of Frenzy And Other Freakish Forays?

Both projects contain stories written by myself and two other writers (different writers for each). Right House On The Left contains stories about evil houses, and my story in that chapbook is an homage to every haunted house story ever written and filmed. It is entitled 'Don't Look In The Little Storage Room Behind The Furnace' and would make a very good film starring Johnny Depp. I urge Hollywood to fling money at me so they can option it. Folks wanting to learn more about the chapbook should visit www.novellopublishers.com.

At The Foothills Of Frenzy is a much more elaborate production. In that one, all three of us contributed several stories apiece, and then each of us wrote a story killing off one or both of the other two, and then all three of us wrote the title story together. Co-author Brian Knight kills me off in one story, and then I kill off the other co-author, Shane Ryan Staley, in a story entitled 'Give Us This Day Our Staley Dead.' This book also contains, among other works, my story 'The Astonishing Secret Of The King Of The Cats,' which is a tribute to every musical ever set in a sewer or dump. There are more than you may realize. The title story is a Nancy-Drew-meets-H.P.-Lovecraft-meets-Caligula type of opus, one which must be read to be believed. Look at www.solitudepublications.com to find out more.

Slime After Slime *has sold out before its release. What sort of things can those who pre-ordered a copy expect?*

Readers can expect a startling and robust range of depraved characters for their amusement. Where else would they be able to find, in one book, The Venereal Avengers? The rock 'n' roll octopus god Kugappa? Santa's murderous elves Smedley and Belvedere? Dr. Seldag and Professor Puthmoor? Mizimba the Internet Witch? A butler named Sputtersworth? The Lactose-Intolerant Whore of Babylon? Cannibal princess Hekuuna? The Beach Blanket Chainsaw Talkin' Pig? Alien porn stars Mocha Sumatra and Jonni Gonad? They are loads of other characters, too.

Not all the stories are funny. There's one story, set in the far future, that's actually rather sad. But, per the book's tile, there's always plenty of slime. For my most loyal readers, I have unleashed the floodgates of my imagination and allowed all sorts of lurid goo to flow over the pages. I should add, I'm using goo as a metaphor and do not actually condone the use of excess goo.

Will Slime After Slime *see a second printing?*

It's a limited-edition collectible hardcover right now, but who knows, maybe someday some publisher will reissue it as a mass-market paperback—if they dare! It's pretty strong stuff.

In Mike McCarty's Dark Duets, *you not only provided the cover art, but you collaborated with Mike McCarty. What do you come away with after a collaboration?*

I've collaborated with many writers over the years, and they've all taught me different things about the craft of writing. Matt Cardin and Michael Kaufmann taught me how to be more serious. Mike McCarty, Jeff Strand, and Mike Philbin taught me new ways to be funny. Mike Arnzen taught me how to be more wicked. I sure do collaborate with a lot of Mikes, don't I? Rain Graves taught me how to be more sensitive.... The list goes on. Collaborating is very much a learning process, and I encourage writers to do it often.

Do you have any magazine or anthology story appearances coming up?

Certainly, yes. Lots. Mike McCarty and I wrote stories for the anthologies In Laymon's Terms, a tribute to Richard Laymon, and also *Aim For The Head*, a zombie anthology. Both of those should be coming out within six months or so, I think. I wrote a story with actress Kyra Schon, who played the little girl in the original *Night Of The Living Dead*, and that will be coming out in *Midnight Premieres* from Cemetery Dance Books. Also, a story I wrote with Matt Cardin, Nightmares Imported and Domestic, will appear in the HWA anthology, *The Dark Arts*. Mike Arnzen and I have a story coming up in Cemetery Dance Magazine—as you can see, a lot of my collaborations find really great homes! I have a story coming up in Kopfhalter! Magazine, and people can always read my online column, 'Four-Letter Word Beginning With F,' in the Features section of www.HorrorGarage.com.

It looks like you mainly concentrate on short fiction, poetry, and some articles. Any novels in the works?

Mike McCarty and I have completed a wild roller-coaster of a horror novel called *Monster Behind The Wheel*, which we've been shopping around to publishers. It's a big, brooding, gruesome tale with a lot of jet-black humor to it. It would make a great movie—Hollywood, are you listening?

What attracted you to the genre of horror to begin with?

As long as I can remember, I've always been attracted to, and often mesmerized by, the strange, the exotic, the extravagant, the dark. My grandmother was an elegant Greek woman who believed in the supernatural, so perhaps I inherited some of that mindframe from her.

I love horror movies—that's what I write about in my online Horror Garage column. Movies are what got me into horror, back when I was a scrawny little teenager. My favorite horror movies include *The Abominable*

Dr. Phibes, Dr. Phibes Rises Again, The Company Of Wolves, The Bride Of Frankenstein, Horrors Of The Black Museum, Theatre Of Blood, and *Werewolf Of London*. All horror movies, no matter how serious, have their moments of humor, whether the writers and directors planned it or not. For example, in *Werewolf Of London*, I think it's hilarious that the werewolf takes a moment to put on a hat. He's a werewolf, fer cryin' out loud—why is he even wearing clothes?

Any other interests besides horror, humor and movies?

I enjoy going to wine tastings. In the past few years, I've made the acquaintance of various friends who have shared their knowledge of fine wines with me, and I find that rather compelling. Basically, wine is just fermented grape juice, and the fermentation has been arrested at an especially tasty point in the process. These tastings are not about getting drunk—they're about savoring the unique character, the subtleties, the craftsmanship of wines. A person doesn't have to drain their bank account to buy a good bottle of wine. I recently enjoyed a fine, reasonably priced Rodney Strong cabernet sauvignon that was very flavorful, with sophisticated hints of cherry and spicy toast. Zed, a New Zealand wine, produces a perfectly affordable sauvignon blanc that is quite crisp, with a zesty, fresh grapefruit tang to it.

What music do you listen to? Goth? Heavy metal?

Mostly high-energy dance mixes, usually British! I especially like all the old '80s Brit pop groups—my favorite is Dead Or Alive. They're still around, still making music. I have every record they've ever done, even from the days when they were known as Nightmares In Wax. The lead singer keeps getting more and more plastic surgery. These days, he looks like a six-foot geisha girl with massive collagen-injected lips. What happens to plump lips like that after the collagen is absorbed by his system? Will they shrink back down, or will he just have really loose lips? I like the Pet Shop Boys—they've had tons of hits of England, though only a few in America. I also enjoy the music of Gwen Stefani, and Scissor Sisters, too.

Which up-and-coming writers do you enjoy reading?

Lee Thomas, who recently won a Stoker Award for his first novel, is a fantastic writer. Charlee Jacob is a great writer—her work is sheer poetry.

All of my collaborators are great—that's why I collaborate with them. My favorite writer who isn't into horror is comedian Lord Carrett—his body of work is his stand-up routine, all the jokes he has told, is telling, and will tell. I think he's the funniest stand-up comedian in the world. His webpage is www.lordoflaughs.com, so check him out.

Do you have any suggestions for other writers that you'd like to share?

Never send out a first draft. After you've finished a story, let it sit for at least a week, then go back in and do some revising. You'll be surprised at all the little things you'll want to change.

Also, as Karl Edward Wagner said to me: Just be yourself. Why try to be Stephen King? The world already has one of him, and he has the headstart advantage! Just be the best you that you can be.

ERIC VAN LUSTBADER

WHEN ERIC VAN LUSTBADER'S first fantasy novel, *The Ring Of Five Dragons*, hit the stands in 2001, the author perhaps better known as the man behind the international thrillers like *White Ninja*, *The Miko*, and *The Sunset Warrior*, to name but a few, delved into the world of the Fantasy series, in this case, *The Pearl*, proving that in that genre as well that he is indeed a force to be reckoned with, and a man of many passions.

In 2004, he also tried his hand at carrying on the legacy of Robert Ludlum's character of Jason Bourne in his novel, *The Bourne Legacy*. This interview was conducted shortly after the release of the movie *The Bourne Supremacy*, and the release of Eric's own Bourne novel.

What kind of research did you do for the tribal dynamic, especially for The Veil Of A Thousand Tears?

I have a good friend who's an Arabist. He travels to the Middle East all the time, speaks perfect Arabic and has even lived in several countries there. I spent a lot of time with him getting to know how Arabs think—Especially the tribal, nomadic Arabs like the Saudis. It was quite an experience and affected deeply how I depicted the tribes in *Veil*.

Several authors have found that they needed to write under pseudonyms in order to stretch out creatively, such as going from international thrillers to fantasy, how have you've been able to avoid this?

I think my fan base is wide and varied enough that they've become used to my going back and forth. After all, I started writing fantasy with *The*

Sunset Warrior trilogy (that subsequently became a series of five novels) before writing *The Ninja*, my first international Best-Seller.

How did the writing of Mistress Of The Pearl *differ from the novels before it?*

It differed significantly because in the middle of the first draft, my father fell ill and died. I thought I'd be prepared for it (he was 90 and had had quadruple bypass some years earlier—an operation from which he almost died), but I was wrong. In the aftermath of his passing, I began to think about love—all the forms of love, not simply romantic love—the love a child has for his parents, love between siblings. The result was that the final version of *Mistress* is underpinned by an exploration of all the forms love can take—some to disastrous effect. After all, which of us has not has his or heart broken or had broken the heart of someone who loved him?

What would your readers be surprised to learn about you?

I've had three careers. I was a public school teacher in NYC, I worked in the music business for 15 years with such greats as Elton John, Bruce Springteen, John Lennon, etc. Through those first two careers, however, I never stopped writing, so I guess it was fated that I become a published author.

What were the genre novels that you read as a youngster?

All the Raymond Chandler mysteries; *Lord of the Rings. Dune*, of course—Frank's exploration of political and religious in-fighting was of great interest to me, a Sociology major in college.

What's your opinion of David Lynch's version of Dune?

The film was dreadful, quite unwatchable, and I didn't care for the recent TV mini-series. I am of the opinion that some stories cannot be adequately filmed. Dune is one of them.

Is there anything new for us to learn about the hermaphroditic Gyrgon?

Tons. You don't expect me to tell you, though, do you?

Are any of your characters based on anyone you know?

Any good writer processes everything he or she sees, hears, loves, hates and fears. These everyday observations get processed and in some form or other come out through the fingertips. I suppose there are bits and pieces of people I know in my characters, but none are actually based on people I know. Rather, they're people I'd like to know!

Some downright bad things happen to your most beloved characters. Does a reader need to actually like a character to be so affected by his/her downfall?

Absolutely. That's one of the keys to good fiction writing. I have no patience for so-called 'great' story-tellers who nevertheless have no idea how to create a real three-dimensional character. Why should I care what happens to any character if I don't believe he or she could exist and don't empathize with the character?

You've gone from Thrillers to Fantasy. Any interest in Science Fiction?

I'm not big on describing hardware; I much prefer exploring the ways in which people interact.

It can be argued SF isn't just about hardware, it can be more about ideas.

Of course. Philip K. Dick is a prime example of this, but hardware does play a huge role in most SF, which seeks to predict (and warn about the dangers of) the future. Fantasy, on the other hand, is more concerned with teaching us the lessons of loyalty, morality, friendship and love—Lustbader's Four Pillars of Fantasy.

Do you have any pet peeves about the genre?

Oh, yes. Epic Fantasy is totally without humor—except for my books, of course! In the beginning, I had the devil's own time convincing my editor to accept Thigpen. But in my opinion without a bit of comic relief, all the action and angst becomes dull and boring.

What do you think about comic-fantasy and all those genre spoofs?

I'm for anything that's good.

What are your plans for your next book—will it be Fantasy or Thriller?

At the moment, I'm at work on an outline for a new Thriller that has me very excited.

20th Century Fox has revived their interest in your novel, The Ninja. *Who would your choice be for casting?*

Well, Nicholas Linnear is half-Japanese, so I would say Keanu Reeves, because he's the right age and he has the right look.

What can you tell us about writing The Bourne Legacy?

I can tell you it was a heckuva lot of fun to write, that I enjoyed every single minute of it, and that I'm extremely proud of it. In fact, it's the Thriller I've been wanting to write all my career: It's non-stop action, but befitting the character of Jason Bourne it's also deeply, deeply emotional.

How did knowing Robert Ludlum as a friend affect the way you wrote Legacy?

I know Jason Bourne inside and out. I don't even have to think which way he'd react in a situation—I simply know. And wherever Bob is now, I know he's as thrilled and proud as I am that his creation has been Bourne again.

Do you have a personal favorite of Ludlum's 'Bourne' novels?

The Bourne Identity was Bob's best novel, period.

What is it about Jason Bourne that makes readers want to continue following his exploits?

First-off, he's a tragic figure. He's lost an entire family—wife and two children. Secondly, he's a man of tremendous integrity immersed in a world of treachery and double-dealing. Finally, he's a man who cannot remember his past. I think this makes him fascinating and, in a way, unknowable. The reader cannot wait to be drawn into his next adventure, because it's sure to reveal another piece of the puzzle that is his former life.

What was writing a post-9/11 espionage thriller like—did you approach it any differently?

Of course. The world is always changing, and your writing has to reflect that. It's interesting to me that in post-9/11 the thriller reader wants to learn about the people who, for whatever reason, want to oppose us. I think very little is really known about Islam and Islamic fundamentalists in this country, and so there are a lot of misconceptions. Part of what I wanted to do when I sat down to plot out *The Bourne Legacy* was to give form and meaning by way of both background and well-rounded characters to those people who were opposing Jason Bourne. I want readers to learn without even know they're doing it.

Do you feel Matt Damon was an accurate portrayal?

I never would have thought of Damon as Bourne, but much to my surprise he created a real-life, flesh-and-blood Jason Bourne right in front of our eyes. Kudos to him, [screenwriter] Tony Gilroy [director] Doug Liman. I understand that the second film, *The Bourne Supremacy* is even better.

Is there anything you'd like to say to Speculative Fiction fandom at large?

It seems to me that back in the day Speculative fiction fandom was more accepting of genre-busting books. Nowadays, everything in the genre is sub-specialized, i.e., Fantasy, Epic Fantasy, Hard Science Fiction, etc. I think this is a shame, because Speculative fiction was born from brilliant writers bent on breaking out of the conventional genres to which they'd been bound for decades.

Does that mean you're opposed to 'genre' label, as some writers are?

Absolutely. People should approach a book for what it is, not seek to put it in a category first and allow that to decide whether or not to read it.

What made you want to make the jump from thriller to starting your own fantasy series, The Pearl?

The question of Technology vs. Spirituality, which is the core theme of *The Pearl* series was simply too big and complex to be able to do in anything but a Fantasy series.

Going back to your first novel, The Sunset Warrior, *what can you tell us about the writing of it, and the inspiration behind it?*

I'd loved SF and Fantasy ever since high school. One day just after I'd graduated college, I ran into an old high school buddy who I hadn't seen in years. It turned out that he was writing a Western series for Avon Books. I thought: Well, if he can do it, so can I! I wrote it on an old manual typewriter my parents had given me for a HS graduation present. I worked so hard and long on it, my father came to my door one day and made me take a vacation!

It seems to me Sirens *is heavier on the psychological aspect of a thriller, would you agree?*

I was a Sociology major at Columbia and at one point was going to become a psychologist. I love dissecting people's motivations—there are always so many layers, and most of them are contradictory.

Having worked in music industry, what sort of music do you listen to while writing?

Right now I'm listening to Franz Ferdinand. The soundtrack to *Lost In Translation* is awesome. Moloko. Bel Canto. Calexico. Paul Oakenfold. An eclectic bunch, and so many more... I must have 20,000 CDs!

What's the continuing appeal of the oriental themes/culture that you have such a passion for?

The Eastern way of life—that is, to let go of everything and accept the chaotic nature of the universe is the polar opposite of Western thought, which seeks (and, of course, fails) to control everything.

PETER S. BEAGLE

PETER S. BEAGLE—AUTHOR, songwriter and the screenwriter who took a swing at adapting J.R.R. Tolkien's masterwork, *The Lord of the Rings* via Ralph Bashski's animated vision—began his writing career at the Bronx High School of Science as a regular contributing writer, followed by a scholarship at the University of Pittsburgh by way of winning a contest by Scholastic Books in 1955. By age 19, he had written what would become a benchmark in Fantasy, *A Fine and Private Place*, and graduated with a degree in creative writing.

A Fine and Private Place was soon followed by *The Last Unicorn*, which not only became a much-beloved novel but also became an equally acclaimed animated feature-length film, now available on DVD. His passion for writing led him to write Ralph Bakshi's 1978 film adaptation of *The Lord of the Rings*, a film that for years seemed the only vision viewers would receive of Tolkien's legendary world of Middle-Earth.

Beagle has also dipped his feet in the waters of the world of *Star Trek: The Next Generation*, and back into his own with a follow-up novelette to *The Last Unicorn, Two Hearts*. His other forays into writing have included the nonfiction *The Garden of Earthly Delights,* the two-volume collections of *Unicorn*-related fantasy, *Peter S. Beagle's Immortal Unicorn* and the novels *The Innkeeper's Song* and *Tamsin*. Peter currently resides in California.

You can find him (unofficially) at peterbeagle.com.

For years, you said you would never write a sequel to The Last Unicorn, *but then came* Two Hearts…*why, after all this time?*

Well, the blunt truth is that I accidentally got prodded into it by my business manager. He wanted me to write a story set 'in the world of *The Last Unicorn*' as a promotional extra for the release of the unabridged *Last Unicorn* audiobook, and he got around all my objections by telling me I didn't have to include any of the characters from the book. And once I started to do what he asked, well, things happened. The truth is that I had never given *any* thought to writing a sequel, but once I began this story that's what came out. I was startled at how easily it came. Maybe because I'm taking another stance altogether, maybe because this time I was telling it from a first person point of view, but as difficult as *The Last Unicorn* was to write, *Two Hearts* was a comparative breeze.

Why is Two Hearts *being published in a limited edition?*

It just seemed like a really intriguing idea to publish a limited hardcover edition as a bonus for the first three thousand people who bought the audiobook. It was something I hadn't done before. I've seen other promotions like it, but the approach was new for me, and that aspect was really appealing.

There's been quite a bit of legal dealing regarding your involvement with both Bakshi's Lord of the Rings *and* The Last Unicorn. *Can you give some details on what's happened?*

With both of them the problems began because I trusted my then-agent. I shouldn't have. In the case of *Lord Of The Rings*, following her advice meant I wound up writing that script God knows how many times, at least eight or nine drafts, for a bunch of never-fulfilled promises and a flat fee of $5,000—the second half of which I actually had to threaten to sue to collect. However you slice it, I was taken advantage of rather badly. Now, my work is what made it possible for Saul Zaentz to complete his film. And the film is what inspired Peter Jackson to read Tolkien, a happy coincidence that has so far directly benefited Saul to the tune of nearly $200 million. So I'm trying, at this late date, to stake my claim—to get Saul to live up to the promises he made and never came through on, all those years ago.

The issue with *The Last Unicorn* is simpler and purely contractual. According to the way my lawyer reads my contract and the financial records, Granada Media International owes me a sizeable chunk of all the money they've been making on the film. They claim otherwise. So we edge closer and closer to court, which is where we're going to wind up unless one side or the other backs down. And I'm not going to back down. People who want to know more should go read the pages they'll find at http://www.conlanpress.com/youcanhelp.

Were you happy with the animated version of Lord of the Rings *and/or* The Last Unicorn?

I thought that the animated *Lord Of The Rings,* was, in an artistic sense, a disaster. I felt the screenplay was extremely good, and I was very proud of having a chance to work with actors like John Hurt and Peter Woodthorpe and William Squires. But I don't think it's much of a movie. I think it might have stood a chance if the second film was made, the way we always planned. But as a single movie I think it's incoherent. A lot of parts got cut up, or shoveled and jumbled together with no discernable pattern or rhythm. And yet it has survived. And I've been told by a fair number of people that they like it better than the Jackson film. I can't imagine saying that or feeling like that, myself, but there you are. As for *The Last Unicorn*, by comparison it is magnificent—at least it follows the story, as much as we could. Some parts of it are better than others.

What did you think of Peter Jackson's film?

I felt it was as good a *Lord Of The Rings* as anybody's every going to get on film. I thought it was a remarkable job, very powerful. Nothing is ever as good as the work of art that you have in your imagination, of course. So many millions of people have their own Middle Earth in their heads, and I've known several who have told me that they were disappointed in the Jackson Films for not living up to *their* personal vision. But in terms of making a film of Tolkien's work, the Jackson movies are it. By the nature of film, I don't see how it could be any better.

Will we ever see a feature-length version of your work,? Maybe A Fine And Private Place? *I remember reading that Richard Dreyfuss was supposed to be in that.*

Dreyfuss was involved in it for a good fourteen years, give or take. For a while the option payments on that were the nearest thing I had to a regular income. But in 2001 we told them they'd have to come up with a full buyout if they wanted to keep it, because we weren't going to renew their option—the amount that had made sense 14 years before was now way too little. And they dropped it, without a word. I've never heard anything from those people again. Them letting go was kind of nice in terms of timing, because it wasn't even two weeks later that Connor Cochran came along wanting to develop the picture. We started working on a new screenplay together, then one thing led to another and he wound up becoming my business manager. Then this last year he set up Conlan Press to do new publishing for me as well. And we're still working on that much-delayed screenplay, reworking scenes, trying to get it right.

I actually do have great hopes for live action versions of both *A Fine And Private Place* and *The Last Unicorn*. There are also other books and stories of mine that I think would make excellent films, but whether or not they'll be made...well, I don't lie awake nights thinking about that. I know better. In Hollywood you just do your best and try to push things towards reality. They'll happen or they won't.

Can you tell us about how you came to write for Star Trek: Next Generation? *['Sarek']*

I'm working on a book called *Writing Sarek* that tells the whole story and goes into lots of detail. But basically it was like this. A science fiction writer named Diana Gallagher called me—at a particularly tight time in my life, financially—to let me know that the third season of the new *Star Trek* was short a couple of scripts. The show was typically house-written, so they very rarely took outside scripts, but now they needed a couple. I literally gambled on selling them something. I arranged to come in and speak, to come down from the Seattle area, where I was living, to meet with Michael Pillar and the other writer-producers. And I knew I was on to something at the point where they stopped taking notes on yellow pads of paper and just started just listening to the stories I was spinning. That's how it happened.

To quote from your song 'When I Was A Young Man,' in The Last Unicorn... *do you feel you have, as the lyrics note, 'Gracefully grown more debauched and depraved?'*

I certainly hope whatever I've done has been graceful. I've always wanted to be graceful and never had to much hope for it. As for debauched and depraved... well, one does what one can.

What attracted you to the genre of 'Fantasy?'

Reading *The Wind In The Willows* when I was in the second or third grade. That was almost certainly the start. My beloved teacher, Margaret Butterweck, sent the book home to me when I was out of school sick (I was sick a lot as a kid). And I knew I'd never read anything like it before, and I just wanted to do *that*. If I had to pick any one book that turned me in the direction of fantasy, more than anything else that would be it.

What is your opinion on the current practitioners of Fantasy?

I don't read a great deal of Fantasy. I mean at this stage in my life I seem to read a lot of history, and I'm reading more poetry than I have for quite awhile. And I love Mysteries, I wish I could write one. But Fantasy? Not so much. There are people I do like very much, and some I admire enormously, like Robin McKinley and Patricia McKillip. My best friend always wanted me to read Guy Gavriel Kay, but I haven't gotten into his work yet. A lot of the time, when I do read fantasy I'm rereading older guys. There are a lot of really good young writers whom I simply don't yet know. I'll make their acquaintance sooner or later.

MICHAEL McCARTY & MARK McLAUGHLIN

Mike, let me start *by congratulating you on winning the David R Collins Literary Award.*

MIKE: Thank you, Cristopher, for the kind words. I was really touched and honored to win the David R. Collins' Literary Achievement Award from the Midwest Writing Center. I don't really see my books as award-winning works, but to be recognized by other writers was one of the proudest achievements in my 25-year writing career as a professional writer. Horror, science fiction and fantasy writers usually don't win that many mainstream literary awards, so this is very special for me.

MARK: Mike has come a long way as a writer and his award is well-deserved. I remember a time, years ago, when he would talk with high hopes of someday becoming the author of a book. Now is the author of several books, with many more on the way, and he always takes the time to encourage and help other authors in both the local community and the world's horror-writing community.

Describe your collaborative novel Monster Behind The Wheel *for those who may be unfamiliar with this wildly entertaining story.*

MIKE: During his childhood, Jeremy Carmichael falls from a Ferris wheel, landing on—and killing—a beautiful woman. Years later, as a young man, he is involved in a horrific car crash. Soon he finds himself transported between the worlds of the living and the dead on an all-too-regular basis.

    Jeremy strikes a bargain— sexual favors in return for reduced car payments—with an older woman, Connie Edmonson, and purchases her car, a 1970 Barracuda. Then all Hell breaks loose—literally. The novel is a surreal helter-skelter ride of thrills, humor, lust, horror and oil changes (not to mention a haunted muscle-car and lots of zombies, too....)

MARK: Jeremy is a highly unusual protagonist. Everything strange happens to him, and there's a reason for that. Jeremy is not like other people, and eventually we learn the reason has something to do with the incredibly powerful River of Time, which runs through the Land of the Dead.

Connie is Jeremy's love interest in the Land of the Living, and the horribly lovely zombie Fiona Bloom is his sweetie-pie in the Land of the Dead. The reader also meets lots of other weird folks, living and dead, as well as a variety of horrific creatures, including the winged things that guard the River of Time and something with the highly appropriate name of Mr. Brown.

What made the two of you want to collaborate on a novel?

MIKE: Mark and I have been friends for over a decade now. We've written many short stories together over the years. Mark had also edited my novella *Liquid Diet*, my vampire satire, which is going to be published from Black Death/Demonic Clown books either in late 2008 or early 2009.

I was working on *Monster Behind The Wheel* as a solo novel and Mark was editing the book for me. He gave me some great advice and guidance. Then Wildside Press offered me a contract for *Giants Of The Genre* and *More Giants Of The Genre*. I was only about half-done with *Monster* at that point, so I asked Mark if he wanted to collaborate and finish the novel, and he did. We wrote and re-wrote so much of the book together, sometimes I'm not sure who wrote what anymore.

MARK: When Mike and I write together, it's like a construction team building a skyscraper. Often he puts in the beams and walls and floors, then I move in and embellish that mighty framework with pipes, wires, furniture, extra doors and windows, even potted plants for the lobby. Sometimes, he'll be working on the foundation while I'm working on the top floor, and then we'll meet in the middle. I defy any construction crew to try that!

When we're working on a short story, we may start with a 1,000-word rough draft that Mike has written. I'll add more characters and plot twists, and then he'll add a little more, and before you know it, the story is 3,500 words long.

At a writing event, a young writer once asked me how my collaborations with Mike worked, and I told him, 'Each of us writes every other word.' Then he had to take off for a workshop, so I never got the chance to tell him I was joking. So somewhere out there, there's a young guy who thinks, 'Wow! Every other word! How do they *do* that?'

As a collaborative effort, what were the challenges involved?

MIKE: Time was the biggest challenge. Both Mark and I had writing careers before writing *Monster* and we had to do our own solo works—short stories, poems, nonfiction articles, etc. We were able to do our solo stuff and still work on the novel as well. It was a great team effort.

The writing of the book went very smoothly. I was writing the book from the beginning to the middle and Mark was working on the end. We met in the middle. Then we switched. He worked on the beginning and I worked on the end. Stylistically, the book seems like it had been written by one person. Sometimes I am not even sure what parts I wrote and what parts Mark wrote, because it flows so well together.

MARK: There would be times when one or the other of us was really busy, and that would bring about some delays. But on the other hand, we were always there for each other, to cheer each other on, and to bug each other to get the lead out! We got the job done because we weren't going to disappoint each other.

Humor and surrealism—both strong points in Monster—*can both be liabilities in horror storytelling. How did you blend those things so well?*

MARK: Mike and I are both wild, energetic guys. That's probably why we get along so well, and have written so much together. We see the humor in everything, and we can also see craziness and horror and just-plain-weirdness in the world around us, too. The world IS a weird, funny, surreal place. Some people say, they'd love to go to another planet to see how creatures on other worlds live. Mike and I would be more likely to say: You want to see strangeness? Alien behavior? Go to different parts of your own city. You don't even have to go that far! Just look at your neighbors!

MIKE: I was a former stand-up comedian so comedy comes natural for me. Plus, I've always been a bit esoteric and that seeps into my writing.

For the surrealism, I am a big fan of such artists as Salvador Dali, René Magritte and Max Ernst. Mark's surreal short stories and poetry have been a big influence on me, too.

MARK: Mike is a natural-born comic—if I've had a bad day, he'll make some funny observation and cheer me up immediately.

Did you ever reach a point in the writing of Monster *where one of you read something the other wrote and said, 'I don't get it?'*

MIKE: Actually it is the complete opposite. I think the thing that Mark brought to *Monster Behind The Wheel* was humor. As a former stand-up comedian, I couldn't let Mark get all the funny lines, so I started writing dark humor as well (including a very long and sick joke in the book).
Mark and I get each other's humor—that's why we're such good friends.

MARK: Another reason we're good friends, and collaborate so well together, is because we work as a team and neither of us is the boss of the other. We don't put a lot of pressure on each other and we don't have a lot of ego trips. So we both are free to write the humorous material that comes naturally to us—we know we won't nitpick each other to death, which would take all the fun out of the writing process.
The protagonist in *Monster*, Jeremy, has the same sense of humor as his creators. And his enemy, the evil Frank, has no sense of humor at all. Boo, Frank! Frank is always trying to control Jeremy, which is, of course, classic villain behavior: trying to make people do things they don't want to do—like die!

There's a good deal of detail to the passion of muscle cars. Are either of you into classic cars?

MIKE: My dad was a mechanic. I've been around cars my entire life. I love muscle cars. The reason I chose a 1970 Barracuda as Monster was that car was completely restyled and re-engineered. It was considered then, and remains to this day, one of the finest muscle car designs from Chrysler Motor Company. The high-performance 'Cuda model came standard with a monster-sized 426 Hemi engine. It was, and still is, a real monster on the road.
I went to a car show in Davenport, Iowa, and saw a black 1970 Barracuda. I had the owner start the engine for me and when he stepped

on the gas pedal, it sounded like a monster roaring. That's how I came up with naming the car Monster.

I've only owned one muscle car, a Dodge Duster from the '70s. It was sweet on the street, and I miss that set of wheels.

MARK: Mike is definitely the muscle-car fan. Over the years, I've driven a dinky red Chevette, lots of beat-up old gas-guzzlers, and an ancient midnight-blue Cadillac. I just drive whatever catches my eye that has wheels. I don't drive muscle cars—I drive flab cars. These days, I hate driving at all because gas costs so much. So I've been riding my ten-speed bike more and more, whenever I get a chance, since it saves money and also helps keep me fit.

What other passions have been fueling (pun sort of intended) your writing as of late?

MARK: Mike and I have always loved monsters, and that has fueled many of our projects. It's fun to write about gruesome, outlandish monsters—the weirder, the better!

You'll notice I didn't say 'big' when talking about monsters. The best thing about monsters is, they come in all shapes and sizes. Mike and I are currently working on a futuristic novel that has huge monsters and also microscopic ones in it.

My solo poetry collection *Phantasmapedia* is all about monsters—32 monsters that live, for the most part unseen, among us. It came out from Dead Letter Press in 2007 and was on the Stoker Award Final Ballot in the poetry category. The second printing is now available from www.DeadLetterPress.com, and I also have a MySpace page for it: www.myspace.com/phantasmapedia. The monsters are arranged in alphabetical order in the collection: the Adipossum, the Brown Creeper, the Control Freak, the Dungfish, the Elefantoccini, the Fire Slug, Glucozoth (the god of candy), the Granddaddy Longlegs, the Heliosaurus, the Internet Witch, the Jellychicken, Kleptomunculi, the Lungpuppy, the Mollywog, the Necromorph, the Oncoloscarabaeus, the Plastozoid, the Polyglotcha, the Quetzalcuckoo, Rat-A-Tattlers, the Sewer Clam, the Theodoptera, the Tumble Roach, the Ultragorgon, the Urban Lamprey, Vyvyka Megamega, the Were-Mannequin, the Xeno Sapiens, the Yellow-Tailed Satanus, the Zumble Bee and the Zzhark.

Also, my story collection *Pickman's Motel* is a hardcover chapbook of Lovecraftian spoofs and satires, from www.DeliriumBooks.com, and it has plenty of ghouls and other monsters in it, including the Heckler in the Ha-Ha Hut, the worst audience member in the entire cosmos.

MIKE: I was just thinking about this very topic a couple of days ago. This year I have three novels schedule to be published. *Monster* is a about a muscle car, *Liquid Diet* is about radio stations and vampires, and *Out Of Time* is about time travel and politics. It's lucky I am a very passionate person—I have many passions I like to write about.

Can you tell us about how promotion for Monster *has been going? Any anecdotes?*

MIKE: Originally *Monster* was going to be published in September 2007 from Sarob Press in Wales—so Mark and I promoted the book throughout 2007. Sarob went out of business before they could publish the book, and so *Monster* is now coming out August 2008 from Delirium/Corrosion Press. You can see the book trailer at our MySpace page, www.myspace.com/monsterbook.

We haven't stopped doing promotion for the book. It seems like one long strange trip. The book has been receiving rave reviews—and even Stoker Award recommendations from reviewers who have read the manuscript in advance. It is quite an honor for both Mark and myself. Between the two of us, we've written story collections, poetry collections, and nonfiction books, but this is the first novel for both of us.

MARK: The promotional video was created by a friend of mine named Steve Couch, who did a fantastic job. The video is on our MySpace page and other choice spots on the Internet. It's fun, figuring out new ways to get the word out about the book.

What can you tell us about your other collaborative books, All Things Dark And Hideous *and* Attack Of The Two-Headed Poetry Monster?

MIKE: *All Things Dark And Hideous* is a short-story collection of our collaborative tales, published in England by Rainfall Books. It features 'Sex, Drugs & Rot 'N' Roll,' 'Military Mite,' 'City Of Two-Thousand Sins,' 'Night Of The Squealers,' 'The Ten-Klown-Mandments' and 'Bride Of Bugboy.' I really love Steve Lines' creepy clown cover—it reminds me of an amped-up John Wayne Gacy, who was Pogo the Clown (he once said, 'I used to love being a clown, it meant you could get away with murder.')

Attack Of The Two-Headed Poetry Monster is a collection of poems written by Mark and myself. There will be something like 100 poems in the book and it should be out pretty close to when *Monster Behind The Wheel* is published. Mark is also doing the artwork. Rain Graves is writing the introduction and Sandy Deluca wrote the afterward. It'll be a kick-ass collection.

MARK: Both of these projects are filled with monsters, freaky pseudo-science, bizarre characters, madness, mayhem, weirdness and wonders. What more can I say? They'd make great Holiday stocking-stuffers!

What other projects are you working on as solo authors?

MARK: I'm working on a solo novel, a story collection, and a poetry collection. Mike's got a full banquet table of literary delicacies coming up—wait until you hear what he's got cooking!

MIKE: I have eight books coming out in 2008 and four in 2009. In 2008, I have:

With Mark:
All Things Dark And Hideous (Rainfall Books, England, short story collection)
Monster Behind The Wheel (Delirium/Corrosion Press, novel)
Attack Of The Two-Headed Poetry Monster (Skullvines Press, poetry book)

With Connie Corcoran Wilson:
Ghosts Of Route 66, Chicago Through Oklahoma (Quixote Press, true ghost tales)
Out Of Time (Lachesis Publishing, novel)

Solo projects:
Little Creatures (Sam's Dot Publishing, short story collection)
Modern Mythmakers (McFarland & Company, nonfiction book of interviews)
Liquid Diet (Black Death/Demonic Clown Books, novella, a vampire satire)

Do you have a favorite work the other has written?

MIKE: That is really hard to answer because Mark has written five poetry collections, five short-story collections and five chapbooks. I'm going to cheat and name one from each category:

From his poetry collections: *Your Handy Office Guide To Corporate Monsters* from Richard Geyer, Publisher. This is sort of like mixing *The Addams Family* with a *Dilbert* comic strip.

From his chapbooks: *Pickman's Motel* from Delirium Books contains three short stories, all set in Arkham, that go all the way from the present back to the Stone Age. I just love this collection to death.

From his short-story collections: *Slime After Slime* from Delirium Books, a top-notch collection of gross-out stories, now available in paperback.

MARK: I would have to say it's Mike's novel, *Liquid Diet*, which hasn't been published yet, but I'm sure it'll find a home soon. It's zany, it's sexy, it lampoons every vampire cliché in literature. I think any vampire who reads it will really enjoy it. I certainly did! (Oops! I've said too much!)

Besides yourself, who would you want to be?

MIKE: Count Dracula, because he gets to bite pretty ladies in the neck. H.G. Wells because he wrote great science fiction and if I had been him, I would have earned a better grade in science class. And Paul McCartney, because he can rock!

MARK: I have no desire to be anyone else. It took a lot of years to become the person I am today—it was a tough job, but somebody had to do it! Why would I want to trade in all that time and effort for another identity?

One of Mike's questions, from the many interviews he has conducted over the years: Any last words?

MARK: Last words? From me? Not any time soon! I love life, I love people—especially my readers!—and I'm going to keep writing, communicating, and sharing my strange dreams and visions as long as I am capable of thought and movement.

MIKE: I'd like to thank you, Cris, for interviewing us, and Mark for being my collaborator. I'd also like to thank Sarob Press and Rainfall Books for publishing our works overseas.

Also, be sure to visit our websites:
   www.myspace.com/monsterbook
   www.geocities.com/mccartyzone
   www.geocities.com/mcmonstrous

Thank you and God bless!

RAY MANZAREK

As ¼ of The Doors, Ray Manzarek made his bones in the music industry as keyboardist in a thinking man's band, one that was not afraid to be literate, and influenced by the free-form style of both poetry and jazz, so it should come as no surprise that he has since found his way into the world of the author, not only in non-fiction (his first work was *Light My Fire*, which detailed his life with The Doors) but in fiction as well, with *The Poet In Exile*, and his latest, *Snake Moon*, a tale of the supernatural published by Night Shade Books.

Not one to rest on his laurels, Ray is also comfortable in the world of film with *Love Her Madly*, and has continued make music with Riders on the Storm, playing the music of the Doors with frontman Ian Astbury (formerly of The Cult) and Doors bandmate Robby Krieger. In November, The Doors will issue a second Boxed Set, entitled *Perception*.

Speaking from his home in northern California, Ray was his usually affable self, quick to joke and share his thoughts about his written work, the Fortieth Anniversary of The Doors, and a vision of his late vocalist, Jim Morrison.

Snake Moon began as a screenplay with Rick Valentine. Can you talk a little about the background to how you came up with the story?

We were both attracted to ghost stories and the Civil War, and we were talking over beer and wine as we often do, and we started talking about a family compound during that time where no news of war came. It was an idyllic existence, and peaceful. They were in love. And because of greed, madness, and lust for fame and strange adventures, the men pay a price for it. Actually, we worked on the story with Rick Schmidlin, who did the reconstruction on Orson Welles' *A Touch Of Evil* and Erich Von Stroheim's *Greed*.

What led to your novelizing the screenplay?

That was Hollywood's decision. We wanted a film, but when we had shopped it around, *Cold Mountain* had just come out and went flopsky, so Hollywood said 'No Civil War movies.' We said 'But it's a small movie, no battle scenes, we can film it in Tennessee or Kentucky, won't cost much.' Hollywood said, 'No Civil War movies!' We said, 'It's an esoteric love story!' And Hollywood said 'No Civil War stories *for the last time, Manzarek!*'

But all three of us loved the story. I said 'This is too good, I'm going to write it as a novel.' I'd still like to see it as a movie, but I understand *Crash* was banging around Hollywood for something like nine years before it got made, and it won the Academy Award for Best Picture (2004)! But you're typical moviegoer is a seventeen year-old on a date, so you're going to have *Pirates Of The Carribean* -type movies more than anything else.

Spectacle over substance?

Right. And it's getting harder and harder for films like *Crash* to get made.

Is that why the chapters in Snake Moon *are short? To maintain the integrity and pacing of the screenplay?*

Yes, exactly. Scenes. I had a friend say 'This is a fast read.' I said 'That's what I was trying to do; write a fast-paced page turner.' The way it was written, everything was said, everything was covered. But the publishers we sent it to all said, 'It's gotta be three-hundred pages to be considered a novel.' I said, 'But it's two-hundred, it's a good, fast read.' I mean, gee, I wish there was more. But you know what Elvis said, 'Always leave them wanting.'

Is that why you picked Night Shade as a publisher?

Absolutely. They said 'Fine, we like mysteries… strange tales.' It was great fun writing it; I was there, standing behind a tree observing these great characters, just watching what they were doing. I'd like to direct it, if it does become a movie, but I don't think that's going to happen [Chuckle].

Do you have a dream cast for the movie?

Oh, man... I couldn't begin... maybe John Malkovich at twenty-eight for Jebber...

Would you prefer unknowns?

Well, you cast unknowns, no theatre will want it... You can say 'I thought I'd cast unknowns in it,' Studios will say, 'Go finance it.' 'Okay, we made it.' 'Who's the star?'

'No one. It's a cast of unknowns.' 'Well, fuck it.' [Laughs]. Same thing happened when we made *Love Her Madly*. Who's in that? Unknowns. I told them, 'It's a dark love story, it's about obsession and darkness.' They said, 'Great, who's in it?' 'People you don't know.' 'Sorry.'

And Sundance... I thought Sundance was supposed to be about small, *independent* films.

Studios see an inroad to profit, and want a presence. Actors want the credibility and the flexibility to say that they've made the multi-million dollar action film, but also that small independent film.

[Laughs] Right. I don't know... Maybe I could see studio films at Sundance that cost under a million to make...

What authors do you like?

I loved John Steinbeck's first... *To A God Unknown*... [Ray's first novel] *The Poet In Exile* is W. Somerset Maugham's *The Razor's Edge*...off he goes on his search, but before he can find what he's looking for... it's the same story, man. Danny Sugarman, a man who worked in the Doors office back in the Sixties, worked his way up to become the Doors' manager, died of lung cancer, fifty years old. [Doors producer] Paul Rothchild... I remember he was planning this big 60th birthday party. No matter what Paul was planning, it was gonna be great, man... he died two months before his birthday. I lost two good Doors friends... And Jim in that bathtub... or not [laughs]. That sealed coffin in the flat... 27 years old... so young, man. You should have more time to find yourself in.

Speaking of the Doors, can you bring us up to speed on Riders on the Storm?

We're going out in 2007. Celebrate the 40th Anniversary of the Doors, worldwide. But not consecutive like the Stones. I don't know why Mick Jagger feels the need to do that… With us, it'll be 'Forty Cities/Forty Years': Ten in the Orient, ten in South America, ten in Europe, and ten in the U.S., concluding in New Orleans, where the Doors last played with Jim [in April '71].

Will this be the last tour?

This may be it, man. This may be it.

Who's playing drums for you guys?

Ty Dennis. Phil Chen on bass. To go from the way we play 'Touch Me' to 'L.A. Woman.' Ty just drives it [chuckles]. And then to go to Ty and Phil *pushing* 'L.A. Woman…'

I had this vision of Jim when Riders last played Paris… I had my eyes closed, and I saw Jim's grave, and out of it comes a hand, like in *Carrie*, only not scary at all. It was Jim. I could hear him say, 'Don't stop, Ray, keep going…'

So yeah, this might be the last tour… like Cher…. [laughs].

Or KISS…

[Laughs] Yeah, like KISS, or The Who… then we go in the studio in 2008. We have lyric contributions from Michael McClure, Michael C. Ford, Jim Carroll… I asked Warren Zevon to send me something, and he sent me two stanzas before he passed away: 'River of madness/Running through L.A.'

Will Ian be contributing?

He might. He's a busy chap.

Will you be performing 'The Soft Parade' live?

The song or the album?

The song.

No.

Any particular reason?

It's a bitch [laughs]. A lot of woodshedding to just sit down and learn it. Ian would have to learn it. It's fatiguing. I'm getting lazy [laughs]. Robby will bring it up, and I'm saying 'Oh, *fuck…*' 'It's easy, Ray. I'll show you.' It's like Senior Wences; [imitates Wences' 'Johnny' voice] 'Easy for you, not easy for *meeee*.' Robby's mind is *sharp*. Has something to do with that IQ… 140… somewhere around there. My wife Dorothy has the same.

What do you have planned for the future?

A script for *L.A. Woman*, a story about a woman and two guys, one representative of darkness, like Dick Cheney, and another of the power of light. It follows her seeking refuge from 'Dewey' Kim, the Cheney character. It takes place in Venice, California.

Any plans to novelize it?

I may have to! [Laughs]. There's *Riders On The Storm*, a story about three guys from UCLA on a quest to find peyote, and come across a church of peyote takers and get mixed up in a murder committed by white supremacists. It's based on people I knew at UCLA. Rick Valentine and I are working on a script about a Native American Indian coming to L.A. to find the man, a trucker, who stole his polar bear skin… a Native American traveling across America. The trucker is going to the South side of Chicago to deliver Alaskan marijuana… the best (chuckles)… Going to the South side Bloods or Crips to deliver Alaskan Chronic… that's a great title.

Thanks a lot for taking the time, Ray.

Hey, no problem, man. Anytime.

PIERS ANTHONY

PIERS ANTHONY HAS LONG BEEN synonymous with speculative fiction, being a leading and influential voice in the fields of both fantasy and SF, with a body of work few can match. More than 60 of his books have seen print, not including his seminal Xanth series (in itself, 25 volumes and counting).

Anthony is also a vocal proponent of both Internet- and self-publishing. His Web site *hipiers.com* has a wealth of links to such publishers, as well as the wisdom of a seasoned veteran in the field.

The author was gracious enough to give his opinions, getting right to the point on matters regarding the business of writing speculative fiction, as well as the status of the genres and how established names have been affected by the present and future of publishing.

What motivated you to write your autobiography, Bio of an Ogre, *and your forthcoming second autobiographical volume,* How Precious Was That While?

I have had about as much adventure in publishing as any writer in my genre, such as getting blacklisted for protesting when a publisher cheated me, then becoming a best-seller, so I felt I ought to tell my story. But things continued to happen, such as my extensive interaction with my readers, so it seemed to be time to catch up with a sequel. The thing is, normally when a publisher cheats a writer, it's the writer's tough luck; he has to keep his mouth shut or get in worse trouble. I was in a position to blow the lid off that situation, including the complicity of a writer's organization, and it seemed that if I didn't do it, no one else would. So I did it. My *hipiers.com* Web site is more of the same; I tell the truth about what is going on good and bad, as much of it as I know. I'm not anti-publisher, just pro-writer.

What can we learn from the story you've lived?

You can learn what it is like to be a writer, and what it is like to stand up for what you feel is right. I have a lot of sympathy for whistle blowers, knowing from my own experience how telling an unpopular truth can make you the target of lies intended to destroy your reputation. The irony is that the public is as apt to believe the lies as the truth. If you want to live a peaceful life, don't say or do anything that isn't socially approved.

Has the Internet affected publishing in a positive or negative way?

Positive, by opening it up to more people.

Does writing fantasy differ from, say, writing science fiction?

Yes—fantasy has fewer rules, and just about anything goes. You don't need to research, so it's easier.

How has promoting your work changed over the years?

Publishers hardly seem to be promoting it any more.

Would you suggest self-publishing to a first-time novelist?

Yes, because that way his work can be read.

You don't suffer from writer's block—is there a conscious effort behind that or is it more of a natural ability?

I once suffered from it, and worked to conquer it. Now I have a system that works for me and just about anybody else, so it's no problem.

Can you elaborate on the system?

I call it the 'bracket' system. When the text stalls, go into brackets [like this] and talk to yourself. State the problem, play with ideas to fix it, and keep doing that—for thousands of words, if need be—until something clicks. Then emerge from the brackets and resume writing text. This does two things: it keeps you writing, which is important for momentum, and it solves your snag. I use it constantly, and it works for me; I never suffer writer's block. Today, with the computer and multiple files, I use a separate file instead of brackets, but the system is the same. When you edit your text later, delete the bracket material; it is like scaffolding for a building under construction, essential in its turn, but never intended to be permanent. Mainly, it's a way to explore your problem sensibly, in a relaxed way, chipping away at it, and that is generally enough.

Example: He took her in his arms and said—[oops, my mind has gone blank! I'm in Writer's Block! What on earth does he say? "Get out of here, you bitch?" No, because he loves her. Say—maybe he could tell her that. What an original idea! I'm a genius!] "I love you." She replied, "I'll believe that when you show me what was in those mysterious brackets." [Oops!]

Stephen King has withdrawn Rage *from print in light of the violence in some schools, viewing such books, in his words, as not a cause but an accelerant. Do you agree, and would you do the same?*

Yes, I think I agree. But it is a complex case, and I'm not sure that censoring anything is ever justified.

What are you currently reading?

Nemo, by Kevin Anderson, a historical fantasy to be published about six months hence. I have an advance copy to consider for blurbing.

Was there something in particular that made you want to be an author?

When I pondered my life course, in college, I realized that writing was what I really wanted to do. That belief has not changed in 45 years.

What's the biggest liability to fiction writers today?

Surviving. 99% can't make it into print, and most who do still can't earn a decent living from writing.

Xanth crossed over in a cameo appearance in DoOon Mode *(Tor)—can we expect another, maybe longer, crossover in a future novel?*

No. D. Metria is angry about what happened.

The character of Colene is quite human in that she has very realistic, maybe dark, faults. Is that sort of personification becoming less common in today's protagonists?

I don't read widely enough to know. I never read of a character like that before, so as far as I know, I'm the only one to do it.

What can you tell us about Swell Foop *(Tor) and* The Dastard *(Tor)?*

The Dastard is now in hardcover, about a man who travels in time to do dastardly deeds. *Swell Foop* will appear in October, about the abduction of Demon Earth, who has to be rescued before his Magic of Gravity fades and folk start falling off the planet. They would be rather angered by that.

You wrote The Gutbucket Quest *(Tor) with Ron Leming and* The Secret of Spring *(Tor) with JoAnne Taeush—what's key to a successful collaboration?*

For me, it seems to be to have my collaborator write the novel, then turn it over to me for revision, as I generally have a better sense of the market. But there are many ways to collaborate.

Where do you see the fields of fantasy and science fiction going?

I'm not sure they have a direction, any more than evolution does. What works, survives.

Any future projects you're excited about?

ChroMagic, my huge fantasy series wherein volcanoes erupt different colors of magic. It is sexy sword-and-sorcery with a vengeance—but no publisher is interested so far. Have I commented on the idiocy of publishers? Consider it done.

STEVEN ERIKSON

TORONTO, CANADA-BORN STEVEN ERIKSON has written five fantasy novels in his epic ten-novel series *Malazan Book Of The Fallen*, the latest being *Gardens Of The Moon*, although it was previously published (as his other works before it), in the U.K. in 1999, where he has spent a good part of his life.

An anthropologist and archeologist by trade, Steven is also a graduate of the Iowa Writer's Workshop, and has seen his *Gardens Of The Moon* be nominated in 2000 for the World Fantasy Award for Best Novel. You may be able to find a copy of his limited-edition novella, *Blood Follows* (published in 2002.) He currently resides in Winnipeg, Canada with his wife and son.

How does it happen that someone with a degree in archaeology comes to write fiction?

I've been asked this many times and now I've finally sat back to think about it, and I think it's that archaeology and fiction (especially something like fantasy fiction) have a lot in common. Both require imagination—I did a fair bit of surveying back then, which is essentially going out into the wilds and looking for sites, and to do that well one needs to re-construct the landscape, working backwards from the present into the past—environmental conditions, drainage patterns, erosion, all that, and then, using common sense, the archaeologist asks him or herself: where would I camp? That's one of the ways of finding sites (sites are also found by accident, of course, and there was a time there in the profession when 'random survey' was big, but it turned out to have very limited usefulness),and it works very well. But only if you have a good imagination, and some sense of the commonality of the human condition, commonality in the sense of what we share as a species. In fantasy fiction, there's a whole world to construct, and its own layers of activity to figure out. For me, it feels the same, and carries with it the same sense of wonder and fascination.

In archaeology, some people are known as 'site magnets.' They find sites where other archaeologists don't/can't. For whatever reason or fortuitous chance, I was one of those site magnets—because I had a good imagination? Maybe. Preferring field work to lab work back then, I treated summers and field projects as paid vacations. I got out into the bush, the wild-lands, and simply thrived. Re-fuelling my imagination, I suppose, and having left an MA program in anthropology to take degrees in fiction writing, my winters were spent writing. So, it was the best of both worlds, for a while there....

What were some of the locales you've visited on archaeological digs, and how did the experience effect your world-building?

Northwest Ontario, south and west and mid-northern Manitoba, mid-north, west, south and eastern Saskatchewan, the city of Winnipeg, and, to throw a spanner in the works, Belize, Central America. In terms of environments, the above included boreal forest, precambrian shield country, aspen parkland transition zones (the fringe between plains and boreal forest), river valleys, plains, ancient beach-ridges (from the now-extinct glacial sea that covered most of central Canada), and, far to the south, coastal, tropical scrubland and forest (although in Belize we were looking at paleolithic and early archaic—two phases of very old occupation, ranging from big-game hunting to just after the extinction of said big-game). Such environments show up in the novels of the *Malazan Book of the Fallen*, naturally, especially the exotic ones, and by exotic I mean environments that are, for many reasons, difficult, almost never seen in motion pictures, hard to traverse, and never obviously majestic (as, say, the uplands of New Zealand).

Years ago I had a number of conversations with Canadian writer, Jack Hodgins, regarding the distinction between 'prairie writers' and 'mountain writers' (and 'urban writers'); while I won't go into detail here since that would take pages and pages, we were in the end able to observe that I was a 'prairie writer' whilst he was a 'mountain writer,' and it had to do with the relationship the writer reveals between him or herself and their chosen environment within a work of fiction—a fundamental and observable difference that infuses the narrative. Put another way, it comes down to horizons. In the mountains those horizons are close, rearing, damn-near right on top of you and ready to tumble down at any moment (it seems)—and that makes for one kind of character (in the story, in the writer him or herself). On the prairie the horizon is so far away it's a hazy smear at the very edge of one's vision—and that makes a different kind of character, and writer. Then there's urban but I won't go into that.

Anyway, I'm oversimplifying here but if I look at my fiction, fantasy as well as all the rest, I can see/feel the way that extended vision suffuses everything I write. My characters squint. They do a lot of walking. They claw their way through thick brush more than they walk old-growth forests. They cross muddy, slow, meandering rivers more often than mountain streams. Of course there are exceptions. There always are. I make a point of them, in fact.

Often—to take another tack on your question—it's not the digs themselves that have the most profound effect—it's the people one works and lives with, it's the excursions one makes into the world beyond (as I did in Central America) that often provides the most vital kind of experience which in turn eventually feeds the writing.

What inspired you to approach Malazan *as a work encompassing ten volumes?*

When the horizons are that far away.... Or, to put it another way, once I immersed myself in the creation of an entire world, it would feel like an injustice to leave it after just a few books—I certainly feel that way. There is a vast history to unravel, and people's lives to follow, and endless themes to explore. I like large canvases.

Were there any concerns specific to the length of the series in it's marketability as your debut work in the States?

Not for me. If such concerns existed among my agents or with my UK publisher, they all showed enough tact to not mention them to me. Individual book length was another matter, but that had as much to do with manufacturing limitations as anything else. I know the German publishers are splitting my books. Concerns about US marketability had more to do with the style of my writing, as I understand it. Odd, given that the US has produced such writers as Robert Ludlum (bestselling writers at that) and Clancy. Too many characters, that kind of stuff.

What led to your decision for the Malazan *series to be a series of self-contained series of stories, which seems to be rather unique in the fantasy setting?*

Oh, I was never a fan of cliff-hangers. Besides, it has to do with the kind of structure I like to create in a novel. Picture a scribbled line of loops, one after another. That's how I write. Circular, coiling ahead. I do that with paragraphs, sections, chapters, parts and the entire novel. All loops. I like my opening scene to find an echo in the very last scene—not always directly, sometimes in theme only—and that gives a sense of momentary closure, I hope. And, with each novel, I try to make a point of exploring a theme or themes unique to that novel. This way I can keep things fresh for me as a writer, and I don't end up retelling the same story over and over again, which is a pitfall writers can fall into if they're not mindful, or if they're overwhelmed by the pressure of previous success.

Will you be working on anything outside the Malazan *universe while the series continues? What can we expect?*

Amazingly, I'm still finding time to write other stuff. Shorter stuff, mostly, under the Erikson name and as Steve Lundin. With the reprint of *Gardens of the Moon* in the US and *Blood Follows* in the UK, I actually have seven books coming out this year: *Midnight Tides, The Devil Delivered, The Healthy Dead, Fishin with Grandma Matchie,* and a hockey novel set in Winnipeg called *When She's Gone* which will be coming out this autumn here in Canada, under the Lundin name. Now, I can't see that happening ever again, but the short novels and novellas are great fun and I'm sure I'll manage at least one a year. They're fun because I can be more blatantly subversive—sure, there's irony and some satire in the *Malazan Book of the Fallen*, but they tend to be more character or scene specific than thematic, whereas I can go straight for the throat in the shorter fiction.

Are there any plans on bringing your earlier works over to the States?

I haven't really thought about it, truth be told. If I run into some kind of financial disaster, who's to say the extent of my desperation?

Your use of the 'Deck of Dragons,' and its use in your books is an interesting detail to the work; any plans on publishing an actual 'Fatid,' or deck?

There were plans, once, a few years back. The snag was with finding an illustrator for the cards. Because the deck is elemental based, it follows the same sort of archetypal-style divination system as a Tarot deck; and Tarot readers have tried it out and liked it. Something like that would be fun, I think.

Given your experience in roleplaying games, will we ever see the Malazan *universe as a play system?*

Again, that would be cool to see, but I've not been approached. The system would have to be implicitly freewheeling, like Steve Jackson's GURPS, with none of the rigid strictures of character classes, or such things as alignments (good/evil/neutral/lawful good/lawful evil etc). I wouldn't mind seeing a computer game version, as well, but something that could allow both individual RP and RTS/turn-based on a grander scale—is such a thing now possible? They're getting close, aren't they?

Are there any significant differences between English, Canadian, and American audiences? What would they be?

Yikes, that's a loaded question! I don't know if I have an answer yet—not enough feedback, nor am I inclined to start categorising it in that way. As far as I take it, there's just readers who tried the series and gave up early on, or who got hooked and are still with me, awaiting the next installment. And among the latter, there's readers who think I can't do characterisation and readers who think I can, readers who think I do bad fight scenes and readers who think I do great fight scenes, etc. A humbling reminder, always, that you can't please everybody; even more humbling, you also can't convince everybody that you know what you're doing and seeing what's there comes from a certain way of looking. I think readers either click in all the way or they don't, and for me, there's no real way of predicting or even affecting that outcome. Oh well.

Do you have any pet peeves regarding the genre?

Don't get me started.

Have there been any particular challenges in being published outside of America, then going into that market?

Well, it took years of trying. My first three targets for Gardens of the Moon years and years ago were all New York-based US fantasy publishers.

Three strikes....

You said that Glen Cook's Black Company *'Single-handedly changed the field of fantasy,' and he has said 'I stand slack-jawed in awe of the* Malazan Book Of The Fallen. The Black Company, *Zelazny's* Amber, *Vance's* Dying Earth, *and other mighty drumbeats are but foreshadowings of this dark dragon's hoard.' How does that feel to have that said about your work?*

It's overwhelming—so many writers I admire and indeed grew up reading have commented favourably on the series, and have helped me in many other ways besides. I was for so long outside the community but I no longer feel that way—and not just writers, but book-sellers, editors and publishers, it's incredible how open and welcoming they are—it's a great feeling to think, rightly or not, that I'm now just another crony at the conventions and conferences, guaranteed to keep the bar-staff awake all night.

What can we expect to see from you in the future?

Hard to say. I'm playing it by ear, but there will always be more obsessions for me to find as a writer. Which is what we all feed on. Sort've like maggots.

RAYMOND BENSON

RAYMOND BENSON MAY BE BEST KNOWN as the fourth official author of the James Bond novels. Including adaptations of *Die Another Day* and *The World Is Not Enough*, and the authoritative non-fiction book, *The James Bond Bedside Companion*, but what is just as much testimony to his talent is the fact he is an accomplished musician, video game designer and director of stage productions.

His work outside the Bond franchise has included the *Black Stiletto* book series as well as numerous mysteries and thrillers such as *A Hard Day's Death*, *Sweetie's Diamonds* and *Torment*. As a Bond and an overall spy genre nut, it was with great pleasure that I was able to conduct this interview.

You can find Raymond online at: raymondbenson.com

How were you approached to take over the literary part of the Bond franchise?

I had written *The James Bond Bedside Companion* in the 80s. When I was researching the book, I went to England and met members of Ian Fleming's family, his business people, friends, etc. The copyright holders liked the book when it came out and we stayed in touch. I did little odd jobs for them (no pun intended) in the late 80s and early 90s. Then, when John Gardner announced that he would no longer continue writing the books in 1995, they simply asked me if I'd like to give it a shot.

Did you have any trepidation about writing new adventures?

I was stepping into very big shoes! Anyone who didn't have trepidations would need his head examined.

John Gardner seems to have taken a lot of flak over how he reinterpreted Bond during his run as author of the franchise. Do you feel some of the heavy-handed criticism was warranted by the fanbase?

It's a large fan base and therefore very opinionated, just as any big franchise fan base is (*Star Wars, Star Trek, Batman*, etc.). You can't please everyone. Every fan has his or her own interpretation of the character in one's head. Bond comes with a lot of baggage. John had his fans and his detractors. I had my fans and detractors. The same is true for the authors who came after me. Even Ian Fleming had his detractors!

How much interaction did you have with the filmmakers of the Bond films?

Not much. Only when I was writing the film novelizations did I work with EON. I went to Pinewood Studios to see the sets and costumes and designs for the gadgets, but saw no filming. I communicated with the screenwriters. The original novels, though, were just between me and Ian Fleming Publications.

Did you have a particular Bond in mind when you were writing the books?

The one that I pictured in my head when I first read the Fleming novels back in the 60s, and it wasn't Sean Connery! I'd say he resembled the John McClusky drawings in the Daily Express comics, but that was before I'd even seen those comics. Every reader imagines his/her own Bond in the part as they read…I had fans tell me "I could hear Sean Connery say those lines!" or "I could hear Pierce Brosnan say those lines!" That's good. When a reader can inject his/her own Bond into the story, then I've succeeded.

Which book of yours do you feel really captured the dynamic of James Bond?

I would like to think they all did!

What should the next direction be for the Bond novels?

That's not for me to say. I had my seven-year tenure, I wrote six original books, three movie novelizations, and three short stories. That's a pretty good run. I don't own the character and therefore have no say in what Ian Fleming Publications decides to do with the franchise.

What do you think of Daniel Craig as 007?

I think he's terrific!

What can we expect to see in the re-issue of the Bond Bedside Companion?

It's the same book as before. I've written a new Introduction, explaining why I can't and won't update it, but I give a brief rundown of what has happened in the Bond world between 1988 and the present.

Will there be any more Splinter Cell *novels to follow?*

Not from me.

What was it like to work with John Milius for Homefront: Voice of Freedom?

That was a good experience, I really enjoyed it. I'm proud of the book, too. Watch this space, there may be more *Homefront* coming in the future. In short, John came up with the idea for the videogame and helped create its universe with the game developers. I came in afterwards and wrote the novel.

How did the character of Spike Berenger of the Spike Berenger Rock 'n' Roll Hit *series come to be?*

I'm a huge music fan (and a musician too) and thought it would be fun to write thrillers/mysteries in that world. There's a lot of humor in the books, references to rock music, cameos by rock stars…they were fun to write.

You've written novels based on the video game Metal Gear. *How did that come to be?*

With most media tie-in work, a writer is approached by the publisher. The publisher and the videogame company (or movie or TV company, depending on what the property is) make a deal together to do a book.

Then the publisher finds the author. Based on my previous work, the publisher hired me to write the two *Metal Gear* books, with Konami's approval.

I was a roleplaying game addict in the 80s, and that extended to the James Bond RPG. What inspired your gaming module You Only Live Twice II?

I was asked by Victory Games to do one, as I was also a fan of the RPG. I believe they gave me the title—*YOLT II*—and I had to work from that. I tied it into the first *YOLT* game with a few bits in Japan, but then took it off to other original places, like Australia.

What was the process for similar games involving A View To A Kill *and Stephen King's* The Mist?

That was such a long time ago! My literary agent at the time got me involved with a game developer who was doing those titles. I was into the text adventure games like *Zork* and was very familiar with them. So I was a natural to be hired, especially for the Bond game. I also did *Goldfinger* for the same company.

You wrote the Pocket Essential Guide to Jethro Tull. *What is the draw for you to their music?*

I've been a fan since the beginning, or close to it, as their third album was my first. I grew up in a time when progressive rock was popular, and Tull's music spoke to me in ways that others didn't. I've always been a fan. Then, much later, when I learned that Ian Anderson was a Bond fan, I contacted him, sent him some copies of my Bond novels, and we became friends. After that, I wrote the book.

You had two novels were published as e-books in 2011: Torment, *a supernatural thriller, and* Artifact of Evil, *a thriller using elements of modern day crime, historical characters, and fantasy. What led to the decision to publish them as e-books, and would readers more familiar with your mystery novels see any change in the dynamics of your writing out of what may be considered out of your usual genre?*

I think so, although I wouldn't say they're out of the usual genre. They're both thrillers. I wrote both novels in 2006 and my agent spent two years trying to sell them to traditional publishers, but as every author in the field knows, not every book gets sold and it's becoming more and more difficult to gets books published. That's why every author I know is now e-publishing backlist titles to which they own the rights as well as never-before-published works that for some reason never sold. I happen to think that *Torment* and *Artifact of Evil* are among my very best books.

The Black Stiletto is the story of a female vigilante in the Eisenhower/Kennedy eras, what made you pick the era and the female protagonist?

That era is hot now! The whole 50s and 60s time period is being explored a lot more now (a la *Mad Men*). I'm very proud of this book. It's the first of a series. The second book comes out in May 2012.

Your material is published at a good rate for fans of the genre, so I have to ask, what's in the future for you?

Certainly more *Black Stiletto!* I'll also continue writing tie-in novelizations to games and movies. I suggest that fans subscribe to my newsletter through my website www.raymondbenson.com and follow me on Facebook and Twitter for all the latest news.

WESTON OCHSE

ANYONE WHO NAMES his Great Danes Pester, Ghost, Palm Eater, and Goblin Monster Dog is already aces in my book, but when you add the punch of winning the Stoker for Best First Novel for his *Scarecrow Gods*. He's also been known as the Gross Out Contest bouncer. Combine that with the fact he is a practitioner of several martial arts and he's married to a genre author, Yvonne Navarro, and you have a pretty interesting subject for an interview!

Weston can be found online at: WestonOchse.com

In my first interview collection, I interviewed your wife, Yvonne Navarro. What's it like living with another Horror author?

Terrific, really. I think it's a pretty rare thing and I'm so glad I'm married to someone who likes what I live, does what I do, and works the craft like I work. We're always talking. We're always communicating. We bounce ideas off each other and commiserate about projects in a way that a non-writer would never understand.

Has there been any talk of you writing a book together?

We just did. Yvonne and I wrote the Y.A. novel *Ghost Heart*, coming this summer from Dark Regions Press. It's the story of a teenage boy and girl who travel into the Black Hills and Badlands of South Dakota, each in search of something dear to them.

How did your latest work, Blood Ocean, *come about?*

This is a long story, but here it is: I don't know where I was at the time, but I do remember that I heard about a new publishing house called Abaddon Books and asked for their bible about *Afterblight*. I sent a quick pitch, and I mean quick, and I got back an email from Jon Oliver, then Editor-in-Chief of Abaddon, now Editor-in-Chief of both Abaddon and Solaris, that he was intrigued about the idea and would I send him a full pitch, which has a sample chapter as well as a chapter by chapter outline. So I found myself working on this for about a month. In fact, I finished the pitch while I was in a hotel room in Alexandria, Virginia, working on my laptop while the Steelers beat the Colts in the Super Bowl.

My pitch at that time was about Native Americans in the Southwest, who must team up with an L.A. gang of biker samurai to fight off the *Radiant Dawn*—the white folks who want their blood. It was a damn good pitch. I sooo wanted to write that book. But the problem was that every Tom, Dick and English Harry submitted a pitch about Native Americans too.

Needless to say they didn't need me.

So I did what every other writer would do in my shoes......I sulked and wrote something else.

Then about a year later, I was at Book Expo America in Los Angeles. My agent and I went around and had some table-side chats with a few of the editors, one being Jon. This was our first face to face. Being an outgoing person—those of you who know me will agree with this—I enjoy face to face conversations. I thrive on them. Jon and I got to talking. He mentioned that he liked my pitch and was sorry to have to pass on it, but why not send him a pitch for a zombie novel.

A zombie novel? It had never occurred to me to write a zombie novel.

But I did. I sent him a pitch and it became Empire of Salt which sold out everywhere and was a smash hit!

But I still wanted to write an *Afterblight* novel. There'd been a burning inside of me that had not gone away. So even as *Empire of Salt* was premiering in Brighton, England at the World Horror Convention, I was verbally pitching Jon a sprinkle of an idea. He told me to put it on paper when I returned to America and send it to him. I think he saw how eager I was, plus, I think I was keeping him from the pub. So whether or not he meant it or not, I took that as a YES, mentally pumped one arm, and began to work on an idea which revolved around an idea of a monkey being surgically attached to a person's back.

And when I returned to America, I wrote the pitch. It took me about a month as everything came together. And to be totally honest, at first he wasn't sure and didn't accept it right away. But like a dog with a dead rabbit, I shook that idea and shook it, and tweaked the pitch until finally he liked it enough to say those magical five magic words—I'll send you a contract.

Velvet Dogma has been called Phillip K. Dick meets William Gibson. Do you feel that's an accurate statement?

Yeah. That's a pretty lofty comparison. I forget who made it, but it fits really well. PK Dick was truly groundbreaking in his ability to forecast social issues and wrap them within the framework of a science fiction story. Additionally, William Gibson is the godfather of cyberpunk, a subgenre of science fiction that I hold dear to my heart. Some hardcore science fiction readers see cyberpunk as the gutter, but I've always embraced it's guerilla-like message. Gibson and Stephenson are the demigods of my Cyberpunk Sci Fi Pantheon and it was my distinct pleasure to write within their strata.

Here's the synopsis: In the year 2040, the world has finally achieved the perfect merging of human and machine by developing a method by which the computer has direct integration into the brain. Called Personal Ocular Devices, or PODS, the interface fits over the eye feeding information directly along the optic nerve into the brain, allowing minds and computers to become one.

But not for Rebecca Mines, who has been held in solitary confinement for the last 20 years. Arrested under the 2002 Patriot Act as a cyber-terrorist for unleashing a program called Velvet Dogma, her parole restricts access to all computers and all but the simplest of machines. Although the government is still fearful that she'll resume her previous profession, Rebecca wants nothing more than to find a place to exist in peace. She has a life to live, and twenty years of personal stagnation from which to recover.

But she discovers that things have changed dramatically since she's been in prison. Not only is organ theft sanctioned, but all of her organs have already been levied to the highest bidder. No sooner does she promise the judge that she'll be a law-abiding citizen, then she finds herself on the run from not only Chinese Black Hearts, eager to confiscate her organs, but the authorities who realize that they've let her out too soon.

You've said you never set out to be a Horror writer. Your body of works shows your command of other genres, but what sort of writer had you originally set out to be? Do you think you've reached it?

I want to be a full time writer. I want to be able to write, support myself and my wife, live a pretty good life, and travel. I'm not going to slow down until I achieve that. I imagine even if I'm able to achieve it, I probably won't slow down even then.

Can you tell us anything about your upcoming novel from St. Martin's Press, SEAL Team 666?

Absolutely! It's a novel about a special SEAL Team whose mission it is to protect America from supernatural attack. Within the book is a loose history of this unit which has been known by different names since before the American Revolution. In the novel, you follow the adventure of a young Navy SEAL who is jerked out of BUD/S training and selected for SEAL Team 666 because of several important factors.

Peter Straub is one of my all-time favorite authors. He read it and just loved it. Here's what he said: "Weston Ochse has always been a wised-up, clued-in, completely trustworthy writer of high-action fiction that deserved a wider audience, and *SEAL TEAM 666* is his breakthrough book. Here, every story-line is as taut as a gunfighter's nerves, and individual scenes pop like firecrackers. I raced through this novel and when it ended, I wanted more."

Who would you consider your contemporaries?

I guess it depends on how you define contemporaries. There's a whole bunch of us who started writing about the same time. We had the same hopes and dreams. The same drive. The same sort of skewed vision of the universe. We met on HorrorNet in a chat room back in 2007. We'd chat about writing and writers, while folks like Dick Laymon, Ed Lee, Ray Garton, F. Paul Wilson and Tom Piccirilli would come by and bestow upon us great wisdom (in all seriousness). We called ourselves the Cabal. We've achieved varying degrees of success. Which is okay because I think as we grow our definitions of success change as we change. Members of the cabal include Brian Keene, Regina (Garza) Mitchell, Mike Hyuck, Mike Oliveri, Feo Amante, Rain Graves, John Urbancik and Tim Lebbon. We have a bond that still holds strong to this day.

Vampires have long been the most popular creature that readers as well as writers gravitate to, but zombies seem to be on the rise, if you'll pardon the pun. What do you think will be the next creature?

Ahh. You want to know the secret. As a member of the Successful Authors Union, I was given this information in a ceremony that involved incense, chanting and naked dancing. Sorry, I can't tell you without the secret high sign.

In all seriousness, I don't think zombies are going anywhere fast (no pun intended). See, the zombie is unlike every other monster in a very specific way. When you write about werewolves, you write about the wolf and how the human fights against the change or embraces it. When you write about vampires, even the sparkly type, you write about the vampire either wanting to suck someone's blood or fighting against it. Both sorts of novels are about the monster. A zombie novel, with very few exceptions, is about people's reaction to a monster. A vampire novel is a monster book and a zombie novel is a people book. Get it?

If you had six months to live, how would you spend them?

I'd live my life like I was Kid Rock channeling Ernest Hemingway with the style of Elvis Presley.

Do you have a "Stranded on a deserted island" book you'd have with you?

There's a book on my shelf that I've always wanted to read. It's big. It's thick. It's seminal. But it's also daunting. It's *Dalghren* by Samuel R Delaney.

What's next for you?

I have several novellas and short stories due. This summer I'm going to be working on a new novel, but I don't want to talk about it until it's done. Meanwhile, I'm going to be promoting *Blood Ocean* and *SEAL Team 666*, hopefully coming to a bookstore or convention near you.

JACK KETCHUM

Jack knows that things in the dark move slow but sure. He knows their names and that they are disturbingly more human than we'd care to admit. Jack brings them out to fuck with whichever head is trying to wrap itself around his work such as his debut, *Off Season,* and *The Box* which won the Stoker for best short story in 1994 and also received an endorsement from Stephen King saying Jack was the scariest guy in America. Between that an impressive body of novels and short stories, he had also been elected as Grand Master for the 2011 World Horror Convention.

Jack can be found online at: jackketcham.net

The Girl Next Door *deals with the disturbing theme of child abuse. What made you want to write on that particular slippery slope?*

People who do this kind of thing royally piss me off. I like to write pissed off. And the sheer scope of the particular crime this was based on—an adult inviting the neighborhood kids in to participate—invited some important themes to explore I think. Herd mentality, corruption of the innocent, secrets, love and regret, heroism and cowardice. Juicy stuff for a writer.

When you wrote the screenplay for Offspring, *did you come across any problems unique to the mechanics of the screenplay? There's the Hollywood cliché, but true, saying that when adapting a screenplay, the first thing you do is throw out the source material?*

Oh yeah, I was about to throw out my own source material. Sure. One of the things that make the films based on my books unusual is the attention the various writers and directors have given to staying as close as possible to the source material. I wasn't about to do otherwise. The major change from book to movie was letting The Woman live at the end, but that wasn't in my screenplay. My screenplay killed her. But director Andrew Van den Houten saw how good Pollyanna McIntosh was in the part and said no, she's gotta live, she needs another movie. And I'm glad he did.

There have been two Offspring *movies thus far. Is this the beginning of a franchise?*

I hate that word. It brings to mind greasy hamburgers. Lucky McKee and I have talked about doing a sequel to *The Woman* at some point, but we agree that the themes and subject matter have to be as unique and unusual as that film. No Jasons or Freddies, please.

With being called "The Scariest Man In America" by Stephen King, does that effect your mindset when you sit down to write?

Not at all. I don't always set out to be scary. Fiction's all about character and story. Some of my stuff's not scary at all, though I'll admit to an inclination in that direction. I'm happy as all hell that Steve said it, though. That comment's still selling books for me.

You handle some of the disturbing or disgusting traits of the human condition, sometimes questioning in The Woman *that monsters can be the anybody, not just the disfigured serial killer. What motivated you and/or continues to motivate you to turn that particular stone over?*

I think I just like reminding people that there are monsters everywhere. You don't have to be a serial killer to be a sociopath, to be minus the empathy gene. You can be a son with his mother strapped to a bed so that he can cash her social security checks. You can be the inventor of a Ponzi scheme. You can be a kid posting vicious hate-mail on the internet. So neighbor, girlfriend, business associate, whatever—buyer beware. Always.

What benchmark, if any, do you use to avoid the explicit from becoming the exploitive?

No benchmark really except my own intuition. I often use a very flat line for the violent stuff, so that it's not all gussied up with adjectives and adverbs. Which, when misused, can be kinda salacious.

The Girl Next Door continues to haunt me. As it was based upon a true story, how did you first learn about it, and what changes were made to fit your vision of a fictional story?

I came upon Gertie and Sylvia first in J. Robert Nash's *Bloodletters And Badmen* and was struck, not only by the crime, but by the photo of Gert. She haunted me, and I knew I wanted to write about her. But the crime took place in Indiana and I don't know a thing about Indiana. Then my mother died and I'd go back and forth from New York to New Jersey for a few months to settle her affairs and get used to losing both her and the home I grew up in. And at some point I realized I could set the story there, on that dead-end street back in the 50s and early 60s. I whittled down the real family to just three boys and posited a boy next door who is witness to the proceedings, pondered how he'd feel about his participation as a grown-up, and told the story from that point of view.

What was the inspiration behind Right to Life?

I read about these idiots who kidnapped a woman in order to bring her to term. Then, a block away from me, we had a clinic over a bank and there were these right-to-lifers picketing every day. I still have one of the little pink plastic fetuses they were handing out in a tray above my desk. The bank eventually refused to renew the clinic's lease. Did I mention that I write a lot from anger?

And, as clichéd as a question this is, I have to ask the scariest guy in America, what scares you?

First, Alzheimer's. Second, snakes. You can read all about the latter in my story of the same name in *Peaceable Kingdom*.

How would you like your tombstone to read?

I sorta want my ashes scattered to the wind. But I guess HE HAD A DAMN GOOD TIME would do.

RAYMOND FEIST

RAYMOND IS NO STRANGER to the successes Speculative Fiction can bring to a determined author. He has been on the New York Times Best-Seller List, thanks to his superlative books such as *Magician, Silverthorn,* and *A Darkness at Sethanon*,which complete The Riftwar Saga, the first series in the Arc that has since become known as the Riftwar Cycle. Following this, he penned *The Serpentwar Saga,* and *The Riftwar Legacy* series which is based in part, on the hugely successful computer games set in his universe, *Betrayal at Kondor and Return to Kondor* which are the basis for the computer games of the same name.

Raymond can be found online at: http://www.crydee.com/

Who are your contemporaries?

Contemporaries? I guess that depends on how you define it. If you mean "people published the same time I am," we can start with Homer and end with whoever has a first fantasy novel published this week. If you mean people who broke in more or less about the same time I did, that list is out there for anyone who wants to look at publishing since 1982. There are some obvious names, Robert Jordan, Joel Rosenberg, George R.R. Martin, etc.

Did the authors you read as a child influence you as much as those you read as you grew older?

Childhood authors influence you more, I think, as they tend to set the paradigm of what you love more than what you admire for craft or being clever or any other less visceral reaction. I grew up on "Boys Adventure Fiction," of the late 19th early 20th Century and historical novels, and that influenced me far more than the fantasy I read in college.

With your experience as an author, is it difficult for you to read stories just for the pleasure of being the reader?

I read for fun. I just don't read fantasy. I read history, biography, politics, spy thrillers, action/adventure.

I know you're an admirer of Shakespeare. Out of curiosity, what do you think of films like Shakespeare in Love *and more recently,* Anonymous?

Haven't seen *Anonymous*, but *Shakespeare in Love* was charming. It worked on several levels, and one of the best was showing non-writers how often writers grind what's around them into the details of story.

What's your opinion regarding e-books? It seems to be the next step in self publishing as well as for those who could be found of the New York Time's Best Seller List?

E-books are here, and they will grow. So, I really don't have an opinion on them. We still don't have a good idea of how they fit into the ecology of the publishing market, but that will come into focus soon. As for the NYTs, they're pretty conservative, so by the time they have a list of ebooks, you'll know they've arrived finally.

One of my favorite books of yours is Faerie Tale. *What went into your building that world?*

Faerie Tale was a challenge, because I took some diverse premises and wove them together into an improbable cloth. The setting was mundane, but the magic was merely a glimpse away. Holding that perspective from start to finish was the hard part. Kids talking baseball one page, then the thing under the bed the next, that was some of the hardest stuff to write I've ever done.

What was it like working with Janny Wurts for the Empire Series?

Janny and I argued a lot, but we always found a better solution for that. She was a great experience as a writing partner, as I learned how to look at things with different eyes. She has an artist's sensibilities and is very visual. I really am happy with how our series turned out.

You once mentioned having wanted to write an "Elmore Leonard" type book, and a Western. Have either of these become closer to becoming a reality?

My non-fantasy projects always seem to get pushed back. Maybe if I win the Lotto I can just write what I want, but for the near future, more fantasy.

What was the inspiration behind the Demonwar Saga?

Demonwar was based on the concept of a route army, but on a dimensional scale. You beat the hell out of the other guys army, and instead of surrendering, they take off. Once that happens, they're not beat anymore, but seriously dangerous like rats clawing their way out of a corner. It was a nice thing to slug into the longer narrative because it's not what it looks like at first glance. In fact, the truth about the *Demonwar* doesn't come out until this very last book I'm writing in the ChaosWar Saga.

What can we expect from A Crown Imperiled?

Crown Imperiled is the 2nd act of a 3-act play, so you'll see bridging action, new sets of problems revealed, and hopefully have fun reading it.

Are there any new clichés in the Fantasy genre?

By its nature, there can't be "new" clichés. They have to be around a while and get used a lot before they're clichés. There may be new trends that will become that, but as I don't read other people's fantasy, I can't tell you what they are.

Which new authors, if any, do you enjoy reading?

Don't read new authors. My reading time is so scant someone needs to hang around awhile before I get to them.

You've created several worlds in a variety of series. Have there been any particular challenges in creating each world as richly unique as you have?

The challenge to world building is to make it "make sense," i.e. each planet has to have an ecology that seems to make sense to the reader, even if an ecologist is doubled up laughing.

What is on the horizon for you, as a person as well as an author?

As a person, seeing my kids off to college (one there already, the other a year away), putting a little by for old age (too late, probably), having as much fun as I can squeeze out of a day, and keep writing until I grow bored with it. For the future, I'll do a non-Midkemian series next, which looks to be a three book package, about which I'll say no more.

SCOTT LEBERECHT, EDUARDO SANCHEZ, & MATT COMPTON

WITH THE CONSTANT "spectacle above substance" approach constantly shoved towards the average moviegoer, complete with stunt casting, a committee of suits who think they're writers, and more Surprise rather than Scary Factor, it's refreshing when small-budget films like *The Blair Witch Project* or *Paranormal Activity* get the attention they deserve. They hearken back to a time when horror meant thrills, creepiness, and God forbid, a story that produces characters unique and true to themselves.

Thus, Writer/Director Scott Leberecht conceived *Midnight Son*, and through the collaboration and help of Producer Matt Compton and some guy named Eduardo Sanchez (Executive Producer) who co-created *The Blair Witch Project*, they were able to give us, the viewer, a small-budget horror film that has its head tilted just a little off to the side…

The cinematic representation of claustrophobic isolation is especially dynamic. Was that an intentional aspect of the cinematography?

SL: Feeling the walls closing in on Jacob was something Lyn Moncrief (Director of Photography) and I definitely wanted to achieve. We selected framing that creates a claustrophobic effect, but we also chose locations that were going to box us in and naturally limit our options. I would say most of it was intentional, but there were definitely times we had no choice.

ES: This was definitely one of the aspects that originally drew me into this film after I saw some raw footage of what Scott and Lyn had shot. They were smart with their angles and locations choices, showing us just enough to make the world work but not over-reaching, which is what a lot of really low budget films do, mostly to their detriment.

What prompted the specific use of the Fright Night *clip as Jacob researches what vampires are?*

SL: I am a sick fan of that film, and I think I watched it a hundred times as a kid. When I was writing the bit where Jacob researches and tests his "vampirism," I thought of the scene where Evil Ed is burned by the crucifix. There are a lot of vampire films that have this moment, but *Fright Night* felt best for us. There is a campy, funny quality to it that contrasted with, and gave some relief to, the heavy tone of *Midnight Son*. There was talk of casting a couple actors and shooting a similar scene, which would have been cheaper than securing rights, but ultimately I felt he needed to watch a real vampire film—something that exists in our world, to ground it in a reality the audience could relate to.

ED: This was one of the first things we told Scott that we'd have to cut out when Matt and I first came on board. There was no way we were going to be able to afford this clip from *Fright Night*. But Scott insisted, found out that the numbers weren't that crazy and we ended up keeping the clip, which in the end, really adds a lot to the film. It's Scott's tip of the hat to a solid classic.

What led to the decision to have vampirism as a disease in the movie?

SL: Truth is, I never really set out to make a vampire movie. It just became the perfect vehicle for a story I wanted to tell about a young man coping with his transformation into something he believes is 'wrong' or 'evil'. Treating it as a congenital illness—rather than an infection by some outside organism—played into the idea of my character being antagonized by his own body. Events like puberty, sexual attraction, and falling in love are all things that happen to us from the inside out. We generally dislike being at the mercy of anything, but when the thing we don't want emanates from within, our self-image shatters. We must cope with a new set of rules, and our identity is temporarily on hold. These are very scary moments in life, and it is always what I wanted to explore.

ED: It's what I really love about the film and why I was so intrigued when I first read the script. There's never the obligatory "fun being a vampire" section that most vampire stories have. In fact, the only character that seems to relish it is the main bad guy in the film, and that kind of morality was what I liked in the script and now in the film. It's a disease, and that's why we really feel for Jacob. It's the glue that holds the story together.

The chemistry between Zak Kilberg and Maya Parish is remarkable from their first meeting onscreen. How did you find these two?

SL: I saw Maya Parish in a short film directed by a colleague while attending the American Film Institute in Los Angeles. At the time, I was writing *Midnight Son*, and thought she could be right for the role of Mary. I approached her after the screening, and said I may have a part for her. Years later, I sent her the script. She loved it and agreed to play the part. Zak Kilberg was led to a website I created early on to raise awareness and support as I we neared production. He sent me a headshot and I thought he looked perfect for the lead role. I was living in San Francisco at the time, and he was in LA. He then shot a video, acting in a scene I had written. I loved it, and wanted to meet him. After that meeting, I knew he was right for the role and didn't bother to audition anyone else. As far as their chemistry goes, I like to think there was some weird metaphysical harmony at work.

Matt, Ed, how did you discover Scott's work?

MC: Ed approached me about it. He had read the script and seen a little bit of footage, and liked both. He asked me if I'd be interested in coming on as Producer, while we would be an Executive Producer (along with friend & colleague Reed Frerichs).

I read the script, and thought it was quite original. I had never seen a vampire story told that way before. Ed, Scott and I met for lunch one day in LA, and he showed us some of the dailies. The cinematography looked really good, and the acting was great. I felt like he had something special here, and I wanted to be a part of it. Almost three years later, here we are with a finished movie. It's feels great to finally be able to show it to audiences after so much work!

ES: I was mixing Seventh Moon at Skywalker Sound and one of the sound editors, David Hughes, approached me about this cool film he was working on, *Midnight Son*. He thought it was really special, so he got Scott and me hooked up. I read the script, saw the footage and was sold.

That's when I contacted Matt Compton and Reed Frerichs to see if they wanted to help and they were impressed with it just like I was. Matt came on as a full producer and Reed and I became executive producers and the rest is history.

The soundtrack is spacious. What led to the decision to take that approach?

SL: Kays Alatrakchi is a brilliant musician. This was our first time working together, and I learned a lot from him. His instinct to keep the music spacious turned out to be exactly the right approach. In order to achieve realism, we shot using a somewhat documentary style, so the score had to exist in a space between the lines—on an almost unconscious level—but it also had to be powerful enough to elicit an emotional reaction. The ability to create music that stands alone, supports a narrative, and somehow does not call attention to itself is big challenge. Kays is one of the hardest working artists I've met in a long time. He embraced this challenge with a truckload of ideas and the courage to walk that tightrope.

ES: Kays is someone Matt and I knew from back in the day in Orlando. He's a great guy and a very talented composer. I think he hit a home run with this score, probably my favorite of his work. Like Scott said, it's just the right mixture of subtlety and power.

Scott, Your appreciation for David Lynch is obvious in Midnight Son. *Do you have a favorite film of his?*

SL: I do appreciate Lynch. I would say my favorite movie of his is *Blue Velvet*.

Judging by his apartment, Jacob's a reader...what's on his shelf and why?

SL: I imagine Jacob reads a lot of fantasy, adventure and science fiction—Jules Verne, Edgar Rice Burroughs, Ray Bradbury, Terry Brooks—anything to escape his lonely, sedentary life. I also imagine he has a lot of pornographic magazines and adult comic books. His favorite would probably be *Ripple* by Dave Cooper.

How did you choose which things could or couldn't harm someone in Jacob's condition? For instance, a cross won't, but sunlight is fatal. They do not have superhuman strength, but their will to live is...well, paranormal.

SL: I don't think Jacob's will to live is paranormal. He just has to do what he must to survive. He is very mortal, and has been thrown a new set of rules to cope with, as a mortal. Writing draft after draft of the screenplay made me realize that anything that made it cool to be a vampire had to go. I kept the blood and sunlight problems because those are the two things I personally would hate to deal with on a daily basis. I believe my unconscious goal was to make the audience feel like they've been lied to all these years, and that being a vampire would, in reality, suck.

ES: Like I said earlier, in *MS*, vampirism is a disease, a sickness that has to be dealt with like any other attack on the body. It was a great choice that Scott made during the process, a completely realistic and unglamorous look at this condition. And besides his thirst for blood and the healing ability, he's just a normal dude trying to deal with the shitty hand that life has dealt him.

I always wonder what other abilities Jacob has that he hasn't discovered yet. Could be a very cool sequel.

Ed, how has being the Co-Creator of Blair *changed your view and vision of horror in cinema?*

ES: Well, it's completely shaped it, really. I wasn't much of a horror person until we did *BW.* I mean, I liked horror films, but I didn't give it any special attention. Now, I have to keep my finger on the pulse of what is out there. And because of *BW*, I feel like I'm a part of this eclectic family. The fans are so amazing and so dedicated to this genre. It never ceases to surprise me. I feel privileged to be a small part of it.

There are rumblings of another Blair *film. What can you tell us?*

ES: We are as close as we've ever been to making another *Blair* film a reality, but I really can't say more. And even that doesn't guarantee that another *Blair* film will be made. It's still very much up in the air. We are making progress, though.

JOE SCHREIBER

Joe's blog is called The Scary Parent, and has written in the Expanded *Star Wars* Universe with *Red Harvest*, and the *Dawn of the Dead Meets Star Wars, Death Troopers,* considered the first combination of SF and H for that franchise. Throw in his superlative work such as *Chasing the Dead* and *Au Revoir, Crazy European Chick*. For some reason, I felt a connection to Joe's view on being a writer of things dark as well as a parent.

Joe's spots in cyberspace are http://scaryparent.blogspot.com/ and http://joeschreiber.blogspot.com/

What's the average day for someone referred to as 'The Scary Parent?'

I get up with my kids at 7:00 a.m.. Hang out with them for a couple hours—they're homeschooled, so I do a bit of that with them—then if there's nothing else going on, start writing around nine. Finish around noon, a little more kid time, then head off to the hospital where I work. Get out around eleven at night. Eat cold pizza and watch *The Hangover 2*, then stumble off to bed. Repeat as necessary.

Are your kids fans of Star Wars?

Not at all. My son's into Super Mario and something called Skylanders. My daughter likes Harry Potter and *Diary of a Wimpy Kid*. They like hanging out with stormtroopers at the book signings, but that's about the extent of it...

How did they react to their father's rather dark take of the Star Wars Universe, Deathtroopers?

They liked the cover, although the posters of it in the basement kind of freak them out. Occasionally they'll ask questions about the story, and they might eventually read it, but I'm not holding my breath. Meanwhile, they draw pictures on the backs of the proof pages that have accumulated around the house.

What can you tell us about the development of what is basically the Horror side of the Star Wars *literary franchise?*

It was an amazingly smooth process. I got a call from my editor at the time, at Random House, who asked if I'd consider writing a zombie *Star Wars* novel. I said yes, and started working on an outline. Lucasfilm had some notes, and I went back and rewrote it, then tackled the book. Eight weeks later, the first draft was done. They were incredibly supportive and encouraging throughout the entire process, a dream to work with, really.

Writing in such a beloved universe where fans are at times rabid and unforgiving, did you have any trepidations about taking Star Wars *into dark territory?*

Not really. When I sit down to write anything, all the pressure that I feel comes from within. Can I pull it off? Can I actually write a story that's going to hold my interest, and develop it all the way through? All that stress goes away once you fall into the story and find your path but until then, it can be pretty scary. I figured that *Star Wars* fans would either like it, or they wouldn't, but first I needed to make sure I did the best job that I could do.

Red Harvest was another dark Star Wars *story. Did its development mirror that of* Deathtroopers? *And is the title a play on the* Star Wars *film codename* Blue Harvest?

The title is definitely a play on *Blue Harvest*. I was contracted to write that book before *Death Troopers* was even released, and there was a lot of back and forth on that one, developing the world of the Old Republic. It was fun to be able to use Jedi and Sith in a zombie environment.

Which character or set of characters in the Star Wars Universe would you like to write a novel about? Would it be a horror story?

Horror tends to be my default mode, so my guess is that it probably would go that way. My favorite *Star Wars* characters are the ones that we'd recognize from our world, or at least our pop culture universe—the inexperienced farm boy yearning for something bigger, the rogue who lives by his own moral code, the tough princess. Having said that, I love writing about stormtroopers. I think it would be great to do another story about the guys who wear the armor, Vader's Fist, encountering something way beyond their pay grade.

Do you have a favorite Star Wars *movie?*

Empire, hands down.

Is there any other franchise you'd like to write for?

Great question. I'm not sure, honestly—although I think an *Alien* novel would be a lot of fun.

The Supernatural *novel you did,* The Unholy Cause, *resonated with me because of the Biblical connection and the noose Judas hung himself with. I know you immersed yourself in* Supernatural *continuity, but was there much research into Judas or the noose? Not a whole lot is out there?*

I'm not exactly the world's greatest researcher. Lazy is probably a generous way of describing it. I'd like to say that I spent hours researching archaic apocryphal texts and ancient books of knots, but that would be a lie. Mostly, I just made it up.

With No Doors, No Windows, *you established an almost Serlingesque pacing to this very patient, deliberate story. It seemed to me your previous novels were a bit faster paced. Did you approach this novel with that intent?*

Absolutely. With *No Doors*, I was very much aware that this would be my last horror novel for a while, and I was taking a shot at the haunted house genre, so I was definitely shooting for a slow-burn creep fest a la Shirley Jackson, instead of the balls-out adrenaline blast of horror like the couple before it. I'm guessing the three or four people who read the thing probably agreed.

A favorite novel of yours for me is Chasing the Dead. *It plays upon some very visceral fears as person and parent. How did you refine such an emotional response without going for the easier aspects that seem to be so prominent in movies and lit?*

I'm really not sure. *Chasing the Dead* was written from my nerve endings, in the most compulsive and direct way I knew how, and I didn't really have anything to compare it to, let alone emulate, so maybe that's why. It's very much the work of a new parent who was working two jobs and didn't have a lot of extra time to mess around. It's raw, almost a bit ugly in its urgency, but that was how I felt at the time.

How is the development of the Eat the Dark *and* Chasing the Dead *coming along? The cliché is that when you adapt material for a screenplay, you toss out the source material...*

I know! I'm adapting *Eat the Dark* myself, and it is quite different from the book. but that's okay—it's kind of the book's twitchier, untrustworthy meth-head brother. But it's a lot of fun. The outlook for *Chasing the Dead* is a bit more nebulous. It's still being developed, and the script I read was quite good, but so much of the process has to do with the guys who handle the money, so we'll see.

Your latest, Au Revoir, Crazy European Chick *is sort of a sideways* Le Femme Nikita *with a lot of humor and aimed at a Young Adult audience. Will we see a series stem from this? Maybe a movie?*

There's a sequel due out this fall, set in Europe, and Paramount has the movie rights with Josh Schwartz attached to direct, so we'll see.

What scares the Scary Parent?

The Visa bill...

CAITLIN R. KIERNAN

WHILE HER FICTION HAD GAINED notice in previous years, in May 1996, Caitlin was approached by Neil Gaiman and editors at DC/Vertigo Comics to begin writing for *The Dreaming*, a spin-off from Gaiman's groundbreaking *The Sandman*. She wrote the book until its conclusion in 2001. She has consistently eschewed the label of "horror writer" but has certainly placed her own dynamic mark on the fiction of the dark and weird.

You can catch her online at: caitlinrkiernan.com

How does a paleontologist become a SF/DF fiction author?

The paleontologist comes to a place in her life where continuing to be a paleontologist ceases to be a viable option, and so she has to turn to an utterly ridiculous Plan B. Luckily, though, the paleontologist is well-read and has some talent as a writer, and people think having been a paleontologist is interesting and so they remember you. But none of this means anything at all unless the former paleontologist is incredibly lucky. Highly unlikely, but weird shit happens all the time. Well, not so much *weird* shit, as shit that is merely highly improbable.

Your first novel, The Five of Cups, *was written between 1992-1993, but didn't see publication until 2003. What's the story behind the delay?*

Well, I did try to sell it immediately after it was written. I almost sold it right off, and it *did* get me my first agent. But it's actually a pretty lousy novel. I was only just learning how to construct a novel, and I was lucky enough that every editor who read it rejected it. All those rejections, they led to my agent, that first agent who's no longer my agent, asking me to write another book. One that wasn't about vampires, please. So, I forced myself to step away from "horror," and I wrote *Silk*, which was, instead, published as my first novel. But over the years, readers had an interest in my "lost novel." It was actually called that. Someone at a con actually offered a friend of mine five-hundred dollars if he could get this person a copy. Finally, all those years later, I let it be published, mostly as a curiosity. So people could see how it began, I suppose. But, truthfully, I can't stand to look at the thing. I try not to talk about that book.

You worked very closely with Neil Gaiman on DC Comics/Vertigo's The Dreaming, *what was it like working with him and getting the chance to play in his universe?*

Neil is wonderful. He gave me some of my first breaks, including the *Dreaming* gig. And *The Sandman* is brilliant. Unfortunately, by the time I was asked to write for *The Dreaming*—a series that never should have happened to begin with—was already hopelessly broken. There were all these readers who wanted *The Sandman: The Next Generation*. And that's not what they got. So this spin-off limped along for sixty issues, most of which I wrote, a few of which I love, before someone thankfully pulled the plug. By the way, I'd asked to leave the series at the fiftieth issue, and was persuaded to stay on. I was told the series would last a long time. Reluctantly, I agreed. Then it died ten issues later. But. Playing with Neil's characters, many whom I loved and still do, that part was marvelous. It's just that working for DC Vertigo was a nightmare. It paid the bills, probably better than my bills had ever before been paid, but the shiny wore off after my first six or seven issues. Neil knows how I feel about *The Dreaming*. I made the best of a bad situation. In the end, it taught me to be a professional, to handle deadlines and what have you. And, yeah, working with Neil was great. There are even a few bits of actual secret collaboration strewn here and there through the series. Mostly, he'd give me permission to write one of the Endless, and I'd ask him to write that character's dialogue.

The Drowning Girl: A Memoir *has a very compelling trailer on your website. Can you tell us about the making of it?*

Well, we're still working on the full one-minute cut, the final. But so far it's been grand. First, it was incredible to see the response from my readers when I set out to crowdsource a book trailer. We set it up on Kickstarter, asking for $1,200, but the donations came to more than three times that. We found our cast and crew, and filmed in Massachusetts and Rhode Island, on location, and almost the whole experience was genuinely wonderful. Sara Murphy, the actor who played Eva, was a trooper. We'd planned to shoot in the summer, but were delayed until the autumn, after the weather turned cold. One scene, which she had to do in the nude on a country road, she did it in a rain so hard we could hardly hear each other over. Then, the next day, we were filming in the Blackstone River Gorge, and the river was freezing. Never mind the current. She was willing to do another nude scene, crawling out of that river. I was standing there expecting to have to go in after her at any moment. Oh, and the first day, Sara walked into three-foot surf at Moonstone Beach. She was amazing. And the footage is wonderful. Nicola Astles, who plays the book's protagonist, Imp, she had the unenviable task of playing out a scene where Imp tries to drown herself, and I fear we almost managed to *actually* drown her in the process.

What can we expect from The Drowning Girl?

It's not like anything I've ever done. I was terrified I'd spent two years writing something awful, something illegible, unreadable. But then Peter Straub read it and loved it. In fact, he went so far as to say he'd never read anything like it before, and that it was my masterpiece. Still, if people go in expecting a genre horror novel, they're going to be very, very disappointed. It's the memoir of a schizophrenic girl who may, or may not, have met and fallen in love with a ghost, and the ghost may, or may not, be a mermaid. Or a werewolf. There's a wonderful line from a Kelly Link story, "Pretty Monsters"—*Stories shift their shape.* And that line sort of sums up the novel. Just when you think it's this, it becomes that. But if you believe it's that, maybe it's this, after all. What should people expect? A book about schizophrenia, more than anything. But also a book about hauntings, about the nature of hauntings. Which may, or may not, make it a ghost story. But not in the tradition that a lot of people have come to expect. Not a book where I'm necessarily setting out to scare you. Go back to *The Turn of the Screw*, or *Rebecca*, or *Gaslight*, or *The Haunting of Hill House*. This is a story about the human mind, and how it shapes reality, how those perceptions of reality are constantly shifting their shapes.

I know you're not fond of being pegged as a 'horror author,' but The Red Tree *has a creepy elegance to it. Are you ever aware of not being a Horror writer when writing a work like that?*

To quote—or paraphrase—Douglas Winter: "Writing isn't a genre. It's an emotion." I write stories filled with horror, terror, awe, fear, wonder, beauty, sorrow, epiphany, and on and on and on. *The Red Tree*, it might all add up to something that instills a sense of dread. Or whatever. But so does *Apocalypse Now*, and people don't generally claim Coppola was making a horror film. For that matter, sort of looking at this problem from another direction, if I buy into the idea that we have to label people "Horror" writers, "Science Fiction" writers, "Fantasy" writers…what the hell do we do with someone like Harlan Ellison? Or Ray Bradbury? Angela Carter? Cormac McCarthy? Kathe Koja? Kurt Vonnegut, Jr.? William Burroughs? Genre is primarily a marketing paradigm, and has very little to do with what any given writer does.

Are there any plans to bring The Red Tree *to the silver screen? Has there been any interest from filmmakers to adapt your work?*

There's been a lot of interest, and there still is. It comes and goes. *Threshold* came very close in 2002. When it all fell apart, well, it was hard enough that I learned to forget about Hollywood. If it happens, it happens. If it happens and the resulting movie isn't shit, that would be wonderful, and I'd be happy. I love film. But it's not something I think about when I'm writing or daydreaming. A producer or a director shows interest, and, well, it's not my job to think about those sorts of things. Anyway, if there are any current plans to film *The Red Tree*, no one's told me.

Do you have a favorite work of yours?

Definitely *The Drowning Girl*. No question. With *The Red Tree* a close second, and my short-story collections *A is for Alien* and *Confessions of a Five-Chambered Heart*.

The narrative tone of your work has been compared to the likes of H.P. Lovecraft and Algernon Blackwood. Do you feel that's an accurate comparison?

Yes and no. I've definitely looked back to Lovecraft, Blackwood, Lord Dunsany, Arthur Machen, Ambrose Bierce, to learn a lot of what I know. The importance of mood, for example. Restraint, for another. But I've never written what could be called pastiche, as some admirers of Lovecraft have done. I'd never do such a thing. Not even if I'm using elements from his fiction. But, too, there are a lot of influences I think have been overlooked recently, because some people want to peg me as one of the new flag bearers of the weird or whatever. The Modernists are a huge influence, especially Faulkner. A lot of poets, more than I could name. Angela Carter and Shirley Jackson have been huge influences, as have Harlan Ellison and Peter Straub. But I could go on like this for hours.

Is it fair to say that Silk *was the book that put you on the map, so to speak?*

I think it's completely fair. It was my first published novel, and it may not have been a bestseller, but it wasn't unsuccessful. I think it led a lot of other authors to expect a lot from me in the future, which was, at the time, terrifying. Honestly, I don't think I lived up to that potential until *The Red Tree*.

As a paleontologist, you have many fossils in your home. Do you have a particular favorite?

You know, I've got cabinets filled with beautiful trilobites and ammonites from all around the world, with dinosaur and mosasaur bones and fossil turtles. But, if I had to pick a personal favorite, it's a tiny squashed trilobite, may five mm. long, on a chunk of shale. I collected it when I was thirteen, and when I showed it to paleontologists at a museum in Birmingham, they were very excited about it and asked me to lead them to the road cut where I'd found it. Which led to my volunteering at the museum. Which led to my working at the museum…and so forth. So much happened because that one tiny trilobite.

What does a typical day entail for you?

If I'm lucky, I'm out of bed by ten-thirty or eleven. I'm a night person. So, I have breakfast and coffee. I read email. I write a LiveJournal entry. Then I answer all that email I read earlier. Then I write. I go weeks at a time without leaving the house. I just repeat this day-to-day cycle. I don't know how I haven't died of monotony. I meet people who see being an author as a glamorous life. And I want to say, you ought to see me sitting at my desk in my underwear—I usually write in a tank top and underwear—and watch me sitting there typing, day after day after day. It's about as glamorous as watching grass grow.

Given an hour over coffee (or beverage of your choice) with anyone alive or dead, who would it be, and what topics would you like to talk about?

I have no idea. Maybe David Bowie, in which case we'd talk about sex and music, Outsider art and what it's like to kiss Catherine Deneuve.

You've called collections like your Confessions of a Five-Chambered Heart *"Weird erotica." How is your "Weird erotica" defined?*

There are things that defy definition. Or that it's just too much trouble to define. I call it *"weird erotica"* because I figured people would want me to call it something. Angela Carter and the Marquis de Sade get together and write a story about a drug-fueled gay masked ball that culminates with a performance of Oscar Wilde's *Salomé* wherein the title role is played by a nude pre-op transsexual. Or, H.P. Lovecraft and Anaïs Nin and Bill Burroughs get together and write a story about a cannibal and her willing victim, who's also her lover, who's being consumed over months and months, and who takes part in the feasts of her flesh. That's *"weird erotica."*

What can you tell your readers about yourself that they probably don't know?

I was a born with a tail. Unfortunately, most of it was removed at birth. All that's left visible is a tiny little nub of cartilage.

WILLIAM NOLAN

WHILE HE IS BEST KNOWN for coauthoring the novel *Logan's Run* with George Clayton Johnson, he also co-wrote the screenplay for the 1976 horror film *Burnt Offerings* which starred Karen Black and Bette Davis. His nonfiction books are of such ambitious studies of a variety of fields and genres *John Huston: King Rebel, Carnival of Speed, The Ray Bradbury Companion, Dashiell Hammett: A Casebook* and numerous others. In 2010, he received the Lifetime Achievement Stoker award from the Horror Writers Association. It was my honor to interview a man whose work I grew up reading.

williamfnolan.com is the place to find him online.

I guess I'll start by asking a popular question of late; What's going on with the remake of Logan's Run?

"They" (the Hollywood trade papers) say that the new version will be produced this year... I'll believe it when it happens (after fifteen years of waiting!). All fingers crossed...

What did you think of the radio production of Logan's Run *in 2011?*

I thought it was well-produced.

What was in the decision making of having Paul Salamoff write Logan's Run: Aftermath?

That was decided by the publisher (Bluewater Productions). Jason V Brock and I acted as Costume Designers and Story Consultants. Actually, the "Future History" section of the first series is all by Jason—even the parts in the comic are his writing, verbatim!

Did you initially imagine the Logan *saga to be the trilogy of* Logan's Run, Logan's World, *and* Logan's Search?

No. I also went on to write *Logan's Return* (a novelette) and am completing another new part of the series, *Logan's Journey* (with Paul McComas). Jason and I are also gearing up to do a major retake on *Logan* as well: *Logan Falls*.

Having written Logan's Run *with George Clayton Johnson, I was wondering if the two of you still keep in touch?*

Oh, sure. We see each other at least once a year. We're still good friends!

You've written other works, does it ever get to you that Logan's Run *looms over anything else?*

Not at all! I'm grateful to have Logan as my "calling card." It's one of the high points of my 60-year career! I'm proud to be "Logan's Papa."

You wrote a film treatment for John W. Campbell's story "Who Goes There?". Having done that, what's your take on the films that ended up being made from Campbell's source novella, such as Howard Hawks' The Thing From Another World *in 1951, John Carpenter's* The Thing *in 1982, and the 2011 version?*

I didn't see the most recent version, but I liked both of the other versions. That said, I think that my version would have made a better picture.

What was it like working with Dark Shadows *creator Dan Curtis for the film* Burnt Offerings?

Dan and I were pals...I worked on seventeen projects with him. We got along fine, and he had great respect for my work. Interestingly, *Burnt Offerings* at the time was just another of our many projects together, but now has a life of its own. I'm proud of it.

The Seven For Space series features a classic sort of gumshoe in a futuristic setting. What inspired that?

I've always loved wild humor. (I discovered S. J. Perelman in high school—and I also love James Thurber.) One of my closest friends is the comedian Stan Freberg, who's a *very* funny guy!

Seven For Space was not only Science Fiction, but also humorous without being mean-spirited towards the genre. Who influences your sense of humor?

Everyone and everything… I find humor everywhere. I read Sheckley and Goulart in SF, and they influenced the *Space* series.

What went into writing How to Write Horror Fiction?

I was teaching creative writing at a college and was asked about horror fiction in particular as a genre. (Another book I did that is worthwhile is the more general writing primer called *Let's Get Creative!*)

Have you ever been concerned that you may be pigeonholed as only an SF writer?

Sometimes. I mean, I've done SF, true, but also fantasy, horror, biography, poetry, crime, comics, and a wide variety of short fiction… And only a handful of those are SF. The label doesn't really fit me; no one label does!

What attracted you to the works of Dashiell Hammett?

I read Chandler first, and I loved his stuff. A friend said to me: "If you like Chandler, you'll dig Hammett." Of course, he was right! I love 'em both: Hard, tough, but poetic. They're the best, I feel.

You're self-confessed movie fanatic. What films have you seen recently that you were really affected by?

I thought that *War Horse* was lovely. *The Grey* was a marvelous wilderness picture…I try to see a new movie each week. (Since age five!) Films have been a huge influence in my life.

Is there a book that you wish you've written?

No, or I would have!

You knew James Dean. What can you tell us about your relationship with him?

I knew Dean only slightly. We met at the road races in California. He was a very fast driver, but he pushed too hard. His death in a car crash didn't surprise me.

Anything you'd like to say to your fans to sign off?

Read Nolan. Thanks!

NANCY HOLDER

NANCY HOLDER IS A MULTIPLE award-winning, *New York Times* bestselling author (the *Wicked* series). Her two new dark young adult dark fantasy series are *Crusade* and *Wolf Springs Chronicles*. She has won five Bram Stoker Awards from the Horror Writers Association, as well as a Scribe Award for Best Novel (*Saving Grace: Tough Love*.) Nancy has sold over eighty novels and one hundred short stories, many of them based on such shows as *Highlander, Buffy the Vampire Slayer, Angel*, and others. She lives in San Diego with her daughter, Belle, two corgis, and three cats.

You can visit Nancy online at: nancyholder.com

With your experience with YA literature, how do you know where to draw the line; where there may be too much grit or too much of an edge to a story?

This is a tough decision, and I find that the older my daughter gets, the more circumspect I become. She's fifteen now. The *Wicked* series is very dark; *Crusade* has dealt a lot with matters of faith and is far less brutal. *Unleashed* is the least dark of the three, and the most recent. Sometimes adult readers object to underage drinking, language, or sex. I don't believe that you have to do certain things you feel are inappropriate because "the story demanded it." But this is a tough question for me to answer right now. My daughter is sitting across from me chuckling because I was taken aback that someone wrote "fucking awesome" in a book review for *Damned*, the second book in the *Crusade* series. I swear all the time, but I have these little pockets of anxiety when I'm around her.

Do you think parents are as concerned about what their kids are reading as much as what they are watching?

The parents I know, yes. Most of the moms read *Twilight* first. And a lot of my daughter's friends don't even watch TV.

DreamWorks has picked up Wicked, *which you co-wrote with Debbie Vigue. How is that going?*

We've gone into turn around. But our agency is still very excited about it and we've learned that *Wicked* never dies.

Do you feel that your early Buffy *novels had an effect on YA genre fiction?*

I think Joss Whedon had an effect on YA genre fiction. I think he made it hip to be honest and smart. I think he showed that heroes can fail badly, and still be heroes. I was lucky enough and honored enough to work with his characters, but he deserves the credit.

What do you think of the current state of genre TV? The Walking Dead, for example. (Although it's adapted from a graphic novel)?

I'm so happy that there's lots of genre on right now. It's a feast of fantasy and dark fantasy. Long may it wave.

Every time someone says the vampire is a dead character, somebody comes along and rejuvenates it. Zombies are the hips thing now, have been for a while…Do you think they'll fade?

I don't know. I've been surprised by their longevity, but why should I be? They're zombies. I wrote my first zombie short story in 1992 ("Passion Play") and I just did a piece of Stephen Jones' zombie trilogy. So the bubble hasn't burst yet.

There are plenty of places for strong female characters in the genre, we had Buffy, Sonja Blue, and characters like Domino Lady. What does it take to create a successful character that resonates with fans as much as those have?

One thing that I've noticed is that because there's not as much history and context about strong women characters, they're taken to task for things we let slide with our comic book superheroes.. Domino Lady fights crime in stilettos and she carries sleeping powder, knockout drops, a hypodermic needle, a Saturday Night Special, and calling cards. Artists are always asking me where she keeps all this stuff even after I mention that there's a pouch in her cape. Why she's wearing heels. Because she's a crime-fighting adventuress, that's why!

Where did the concept for the Domino Lady come from? She's rather esoteric in a fan way.

The Domino Lady is a pulp character from the 1930s. She only appeared in six stories but she's such a vixen that her story has continued. She was only one of a handful of sassy dames who did the things bazillions of male pulp characters did.

When you wrote The Screaming Season, *you watched a horror movie every morning during the writing of it. Could you name a few?*

A Tale of Two Sisters; El Orfanato; all the *Ring* versions, Japanese and American; same with *Grudge: The Others; The Innocents; The Haunting; The Shining; Memento Mori*; lots and lots of J-horror. *Kwaidan*.

Did watching them in the morning affect the tone of the storytelling?

I watched movies and listened to horror movie soundtracks until I felt scared. Then I tried to stay scared all day. If it started to wear off, I watched a couple of key scenes from *A Tale of Two Sisters*, which is on my computer. I couldn't watch any of these movies after dark because I couldn't sleep if I did!

Do you have any other writing habits like the horror movies?

I write to music whenever I can. I have tons and tons of horror soundtracks and I listen to them constantly while I'm working. I just finished a *Teen Wolf* novel. The new TV show is fabulous and I can't wait for the next season. It's sexy and scary, funny, and involving. They tell you all the music that's used in very accessibly playlists—*Teen Wolf* is on MTV, so duh! I'm so glad I got approached about writing the book because I probably wouldn't have watched it. I'm getting ready to write a dark nursery rime for *Two And Twenty*, edited by Georgia McBride and company. My nurse rhyme is "The Lion and the Unicorn," about the accession of James VI of Scotland to the English throne. And I'm super excited to announce that I've been working on a Buffy coffee table book. It's going to be gorgeous.

A lot of the horror genre has relied on stoking the fires of simple fears, sometimes ones from childhood. They continue to resonate with readers and watchers over and over again. Why do you suppose we have still have yet to outgrow the Thing From Under the Bed?

I think those kinds of fears are so primal that they live in the reptilian brain, and we can't get rid of them ever. They're as much a part of us as our DNA. Lucky for us horror writers.

How do you choose an author to collaborate with? (And yes, you can take that as a completely unveiled attempt to get your attention)

Again, may I saw how gallant you are. I'm friends with a lot of writers and if I think we might be compatible to work on something, I suggest it. With Debbie Viguié, she was a student of mine at the Maui Writers Conference. Her talent was blazing. I needed someone to help me write *Wicked* and Debbie was the one. We've just celebrated our tenth year writing together, and we've sold eleven novels and one short story. Debbie also has her own career, as I do mine. As I'm writing this to you, I'll be seeing her in about 7 hours for breakfast at Gallifrey One, a Dr. Who convention, here in L.A. She flew out from Orlando to be here and I can't wait to see her.

Last question; how would you like your tombstone to read?

SHE WAS A GOOD WRITER AND A GREAT MOM.

TAD WILLIAMS

TAD WILLIAMS HAS HELD MORE JOBS than any sane person should admit to—singing in a band, selling shoes, managing a financial institution, throwing newspapers, and designing military manuals, to name just a few. He also hosted a syndicated radio show for ten years, worked in theater and television production, taught both grade-school and college classes, and worked in multimedia for a major computer firm. He is co-founder of an interactive television company, and is currently writing comic books and film and television scripts as well as novels.

Tad and his wife, Deborah Beale, live in the San Francisco Bay Area with their children and far more cats, dogs, turtles, pet ants and banana slugs than they can count.

The Dragons of Ordinary Farm was co-written with your wife. How was the experience of not only collaborating with your wife, but writing a story for younger readers?

Collaborating with anyone is interesting, but collaborating with a spouse is even more so. Deb and I are very different in our habits and approach so it's been a challenge, but I've loved having the chance to work on something with her.

What can you tell us about the sequel, The Secrets of Ordinary Farm?

It elaborates on the events in the first book, answering some questions and raising some new ones, but there's also a whole adventure that begins and ends in this volume, so even if you haven't read the first you can enjoy this one.

What was it like penning comics for D.C. Comics?

I've always loved comics, so getting to write some was fun. I would have liked to have taken a longer shot at *Aquaman*, but that wasn't the way it worked out. That was my only real frustration. But just being able to set some things up that I hope future *Aquaman* writers will use—way cool.

Will you take readers back to Osten Ard?

I plan to, if not in the exact ways they expect. I'd like to do a collection of short stories, tied together by a central framing story. I've been waiting to get to that for years, so we'll see…

For many of us, Tailchaser's Song *holds a special place for us, given that it was published some time ago (1985), do you have the same feelings for it now as you did then?*

It's so far back I can barely remember the me who wrote it, but of course it's my first book and will always be a sentimental favorite. It's being made into an animated film by a company called Animetropolis, which is very exciting.

Given the current state of printed books, chains like Borders closing, and the rise of e-readers, what do you think the fate of the bookstore or the printed page will be in say, ten or twenty years?

I suspect regular paper books will become more and more of a prestige item—something for collectors and lovers of fine work. More and more people will be reading electronically. That said, I don't think old-fashioned books will disappear, anymore than acoustic instruments did after synthesizers came along.

What went in to the decision to publish Shadowmarch *exclusively online?*

I just wanted to do something different and I was interested in both the internet and the concept of serialization. I'm still interested in both. Maybe I'll do another online novel one of these days.

Shadowmarch is clearly a universe that can expand to no real set end. Can you tell us about what's next?

I've just finished my next book, *The Dirty Streets of Heaven*, the first of three (but not a trilogy, because they're also meant to stand on their own) about Bobby Dollar, an earthbound angel caught up in the cold war between Heaven and Hell. I'm really enjoying them. They're a bit more adult than my other books—more sex and swearing—but they're also funny (I think) and will be fun to read. Lots of monsters, demons, and weird ideas.

Do the villains in your books, say Johnny Dread, think of themselves as villains? Do you approach the creation of antagonist differently than protagonist?

Everybody is the hero of his or her own story. That includes villains. Hitler didn't think, "How can I screw up the world?," he thought, "How can I make the world perfect for people like me?" Same result, but that illustrates the difference in approach. Sadly, most villains either think they're heroes—which would be Ineluki in my *MS&T* books—or are sociopaths who don't care about anyone else, which would be Dread. Either way, they don't spend a lot of time wondering how their opponents see them.

What made you write the Christmas story, "The Sugarplum Favor?"

Had an idea and it was a few days before Christmas so I thought it would be fun. I like writing short, and if I've got a chance I'll knock one out. I'd like to do more.

How much of you is in your characters?

A little of me is in all of them, and there's a lot of me in some—Renie Sulaweyo, Prince Josua. I try to use what I know, so almost every character is going to be tested against my own personal truth—"if this was me, would I act this way?" It means putting oneself in some strange shoes occasionally.

Has there been any interest to have your books adapted to film?

Besides the aforementioned *Tailchaser* animated film, the *Otherland* books have been optioned for a film. I don't have much information about it yet, except that the producer has done good work and seems to get things done. Fingers crossed.

You've mentioned you'd like to work with George R. R. Martin. Has that come any closer to being a reality?

George and I are both pretty busy. Maybe when he finishes his current story (hah!) we'll find a chance to do something.

How does the creative process start for you?

There's no set rule. Ideas bounce around in the back of my mind. Those with staying power usually begin to create or draw other ideas, combining and growing until I can't avoid them any longer. Then I begin to think about whether I want to do something more concrete with them. If they last through that process, they join the line of things I mean to turn into books or stories.

KATHE KOJA

WHILE SHE IS A PROLIFIC AUTHOR of short stories, most of her short fiction remains uncollected. Koja's novels and short stories frequently concern characters who have been in some way marginalized by society, often focusing on the transcendence and/or disintegration which proceeds from this social isolation (as in *The Cipher*, *Bad Brains*, "Teratisms," *The Blue Mirror*, etc.). Koja won the Bram Stoker Award and the Locus Award for her first novel *The Cipher*, and a Deathrealm Award for *Strange Angels*.

Kathe can be found online at: kathekoja.com

You've swung between YA and Horror. Have there been any troubles in your publishing one or the other because of your previous work?

I started out writing SF, then moved into horror, contemporary fiction, YA, and now with *Under The Poppy* and its sequel, *The Mercury Waltz*, historical fiction. To me the concept of genre is like attending a party of gorgeous strangers—who will you meet there, what fun will you have? So far, no one has given me the bum's rush from any of the parties based on my attendance at any of the others.

Would it be fair to call your Horror work as 'Splatterpunk?'

Some people have (and do), but I don't.

What's the last book you read?

Puppet: An Essay On Uncanny Life by Kenneth Gross. Mysterious, emotional, and involving; I highly recommend it. I've just started reading David McCullough's *The Greater Journey: Americans In Paris*—really good stuff.

For fiction, I'm a judge for this year's Ferro-Grumley awards, so I'm reading the list there. No comments, of course, till the judging is done, but I've definitely found a couple of bylines to cherish.

Your YA Fiction seems to attract the 'goth' kind of crowd rather than the somewhat geeky crowd that Harry Potter captured. Do you think that's accurate?

I'm not sure—a book finds its reader, and vice versa, in ways that stay at times inside the bounds of previous taste, and sometimes not at all. That's why I'm always flummoxed when a parent asks me at an event, "Which of your books will my daughter/son/nephew/godchild like?" How in the world could I know that?

Does your inspiration for writing come from one constant source, or does it differ from work to work?

Everything I do starts with an image—for *Under The Poppy*, it was a man, a performer, on the road with his troupe of *outre* puppets; for *Buddha Boy* it was a boy in a wild t-shirt, looking down a stairwell at another boy below. The image intrigues me, I start to learn more about it, other images accrete around it—and sometimes, a book results. Not always, but sometimes.

And writing itself is pretty much the way I live in the world: I have to write, I love to write.

What kind of feedback have you received from your younger fans?

Honest, heartfelt, perspicacious, and humbling.

You adapted Under the Poppy *to a stage show. What went into the adaptation of it?*

An enormous amount of work! So far, we've done three Poppy events—the first at Motor City Pride, the second called "The Company We Keep" during the People's Art Festival, and "Love is a Puppet" as part of "Victorian Opulence" at District VII Detroit.

The first was an introduction to the concept of the Poppy, the next two were the story of Istvan on the road, and this performance takes us into the world of the Poppy itself, with floozies, love, and darkness—and multimedia accoutrements. And yes, there will definitely be puppets... Each is part of the whole narrative of the Poppy story, and each builds on the last, onward to the full event, which will be immersive and all-encompassing. It's an amazing and exciting way to retell the story, and so much more fun than plunking an audience into seats and saying "Just sit there and watch."

You worked with Joe Stacey on the music of the stage show. What made you choose him and what went into the collaboration?

Joe Stacey and I met through a mutual friend (hi, Aaron!), when the book trailer for *Under The Poppy* was being created. I gave Joe the lyrics and a few vague ideas, and he knocked it out of the park.

We began talking about the larger show, I gave Joe a working version of the script, and again, he created amazing work: "All the World Loves a Lover," "Is It Real"—and scored what will be the projections/visuals for the show, too. Joe is a fantastic performer as well as a composer, and he plans to play live in that show.

Most recently, we worked together on the book trailer for the ebook release of my first novel, *The Cipher*, coming this spring. Joe had read the book, saw the first edit of the film (yes, we shot on real film), and yet again, came up with something memorable, fierce and otherworldly. It's a privilege to work with someone so talented.

One of the most compelling story devices in Under The Poppy *is the use of rather unique puppets. What inspired you to use them?*

They are rather unique, indeed, and some of them even anatomically correct... Again, I saw Istvan on the road, this performer with his troupe of four actors, *les mecs*; then I saw another man, Rupert, and knew that they loved one another; and I followed them both from there.

The puppet as character/actor in a novel is a wonderful construct, because there's nothing a puppet can't do, become, or represent. The more I read and learn about puppets, the more I respect them.

Is there a type of genre you'd like to write that you haven't yet?

I would love to do a picture book with very few words. A very difficult and demanding process, like haiku. Maybe someday.

I've had two cats, both rescues, and so a work like Straydog *has a particular resonance for me. Was there a particular reason you wrote it?*

I'm so pleased to hear about your rescues, and to know that *Straydog* spoke to you—all of our cats are rescues, too. I do volunteer work for some animal rescue agencies, and that experience certainly went into the story, but I didn't consciously say "I'm going to write about the plight of feral animals." There was an image: a girl with a notebook, who turned out to be Rachel, and Grrl, the dog she loves and tries to rehab. And *Straydog* was a short story at first, called "straydog," that I wrote for *Cicada* magazine, and that my agent, Christopher Schelling, suggested I might want to expand into a novel: "There's a lot more there," he said, and he was right.

Do young women approach you for advice on anything because of your YA work?

You mean writing, or life? The first I'm qualified to expound on, at least from one particular perspective, and I enjoy talking to younger writers more than any other group in the world. The second is a different matter and one I would be very careful about.

Was it difficult to switch from an 'adult' genre to YA?

Nope.

Is there a particular novel in the Horror genre that to you, defines the word Horror?

There are horror novels I love to go back to—*Dracula*, Shirley Jackson's *Hill House*, *The Shining*—and some of M.R. James' short fiction that, no matter how many times I read it, continue to frighten and disturb me: not with what might be happening in the darkness, but what is.

What is currently happening with the film version of The Cipher?

The film version of *Cipher* is in the development phase—the production team is nailing down the script, working on financing, attaching talent, and so on. Hollywood is its own terrain, but I have great confidence in the team's vision and passion for the project—and its smarts. I'll share more news on my blog as it happens.

I enjoyed Kink for its approach of a normal person in a decidedly unreal situation and the subtext of the human condition or am I reading too much into that?

I hope everything I write has that subtext—it's our terrain, as readers and writers. Though *Kink's* always been called "contemporary fiction," to me it's a horror novel, as is *Going Under*, one of my YAs, and for the same reason: the depiction of human need and greed as a black hole of selfishness that recognizes no boundaries, and counts no one as its equal. The landscape of hell.

Skin, to me, was an unflinching look at what I suppose could be called an alternative lifestyle, but very dark and humorless. Was it planned that way or did the spine of the story dictate it could be no other way?

When *Skin* was published, in 1993, some people on reading it were amazed that anyone could want to actually piece himself/herself at all, and why in the world would anyone write, or read, about such a weird and fringey culture? Recently someone showed me a reader's comment on *Skin* that said "Oh, piercing is so dull and *passé*, everyone's been there done that!" To me, that's pretty humorous.

You've that in Headlong, you were most like the character of Hazel. Who are you like in say, Skin *or* Under the Poppy?

It's definitely hard for me to think in those terms—I believe an interviewer posed me a strict either-or on Hazel and Lily. :) The characters in the novels are who they are, not modeled after anyone, including me. If I'm anyone in *Under the Poppy*, it would probably be Pan Loudermilk.

Was YA a genre that was as clearly defined when you were a teen as it is now? Would you say the genre is clearly defined?

In a marketing sense it means one thing, to an individual reader it means another; there are some adult readers who won't pick up anything labeled YA, sadly.

But back in the day there was no shelf for books specifically meant to explore the years of adolescence—there were children's books, and then there were adult books. S.E. Hinton is a golden exception, and there were a few voices out there, but nothing like the deluge now. A golden age for YA readers, whatever their own chronology.

What can we look forward to in the future from you?

I hope pleasure and surprise… *Under the Poppy* will be out in paperback this fall, *The Mercury Waltz* early in 2013. I'm working on another book but it's too early to talk about. The *Under the Poppy* show is projected for fall 2012, in Detroit; come and see! And I'm planning a work on the poet and playwright Christopher Marlowe, but what form that will eventually take is still a mystery. I love mysteries.

TIM PICCIRILLI

TOM PICCIRILLI IS THE AUTHOR of more than twenty novels including: *The Last Kind Words, Shadow Season, The Cold Spot, The Coldest Mile*, and *A Choir of Ill Children*. He's won two International Thriller Awards and four Bram Stoker Awards, as well as having been nominated for the Edgar, the World Fantasy Award, the Macavity, and Le Grand Prix de l'Imaginaire.

Tom's website is: www.thecoldspot.blogspot.com

With Every Shallow Cut, *your narrative is sometimes stream-of consciousness, and other times erratic. Did you have any particular problems in writing it because of this style?*

I think that's how most of us live our lives, so it was a more natural mirror for an authentic personality of someone on the edge. His mind wanders, he drifts through life, he thinks about the past, fears and anger and frustrations constantly tug at his attention. So it was easier to write if anything because a writer is always trying to give the impression of a character's natural mental state. Writing the story and backstory at the same time just allowed me to create a more fully sympathetic and understandable protagonist.

I've noticed that a lot of Horror-based authors such as yourself tend to go into writing Crime or Noir novels. What's the attraction?

Horror seems like a young man's game to me. It's full of fantasy and uproots the reader from full realism. But the older a writer gets I think the more authentic and realistic topics he finds to write about. The topics are still dark, and the basic conflict remains good versus evil, but crime/noir seems to focus our perception inward and backward, rather than outward and forward. They are stories of personal character, personal fears, disappointments, regrets, needs, and the grays of life, rather than the more obvious black versus white, good and bad, details of circumstance rather than of enduring life.

I enjoyed the novella You'd Better Watch Out. *What made you choose the first-person narrative in a book about a young man from a tragically broken home to become a hitman with some serious demons to deal with?*

Because first person was the more immediate way to tell the story. I wanted readers to understand t his guy who was a very complex protagonist. He was evil, in his way, but I wanted readers to sympathize with him, and so I had to show his background, the terrible events of his childhood, and show how he was, in effect, created from these circumstances and incidents, how he lived with them, how he released them.

What are your feelings about the Horror genre as it stands today?

I hardly read any nowadays. Most of it doesn't feel very real to me. It deals with subject matter that doesn't interest me much. Like I said, I prefer realistic fiction to the more fantastical sort. Maybe the wheel will turn again and I'll start reading more horror, fantasy, and science fiction again, which are the genres that made me first fall in love with reading when I was a kid. But as it stands, I read primarily crime fiction and non-fiction at the moment.

I have to admit, I loved the title of your work, Fuckin' Lie Down Already. *Jack Ketchum was quoted as saying, "This is a small masterpiece. It's said that the devil's in the details and Tom got all the details exactly right. I always said Pic was one to watch. Fuck watching. He's utterly there. A voice to listen to and learn from." Does that kind of praise change your mindset while writing?*

It was very generous of him to provide that blurb, but positive reviews/praise/criticism, none of it tends to change my mind set at this point of the game. I have my voice, I have my material, I have the themes and wells of creativity from which I draw. The writing is its own creature. It feeds itself, it goes places that I might not necessarily want to go or even understand. The act is a kind of fusion of conscious will and desire and unconscious need and driving force.

The Last Kind Words follows the dynamics of someone being raised in less than ideal circumstances. Why is that such a powerful element for you to use?

Backstory is story. History is what brings us to the present, it makes us who we are. Drama and conflict are what make darker characters darker in the first place. It's more interesting for a protagonist to have to go through some kind of traumatic event or events as a kid. We've all had them, we've all suffered through them, and they leave their scars and their marks. We live with those scars and those demons. They follow us, they are us. Drama is the pearl built from the grain of sand of pain.

Which of your books would you recommend new readers to start with?

LKW is my most recent novel and seems to reflect who I am as a writer at the moment. We're all always changing and all always learning, but everything I've learned as a writer has gone into that novel. It's very representational of me as a person. My sense of humor, my regrets, my disappointments, the great motifs of myself.

As a fan of Asian cinema, what drew you to that particular style?

Asian cinema seems to embrace all manners of kinks and oddity and uniqueness. They understand the greater circumference of life. Their movies are totally insane, way over the top, but honest, at a primal and basic level. There's less need to project perfection or heroism the way American cinema seems to do. Here, we're so terrified of always providing good examples. In Asian cinema, it's enough just to try to tell an honest story about flawed people, sad people, driven people.

You have over twenty books to your credit, and have won the Stoker and the International Thriller Writer's Award. Looking back, did those achievements happen as fast as they seem to have?

They don't seem very fast to me. In a 100 word bio they might add up quickly, but we all know that is distilled from the grinding of life. You work. You keep working. You put out product. You tell one story after the next. Sometimes people like what you do and there's some validation along the way, awards, praise, or other kindnesses. But just like every Joe doing his job every day, you do it because you have to do it, because it's the job to do, and the accolades are few and far between.

I once heard Harlan Ellison say that it's more important to be a plumber than a writer. Do you agree?

In a manner of speaking, sure. When the house is flooding, you don't need some creative outlet. You don't need to read a book or watch a movie. You need to get somebody over to your house to fix a busted septic pipe right now. Art is a necessity but it's also recreational, it's food for the soul. It's not an immediate necessity like some other things might be. And so a writer isn't as important as some other jobs might be in certain circumstances.

To me, your writing is reliably dark without always having to resort to blow-by-blow dismemberment. How do you establish this as an author? Does the voice of the Horror or Crime fan speak up and guide you so to speak?

It's all about emotional context, not the hacking off of limbs. We all have to face our dark nights of the soul. Tragedies, social terrors, personal upsets. You show the darkness by understanding the darkness, our shared darkness. Writing is all about finding common ground between the writer and the reader. The insider and the outsider. A writer gambles that he knows his audience, that the audience is, in fact, very much like himself. I'm guessing that I can tell stories full of enough elements that hit you in the same way they hit me. Whether that's drama or humor or horror or whatever, that's the whole objective. A stand-up comic tells his jokes because he figures you'll understand his observations. You'll have seen similar things, you'll look at the world the same way he does. We have the same basic understanding of the world at large.

The Last Kind Words resonated with me not only because of the dynamic storytelling, but because of its portrayal of the human condition. Was that something you intentionally used as a thread, or was it just in the subtext of the story and the characters in it?

Well, I don't know how you write without somehow dealing with the human condition. What else is writing? So, sure, it was intentional, I don't know how you talk about humanity as subtext, by accident in fiction, without intending to do so. In any case, as mentioned earlier, I'm always trying to find common ground, to draw the reader in because these are subjects and themes and context that we all share. If something disappoints or frustrates me, then chances are it'll do the same to you. The "story" as such is just to propel the commentary about all the other stuff that goes along with it. The story is the smallest part of the tale, if that makes any sense. It's the discussion on life and love and poetry and pain that's the real steam that drives the engine.

What are you working on now?

A sequel to *LKW* and a number of other projects. Novellas of one sort or another, new short stories, and a couple of standalone novels in various states of completion.

KEVIN J. ANDERSON

KEVIN'S GOT THE ENVIOUS STATUS of having forty bestsellers. He has written spin-off novels for *Star Wars*, *StarCraft*, *Titan A.E.*, and *The X-Files*, and with Brian Herbert is the co-author of the *Dune* prequels. His original works include the *Saga of Seven Suns* series and the Nebula Award-nominated Assemblers of Infinity. Some of Anderson's superhero novels include *Enemies & Allies*, about the first meeting of Batman and Superman and *The Last Days of Krypton*, telling the story of how Krypton came to be destroyed and the choice two parents had to make for their son.

You stepped into a pair of large shoes when you took up the Dune *series with Brian Herbert. What was involved in becoming part of that legacy?*

We told the story in detail in an Author's Note in *House Atreides*. It's been close to 15 years ago now, when Brian and I first made contact. I had always been a huge *Dune* fan, and Frank Herbert had left his great chronicles unfinished. Brian was a successful writer in his own right, and I had plenty of credentials. Together, we used our love for *Dune*, studying the original novels, and a lot of Frank Herbert's notes to carry on the story. The recently released *Sisterhood of Dune* is our twelfth novel together in the series.

I enjoyed the novel Enemies and Allies, *which featured Batman and Superman. How did you approach creating the story for these iconic characters?*

I had already done my first DC Universe novel *The Last Days of Krypton*, which got me fully immersed in the Superman saga, but when I delved into *Enemies & Allies* I tried to get into who the characters were as *people* in the real world, Clark Kent trying to be a normal guy knowing he's a great superhero……but Bruce Wayne, I think, really considers himself as a dark vigilante and only pretends to be a rich socialite.

What comic book character would you like to write about?

Already done! Batman and Superman would have been my first picks.

Terra Incognita shows a world that features very few of the expected tropes one may expect from Fantasy; very little magic or Conan-like characters on epic quests for the Chalice of the Great Something. It's all very organic; Was there a conscious effort on your part to sort of step away from the accepted norm of the genre?

I was inspired by the legend of Prester John and his great land across the sea. I didn't want to write a fantasy with bearded wizards waving magic wands; in *Terra Incognita* there are sea serpents, but they're just scary animals. However, there is some magic, and unexplored landscapes, and great quests, which gave me the ability to explore real gritty religious conflicts and intolerance—in a way that would be more demonstrative than if I used real countries and real conflicts. It's more of a historical epic, but set in an imaginary land.

What motivated you to have a soundtrack composed for Terra Incognita?

The two rock CDs are actually more like crossover albums, telling part of the story in a rock-opera fashion. Much of my writing had been influenced by music—Kansas, Rush, etc.—and because the record producer and label owner of ProgRock Records was a fan of mine, we had the opportunity to do something innovative, with a rock CD and a novel written by the same author. And I think both turned out very well, it was a great experience to work on.

You've written over one hundred novels at this point, having seen your first novel Resurrection, Inc. *at the age of twenty-five. That's quite a feat. To what do you attribute not only the sheer number, but your continued success?*

I love to write. I love to tell stories, and I keep thinking of stories—I never get tired of it. All I've ever wanted to be was a writer, and I work hard so I don't have to find a different career!

You've played in the universes of the likes of Chris Carter, George Lucas, and Frank Herbert. Are there any other 'prefab' universes you'd like to participate in?

I am a writer, but I'm also a fanboy at heart, so I loved the movies, TV shows, and classics of the genre. Right now my plate is so full of projects that I really love, I can't think of anything I'd rather be doing. If only there were more hours in the day, and at the keyboard.

Your short story, "Prisoner of War" is a sequel to Harlan Ellison's "Soldier" from The Outer Limits. *How did you come to write that, and was Harlan involved at all?*

When I approached Harlan with the idea, he was initially skeptical, said he never had any interest in doing sequels to something he had already written, in fact saw no point in them. Then I pointed out to him that he had created a fascinating and complex universe for "Soldier"—So, Harlan, are you saying that there's only *one* possible story to tell in that whole universe? So he decided to let me take a crack at it. He provided the introduction and his original script to "Soldier" and I wrote the sequel story "Prisoner of War." [The original book publication with Harlan's part, *Outer Limits: Armageddon Dreams*, is very rare and hard to find!]

What went into the process of the current Dune *novel,* Sisterhood of Dune?

This one is the origin of the Bene Gesserit Sisterhood a few decades after the Battle of Corrin. Since this is the 12th one, Brian and I have our process down and we know what each person is supposed to do. It was very smooth.

How many more Dune *novels can we expect from you and Brian?*

Sisterhood is the first of a trilogy, so we have two more of those, and we've got our own original *Hellhole* trilogy to wrap up—that maps out the next five years or so.

I've always enjoyed the stories of Jules Verne, so naturally I was drawn to your Captain Nemo, *which covers a considerable amount of backstory for a classic literary character. What went into the writing of it?*

I loved that book! It's one of my favorites of all my novels. I grew up reading Jules Verne, and *Captain Nemo* allowed me to reread all those classic novels, tie together all the Verneian story threads, and create my own homage. *Captain Nemo* took me more than three years to research and write, and I am very pleased with how it turned out.

What are your five 'desert island' books?

Lonesome Dove by Larry McMurtry, *Dune* by Frank Herbert, *Lord of the Rings* by Tolkien, and then I'll probably toss in two books from my "To Read" stack, so I have something new and fresh to read.

Are there any of your fellow Star Wars *author whom you especially admire?*

I worked closely with a great many of the *SW* writers and comic writers when I was working on my novels. Dave Wolverton, Mike Stackpole, Timothy Zahn, Tom Veitch, and the artists Dave Dorman and Christian Gossett. We were all part of a very fun team at Lucasfilm—some of the most fun I've ever had.

Which one of your characters would you like to have a long dinner conversation with and what would be served?

I think that would have to be Captain Nemo...and we'd probably have steak, because he's probably tired of seafood!

Hellhole *is a novel you wrote with Brian Herbert that was your own collaborative creation. What was the collaborative process like to build that particular world?*

We had worked so well together on 11 *Dune* novels, so it was time to try our hand at a universe of our own creation. We had created many different planets, histories, and characters in *Dune*, so we were well prepped to create *Hellhole*. It took a lot of brainstorming, character building, and plotting. We're just finishing the second novel in the trilogy now, and are still building the universe.

Anything you'd like to end with?

Just to point out that we're releasing many of our out-of-print and hard-to-find titles as eBooks—including many Frank Herbert titles—at wordfirepress.com. It's a new opportunity to put classic works back into print.

STORM CONSTANTINE

STORM CONSTANTINE IS AN internationally-published author of over thirty books, both fiction and non-fiction. She is the founder of Immanion Press, originally created to keep her back catalogue of novels in print, but which now publishes many other authors. Best known for her Wraeththu novels, involving an androgynous and powerful race of beings that arise from humanity, Storm has also written non-fiction titles, some of which are available from Immanion Press. Storm is also a teacher of creative writing, an editor and a Reiki Teacher, among many other interests.

You were brought up reading mythology rather than genre Fantasy. What sort of effect do you think that has had on your work?

There wasn't an awful lot of genre fantasy available when I was very young, certainly not for children, so mythology was the most fantastical literature I had available to me. The stories inspired me and I loved to create 'sequels' to the old legends. In a way it was a kind of mythology fan fiction!

What can you tell us about the magical work that you've done?

I could write a book on that, so it's difficult to paraphrase. I've delved into many aspects of magic over the years, and I suppose the culmination of all this exploration and learning was creating my own magical systems, such as Deharan Magic and the healing system Sekhem Heka. I love pop culture magic and creating new systems. I suppose it goes with my whole bundle of creative urges generally.

What was the road that led you to using hermaphroditic and androgynous figures in your work?

It goes back a long way, but I can't say when the exact moment was that I became interested in the androgyne as a magical creature. I wrote stories and poems about proto-Wraeththu way back in my teens.

There have been Tantric touches in your work and explorations of the energy it creates. What caused you to explore the element of sex magic? Is it more symbolic than literal?

Everything I write just emerges from me without any conscious decisions being made over content. Quite often people read meaning into my work that wasn't put there deliberately, but patterns emerge in a novel that seemingly have a life of their own. I've always regarded sex as sacred, so it disappoints me that for many it is meaningless beyond basic gratification. With the Wraeththu books, I explored sexuality as a magical force.

You've said that vampirism is a metaphor for oral sex and a kind of Russian roulette when it comes to dealing with the fangy types. What would you say creatures like say, the werewolf, are symbolic of?

To me it is simply the beast within. We are all werewolves at heart. It's just that some choose not to show it!

I may be getting off track here, but as you've referred to things such as the Dead Sea Scrolls being an inspiration, have you read such things as The Gospel of Judas?

No, I haven't read that particular text.

What is your muse?

She's a capricious beast who sometimes takes protracted holidays for no good reason!

What have been some of your most memorable paranormal experiences?

These stories are all too long to relate here, because they'd need to be told in context. Let's just say I've experienced some inexplicable stuff over the years. Whenever I meet someone new, one of the first things I like to ask them when there's chance for a good long chat is 'what's the weirdest thing that ever happened to you?' It's amazing how many bizarre stories come out, from the most unlikely people.

Where does your passion for Egypt come from?

It's been with me since before I went to school. My first ever story concerned a fox who went back to ancient Egypt. I think I was affected deeply by the Bast scene in *The Three Lives of Thomasina*, which in all other respects is a rather cheesy old Disney (I think) film. But there is this one scene where the cat 'dies' and goes to the goddess, only to be reborn. That was it for me I think. I was obsessed by cat-headed women as a child and made up lots of stories about them. I imagined being one: her name was Rhodora and she had a blue mane.

What made you create your own publishing company, Immanion Press?

A; At first it was simply to bring my Wraeththu books back into print—the original trilogy—and to provide a UK publication for the second trilogy. It just grew from there.

One of the classes you've taught was called 'Tarot Without Tears.' Could you explain the meaning of the title?

There's no great meaning to it really. It just refers to the fact that there is a lot of memorizing to do with learning to read Tarot, so it can be rather a chore. The system I use to teach it involves mnemonics to help people learn quickly.

Are there any plans to publish your artwork in a collection?

Not at the moment, because I have so many other projects on the go. I might consider it in future.

What went into the world-building of The Wraeththu Histories?

Not a great deal to begin with! I was more obsessed with the characters than their environment, but over time, I fleshed out the world and gave it a firmer foundation. When I released the 'author's cut' versions of the original trilogy I put some of this material into the books to make them stronger.

One of the most striking books of yours to me is Mythangelus. *What inspired you to pursue angelic themes such as those?*

I have always been intrigued by angels, but distinctly not the fluffy kind. Over the years various story ideas have come to me, and I collected them together in that particular anthology. When I brought out the four story collections I attempted to put those with a similar theme together as much as possible, although there was inevitably some overlap. One story, "The Oracle Lips," actually found its way into two of the collections, completely by accident. I didn't realize this until a reviewer pointed it out!

Did you layer in Pagan-based worship in Sea Dragon Air, *or was it you built for the people to believe in?*

The religious systems in the *Magravandias* trilogy were created for the story. I didn't regard any of them as being "Pagan" (in a modern sense) as such. It was a fantasy world, and those were simply the beliefs held by its inhabitants.

Do you feel the success of books like Sign of the Sacred, *and* Hermetech, *overwhelm works like* Magranadias *series?*

Yes, to a degree. It's particularly noticeable in the ebooks I've brought out. The *Wraeththu* books are the most popular, followed by the *Grigori* trilogy, then *The Thorn Boy*, the Magravandias story collection. *Burying the Shadow*, *Hermetech* and *Thin Air* are also available as ebooks but they don't perform as well as the others. There are still a number of books I've yet to republish through Immanion, and these will also become ebooks eventually. I only got the rights back for the *Magravandias* books last year.

How did you come to work with Michael Moorcock on Silverheart?

He had a first draft for the book and didn't have the time to complete it, so asked me to do so.

What do you do to relax?

Listen to music, watch movies, play World of Warcraft, spend time with friends.

Your last non-fiction book was 2008's Sekhem HekA Natural Healing and Self Development System. *Will we be seeing any more NF from you?*

I'm currently working on the second book of the Deharan Magic system, *Grimore DeharUlani*. This is co-authored with Daniel Marcheschi, with input from his Nayati forum members and also the Wraeththu magical group in Second Life. There's a lot of fascinating material out there now, from people who began working with the system when the first book came out. The second book will include some of this material.

What are you working on now? Anything to promote, rant, or talk about?

Apart from the *Grimoire Dehara* I just mentioned, I'm also in the process of compiling two more anthologies. The first is the second Wraeththu Mythos short story collection, called *Para Imminence*. This will include at least one new story from me, and hopefully two—if I get the time.

The second is a sequel to *What a Long Strange, Trip It's Been*, which was an anthology of articles and stories about *World of Warcraft*. I'm currently taking submissions for both of these books if anyone is interested in contributing. There are guidelines available. People can mail info@immanion-press.com to ask for them.

I have a short story to write for an anthology based around "real" magic, i.e. not fantasy magic, and there are also a number of Wraeththu novellas and stories I've got half completed that I'd like to finish and bring out as a book. And I would dearly love to write a new novel. I've got so many ideas, notes and stray chapters I've written, but have so little time to get a good long run at anything. With full length works, I prefer not to have a lot of distractions that get in the way, but unfortunately with working on Immanion and its projects, my time tends to get eaten up.

DARRELL SCHWEITZER

DARRELL SCHWEITZER IS THE AUTHOR of about 300 short stories and the novels: *The White Isle, The Shattered Goddess* and *The Mask of the Sorcerer*. Along with George Scithers and John Betancourt, he refounded *Weird Tales* magazine in 1987 and continued to co-edit the magazine until 2007. He won a World Fantasy Award as co-editor of *Weird Tales*, along with Scithers.

Over the past few years. We've seen a decline of short fiction markets that have legs. Do you see this as a decline in interest in short form fiction? How do you feel about the present state of the speculative short story?

Have we? Ralan.com and such places suggest there are more short fiction markets than ever. I can remember when there really *were* less than a dozen in the whole field. Today we have magazines, anthologies, paying (pro quality) websites like Card's *Medicine Show* or Tor.com, so I am not convinced the short fiction market is declining. I must also point out that Marvin Kaye and John Harlecher seem poised to revive *Weird Tales* and restore its weirdness.

What do you think of today's speculative fiction with regards to the short story?

See above. I don't get to read as much of the current stuff as I would like. One's broader interests do get in the way. I confess the book I most recently finished was the world's oldest novel, *Callirhoe* by Chariton. Greek historical romance, written between about 25 BC to 50 AD. A genuine genre novel no less. No, I did not read it in Greek. I am afraid I shall have to revise my own claims. Romance, rather than fantasy is the oldest of prose genre forms. After that, I must turn to something more recent, a Tim Powers book I am reviewing for *Dead Reckonings*.

All I can say with confidence about the contemporary SF short story is that good stories are still being written and published, and no form is dead as long as it is still being produced. Ignore the doomsayers. The last time someone told me that SF had exhausted itself and could no longer be written, Cyberpunk happened the following year. If the field seems in the doldrums, it will renew itself.

E-media (Internet and e-books): Friend or foe to the integrity of writing?

None of the above. If you read *Moby Dick* on a Kindle you are still reading *Moby Dick*. The internet may make piracy easier, which is another matter, but good writing is good writing and its integrity resides with the writer. In a publishing scene, I expect the mass-market paperback to disappear and be replaced by the e-book. But the hardcover, trade paperback, and paper magazine will continue to exist.

What do you feel is the next step in speculative fiction?

See above. SF renews itself every few years. I think the new *Weird* has run its course and Steampunk may soon have difficulty keeping its pressure up, but something else will happen. We are always waiting for the Next Big Thing, confident that there will be one.

Who are some of the more exciting up and coming authors you've seen lately?

Keep an eye out for John Fultz, Theodora Goss, and Holly Phillips. Also I very much enjoyed *The Postmortal* by Drew Magary, which is a Philip K. Dick Award finalist this year. I was one of the judges, but I cannot tell you what won until it is officially announced, or else I would be ritually strangled. (We judges are followed around by officially-appointed Thugees with scarves. I bet you didn't know that.) This relates back to my feelings about the state of the field. I was a PKD judge in the last year. I am really sick of steampunk zombie noir ......I notice that most of the really creative stuff these days is, like the Magary book, not actually being published with the science fiction label on it. Science Fiction has really gone mainstream, and hopefully this mainstream SF may feed some vigor back into the genre, which has way too many military SF or zombie series right now.

What originally drew you to the dark side of fiction?

One for the very first adult level books I ever read or wanted to read (age 12) was *Dracula*. It's a natural affinity.

What keeps you going in the writing gig? What excites you enough to motivate you?

Certainly it isn't making a living, because I have never done that with writing. What excites me is the act of creating a story good enough that I like it and have a pretty good idea that other people will like it too. As I have sold over 300 stories by now, I may be able to trust my judgment a little bit here.

Vampires or zombies? Why?

I've written one real zombie story, "The Dead Kid," which is in *The Living Dead* (JJ Adams, ed) and a very small number of vampire stories. I am probably best known in that "field" for the two "Kvetchula" stories which may well be the best Jewish vampire stories written by a Gentile in the past several years. My (Jewish) mother-in-law, aged 82, read "Kvetchula's Daughter" and pronounced it "Funny as hell." "Why?" for whom? For me, when something starts to become a cliché I start getting silly. Certainly good vampire and zombie stories can still be written, but horror can be about something else. The best path may be back to basics. Vampires as evil. Zombies actually based on Haitian folklore rather than on George Romero movies.

Real vampires do not sparkle, of course.

Will you be publishing an updated Neil Gaiman Reader *or* The Thomas Ligotti Reader?

I would like to update the Ligotti reader because by a ghastly accident a chapter which was supposed to be in the book isn't. But I don't know that the publisher is going to let me. The old edition just keeps on selling. If there is enough interest, I could always do a second volume. The Gaiman Reader, I am sorry to say, was not financially successful. I would need a new publisher. Wildside took a bit of a bath on that one. The irony is that for all Gaiman has a zillion times more fans than Ligotti, Ligotti criticism is a mature field, and I don't think Gaiman fans are really ready for lit-crit yet. The Gaiman equivalent of ST Joshi will write great articles when he is 40. Unfortunately, right now he is about 25.

What led to your editing The Secret History of Vampires?

This is actually a good story. About the time *Alternate Kennedys* came out I started to joke that *Alternate Historical Vampire Cat Detectives* was only a matter of time. (I have written and published a story that would have fit into that book. Look up "The Adventure of the Hanoverian Vampires.") Anyway, at a party I started to kid one of the late lamented Marty Greenberg's assistants, "You know, alternate history sells and vampires sell, so how about Alternate Vampires, in which Elvis, Elizabeth Tudor, or whomever are vampires?" I thought I was joking. He thought I was pitching. He said, "Well, we're doing something like that already, but maybe in a year." Meanwhile, they came out with *Celebrity Vampires*. A year later the topic came up again—I had actually been called up about a Lloyd Biggle story because I am the agent for the Biggle estate—and before I knew it I had actually talked them into trying to sell the book, with the refinement that it was going to be Tim Powers style "secret history" rather than alternate history, with vampires. Then DAW went for it. I would be quite happy to do a second volume, if DAW is interested.

How did Tales from the Spaceport Bar *come to be?*

This was George Scithers' idea. Ironically, neither of us ever hung out in bars much, or drank beyond a very minimal level. I still do not know what to order in a bar. It's a social skill I will probably (at age 59) never really learn. But there are a lot of good bar stories, and George knew that I could find some he hadn't thought of, so we collaborated on two volumes of them.

Your interview collection Speaking of Horror *had some heavy hitters in the genre. Who are some of the writers you'd have in a second volume?*

I am going to have a second volume as soon as I can get the files assembled and turned in. Peter Straub, Gahan Wilson, Chet Williamson, Lisa Tuttle, Ramsey Campbell, Brian Lumley (again; the interview from HPL's Mag

#3), Brian Hopkins, Sephira Giron, F. Paul Wilson… I have a rather long list to draw from. The irony is that I don't get to do horror interviews much anymore, as I do not seem to have a market for them. I still review SF writers and editors in every issue of Card's *Medicine Show*. I do not know if the new, revived *Weird Tales* will ever go in for interviews.

What are you working on now? Anything to say to your fans?

I owe various people short stories. I am also working to scan, edit, and assemble a file of the companion stories to *The Shattered Goddess*, into a book called *Echoes of The Goddess*. These are dark/mythic fantasy stories set in the remote future. The Donning Co. was supposed to publish the book in the mid-'80s. Now I can get a Wildside/Borgo edition if I buckle down and assemble it. Alas, my scanning skills and software are such that scanning is scarcely better than retyping. All the stories predate my owning a computer. The good news is that but for an occasional clumsy phrase, I still like the stories.

If my agent can sell my young adult novel *The Dragon House*, I would like to write a sequel. But that has not happened yet. The sequel would be the world's first humorous (or somewhat humorous) Cthulhu Mythos novel for teens. Just what the world needs. My most recent sale was a story to Joe Pulver's *Grimescribe's Puppets*, a Thomas Ligotti tribute anthology. I am working on an anthology myself, about which I must be vague at this point because it is almost entirely invitational and I do not want to be deluged. I've also recently sold stories to volumes 2 and 3 of ST Joshi's *Black Wings* (of Cthulhu) series, and to the new *Weird Tales*. I wrote something for their Elder Gods issue , but they decided to use something else of mine in that issue, so the story I actually wrote for the occasion will appear later. The forces of the marketplace seem to be pushing me in a Cthulhuoid direction right now. A collection of my Cthulhu Mythos stories is inevitable as soon as I have enough available for reprinting to fill a book. Believe it or not, I have not spent years and years writing Lovecraft pastiches. I did no serious Mythos fiction until quite recently.

BRIAN HODGE

He's written an armful of novels or horror/crime, nonfiction that shows no signs of slowing, and about 100 short stories. He has seen numerous finalist slots for the Stoker, the World Fantasy Award, and the CWA Dagger Award, and obtaining the International Horror Guild Award for outstanding short fiction, *With Acknowledgments to Sun Tzu*.

Brian is online at: http://www.brianhodge.net and http://warriorpoetblog.com

What is Horror's biggest asset: the scare, or the exploration of the darker topics of the human condition?

For my money, Column B, definitely. Exploring the human condition is the highest goal of any kind of storytelling. Or should be, most of the time. Not that you can't make room for something purely frivolous. But if all you're doing is conducting an exercise in stringing together a sequence of technical tricks to keep someone reading, without getting into your own deeper thoughts or feelings on anything, observations from your own life experience … that's not something I'd be much interested in reading. Or if I read it, it probably wouldn't strike me as in any way memorable.

That issue was at the heart of my all-time favorite piece of reader mail. I've never liked the term "fan mail," because I'd rather think of it as a lateral dialogue. But it was from a Florida prison convict. He'd been in for decades, I guess. He said he'd read 20,000 books in that time, and upon reading *Prototype*, it was the first time he'd ever felt compelled to contact the author. He wanted to tell me that my gifts were wasted on fiction and that I should turn to nonfiction philosophy, something like that.

How sweet is that? Saying, in essence, "You did this so well you shouldn't do it anymore." But of course, fiction is where those sorts of explorations come most alive for me.

Spirituality in a variety of forms is a thread through several of your books. Why is that?

I'm afraid this one is going to follow a lot of tributaries. At the heart of it, your art or craft is invariably going to reflect your interests and obsessions. As well, for a lot longer than horror has had to make room for, say, slasher movies and the likes of *Saw* and *Hostel*, it's had a metaphysical component, with other realities and dimensions, so the spirit side is much older turf, and certainly more expansive.

But why the draw, on a personal level? It's just a fascinating realm to explore. There's no end to the tangents and permutations. It's like a Mandelbrot set: The closer you look, the more it unfolds. And, arguably, nothing has had more influence on shaping human history. Some might make a case for things like disease and technology, but to me, all that is vying for second. Although at this point you really have to start making a distinction between raw numinous experience, and the institutions and dogmas set up to corral and control and own it. You ask about exploring the darker side of the human condition? Ultimately, what's darker than these institutions and dogmas when they run amok? What's more terrifyingly relentless than people convinced their god is telling them to subjugate and kill? What's worse than the idea of some capricious force that toys with you for amusement, or regards you as less than you might regard an ant that meets your shoe sole?

Plus, I've always been relentlessly curious about what's on the other side of the veil, and the mechanisms of interactivity back and forth. I've had a number of intriguing experiences, some of which I've sought out and some of which have just happened, and most are personal enough that I'd rather keep them to myself, but here's one that's kind of delightful:

Before Doli and I could move to Colorado, we first had to sell her house, and it wasn't moving. It was on the market for the better part of two years. Then somebody gave her one of those St. Joseph statues from the gift shop of the local Catholic hospital. You know, those cheap plastic statues you bury in your yard, and it's supposed to prompt the sale of your home? Now, by this time, I'd already written stuff like "The Dripping of Sundered Wineskins," so, to put it lightly, it wasn't like I had a particularly reverent attitude about the whole thing. But the place sold within two or three weeks.

That's not even the really cool part. I have this friend, Denise, that I've known since junior high. We'd run into each other every so often, and she'd come to my earliest book signings, but overall, we're talking very infrequent, random encounters. Then one night I dreamed that she came to visit me in a jail cell, and let me out. Less than a week later, she showed up to look at the house, and bought it.

What's going on behind things like that? With the statue, sure, you can dismiss it as coincidence, but then, it's been a coincidence for a great many frustrated home sellers. You could think of it as a process-oriented equivalent of a tulpa—something that takes on an objective reality after the belief in it reaches a kind of critical mass. Or something like one of Rupert Sheldrake's morphic fields. And the dream, well, that's like a wink from the universe, which definitely seems to have a sense of humor sometimes.

I just try to stay open, and can't see the universe as a hostile place—quite the contrary —unless that's how you choose to relate to it, with hostility and fear as a kind of programming language. So when I'm in that mode as a writer, I guess what I'm really doing is just spinning cautionary tales: Be careful what you believe in, because you might get it, and in ways you don't expect.

You're also a musician; what sort of music do you enjoy, and what would the first-time listener of your music be able to expect?

Well, musician may be pushing it. Sound deformer, that might be more like it.

I listen to a lot of ambient music, all sorts of sub-genres, because I find it easiest to work to. It's moody, it's atmospheric, but it's not intrusive or distracting. Beyond that, it gets pretty varied: classical and baroque, Nordic black metal, apocalyptic folk, gothic-industrial, Celtic, Tuvan, didgeridoo, soundtracks to sword movies, and the list goes on. Perennial favorites include Steve Roach, Fields of the Nephilim, Skinny Puppy, Nine Inch Nails, Courtney Love, Dimmu Borgir, Tom Waits, Gary Numan, Loreena McKennitt, Ordo Equitum Solis, Sol Invictus, Rush. Right now I'm on a Rammstein kick. Before that it was vintage Tangerine Dream.

As for my own efforts, again, I tend mostly toward the ambient direction, kind of soundtrackish at times. Painting with sound is a good way to describe a lot of it. Sometimes it has ties to my writing; sometimes not, and it's like doing aural landscapes.

As a gearhead from the Eighties, I feel compelled to ask you about your rig, and how has it changed through the years?

Not surprisingly, it's become a lot more computer-centered. The earliest pieces I had were these analog castoffs you could pick up cheap after the first digital instruments emerged: a Moog Prodigy, an ARP Solina String Ensemble, a Yamaha CP-30 electronic piano. I sold all of those for nice profits when vintage analog gear started to enjoy a resurgence. A Memorymoog drifted through for a few years, too, then I sold that to a collector in Germany. It'd be cool to still have them—well, not so much the CP-30— but you can't keep everything.

With the early gear, I didn't have a way to record anything, until Roland came out with their VS line of digital multitrack recorders. Compact marvels at the time, but now, even those seem rudimentary compared to programs like Logic, which I run in an 8-core Mac Pro. Around the same time I got a VS-840 workstation, I got a Roland JP-8000, one of the first virtual analog synths—still have it, still love it—and since then, it's just built up from there, into that ridiculous gear list I have on my web site. I do still love the hardware synthesizers and modules, but now I mostly get things rolling with software synths and sample libraries. It's all just so seductively self-contained. The last two bits of hardware I've bought were USB MIDI controller keyboards: a Yamaha KX8—I'd been waiting years for Yamaha to put their piano action in a pure controller—and an Akai MPK49, which has an excellent control surface.

Was there one particular moment when you decided to pursue an outlet in music?

Not really. I had lessons in clarinet and piano when I was a kid, and more piano in college. It's just something that's always been there, to one degree or another. What triggered its current degree was when my novel *Wild Horses* sold at auction. I had this nice fat influx of cash, and decided to hit the reset button on my gear set-up. I have this saying that came out of that: "Success in one field of creative endeavor should fund the ongoing abuse of another."

The only definitive moment was when I took up the didgeridoo. The first Steve Roach album I heard was *Australia: Sound of the Earth*, which features an aboriginal didge player named David Hudson. He is to the didge what Eddie Van Halen is to the guitar. Hearing that, my reaction was like, "I have GOT to make this sound!"

What makes your expansion of the Horror genre as you see it attract the fanbase you have?

I can only echo feedback I've gotten from readers and reviewers and editors. Probably the first thing comes down to characters, the work I put into trying to make them as real and compelling and three-dimensional as I can. And that there's a definite emotional connection to them, and what happens to them. Also, that I try to avoid the obvious, the predictable. That I usually strive to be writing *about* something, not solely escapism that's only operating on the surface. For some readers, at least, that I've never stopped working to refine my prose style into something that's smooth and effortless, sometimes rhythmic and lyrical. None of which has anything to do with horror per se. It's all to do with the craft of writing, period.

What led to the writing of Wild Horses? *It was quite a departure from what readers had, up until that point, had been expecting from you.*

That came after the years I spent under the Dell/Abyss imprint, where I'd done four novels, each one grimmer than the last, culminating with *Prototype*. As weird as it may sound, I hadn't learned, at that point, to protect myself from my own material, the places I was going emotionally to do the work. It was like the writing equivalent of method acting, where you *become* the role. It was taking a real toll, and *Prototype* was the nadir of that. I've seen and heard all kinds of assessments about *Prototype* in that regard. Writer Edward Lee called it the most depressing novel he'd ever read, if also the most illuminating, for that reason. My editor on it, Jeanne Cavelos, called it unbearable. Someone else, the novel *not* to read if you're feeling suicidal. More recently, one of my physical instructors said that, in terms of bleakness in everything he's read, it runs second only to Cormac McCarthy's *The Road*. It's not just me reacting that way.

So I came out of *Prototype* with two problems. I had to do something different for my own well-being. And even if that weren't a factor, it still felt like if I tried to go any deeper, it was going to turn into self-parody. The only option was to ricochet in another direction entirely…something that also appealed just for a change of pace. Fortunately, I'd done this longish crime piece called "Miles To Go Before I Weep," which at the time was unpublished, because the book it was supposed to go into fell apart, as did the second one. It was the core of Allison and Tom's story, and I realized I wasn't ready to turn loose of these characters yet, and that there were more waiting under the surface. So that was the road that beckoned, and grew into *Wild Horses*.

Your novel, On Earth As It Is in Hell, *takes place in the Hellboy canon. Had you been a fan of the comics or movies? Were you envisioning either medium when writing?*

By then I was a fan, yeah. The roots of this go back a few years earlier, when Dark Horse Comics did an anthology of Hellboy short stories, called *Odd Jobs*. The editor, Christopher Golden, invited me to do something for it, and at that time, no, I wasn't familiar with the character beyond seeing the covers in comic shops. They sent me some stuff, and it clicked with me, so despite the crash course, I thought I could do it justice.

In a situation like this, where I get asked to play with somebody else's toys, I look for overlaps in interest. It was obvious that Mike Mignola, Hellboy's creator, has an interest in folklore of the British Isles and Europe, and that was something I could tap into, so I did a story called "Far Flew the Boast of Him," which is a phrase from *Beowulf*. At least from the translation I reread to do the story, which has Hellboy encountering a reincarnated Grendel after he's slaughtered a group of medievalist battle reenactors.

A few years later, come to find out, that story is one of Mike's favorites among other people's uses of his character. Apparently he felt I really got the feel and flavor of things. The success of that first Hellboy movie led to Mike setting up a deal with Simon & Schuster to license the rights to four novels, and of course they needed people to write them. On the basis of that story, I was on the short list. The novels were rooted in Mike's own version of his universe, rather than the film version—there *are* differences—so that's what I was staying true to.

Prototype *may very well be one of the best examples of what could be referred to as 'Thinking man's Horror.' Would this be an accurate statement from your point-of-view?*

That's such a nice compliment, I could hardly be so rude as to disagree, now could I? Yeah, I'd hoped it would be food for thought, and the fact that there's nothing supernatural about it, that it involves a chromosomal mutation and some rather Jungian concepts, maybe that helps.

How did you get involved with the mosaic storytelling in Zombie Apocalypse! Fightback? *Can you tell us what the story will be about?*

These books are the brainchildren of editor Stephen Jones, and they straddle a weird line between novel and anthology. Steve's approach has been to conceptualize each book's direction, and the individual segments that make up the whole, then match each segment to the writer he feels will open it up and bring a unique strength to it.

The section he wanted me for focuses on sport fighting with the living dead. Or as I think of it, the UFC with zombies. Steve knew that I have an interest in combat sports, and some knowledge there, and some experience with the training and sparring, so that made me the go-to guy.

That was my main contribution to the book, but I also did a shorter piece that helps recap the origin material from the first book, from a different angle. This one was an improvisation, almost, after I sent Steve an article about a medieval plague pit excavation going on in London that dovetailed with what he'd already conceived. It was funny—here I am in Colorado, reading the *New York Times*, sending Steve news on an archaeological dig in his own city, which he wasn't aware of. I'd only thought he might file it away for possible future reference with the third book, but he came right back with another commission: adapt it, run with it. It worked out well, too. He says it fits in perfectly.

What can we expect from Without Purpose, Without Pity?

It's a good-sized novella, the longest thing I've done that doesn't break the usual word-length finish line that constitutes a full novel. It's set in the near future, to give enough time for the real-life aspects of the core premise to play out to their worst-case-scenario conclusion: that Las Vegas is an unsustainable city because of its escalating water needs relative to the dwindling available supply. Just yesterday I saw an article on how the Nevada state government has approved a plan for Vegas to begin pumping in groundwater from rural areas 300 miles away, at a cost of between $3- and $15 billion. You have to love that fivefold margin of error. So the ranchers and Indian tribes get screwed, of course, but on the bright side, one of things making out great would be, and I quote, "a new, golf-course-based city in Coyote Spring Valley in the Mojave Desert."

Where's a good, low-level asteroid strike when you really need one?

I digress. The novella: It's an odd mix of elements. This future dystopian aspect, but there's also this Lovecraftian element that's asserted itself after the socio-economic and environmental collapse. And it's told through the world of boxers, in particular what's going on with a former heavyweight contender whose limbs have started to mutate. Plus, as a bonus, it has the weirdest Thai rope fight ever conceived.

What inspired you to write "With Acknowledgments To Sun Tzu" from your collection, Picking The Bones?

I originally wrote that for an anthology themed around art and artists. After the invitation to contribute came along, I went through my usual contrarian thought process. That is, when there's a unifying theme, there's also usually an obvious direction to go in, and I try to avoid it like the Ebola virus. This tactic has always served me well. In this instance it meant throwing out the usual notions of art and artists and the like. Then I got to reflecting on the title of the Sun Tzu classic, *The Art of War*. OK, what if you took *that* to mean a medium of expression? Not long before, I'd watched a documentary on combat photographers, and it's such an outlier culture, you know—they're running into places that every other civilian is trying to run away from—so to me that automatically made for an interesting dynamic. Plus I've done a number of works in which whatever terrible things may be going on the surface reality, they're still just ripples above these vast, powerful currents flowing underneath, and this fit right into that, as well.

In your bio, you talk about how when you were young, you would scribble on bits of wood and attach them to trees, 'Apparently trying to communicate something to whoever might come along later.' What would you have done if whatever or whoever had come to discuss this with you as a boy and/or as an adult?

That's a good question! I never thought of that. I mean, when I wrote that line I was thinking of it in mundane terms, but the way you're asking it makes it sound more mysterious, more esoteric. Which is just as valid. Who knows what was going through my head at the time, what I thought I had to say before I even knew the alphabet? And who's to say that some sort of contact hasn't happened, and I didn't recognize it for what it was? There *is* the other anecdote I paired that with, about the bullets, and that retroactive sense of somehow being guarded, being protected from my own childish ignorance. Maybe that's how these things work: with great subtlety.

You're a practitioner of Krav Maga; what made you pursue that particular form of self-defense?

We might need to define that a little more, for clarity's sake. Krav Maga is the hand-to-hand combat system of the Israeli Defense Forces. I'm in my fifth year of it, and when I started, I was looking for a different way to work out. I was bored with years of running and looking for new ways to lift the same weights. I'd seen the sign for this place, and my friend Nickolas Cook had taken up Krav several months before in Arizona, and spoke highly of it, so I went for a sample class. I spent the first 20 minutes wondering what I'd gotten myself into, but by the end of the hour I was laying down ink for a year.

My thinking at first was like three birds, one stone: I'd get great workouts, with zero chance of boredom, *and* be picking up a valuable skill set, *and* it might expose me to material I could use in writing. All true. But it's gone a lot deeper than that. When you stay with something like this long enough, committing to it and internalizing the subtler aspects and tenets, I fully believe it can make you a better person, in a lot of ways.

I appreciate the background of it. The early foundations of Krav were laid down in Eastern Europe in the 1930s, by a man named Imi Lichtenfeld. He wanted a way to equip his community with a direct, effective means to deal with attacks by Nazi thugs. As such, it's not strictly a martial art, but a system that draws from a variety of traditions—boxing, kickboxing, Muay Thai, Brazilian Jiu Jitsu, escrima, military weapons applications, etc.—and even now it continues to evolve and refine, so I like that fluidity. And where I train, the lineage is very direct. Imi introduced it to the U.S. in the 1980s through a guy named Darren Levine, who was the chief instructor for the owner of my school, James Hiromasa, who's an internationally renowned instructor in his own right.

Plus it's full of great people, instructors and fellow students alike. In my years with it, I've never seen anyone come to it with a bad, or bad*ass*, attitude. Not once. People seem to get the humility aspect of it right away, and maybe a little later, the service aspect, the guardian aspect. I did some more advanced training with several specialists a few weeks ago, and one of them, his metaphor for us is sheepdogs: pack animals with a high regard for the safety and well-being of others.

What is next for you?

There's quite a lot in the works. We've already covered *Without Purpose, Without Pity*, which is just now becoming available in early digital format, with the hardcover edition coming in a couple months.

I'm putting together my fifth collection of short fiction, called *No Law Left Unbroken*, which rounds up my crime-oriented shorter work, along with some new stuff. We're experimenting with this one as a digital-only release, with print-on-demand, I think. I'm also past the midway point of converting my backlist books over to e-book formats. That process is going smoothly now.

Cemetery Dance is doing a big fat hardcover edition of my early post-apocalyptic novel *Dark Advent*. I did an extensive polish of that one, to the extent that it's a brand new draft. Not a different novel, but it was such early work that I really wanted to take the opportunity to make the immaturities of execution grow up a little.

Distinct from that, but related, CD is also planning a special end-of-the-world issue of the magazine, in which various authors who've wiped out the world already contribute do it again, in shorter form. There are a couple-three other short fiction appearances on the horizons, as well.

And, finally, there's the novel-in-progress, that's been taking way too reprehensibly long. It's already longer than eight of my previous ten novels, and should easily surpass *Dark Advent* and *Deathgrip* by the time it's done. Most writers seem to have one of these at some point: the one that turns into your Mount Everest, your Tour de France. It's yet another departure, which has been a big part of the challenge.

PAUL DI FILIPPO

PAUL DI FILIPPO HAS BEHIND HIM hundreds of short stories, some of which are to be found in *The Steampunk Trilogy*, *Ribofun*, and *Lost Page* and his novella, *A Year in the Linear City*, was nominated for multiple awards. Another collection, *Destroy All Brains*, is a rare treasure. And if you can find it, do yourself a favor and buy it!

You can find Paul at http://paul-di-filippo.com

What led to the writing of "Waves" and "Smart Magma?"

This story is actually the second in a highly abbreviated series. And both pieces were commissioned by wonderful editors, so they deserve a lot of the inspirational credit. First, Lou Anders was putting together an anthology titled *Live Without a Net*, the premise for which was worlds and futures with non-computer-based internets. I came up with a piece titled "Clouds and Cold Fires," in which computing power was distributed literally across the skies, embedded in meteorological phenomena. Moreover, those computational powers were Singularity-powerful. Additionally, most of humanity had gone post-human, leaving Earth to uplifted animals and the dregs of our species. Having written one adventure in this venue, I had a few years pass until Mike Ashley asked for a contribution to THE MAMMOTH BOOK OF MINDBLOWING SF, one of several original stories in a reprint book. I had implied further adventures for a new generation of characters in "Clouds," and also felt there was more in this venue to explore, so it was off to the races!

With works like Wikiworld, *how do you combine a bit of satire with good old-fashioned humor?*

Humor is always better if it has a bite, and satire often provides the fangs. The baseline human situation is always pretty absurd—our bodily limitations, our emotions, our aspirations, our vices—but if you can add in something topical and give it an unexpected surreal twist, then you often have a powerful combination. So my recipe is to find something topical and see what kinds of comic characters best match the theme.

You've done quite a bit of e-publishing. With the ability for writers can have now to present their work for all to see, do you see any liabilities of electronic media v. traditional print?

I actually consider myself behind the curve with e-books. Out of my roughly thirty print volumes, only about one is available electronically (*Cosmocopia*) as well as a smattering of shorter works. I'm very happy to offer my work on any platform that appeals to readers. But personally, I still prefer hardcopy for my own pleasures. Having said that, I should also announce that Richard Curtis is working to port almost all my short fiction over to his E-reads venue. So stay tuned!
    http://neconebooks.com/byauthor.htm
    As for liabilities versus advantages for readers and authors both, I think the latter outweigh the former, so long as we can sustain a technological civilization. But if bad times come, my bet is on paper!

Fuzzy Dice is (at least) eclectic storytelling. How did you manage to work through 144 Chapters with a story that changes approach and style in a cavalier way?*

My role model here, as I've said publicly before, was A. E. van Vogt with his famous writing advice to "do something new every 750 words." I always loved van Vogt's stuff and wondered if I could emulate him. Of course, infamous idiot savants like Harry Stephen Keeler often did the same thing, with charmingly disastrous results. Hopefully, I came across more like van Vogt than like Keeler! It was a challenge, but actually proved liberating and fun, trying to warp the plot every thousand words or so, and come up with zillions of neat ideas. Can't do it every outing like AEvV did, but once was a blast.

How does your admiration of Thomas Pynchon affect your work? Do others see Pynchon-esque touches in your work you didn't know were there?

I truly believe that in 100 years, Pynchon will be seen as the Dickens of the 20th and 21st centuries. Not in the sense that he embodied the same writerly flavors as Dickens, but in the sense that both men were utterly emblematic of the zeitgeist and tapped directly into the strongest currents. Having this admiration and estimation of him, I have naturally sought to try to incorporate some of the things he does, in search of similar effects. So I can point out to you deliberate pastiches of mine, like "Karuna, Inc.," which is modeled on *The Crying of Lot 49*. But undoubtedly, since he's shaped my worldview so strongly (I first encountered him in college forty years ago, when my favorite English professor offered extra credit for reading *Gravity's Rainbow*), there are lots of unconscious emulations of him in my work as well. Heck, just the silly character names alone are rampant!

Which five books would you want if you were to be stranded on an island?

That's a tough one! Here goes, anyhow!
 Walden
 Leaves of Grass
 Gravity's Rainbow
 Dhalgren
 Little, Big

You've said, "I am always threatening to write my great 'horsepower SF' novel starring Bishop Berkeley, The Philosopher's Star. Please be patient." How much closer has that come to being a reality?

Do you know the distance from here to the Oort Cloud? I'm now somewhat beyond the orbit of our Moon on my way to that distant destination.

You've referred to yourself as a "Willy-nilly Buddhist." Can you define the beliefs of the aforementioned Buddhist?

Well, my personal Buddhism evolved this way. I read scores of books on Buddhism. Then I practiced at a Buddhist temple for several years. Then I threw everything away except "Be kind!"

Ciphers contains a great deal of Buddhist lore. Are all of your works united by the thread of your beliefs in some way?

I try not to let any one particular lens or filter color my writings, but of course it's almost impossible to separate one's ideology and morality and ethics and biases from the process of fiction creation. Still, I like to think that I can inhabit mindsets and worldviews that are totally alien or antithetical to my personal preferences and write fiction from that viewpoint. Isn't such selfless empathy part of the writer's essential kit?

Ciphers also starts out with the words "Am I live, or am I Memorex?" Do you feel that not only noting a catch phrase, but a particular manufacturer hurts the legs a given story may have with a sort of pop-culture reference?

That's a tough line to walk. *Ciphers* is indeed overstuffed with very transient allusions that may well be impenetrable to new generations of readers. But you always hope the underlying attractions of the tale allow such readers to blip over what they don't get, or even motivates them to do research. I watch tons of old movies from the 1930s and 1940s and there is often dialogue that references outdated cultural touchstones. But generally, my appreciation of a well-constructed and well-acted film is not ruined by such minor hurdles.

Ciphers is a "Rock and Roll Mystery." With that in mind, what kind of Rock music do you like to listen to?

My mate Deborah and I have a goal of listening together to one new CD every day, and I try to keep the playlist very eclectic. One day might be Angelique Kidjo, followed by Frank Sinatra, then Foster the People, then Charles Mingus, then Coldplay, then Springsteen, then Richard Bona, then Gregg Allman…and so forth. Old to new, rock to jazz, pop to American Songbook. About the only thing I can't groove to is hip hop. Just got a tin ear for that genre.

Has your SF writing caused any sort of inner conflict with yourself in light of Buddhism?

Not so far! Buddhism offers a big spectrum of role models. So long as I keep Ikkyu in mind, I can't go too far wrong.

What are you working on now?

Literally this moment, I have to start a steampunk story to accompany my GOH appearance in Italy at Italcon 2012. It will be set in Venice and titled *A Palazzo in the Stars*. After that, I hope to get a novel off the ground. It's been too long since I've worked at those lengths.

What do you see on the horizon for the SF genre?

Damien Broderick and I wrote a book that is due out soon, titled *Science Fiction: The 101 Best Novels 1985-2010*. Doing that survey showed me the immense accomplishments of the past few decades and made me confident that the genre will continue to perform superbly. As for specific trends, it's hard to say. Ernest Cline's *Ready Player One* seemed to me to represent a new type of SF, savvy about gaming culture and the internet in a new way that some older works aren't. Maybe we're just starting to get some new "voices under 30" that will do amazing and unprecedented things.

Anything you'd like to tell your readers they may not already know about you?

I make a mean dish of carbonara! The secret is parsley.

STEVE RASNIC TEM

STEVE'S SHORT FICTION has been compared to the work of Franz Kafka, Dino Buzzati, Ray Bradbury, and Raymond Carver, but to quote Joe R. Lansdale: "Steve Rasnic Tem is a school of writing unto himself." His 300 plus published pieces have garnered him a British Fantasy Award and nominations for the World Fantasy and Bram Stoker Awards

You can find Steve's blog here: http://www.m-s-tem.com/tems/blog1.php/home

Do you feel that the simple tag of "Horror" applies to your work?

"Horror" is a rather broad brush, and not a very useful description except when applied to certain short stories which have an obsessive, singularly emotional sort of effect. As a label it becomes particularly problematic when applied to the novel, because some greater context is required or the horror has no meaning—in fact it may seem a bit silly. At the longer lengths I think we need to know what is being risked, what is it that may be lost. The whole of human experience needs to come into play—at least if it's going to be a good novel. When we look at it in those terms "horror" becomes but one aspect of a writer's body of work. I think that applies to most writers—not just me.

When did you start pursuing writing as a serious career move?

I'd graduated from VPI in Blacksburg with a bachelor's in English Education. Not a terribly useful degree since I'd decided I didn't want to teach. I'd always wanted to be a writer, so I decided to find out if I could become one. I had no idea how to do that, so I applied to various graduate programs in Creative Writing, just to see what would happen. I was accepted into a few, but Bill Tremblay, a poet at Colorado State University, decided I was some sort of "southern surrealist" and wanted me in his program, so I went out there. That was my first step toward writing as a career, back in 1975.

What sort of reading matter did you have around the house when you were growing up?

Very little. I'd bought comics with my allowance, but the only books we had around the house for a long time were a bible and some *Reader's Digest* condensed books which seemed to accumulate like randomly acquired house decorations, but which no one ever read. Almost no one in our small Appalachian farming community had any appreciable number of books. My grandfather was an exception, having inherited a couple of hundred dusty volumes from my great-grandfather—including some ghost stories. There was also a few hundred "trashy" crime and western paperbacks stored in wooden crates that belonged to a cousin. I read those when I visited—even though they were off-limits.

At some point my mother talked my dad into getting a set of encyclopedias, but I was primarily interested in the set of children's classics that came with them—*Robin Hood, the Tales of King Arthur, Huck Finn, Sherlock Holmes*. I read those volumes multiple times.

What makes Horror fans pursue the dark side of storytelling?

Horror fans like dark fiction for a variety of reasons, depending on age and experience. Some people simply enjoy being scared; for others it fulfills a spiritual need. I'm sure for some younger readers it's just the notion of being contrary to everything ordinary people consider good and heroic—it's yet another way to piss off their parents. Some find it therapeutic. I think for a lot of people horror entertainment is a rehearsal for tragedy—both tragedies past and tragedies to come. One of the interesting aspects of that dynamic is that some readers prefer horror whose specific circumstances remind them of their own. For others that's the last thing they want—they're seeking to escape those troubles. Horror provides them with a safe place to deal with those materials.

What sort of things would we see as a fly on the wall when you collaborate with your wife Melanie?

It would be like watching paint dry I'm afraid. We'll talk about a project in general at first—at dinner or during some lull, and then the rest is just passing the story back and forth via email, rewriting each other and advancing the story incrementally until it's done. A lot of improvisation goes on. And compromise.

Daughters, *co-written with Melanie, is a delightfully written story which deals with the loss of magic and the rise of technology. Is the book a parable reflecting our own modern world?*

Ah, *Daughters!* It was great fun to do, but it's a book of ours very few have ever read. At least we have it available as an ebook now. Yes, it's very much in parable mode, but it's as much about psychological states and human development as it is about modern culture. I think human beings start out with a whole lot of magic in their heads, which is gradually pushed out as they use technology. But the imagination—which for me is another way of saying "magic"—is essential, I think, to becoming a well-rounded human being. But you have to make this journey from the superstitious to the creative. The key is finding a way to allow logic and the imagination to co-exist.

What is your opinion on the state of Speculative Fiction these days?

I think there are more fine writers working in the field today than ever before, and they come from a range of backgrounds. This means a variety of styles and approaches and ways of viewing the world. We're seeing more and more writers from overseas and from other cultures. And we're seeing more writers who actually know how to write fiction, as opposed to writers with great ideas but whose prose is stilted and whose characters are cardboard.

What other art form would you like to pursue?

I love to draw and paint. I make no claims for my talents in that arena, but it's something I enjoy doing.

What inspired Deadfall Hotel?

I've always loved stories concerning haunted architecture, and I'm fascinated by buildings in general—the infrastructure, the electrical and plumbing systems, how they're maintained, how variations in space and color and lighting and furnishing can affect us emotionally, how we can make those spaces our own. The whole psychology of the house and how these structures evolve as substitutes for/elaborations on the womb, and the greater sense of a "body" we all live inside.

All this went into *Deadfall*. I wanted, in a sense, to write about the ultimate haunted hotel, which could also serve as a metaphor for horror fiction in general. I wanted to create a vessel which could contain as much of this as possible.

Among the Living strikes me as a great example of economy of storytelling without sacrificing the texture of the story or characters. What influenced you most in this type of writing?

The novelette and the novella are the perfect lengths for horror fiction, I think. They're short enough that they can sustain a certain obsessive focus and intensity. And yet they're long enough that you can explore various aspects of the same idea, ring complications on those ideas, and develop your characters more fully than you might in a short story. Too often the additional length of the horror novel makes that obsessional quality seem strained. And in the novella/novelette the length of the piece forces you to use a pretty tight, predetermined structure, which helps avoid that "sagging middle" syndrome you so often get in the novel.

The Book of Days took an interesting tack in storytelling in that each day, a man tries to resolve his own sanity. What was the inspiration for the subject matter and format of storytelling?

The format was driven by the circumstances of the writing. I wrote the first draft on the old GENIE online bulletin board system. There was a section of the board set aside for professional genre writers, and Bruce Holland Rogers started this "Steve Rasnic Tem" discussion topic. So he gave me this venue, and I wanted to make use of it, preferably daily so people would have a reason to visit it. And I wanted it to be something creative.

So I needed to come up with a project that had more-or-less logical small daily units, which could be improvised in the composition. Improvisation seemed important because of the time constraints, and because I was seriously interested in improvisational working methods at the time (I still am). So I thought of a diary format, and to spark the improvisations I thought of these "This Day in History" snippets you could find on calendars and in daily newspapers.

Finally I tried to think about what kind of person would feel compelled to write such diary entries. The novel naturally evolved from there.

A bulk of your work revolves around normal people in decidedly abnormal situations. Do you feel that's an accurate observation?

More or less—that's the standard circumstance, certainly, for most genre fiction. The only way I might refine that description is that I think my characters tend to discover during the course of the story that the abnormality, in fact, is in them, and that "normalcy" is a bit of an illusion.

Are there any authors new to the scene who scare you?

Scare me? Well, a lot scares me. But the newer writers who really interest me include the Simon's—Unsworth, Bestwick, and Stranzas—and writers like Gary McMahon, Laird Barron, John Langan, Catherine Valente. But there are *so* many.

What are you working on currently?

I have a science fiction novel in progress—*Before Oblivion*, a couple of YAs, an expansion of my "zombie" story *Bodies & Heads* into a novel, a number of other things.

Was there a particular story you read as a boy that made you realize, "Yes. I want to be a writer?"

It was actually a collection of folklore that first made me think I wanted to be a storyteller: a collected tales of Paul Bunyan and Pecos Bill in the school library. Books were an unusual presence in my area of Appalachia when I was very young, but the school library (there was no public library in my county at that time) had a good selection of fairy tales and folklore which I read my way through. After those it was Jules Verne, which solidified the desire. Much later I read Kafka's story "A Country Doctor," a hugely influential piece for me—I think that's when I really knew the direction my fiction would take.

What's missing from today's genre fiction?

There's nothing missing, if you look broadly and deeply enough. I think we're in a golden age of genre fiction, especially short fiction. I don't think we've ever had so many good writers, trying a wide range of stories, and bringing excellent technique to the enterprise.

What went into the creation of your first novel, Excavation*?*

People had been telling me for a while that I should write a novel, that novels were essential if you want to make any headway as a writer. I had two manuscripts I had been working on—one since high school and the other from my college days (these became *Blood Kin* and *Ubo*, respectively)—but I didn't think I had the control yet to finish either one successfully. Then I wrote this short story, "Excavations," and submitted it to Marion Zimmer Bradley for her magazine. She admired the writing, but thought it was really meant to be a novel, and after re-reading it I agreed. That short story, and a narrative poem "The Bear Hunt" which was the early incarnation of one of the chapters, were published in the special hardcover of *Excavation* that Delirium Books issued in 2006.

As with most of my work I've both liked and disliked that novel over the years. It has many of the hallmarks of a first novel—the main character a bit like the author (but more troubled) who feels compelled to journey back to his birthplace and reconnect, and the enthusiastic, energetic, but sometimes uncontrolled prose. But in the final analysis I think it still holds up very well, and I still admire a lot of its original imagery.

Do you have a preference between the formats of short story vs novel-length work?

They're two very different animals. I still enjoy writing the short story a lot more—they're so varied, and you can stretch your muscles in so many different ways, and I get a certain high when I finish things, and you of course get more completed work with a short tale. But I like the challenges of the novel—especially the structural ones, and that you can tackle some huge subjects. They're just exhausting to write.

What compels people to write in the Horror genre? Does it share any of the traits that non-writers have for it?

I think it's the thrill of dealing with very real emotions and situations which may be somewhat taboo to talk about in polite society. It's also a way to deal with dangerous behaviors in a safe way. You can read or write about them—you don't have to try them out in real life.

What are some of the books you have waiting to be read?

I always have a hundred or so books I want to read next. The current stack includes: Ken Liu's new collection, Mark Haddon's collection, Oates' collection The Doll Master, First Born of an Ass by William Joyce, Kit Reed's Where, Noctuidae by Scott Nicolay, Lucia Berlin's A Manual for Cleaning Women, Claudia Rankine's poetry collection Citizen, a book on Buddhism by Ken McLeod—Reflections on Silver River, Stephen Graham Jones' Mongrels, and many many more.

Is it important for aspiring Horror writers to read specific works in or out of the genre?

Aspiring horror writers need to read as much in and out of the genre as possible. If you want to learn to write good short stories read at least 1000 short stories carefully and consciously, both in and out of the genre, paying attention to structure, beginnings, and endings. Make a list of books off the HWA recommended reading list, along with the one in Stephen King's Dance Macabre, and recent Shirley Jackson Award nominees, etc. That would be a good start.

Do you think genre writers have gotten a bit more respect over the past ten-to-fifteen years or so?

From the mainstream and literary circles? Not really. I think this fiction will always be marginalized and out on the edges of things. In part because of the emotional content. The work isn't emotionally "cool" which means some people won't take it seriously.

You've written several books with your wife, Melanie. Is that something you'd recommend to other writer-couples?

Only if it feels safe to criticize each other's work. The idea is that you're making a new third voice that's a bit different from your individual voices—so you're sacrificing a little bit of yourself for that new voice. And sometimes a couple's individual aesthetics—their sense of what is good versus bad writing—may be at odds. That won't work in a collaboration unless you find a meaningful compromise.

How did you and Melanie decide who would write what?

Sometimes it was simply me taking the male POVs and her taking the female. Or we might reverse that. Other times we alternated scene by scene or chapter by chapter, each editing the other before contributing their bit.

We've seen the tropes of vampires continue to do well throughout movies as well as the written word. Zombies appear to be the in thing now, but do you think that will change or that another creature/trope will come along to take its place?

It's always changing, and pretty difficult to predict. I suspect, given the tensions of the times, that we may see more environmental horror and apocalyptic horror. And more blending of sf and horror themes. A lot of people are rather tense about politics and the future of our country and the world. Not a lot of optimism out there at the moment

Is there a genre you'd like to write in but haven't?

I've tried most things—fantasy, sf, crime, western, local color, YA, contemporary realism. If there were a larger market for noir/crime short fiction I think I would write a lot more of that. I'd also like to do more YA and comics work. And at some point I'd like to publish a mainstream, more or less realistic novel.

Are there any contemporary writers you think more people should read?

More people should read Joyce Carol Oates, Ron Rash, Richard Kadrey, Fred Chappell. And everybody should read Toni Morrison and Cormac McCarthy.

Your characterizations are vivid and uniquely your own. What went into the process of creating that strong a dynamic in your work?

I believe that, particularly in stories of the fantastic in which you've developed a certain level of strangeness in the narrative, there's a tendency to read the story as if it were an unfolding dream. The psychologist Fritz Perls suggested that everything in a dream *is* a projected aspect of the dreamer. Using this Gestalt approach to dreams, the therapist encourages clients to view each object in a dream as part of themselves.

Usually when I create a story it's a process of discovery. Especially if it's based on an anthology call of some sort I may start with a theme and I begin to write down some thoughts and images inspired by that theme and inevitably I'll write down something that sounds like a bit of dialog or a snippet of someone's thoughts and I start wondering who would say or think such a thing. So for a time I focus on writing down more things that same person may think or say until I start getting some glimpses of the setting they're in. Maybe it's indoors or outdoors, maybe there are other people or significant objects with them. I'm assuming during this process that whatever they see, wherever they are, is specific to them and their experience in the world. These things characterize them. They mirror certain internal states of the character. So this feedback process begins to develop where the landscape and the developing tone of the language tells me more about who this viewpoint character is, and in turn as I know more about the character I know what things and events will exist in his or her universe. Eventually I arrive at the emotional heart of whatever it is I'm writing, and generally that tells me what the story is really about, and at that point I can begin my first real revisions.

I know it sounds terribly inefficient, but I find that the efficiencies gained by having the plot and setting and character reflect one another tend to make up for it.

To what do you attribute the strength of your career?

I'm persistent, and ambitious (at least artistically) and I enjoy the actual process of writing. I think most people who find the process too laborious tend not to last long.

But persistence is really the key. You have to be able to stay at it year after year, even during those periods in which you're not selling much and no one seems that interested in you. You take advantage of those periods by trying new things and stockpiling work until the market is more interested in what you have to offer

What do you have planned for the future?

The last thing Melanie and I wrote together was a handbook on writing, *Yours to Tell: Dialogues on the Art & Practice of Fiction*, which will appear soon from Apex Books. It pretty concisely represents everything we know about writing fiction.

And I'm really excited about my forthcoming novel *UBO* (Solaris, January 2017), a dark science fictional meditation on violence and its origins, featuring such historical viewpoint characters as Jack the Ripper, Stalin, and Heinrich Himmler. I've worked on this book, off and on, for decades, and I'm very proud of it.

Any last words?

But if I reveal them now, they wouldn't really be my last words, now would they?

NORMAN PRENTISS

NORMAN WALKED AWAY with a Stoker for Superior Achievement in Short Fiction for "In the Porches of My Ears." His first novel, *Invisible Fences*, was published by Cemetery Dance and his short prose has been seen in *Tales From the Gorezone*, and *The Year's Best Dark Fantasy and Horror*, among many other collections and anthologies. His essays on Gothic and sensation literature have appeared in *Colby Quarterly* and *The Thomas Hardy Review*.

Norman's little piece of Cyberspace is: normanprentiss.com

You've been referred to as one of the genre's rising stars. Does that get in your head in a negative way?

It's an incredibly flattering thing to hear, especially in light of how much respect I have for other writers described with similar words. As far as anything negative: maybe it's a tough label to live up to, putting a bit of pressure on? I don't really think of it that way, though. I'm mostly trying to live up to my previous book or story, to write something I'm proud to put my name on. That's where the real pressure comes, for me.

Having won two Bram Stoker Awards, does that have an effect on the process of your writing?

Not really—not in any direct way, at least. The one thing that has happened is that I've been invited to submit work to different markets. That hadn't happened before, so I'm sure the Stokers played a part there (in addition to my appearance in Ellen Datlow's and Paula Guran's Year's

Best anthologies). When you're invited to submit, there's definitely a different kind of process: you really are thinking about where a story is going to *go*, and the invite itself might influence the story you write. A good example would be one I wrote for the recent Zombie vs. Robots anthology, *This Means War!*, a gig I owe to Paula Guran for recommending me to the editor. I'd never done a zombie *or* a robot story, so the great thing about the project is that it inspired me to do something new. Plus, Jeff Connor at IDW, the book's editor, was so generous with incredible, detailed feedback, and that helped me take the story to new levels. I love how the story came out, but I never would have written it—or even known how much I'd *want* to write it—without being asked.

With "Four Legs in the Morning," did the story or monster come first?

I'm going to say the character of Dr. Sibley came first, then the title—and the story and the monster kind of followed from there. I'll leave it at that, to avoid spoilers!

Will we be seeing any more of Dr. Sibley?

Definitely. Although, part of the idea is that you don't actually *see* Sibley that much. He's in the background, at the periphery of his own stories. The one I'm working on now is called "The Future of Literary Criticism," and it's a kind of origin story—Sibley's early years, when he's on the academic job market.

Childhood trauma and the effects it has on adults as they mature in Invisible Fences. *What was the reason you picked up that kind of narrative thread?*

The novella grew out of a poem I'd written many years before, where I explored the idea of life-events staying with you as you try to go on with your life. For *Invisible Fences*, I thought in the back of my mind about the horror movie cliché where a family moves into a house, and learn that it's haunted. In that scenario, the ghost is a stranger, and the family's main crime is that they've made a bad real estate decision. For me, it's not as scary to be in a house haunted by somebody else's ghosts. They need to be *your* ghosts to be really scary.

What led to the decision of your using older characters in your work?

I hadn't actually thought about this, so that's a good question! Maybe it has to do with my own age? I'd rather attribute it to my temperament, and my sense of what types of story I want to tell. Older characters have a wealth of life experiences to haunt them, and they collect more things to worry about over the years. But I like how scary and strange the world can be for children, too, and have done a lot from that perspective (including the first half of *Invisible Fences*).

Has the Internet reduced the attention span of the modern reader?

Yes.
    People said the same thing about MTV and movie editing. Pace, in print or film, is one of my most important criteria—at the same time, I like a story that builds, so some things I like might seem slow for some readers or viewers. That's what critics call "a deliberate pace," when they're being generous. If the work has atmosphere, or a fascinating tone, that keeps me interested.

"In the Porches of My Ears" was not only a Bram Stoker winner, but a story with a great deal of heart some may not expect. What led to the writing of it?

Some friends of mine had a movie-going experience of sitting behind a narrating couple, and I latched onto that idea. What I looked at my story ideas, I realized that I often take something from life and make it worse. That's what horror writers do. That's what pessimists do, also, but there you go.

Can you tell us about the status of your long-awaited novel-length work?

I've got several in the works, but the one I'm aiming to finish first should be completed this summer. There's a story called "Beneath Their Shoulders" that would be a kind of sneak-peek of the longer work: that story will be in an upcoming anthology from PS Publishing.

What's on the horizon for you, Norman?

More stories here and there, including the *Shocklines* anthology from Cemetery Dance, and a Halloween story for another upcoming anthology. I'm doing a mini-collection of children-in-danger stories

(3 reprints and 3 or so originals), called *The Book of Baby Names*—probably an ebook. And I'm really excited about an upcoming novella from Delirium called *The Fleshless Man*—that's set to be announced in July, with a print date of September. I've gotten some incredible early feedback about this book, and I can't wait for more people to get a chance to read it!

CHET WILLIAMSON

SINCE 1981, CHET has published twenty-five books and over a hundred short stories in anthologies and magazines as diverse as *The New Yorker*, *Playboy*, and *The Magazine of Fantasy and Science Fiction*. He is a playwright as well as an author and actor. That's his voice reading the audio versions of the works of Michael Moorcock, Tom Picirilli, and many others.

Find out more at: chetwilliamson.com

What led to your acting in Joe Lansdale's Christmas with the Dead*?*

Joe called me and asked me if I'd be interested in doing a small but really good part in a film that he was producing. It was a crazed preacher, a cult leader really, who, in a post-zombie-apocalyptic world, gives Holy Communion to zombies by feeding them real flesh and blood. Sounded like something I'd love to do, so I sent Joe a video of me doing one of the scenes so that he and the director, Terrill Lee Lankford, could see it. They liked it enough for me to fly down to Nacogdoches, Texas, where the film was going to be shot, and spend two days reading with Lee and learning the basics of film acting. Though I've done a lot of stage acting (I've been a member of Actors' Equity for decades), I'd never done a feature film. Lee taught me more in an hour than I'd have learned in years of acting school. He just cut right to the chase, and I got what he was saying. The film was based on Joe's short story, and his son Keith wrote the screenplay. His daughter Kasey plays Ella, and his son-in-law, Adam Coats, plays the goofy neighbor Ray, so it's a real family affair. Joe's wife Karen even co-produced. It sounds like a back yard film, but it isn't. Lee got fully professional performances out of some people who'd never acted before, as well as some who were experienced film actors, and the film turned out great. It's funny, but also creepy and touching, and the characters really have that Lansdale charm. I've been to a few public showings, one at NECON, a small horror con, and audiences seem to really love it. I only shot for a week—in 110-degree weather in an East Texas July!—and I tore a blood vessel behind my larynx while I was screaming during the scene where I'm getting...um, chowed down on. Had to have a little surgery to fix it, but I'm finally back to normal. The whole experience was worth it, though!

I'm a big fan of The Final Verse. *Was there anything in particular that inspired the story?*

I've always been a fan of roots music, like The Carter Family, Jimmie Rodgers, Bill Monroe, and other bluegrass and early country music. My son Colin moved from classical violin to bluegrass fiddle when he was in junior high, and I used to accompany him on guitar in fiddle contests (he won a lot of them). I've always liked Celtic music too, and played for about seven years in a Celtic duo called Fire in the Glen (CDs still available at the website!). But what really triggered the story was when Tom Monteleone asked me to do a recording of one of my stories for Borderlands Press. It would have been a CD/chapbook combo, and I thought about doing an original story rather than using a reprint, something I could write to be heard rather than just read. So I came up with the story idea, and then wrote an actual song, both lyrics and music, that was integrated into the story. I recorded it in Tom's home studio, but about then the economy took a bad turn and Tom had to cancel some projects and gave me back the story. I sent it to Gordon Van Gelder at *The Magazine of Fantasy and Science Fiction*, and he bought it for the magazine. Ellen Datlow then picked it for her *Best Horror of the Year* volume, so its readership turned out to be much greater than it might have been originally. I still plan to rerecord it at some point.

Tell us a bit about your acting career?

I feel like I've acted since forever. I did tons in high school and college, got my Equity card in my twenties, and did primarily business theatre and summer stock. Then I started writing as a result of the business theatre, and gave up acting for nearly thirty years. In 1986 I got involved in a playwriting group, primarily just to work with people again, since writing is such a lonely occupation, and did a few readings. On the basis of that, people told me I should audition and act again, so I reactivated my union card and got some great gigs at some local theatres that use Equity actors. I've done Bottom in *A Midsummer Night's Dream*, Dylan Thomas in *A Child's Christmas in Wales*, and if the pieces fall into place, it looks like a performing arts group I currently chair, Creative Works of Lancaster, will be doing *The Woman in Black*, in which I'll do one of the only two roles. I've also used my acting chops to narrate audiobooks for Crossroad Press. I've recorded a number of my own works, but also novels by Michael Moorcock, Tom Piccirilli, David Niall Wilson, Irving Wallace, John Skipp and Craig Spector, Zoe Winters, and others. I recently finished doing Joe Lansdale's *The Magic Wagon* and Neal Barrett Jr.'s *The Hereafter Gang*. All are available at audible.com

What makes an actor want to pursue the considerably more solitary role of writer?

The ironic thing is that I went into writing because I thought it was a more stable profession than acting. The more fool I! And of course, with writing you can play all the roles in your story. You become the director, the writer, costume and set designers, and all the actors. That's a pretty heady assignment for a former actor who only played one role at a time!

What went into the creation of a... unique character such as Henry Watson Fairfax?

Fairfax, who appears in my story, "Excerpts from the Records of the New Zodiac and the Diaries of Henry Watson Fairfax," was born from my desire to write a story about how businesses and businessmen gobbled each other up. I guess it occurred to me: what if it got to the point where they really gobbled each other up? I was inspired by a copy of *Records of the Zodiac: 1915-1928*, a dining club of the super-rich. Everything just clicked into place, and I had a great deal of fun working out the menus for each meal, as they got more and complex and, um, expensive.

With Siege of Stone, *the Searchers series ends. Will you ever go back to that world?*

Very doubtful. It was quite unlike me to do a series in the first place, but I did so at the request of a publisher. I see the Searchers series, however, as one long novel in three parts rather than a series. Due to terrible covers on the original paperbacks, and a lack of promised promotion on the publishers' part, each book sold fewer copies than the one before (and since they cut the print run on each subsequent volume, that was a self-fulfilling prophecy).

Ash Wednesday was reissued in ebook format, containing material that was not used in the original publication. What happened that led the original publisher to want a different ending?

David Hartwell was the editor of the book, and he felt that it should end with what he referred to as the birth screams of a new world. I preferred to end with the more thoughtful and quieter final chapter, which resolves, at least metaphysically, the main questions, but bowed to David's judgment, especially since it (and Soulstorm) were my first book deal. Later on I might have dug in my heels. I thought it was too much of a horror movie shock ending, and some critics felt that way as well. Still, the book was well received and is considered a minor classic today. I did have the final chapter printed in Footsteps, a fanzine, and it now appears in the ebook, back where I always felt it belongs.

Ash Wednesday also uses the ghostly characters as embodiments of sin occurring in the physical plane of existence. Is Horror best suited for that kind of moral mirror?

I really think it is. I've never written horror just to scare. That's too easy to do. I always feel that if I haven't provided a deeper subtext of some sort, I've failed. There has to be something for the reader to take away and think about other than just frightening or horrific scenes. If you read my short story collection, *Figures in Rain*, (now available as an ebook, much less expensive than the Ash-Tree Press hardcover), you'll find a wide array of stories dealing with moral ambiguity (as well as some good scares, of course!). I think ghost stories in particular provide great opportunities for metaphor.

How did Soulstorm *come to be? How did you keep the haunted house theme tense yet subtle?*

Soulstorm was my first novel, and, as such, I wanted to work within a relatively small canvas. I've always been a fan of good haunted house novels, like *The Haunting of Hill House*, *Hell House*, and *The Shining*, so

I figured that the scenario was perfect, with a small cast of characters in a limited environment. I tried to make the horror in the story as much psychological as overt, which I think helps contribute to the tension.

Robert Bloch, author of Psycho said about Soulstorm; *"Williamson has written a real chiller…an enchanting evocation of evil…Crammed with weird insights into a terrifying supernatural intelligence and moments of literally monstrous murder that will make your old nightmares seem tepid and drab." How does such praise effect you?*

Bloch was one of my primary influences, so having those words come from him was quite nice. One of the great things about starting out was having some of those writers who I grew up reading saying good things about my work. I recall Fritz Leiber praised *Ash Wednesday* in Locus, and to me he was a giant, so those things mean a lot, and spur you to try and do good work.

Zombies or vampires?

Neither. I'm bloody sick to death of both. I think horror writers should agree to put both vampires and zombies in the "To Be Revisited at a Later Date" pile. But then that would eliminate about 97.6% of all the horror being written and published (and mostly self-published) today. And that would be a good thing.

What are you working on now?

I'm halfway into a noir novel set in 1953. It deals with lust, crime, heroin, betrayal, and a very special semi-supernatural talent. It's something different for me, and I'm enjoying the hell out of it even as it occasionally drives me insane. And there's not a zombie nor a vampire in sight.

Anything you'd like your fans to know?

Just that most of my backlist is in print from Crossroad Press and in the Kindle Store, as well as all other ebook stores. *Defenders of the Faith*, a horrific suspense novel, is my newest print book, also at Amazon. Folks can friend me on Facebook and follow me on Twitter (I'm @chetwill). Thanks!

NANCY KRESS

NANCY BEGAN WRITING in 1976 but has achieved her greatest notice since the publication of her Hugo and Nebula-winning 1991 novella *Beggars in Spain* which was later expanded into a novel with the same title. In addition to her novels, Kress has written numerous short stories and is a regular columnist for Writer's Digest. She is a regular at Clarion writing workshops and at The Writers Center in Bethesda, Maryland. During the winter of 2008/09, Nancy Kress was the Picador Guest Professor for Literature at the University of Leipzig's Institute for American Studies in Leipzig, Germany.

In Interspace, her blog is nancykressblogspot.com

As a writer of both Science Fiction and Fantasy, do either one have a particular appeal?

They have different appeals. SF requires more logical thinking, as one extrapolates from where we are now—technologically, socially—to where the story is going to be set. With fantasy, the appeal is letting one's mind go free of the present and devise settings and situations that don't have to be related as much to here and now. For both, however, I think that the characters are what matter the most. People are not following George R.R. Martin's *Game of Thrones* because of the War-of-Roses setting, but for Tyrion, Daenerys, and the rest,

Were there any female authors that influenced either your dynamic style or simply your decision to write? Was there even a distinction between female and male authors?

Ursula Le Guinn had an enormous effect on me. Not because I write like her, but because she represents for me the ideal blending of character, idea, plot, and that lovely and eloquent prose.

Do you see the advent of e-books and the glut of self-publishing to be perhaps the mid-list?

Right now, self-published e-books are turning the Internet into one gigantic slush pile, with readers not knowing if a book by an unknown is good or not until they buy it. Previously, editors filtered the glut by what they chose to publish. It's the Wild West out there now, and nobody knows how it will settle out. Personally, I love my Kindle and both read on it constantly and am making my own backlist available in e-form.

Do you think that e-readers will allow for more people to (God forbid) embrace reading as a primary source of entertainment?

No. People who always read, will continue to read. Those who don't read, won't. It's not the medium that determines that; it's the personality.

You've said that in your story "Fountain of Age," you discovered your inner criminal. What was that unique-sounding experience like?

All that any writer has to is his or her own experience. If you've never committed a murder and you're writing a murderer, you draw on the times you felt angry enough to commit a murder. To create Max Feder in "Fountain of Age," I imagined what it would be like to commit cheerful thievery, with no stabs of conscience about it. Would I ever do that? No. Probably not. I don't think so. But…There is Max, drawn out of me.

What went into the world-building of the Beggar's Trilogy?

For years I had read two writers with opposite thinking about economics—Ursula Le Guin's ethical anarchy in *The Dispossessed*, and Ayn Rand's Libertarian Objectivism. Neither seemed plausible to me; that was one strand contributing to *Beggars In Spain*. I need a lot of sleep and envy those who do not; that was another strand. Who knows what else? My world-building is partly intuitive, and pieces of one's own life, sometimes disguised and sometimes not, end up in one's novels.

Beggars in Spain won both the Hugo and Nebula awards. What sort of effect did that have on your writing?

None. Writing goes forward despite awards, stalls despite awards, turns out well or not despite awards. The Hugo and Nebula had an effect on my emotions, however—it's sweet to have validation that other people like the stories one is offering.

Your work in Science Fiction has the thread of humanism with the confines of technology. Is that something that was an intentional theme?

I think all SF has that theme, in that it has characters ('humanism") and technology, whether the tech is spaceships, future weapons, biotech, time travel devices, or the discovery of fire.

After the Fall, Before the Fall, During the Fall *is your latest novel to date; what can your readers expect from it?*

The book, which is actually a novella (38,000 words), is about survival. The story moves back and forth between present day and a future in which much of the Earth has been destroyed, and everybody is mistaken about who did it. There are aliens, adolescents, FBI, and one of my own favorite characters, Pete, whom the reviewer on Tor.com calls "heartbreaking and unforgettable." I hope readers find this one, because I think it's one of the best things I've written in a while (not that the author is always a reliable judge!)

You've also written about the act of fiction writing in your book Elements of Fiction Writing and Dynamic Characters. *What made you throw your hat in that particular ring?*

For sixteen years I wrote a column on writing fiction for *Writers Digest* magazine. My three books on writing grew out of my columns.

Given the choice, would you rather eat dessert first?

No. I believe in delayed gratification, and in the joys of anticipation. A good crème brulée deserves to make a grand entrance at the end.

MIKE RESNICK

ACCORDING TO *LOCUS,* Mike is the all-time leading award winner, living or dead, for short science fiction. He is the winner of five Hugos, a Nebula, and other major awards in the United States, France, Spain, Japan, Croatia and Poland. He is the author of 68 novels, over 250 stories, and 2 screenplays, and is the editor of 41 anthologies. His work has been translated into 25 languages. He was the Guest of Honor at the 2012 Worldcon.

Mike can be found online as @ResnickMike on Twitter or at www.mikeresnick.com.

How did the Lucifer Jones stories come to be?

Lucifer Jones was born one evening back in the late 1970s. I was trading videotapes with a number of other people—stores hadn't started renting them yet, and this was the only way to increase your collection at anything above a snail's pace—and one of my correspondents asked for a copy of *She*, with Ursula Andress, which happened to be playing on Cincinnati television.

I looked in my *Maltin Guide* and found that *She* ran 117 minutes. Now, this was back in the dear dead days when everyone knew that Beta was the better format, and it just so happened that the longest Beta tape in existence at the time was two hours. So I realized that I couldn't just put the tape on and record the movie, commercials and all, because the tape wasn't long enough. Therefore, like a good correspondent/trader, I sat down, controls in hand, to dub the movie (which I had never seen before) and edit out the commercials as they showed up.

About fifteen minutes into the film, Carol entered the video room, absolutely certain from my peals of wild laughter that I was watching a Marx Brothers festival that I had neglected to tell her about. Wrong. I was simply watching one of the more inept films ever made.

And after it was over, I got to thinking: if they could be that funny by accident, what if somebody took those same tried-and-true pulp themes and tried to be funny on purpose?

So I went to my typewriter—this was back in the pre-computer days—and wrote down the most oft-abused African stories that one was likely to find in old pulp magazines and B movies: the elephants' graveyard, Tarzan, lost races, mummies, white goddesses, slave-trading, what-have-you. When I got up to twelve, I figured I had enough for a book... but I needed a unifying factor.

Enter Lucifer Jones.

Africa today isn't so much a dark and mysterious continent as it is an impoverished and hungry one, so I decided to set the book back in the 1920s, when things were wilder and most of the romantic legends of the pulps and B movies hadn't been thoroughly disproved.

Who was the most likely kind of character to roam to all points of Africa's compass? A missionary.

What was funny about a missionary? Nothing. So Lucifer became a con man who presented himself as a missionary. (As he is fond of explaining it, his religion is "a little something me and God whipped up betwixt ourselves of a Sunday afternoon.")

Now, the stories themselves were easy enough to plot: just take a traditional pulp tale and stand it on its ear. But anyone could do that: I decided to add a little texture by having Lucifer narrate the book in the first person, and to make his language a cross between the almost-poetry of *Trader Horn* and the fractured English of *Pogo Possum*, and in truth I think there is more humor embedded in the language than in the plots.

You said a few years back that you had wanted to write a Western; Has The Doctor and the Kid *fulfilled that ambition?*

Actually, *The Buntline Special*, which preceded *The Doctor and the Kid*, fulfilled it. I'd always wanted to write a novel about Doc Holliday and Johnny Ringo, the only two college-educated gunslingers in the West, and this gave me the opportunity. I hadn't planned to have steampunk, zombies and vampires in it, but what the hell, at least I got to write it and it was a lot of fun—and successful enough that I signed to do three more, of which *The Doctor and the Kid* was the first of them.

Are there any authors outside the genres of SF and F whose work has influenced you?

Sure. My Harry the Book stories are (I think) exactly what Damon Runyon would write if he were alive today. Raymond Chandler certainly inspired my mystery novels, and Craig Rice's madcap comedy/mysteries were at least partially behind the John Justin Mallory novels and stories. (Her hero is John J. Malone; notice a similarity?) There are probably hundreds of other influences, but the ones I'm most aware of are Thorne Smith, Alexander Lake, and Nikos Kazantzakis. And Robert Ruark. And Joseph Heller. And, and, and…

You are very much a fan of the genres you write in. How has being a fan affected the way you view books or movies in that genre?

It's probably made me more critical of the movies. I recently was asked to list my 100 favorite movies. The only science fiction film on the list was *Forbidden Planet*, which was 96th.

I got tired of having my intellect insulted on a nightly basis, so I gave up watching television in 1982. Oh, I still watch the news, and some sports, and some old movies, but I haven't seen an episode of a network series in literally 30 years, I've missed most of the science fiction series that everyone talks about, and between you and me, I do not feel culturally deprived.

The one thing that changes when you become a professional writer, is that you don't read for pleasure any more. You *try* to, but you are always analyzing. If a story works, you have to figure out why and how…and if it doesn't work, you have to dope out why not so you can avoid that pitfall.

The Starship series has managed to balance a kind of sweeping Space Opera with the asset of dynamic characters, the emotional voice, as well as the sense of adventure. I think that's a hard trick to pull off whether in books or movies.

I agree. I wanted to write a military series in which brains were more important than high-tech weaponry. I don't think the Good Guys fire five shots in the first two books.

And speaking of characters in general, when I got into this field I was told that what separated science fiction from all other categories of fiction were ideas, and that in our field they were more important than characters. I thought it was bullshit when I heard it, and I think it's bullshit now. And I can't tell you how glad I am that Ray Bradbury and so many others who preceded me proved it was.

Stalking the Dragon is sort of Mystery turned on its ear. Was that the way it had been intended from the start?

Absolutely. Actually, that's the third book in the series, following *Stalking the Unicorn* (1987) and *Stalking the Vampire* (2008). And this summer there'll be a collection of the Mallory stories, *Stalking the Zombie*.

It was back in the mid-1980s that I decided, after all my science fiction novels, it was time to write a fantasy novel. Now, I happen to loathe magical quest stories with Lords, Ladies, archaic English, and enchanted swords, and they were so popular at the time that one of my colleagues (I think it was Bob Silverberg) invented the term "elf-and-unicorn trilogy" as a pejorative.

I got to thinking about it, and decided that my novel should have an elf and a unicorn and be the farthest thing anyone could imagine when they heard that term, so I set it in present-day Manhattan—not the Manhattan you and I visit, but the one you can only see out of the corner of your eye, and which vanishes away when you turn to face it head on. It's a Manhattan populated by lecherous elves, incompetent magicians, entrepreneurial goblins, and the like, and boasts structures such as the Vampire State Building and Madison Round Garden.

How did your involvement with Tarzan Alive *come to be?*

I got into fandom and prodom through the Burroughs door. I was the assistant editor of *ERB-dom* when it became the only Burroughs fanzine to win a Hugo back in 1966, and that same year I sold my first sf novel, a Burroughs pastiche.

Move the clock ahead a few decades, and the University of Nebraska Press asked me to write an introduction to *The Land That Time Forgot*. I guess they liked it, because not too long after that they asked me to introduce Phil's *Tarzan Alive*.

Tales of the Velvet Comet *is a favorite series of yours for me. Will we ever see more?*

No, and for a reason that might surprise you. I enjoyed writing that series, and I have no problem with the subject matter. But each book had to reintroduce the Velvet Comet and, in essence, give you the floor plan yet again, since 100% of the action took place aboard it. And I got so sick and tired of finding new and interesting ways to describe the same damned ship over and over again that I decided the series was finished, that I just never want to describe the layout of the Comet again.

What led to your interest in Africa?

Not Burroughs, oddly enough, but a wonderful writer named Alexander Lake, who was a white hunter during the first third of a century. I was thrilled to be able to bring his two books, *Killers in Africa* and *Hunter's Choice*, back into print a few years ago in The Resnick Library of African Adventure, which I edited for Alexander Books.

You are the all-time leading award-winner according to Locus, with no less than five Hugos and a Nebula. Does that kind of recognition help or hinder an author?

It can't hinder you, as long as you remember that if you stand right outside the hotel ten minutes after you win a Hugo or a Nebula and ask the first 100 people who walk past if they know what the Hugo or Nebula *is*, you will be exceptionally lucky if even one of the hundred knows.

If you have any books out, winning won't affect your advances, because they're based on your track record…but it'll help selling foreign rights, since you don't have a track record at many of those houses (and if you do, it can probably be credited to or blamed on your translator). The award is a shorthand way to show a foreign editor that you're a class act and a Prestige Item.

What are your thoughts on the state of speculative fiction, in film as well as print?

Like most fans, I couldn't wait for Hollywood to develop CGI so you could *believe* scenes in space, or on other worlds. So they developed it—and now it substitutes for plot and character, and I think science fiction movies are as bad as they ever were. I also resent the fact that for the past decade or two, the comic book has been Hollywood's Intellectual Source Material of Choice.

Just as I think that they have no idea how to make a good science fiction film, the same has *never* be true of fantasy films, from *The Wizard of Oz* and *Portrait of Jennie* right up through *Field of Dreams* and *The Wonderful Ice Cream Suit*. I'm no fan of Tolkien, but I suppose the films were made about as well as they could be made. I just wish I knew why the same industry can't put the same quality into science fiction.

As for the literature, some of it's brilliant, most of it's readable, some of it's dreck. Same as always.

How would you like your tombstone to read?

Well, I'd like them to spell my name right.

Truth to tell, I don't plan to have a tombstone. Or a grave. My will requests that I be cremated. Same with Carol, my wife of half a century. I'd like our ashes mingled, and after that I don't much care what's done with them.

DONNA BURGESS

Donna Burgess may be a voice in the fields of dark fiction and poetry, enjoys surfing, playing soccer, and painting and has a deep affection for all things Monty Python and low-budget horror flicks. Over the past fifteen years, her fiction and poetry has appeared in genre publications such as *Weird Tales, Dark Wisdom, Sybil's Garage* and others. She has been married for nineteen years and has two children.

Her Twitter feed can be seen at: twitter.com/horrorgirldonna.

Do you have a routine when you write?

Not really. My schedule is different every day, so I just sit down and write when I have the chance. I do keep a notebook with me, so I can write scenes, etc. when I'm not in front of the computer. I'm nuts with outlining, however. Some writers can just sit down and see where the story takes them. I like to know where it's going from the beginning. (Of course, it can always take a detour!)

What kind of writing haven't you done that you'd like to?

I'd like to do some near-future science fiction and some Steampunk. I'm actually kicking around ideas for both, so hopefully, I'll hit on something that I'll think is worthy of readers' money and time.

An hour over coffee with anyone living or dead; who would it be with, and what would you like to talk about?

Either Stephen King or Bruce Springsteen. I'd probably spend the hour gushing over how awesome they are like some little fangirl.

You did a month-long blog tour for Darklands. *That sounds rather different from what a signing tour would entail?*

It consisted of interviews and guest blog posts, mostly. I believe there was also one live chat. It was fun, but it was also difficult. I'm terrible at coming up with interesting topics for blog posts, so that was a challenge. One problem I had was the misimpression that *Darklands* was urban fantasy or paranormal romance. Readers expecting that kind of novel were not happy to get a book laced with blood, violence and horror.

Do you see the Twilight *series as competition?*

Not at all. Readers who love *Twilight* probably will not like my vampires. And vice versa. I wanted an anti-Twilight novel. My vamps are tough, conflicted and brutal. Plus, my characters haven't been in a high school in quite a while.

The vampire is a constant in the Horror genre. Do you see any other sort of creature that may be just as ubiquitous?

I think the same goes with almost any supernatural creature nowadays. I've read stories about zombies in love, harpies, were-creatures. All it takes is some imagination and creativity to make a creature your own.

What attracted you to Horror?

I've always been crazy for scary stories. When I was small, I wanted to read the scariest fairy tales—*Jack the Giant Killer, Rumpelstiltskin*, etc. Also, my parents loved to go to those all night drive-in horror flicks when I was small. I was raised on Christopher Lee, Peter Cushing, and Vincent Price. On television, I remember watching the *Night Stalker* (albeit, very briefly). I still eat up horror books and movies as fast as I can.

What led to the writing of the three stories in Breaths in Winter *and your collaboration with Alicia?*

Well, Alicia (my lovely daughter) did the cover art. She is an art student at the Art Institute. As for the stories, I think all three of those were written in a continuing-ed creative writing course at Coastal Carolina University a couple of years ago. All the other students were retirees, writing memoirs or light vignettes for fun. I'm sure they all thought I was somewhat demented, writing the things I did.

Dead Girl's Blog is... well a book written in blog for from the perspective of a living dead girl. Where did the inspiration for that come from?

I just thought about how awful it might be to slowly turn into a zombie. *Dead Girl's Blog* is a short story, but I am expanding on the characters and idea with the novel I'm currently working on. It's called *Notes from the End of the World* and will be written in a journal form, but will also have graphics included. It'll be sort of a novel/scrapbook. Alicia will be providing the graphics.

With "Abigail", you have published a short story as an e-book (for want of a better term). Do you think more authors will take this route, or opt for collections?

Short stories do not sell as well as novels and novellas. Collections are a good way of "repackaging" your work—then you have two routes for selling a story instead of only one. As an indie, it's imperative to get more work out there. We need that "virtual shelf-space," as Mr. Konrath puts it. The more shelf space you can take up at Amazon, the more opportunity to find readers. I'm also a big believer in the Dean Wesley Smith method of getting out quality short stories and getting some sales from each one of those every month, rather than placing all your hopes on one or two titles.

Would a self-publishing author have any more of a problem selling an e-book collecting short stories, or a single, novel-length work?

From my experience, novels sell much, much better. But that can be different from author to author. Hugh Howey's *Wool* is fairly short, but he's killing it in sales. I do believe series ebook sell better than standalone stories lately.

Has technology changed the way authors interact with fans in a significant manner?

It seems to have made authors more accessible to fans. Readers (I'm not sure I've sold enough books to call my readers "fans" yet) can interact via Twitter and Facebook, which is nice for most of us. My readers have been so nice, so I'm grateful for that.

You like to surf; what kind of board do you prefer? Any particular waters you'd like to surf?

I have a funboard, which is 6'4" and a 7'6" longboard. I much prefer the longboard. Our waves here in Pawleys Island are nice, but not huge, so the longboard it better for minimal surf. With the longboard, when I catch a decent wave, I can ride forever before bailing.

How did Naked Snake Press come to be, and where did the name come from?

Naked Snake Press just came from wanting to publish little-known authors and the need to create contacts with other writers. I honestly cannot remember how the name came up—it just sounded sort of cool. With the rise of ebooks, I have renamed the company E-Volve Books, in hope that I'll be taken more seriously.

You've noted that publishing has changed a lot just over the past decade. What sort of changes do you think we'll see in another ten years?

I think the need for traditional publishers will continue to decrease and more major authors will make the choice to self-publish. I believe ereader prices will drop and more and more people will have them in their hands all the time—much like an iPod. Personally, I'm hoping for some sort of color e-ink technology. I love my Kindle Fire to death, but I can't read it outside in the sunshine.

Anything planned for the future?

There's *Notes from the End of the World* (*Dead Girl's Blog*) and hopefully, a Southern paranormal novel out before the end of 2012. Plus, a few short stories.

Thanks for having me, Cristopher. Cheers!

ROGER PRICE

ROGER WAS AN ENGLISH television producer, who was also active in Canada. He created the children's science fiction series *The Tomorrow People, Junior Points of View* and the Canadian sketch comedy *You Can't Do That on Television*, which became hugely successful on Nickelodeon in the United States. Roger isn't known for his interest in participating in interviews. Luckily, he made me look good. Now retired, he lives in France.

In television, British Science Fiction has, in addition to The Tomorrow People, *given us fare as* Dr. Who, Blake's 7, *and* Red Dwarf. *How does English Science Fiction differ from American Science Fiction?*

Much lower budgets and less time to shoot.

Were there any particular influences you took while developing The Tomorrow People?

Slan by A.E van Voigt. *The City and The Stars* by Arthur C. Clarke. *The Midwich Cuckoos*—British film of the early 1960's. *Journey into Space*; a BBC radio series in the 1950's. Dreams of freedom during miserable nights and days incarcerated in a British Boarding school.

What led to the decision of re-imagining the series in the '90s?

Persistent pestering by Gerry Laybourne. I never wanted it back.

The original characters returned in the radio plays from '01–'07. Why did you go back to those characters?

What radio plays? First that I've heard about it. Is that my lawyer calling me back?

I understand that the original idea for the ending of Season Three was to kill off the leads on the show, but was never filmed. Can you tell us how the heroes would have died? Do you look back and still think it would be best to kill them off?

The original idea for the ending of every series was to kill them off. I always wrote a scene in which they perished gruesomely. It was therapeutic. I think in series three I left the pages in the screenplays until the first read through as a joke. It may have been that we were doing the read through on April 1st. I don't know. So the legend started.

Sometimes I wrote those endings to spook Thames TV Executives as it was one of their most successful series. In the end they had to let me do comedy series as well, just to stay sane.

And obviously that was a precursor of *You Can't Do That on Television!* My job was to produce and direct television shows. I started when I was 21 years old with a raw and gritty film series about a gang of semi delinquent kids in the east end of London.

Season Six saw changes in not only the jaunting belts, but a new Lab set. Was there a particular reason for these changes?

The old stuff got destroyed in a fire, not much of a fire but the sprinklers went off and the fire fighters sprayed everything. Maybe they also stole the jaunting belts and the Stun Guns. Quite probably.

The Tomorrow People took a creepy, almost surreal turn with "The Living Skins." What was the inspiration behind that particularly different arc?

It was a half baked satire on the fashion industry.

Who or what were your main competitors during the original run or the show?

Whatever the BBC put up against us. They always tried to schedule something strong. There were only 3 TV channels in the UK at the time, ours and 2 BBC ones. They had the cards stacked in their favor and much more money (public money), but we always won the ratings battle.

Do you enjoy any particular Science Fiction these days?

No. And I have not been big on science fiction since I left my teenage years behind. I was Thames TV producer/director/writer (So it said on the contract) and I was asked (told) to come up with an answer to *Dr Who*. At the time he was being played by the BBC as a sort of benevolent old wizard. He was old so I went with youngsters. *Dr Who* famously had a Police Telephone Box because they could not afford to build a space ship. We had even worse budgetary constraints. *The Tomorrow People* was an assignment. I carried it out to the best of my ability.

The TP *novel* The Visitor *differs in several points from what the series became. Were you pleased with how the changes played out for the TV series?*

I made the TV series. It was my responsibility. That book and others were written after the series had started and as part of the deal and published by the publishing wing of Independent TV in Britain. They would have preferred all the books to be different. I didn't have the time. I was allocated (By Thames) two weeks to write each book.

With the radio series, many of the original television cast were brought back in to reprise their roles. Were you satisfied with how that went, and would you have liked to see any other regulars return for the show as well?

I have never heard it. But I was only joking about the lawyer. I knew about it, but only after the event, and it was okay by me *if* the old cast wanted to come together and do it. I would not have agreed otherwise. Or I would have sued except Nick Young pacified me.

Are there plans to make the TP novels more readily available to the US?

Would they sell? Show a publisher the smell of money and they may be published, otherwise not. Even science fiction is a business. I know that sort of thing always comes as a shock to fans. But it's true.

What do you like to do in your spare time?

Walk my dog, mostly, see the grandchildren, work around the garden and fields, occasionally play with my model railroad layout and or video it. Sometimes I make amateur videos for my model railroad club.

Would you have any interest in continuing TP in a novel form or comic?

No. There was a comic strip in the 1970s, which I wrote the scripts for until it became just too much effort. There were also several books at the same time, I forget how many. You can still find them on Amazon.

I have recently realized that in my fiction, there is some aspect of poetic reference in most of what I write, whether as subtext or not and that the "Doomsday Men" story arc with TIM and John reciting Siegfried Sassoon's "Base Details" could very well have been the start of it. Was the poem something that occurred to you during the creative process or had you been looking for a way to use it?

Hey, you're getting out of my depth here. I was a TV Producer; you know one of those selected by IQ test—If you score in double figures you're way too interlekshull. Famous for having the intellectual capacity of a woodlouse and the attention span of a gnat.

I got one of these literary questions from a BBC interviewer once and I'm afraid I said "Books are for writing, not reading." Having said that I did like poetry. It's about the only thing I ever won a prize for at school, about the only prize I ever won anywhere. My Principal (The Herr Direktor) underlined one phrase in the prize book. He said it was me: *Ein Kind mit Augen auch, die lustig lachen*—a child with laughing eyes. But I never wrote poetry in English. When I was sent to boarding school in Britain "To learn to speak your own bloody language" as my father put it, the teachers encouraged me to write humor, even directed me towards writing for TV. One got me a typewriter because my handwriting was so bad. So yeah, whatever that poem was it probably did influence me for a bit. But those poems that stay with me into old age are all in German.

Are there any particular TP episode you are especially proud of?

Yes, but I forget the title, along with I also forgot why I came upstairs just now. After Thames TV let me make comedy shows, which later turned into *You Can't Do That on Television*. The *TP* stories ceased to be silly and became quite satisfyingly dark. My favorite was probably "The Dirtiest Business", but there was also another where the British military start to kidnap Tomorrow People. I forget the title of that one. God that was sinister.

Bringing up "The Dirtiest Business," it was certainly one of the darker shows as The Tomorrow People *went on. It looked as if when the plots became more serious, the change was global in production; writing, directing, and cinematography all seemed to be especially sharp all at once. Was that intentional or just the way the cards fell, so to speak?*

Of course that road led eventually to *You Can't Do That on Television!* And that was the end of *The Tomorrow People*. I don't know why I went though, I already had *You Can't Be Serious* at Thames which was *YCDTOTV* in all but accents and name. Even had the slime. And the kids were fantastic. Well Nigel was one of the Tomorrow People. We did have one conflict with him and another with Mike when I had them in one studio doing comedy and the Tomorrow People needed them in the other fighting aliens or bad guys or something. That needed some fast costume changes and lost lunch breaks, poor little buggers. But when I got my claws into a kid I was reluctant to let go. They were in everything I made. Mike was at one time in three series at once. And he had pop concerts to perform. Look for the Victorian Child chimney sweeps on *Horrible Histories* on YouTube. My daughter says I was The Shouty Man.

Roger, I thank you for granting this rare interview. Is there anything you'd like to say to your fans in parting?

When I was about 12 years old and listening to lots of radio drama serials all the ones that I liked ended with the same announcement. "Written and produced by Charles Chilton" So I wrote to him at the BBC asking how I could become a radio writer producer like him. He wrote back saying that if I was only 12 I did not want to become a radio producer I wanted to become a TV producer, as that was where the future lay. So I found a friend's granny who had a TV and studied it. TV sets were rare in Britain in those days. I thought the children's TV aimed at my age group was boring patronizing crap, while the radio shows like *Riders of the Range* and *Journey into Space* as well as *The Goon Show* were fantastic. I decided that when I grew up I would try to bring the imagination stimulating magic of radio to television.

Always try to achieve your childhood dreams.

Did you know that *Tomorrow People* actor Mike Holoway also worked as a comedy actor and prototype for Justin Bieber in the 1970s?

It was a business. What more can I say?

CHARLES DE LINT

DE LINT IS BEST DESCRIBED as a romantic—a believer in compassion, hope and human potential. He is known as a master in the field of contemporary fantasy, helping to pioneer the genre with his groundbreaking novel *Moonheart* (1984). His vivid portrayal of character and settings has earned him a vast readership and glowing praise from reviewers and peers alike.

His numerous awards and honors include the World Fantasy Award, the Canadian SF/Fantasy Aurora Award, and the White Pine Award, among others. Modern Library's Top 100 Books of the 20th Century poll, conducted by Random House and voted on by readers, put eight of de Lint's books among the top 100.

The proverbial Renaissance man, de Lint is also a painter, poet and musician. His storytelling skills shine in his original songs, several of which were recorded and released in 2011 on his CD, *Old Blue Truck*. A multi-instrumentalist, de Lint performs with MaryAnn (also a musician). His main instruments are guitar, harmonica and vocals, while hers are mandolin, guitar, vocals and percussion.

How did you get started as a writer?

It's just something I've always done. For as long as I can remember I've made up stories—originally just to amuse myself. I'd write long narrative verses and lots of songs, making up worlds and mythologies, sharing them with friends and penpals. I never really thought of it as a career option until I met the writer Charles Saunders and he urged me to submit some of my stories to the small press market. This was pre-Internet. If I was doing it today I'd be going the ebook and print on demand route since it makes so much sense. But back then there was a huge market for short stories in small press magazines published out of people's basements and apartments.

How does your music and art relate to your writing?

It depends on whether you mean my own or that done by others. That done by others inspires me, the same way that good writing does. My own art and music serve a different purpose that still relates to my writing. I think of all the arts as storytelling—or at least that's my approach to them—and the more mediums I embrace, the larger my palette. Specifically, visual art has taught me how to view the world and then translate what I see into prose—what to leave in, what to take out, what to make up. Music has taught me about the rhythm of the language as I put it on the page.

Are there particular writers who have influenced your writing?

Good writers inspire me *because* they're good; I strive to leave with my own readers the same emotion I get when I finish their wonderful books. I think it's for others to say if those writers have left a stamp on my own work. So let me instead point to some writers that always leave me feeling fulfilled, yet hungry for more: Alice Hoffman, Andrew Vachss, Robert Crais, Peter S. Beagle, Patricia Briggs, Barry Lopez, Gary Snyder, Patricia McKillip, William Morris, Lord Dunsany, Bob Dylan, Russell. This is just off the top of my head the list could be much longer. I also delight in finding new voices. A couple of more recent discoveries include Ben Aaronovitch, Stina Leicht and Kevin Hearne.

You've done some shared-world novels. How did you come about doing those stories?

It's always from being invited. I haven't done many but the one I'm always happy to return to is Bordertown, which recently came back from a thirteen-year hiatus with a new collection of stories.

You often write using characters who have a bit of an edge; they've knocked around a bit. What goes into writing those characters?

I'm interested in the outsider. Probably because I've been one for much of my life—at least that's my perception—or because so many of the people I know, now and while growing up, marched to their own drum. Artists, musicians, criminals, street people, the new tribal folk... they tend to approach problems and solve them in a creative manner, which always makes for a good story. And of course *why* they're on the outside is good story before you even add your own plot.

You are drawn to the Sonoran desert. Can you tell us what it is about this place that resonates so strongly with you?

I don't know if I can put it into words. I just know that the first time I stepped out of the airport in Tucson many years ago I felt like I'd come home. I've always been attracted to badlands. There's something so immediate about the dangerous terrain and that huge sky overhead. The connection might have been ingrained into me from spending some of my formative years growing up in Ankara, Turkey, and wandering around in the red dirt hills outside of town. If it wasn't for the lack of health care in the States, I'd probably move there. But as it is, I could never afford health insurance.

I loved Eyes Like Leaves *and its mix of Celtic and Nordic mythology. What led you to write it?*

To be honest, I wrote it so long ago that I can't remember how I developed the various elements. I do remember that I wrote it back when the whole high fantasy field still felt fresh and I loved every minute of it.

In The Painted Boy, *there are a number of story details, which thread throughout the narrative; Chinese lore, Santo del Vado Viejo, and Arizona itself. Was it challenging to keep all that straight when writing it?*

I approach my story characters the way a method actor approaches the characters they portray in film or on stage. Because of that—once I figure out who the character is—I find it very easy to keep it all straight. When I'm writing from their points-of-view I *am* that character and just as I don't forget the elements of my own life, I don't forget theirs while I'm in the story. So it's pretty easy. What's hard is discovering who the characters are in the first place and finding their voices.

Could you tell us about your next book that's coming out, and the ones that you're working on now?

I've been working on a Young Adult series for Razorbill Canada called Wildlings. The first book *Under My Skin* came out earlier this year and I'm working on the second one now for a 2013 release. *Under My Skin* is only available in Canada from Razorbill; for the rest of the world the ebook and print edition are available through Amazon. Next year will also see the release of *The Cats of Tanglewood Forest*, an expansion of *A Circle of Cats*, a picture book I did a few years ago with Charles Vess. I added some 40,000 words and Vess has done fifty new paintings for the book.

After that I still have a third and final Wildlings book to write and I hope to record another CD of original music when I can afford the studio and production costs. I'm also in the midst of getting my older novels and stories available as ebooks. Some of them are already available from Amazon and Smashwords and I hope to have many more of them available this fall including some new stories that haven't been published before.

SANDY DELUCA

HAVING AUTHORED THE NOVELS *Manhattan Grimoire, Settling in Nazareth, Descent* and *From Ashes*, in addition to writing critically acclaimed novellas such as *Darkness Conjured, Reign of Blood* and *Into the Red*. She penned several poetry collections, including *Burial Plot in Sagittarius*, which was a finalist for the Bram Stoker award.

She has written under the pseudonym Autumn Raindance and her work has also been included in the occult book *To Stir a Magyk Cauldron* by Silver Ravenwolf.

Sandy is also a painter who exhibits her work in the New England area. She spends her days painting, writing and caring for several beloved felines.

Both aspects of Sandy can be found here: sandydeluca.com

Writing, poetry, illustration. You seem to wrestle a trio of muses! Which discipline is the one that has the loudest voice?

They're all very loud, but I'll break it down. At present painting provides my greatest source of income and it also makes up a great deal of my social life, as I am involved with many local galleries and exhibit on a regular basis. At this time I'm not really an illustrator—an artist who creates work to accompany someone else's vision. There are many out there who do that much better than I. If a writer or publisher sees a piece I've created and wants to use it then I have no objection and occasionally I'll do a piece for a friend. But I normally paint what I feel and see. My visual art is very personal.

The writing muse refuses to be silent. I make the time to work on my fiction everyday. I love poetry and that muse needs awakening every now and then, but it flows nonstop when it comes to me.

In which order did those muses arrive in you?

The painting muse arrived one day when I decided to create a family portrait on my mother's antique table. I was around three.

What is it about horror that makes it appeal to us, whether as artists or admirers?

On a personal level I am curious about the dark and the mysteries of life and death. I want to know what's inside the killer's mind, what do wicked mystics do and say when practicing their magic and what really happens after we die?

Who are some of your influences in the arts you participate in?

Writers: Greg F. Gifune, Kathe Koja, Darcey Steinke, Rob Dunbar, Lee Thompson and Tom Pic are some of the best around today in my opinion. James Leo Herlihy, James Dickey and James Baldwin are authors I read and reread for inspiration as well.
    Painters: The German Expressionists, particularly Max Beckmann, have inspired me a great deal. I also love modern movements such as Pop Surrealism or Dark Pop. Shawn Barber and Fred Harper are two great artists who come to mind.
    Poetry: Silvia Plath, James Dickey, Emily Dickinson, Charlie Jacobs!

Your novels incorporate the human condition with elements of the horrific. Is this a conscience process?

My characters often take over and the process evolves as they speak. I love to explore the dark side of the human condition and blend it with the supernatural. I have a collection of occult and supernatural books I've been piecing together for years. I have magic books bought in darkened bookstores in Salem, Massachusetts and devilish books I've found on back shelves at the Strand in New York City. The research helps to move my work along as well.

What led you to using experiences like unplanned pregnancy or surviving cancer?

Darkness Conjured was partly inspired by the stigma an unwed mother experienced back in the day. There were several "homes" where these women literally "hid" during their pregnancies in my area. One in particular was said to be haunted, so my imagination went wild.

From Ashes was inspired by my own battle with cancer. It was written while I was undergoing chemotherapy.

Descent seems to be the most popular book of yours. To what do you attribute that?

It's my longest published work and perhaps the most visceral.

Manhattan Grimoire dealt with a lot of themes, not only the unpredictability of the weather, but possession and visions. Was this active tangle of plot threads easy to navigate when writing it?

Writing is never easy, but again, the characters helped me along the process. Lots of *MG* came from journal notes. The character Rico was inspired by a knock off purse vendor I encountered one day in the city. Fragments like train rides to and from New York and churches I'd seen in Harlem were woven into the novel. I'd researched old grimoires as well.

Is there another genre you want to explore in the future?

I'd like to do some mainstream fiction and perhaps some true crime.

Can you share anything about your upcoming projects?

I'm presently working on a new novella. It's based here in New England and it looks as though it'll be my darkest yet.

Thanks for doing this interview. I truly enjoyed it.

NANCY KILPATRICK

WRITER AND EDITOR NANCY KILPATRICK has been called by *Fangoria* Magazine as "Canada's answer to Anne Rice" and she has published 18 novels, 1 non-fiction book, over 200 short stories, 5 collections of stories, and has edited 12 anthologies. Nancy has been a *Bram Stoker* finalist three times, a finalist for the *Aurora Award* five times and, in addition to winning several short fiction contests, won the *Arthur Ellis Award* for best mystery.

Tell us about Nancy Kilpatrick the editor and Nancy Kilpatrick the author.

I'm a rather ordinary person in some way, and a freak in others, but I think all writers are freaks. We dwell so much in our heads that we're not as much a part of the 'real' world as most people. Like many of my peers, I tend to get lost in the imaginary world and forget about the mundane, so dishes, laundry, food even gets forgotten about or delayed.

I love living in my fantasy realms and working to craft them so that they are understandable and have meaning to others. I do the same when I'm editing, but there's almost no focus on me, it's on the writers and their stories and I see my job as being to help them make the story sparkle and then to bring the story ideas together into a cohesive form, the anthology.

Because I'm so occupied with writing, I'm kind of boring as a human being. I try to do things, go places, and I love travelling. But I'm not a terrific conversationalist. I've never been good at 'small talk'. I was shy when I was younger and I've learned to push myself forward and can talk in interviews, etc. but I'm never really comfortable. I'm a one-on-

one person. That's where I feel most comfortable, being with one, and sometimes two people, but I'm not a crowds type, I hate parades and concerts and any events that draw hundreds and…god, quaking at the thought!… thousands.

Meet me for tea, or a drink, and I'm all yours. Drag me to a packed museum, or a sports event, and watch me shrivel! The Incredible Shrinking Writer! Ha!

You've written and edited a great number of stories regarding vampires. Is there any other creature of the night (or day) that you'd like to give more time to?

I adore zombies. I'd love to edit a zombie antho but there's so much the same about zombies and it's hard to find a new take, though I think I have found one in a new novel I'm writing. Most of my novels have either been vampire or general horror and while I've written a few zombie short stories, this is the first zombie novel I've tackled. I kind of like werewolves but I guess I'm old-fashioned about them. I loved Gary Brandner's *The Howling (1, 2, 3)*, that sort of thing, and would love to see an updated version of these stories. Or someone to do Guy Endore's *The Werewolf of Paris* as a movie, sticking to his book. I also liked *Wolfen* (not the same, I know). And *Cat People* (yes, far from wolves now and drifted from books to film). I'm enamored with ghosts and possession stories. There are a lot of supernatural creatures that haven't been given much sway in fiction and could be. Dawn Dunn wrote an erotic ghoul story for one of my anthos years ago that sticks with me. This fall, I have a new antho out which is all about Death as represented in the medieval *danse macabre* artwork.

What books would you have on your Top Five Most Influential?

Well, I generally don't have a top anything list, and kind of hate lists in general. One novel I loved was *Perfume* by Patrick Susskind. Also loved *The Catcher in the Rye, Frannie & Zooey* and the other two books by Salinger. Shirley Jackson is a favorite, particularly her exquisite story "The Lovely House". I don't like commenting too much on living authors, since too many are friends and people's feelings get hurt. Let's just say it's rare I've read a book I haven't found some value in.

To what does the vampire owe its longevity in all its mediums? There seems to be a never-ending cycle of their stories.

As I've said for most of my life, the vampire is an archetype (see Carl Jung for a definition) and that means it's in our collective psyche. The vampire has and will endure. One thing I loved doing was editing *Evolve: Vampire Stories of the New Undead,* and the next one *Evolve Two: Vampire Stories of the Future Undead.* Both of those books bring the vampire into the Now. They are stories for adults, not Twilight, not YA, but the vampire that has evolved in literature from its first mention until today, and into the future. These books, I believe, give a good insight into how the undead have moved along with humanity, how we view them and present them so that they remain with us. Anyone who seriously loves vampire fiction should get these two anthologies.

Will there be a third collection in the Evolve Series?

No, just the two. People have suggested I do a three, but I've done all I can with the vampire for now. One suggestion was to edit an antho called *Devolve,* but those are the vampire stories that have already been done in the past. I like fresh. As I said, I'm onto other anthos. *Danse Macabre: Close Encounters with the Reaper* focuses on the *danse macabre* Death. The stories cover a range of time and space and place and many are set today. It's a lovely book with superb writing, and I think readers will find the stories extraordinary in a variety of ways and my hope is to introduce the artwork to readers.

When editing, is there anything in particular that you look for in an author's work that you're drawn to?

I read a story first as a reader. Naturally, I'm drawn to certain styles—we all are—but I do have a range and my tastes are fairly eclectic. If I love a story, it's in. If I like it quite a bit, likely also in. If I like it but it has some problems, I get back to the author and say what doesn't work for me and perhaps make suggestions for a rewrite. Editing is personal.

A lot of people who slap the word 'editor' onto a book don't edit, they simply acquire. Of course, if it's a reprint anthology, you're buying a story that's already published so you take it as is. But I do anthos of original stories and that means the stories might need work. They also need to be part of the anthology theme as I envision it. There are plenty of stories available about Death but my vision is specific to *Danse Macabre* because I adore the artwork, which dates to the 1400s, and I wanted to present that approach to death, the dead leading the living to demise in various ways, a kind of dancing to the end of life. Get the book. You'll see.

What draws you to the 'Dark Side,' as it were?

I'm probably a functioning sick individual who would be either psychotic or a serial killer if I wasn't a writer/editor. A joke. Sort of. I think the dark side is far more interesting than the light side. What's in the light is clear and obvious and very predictable. Think about it. During the day you see all. At night, you can barely see, so anything can be there. The dark is the realm of imagination and inspiration for me. Anything can happen in darkness and it might not be completely clear or understandable enough to explain. It's thrilling, chilling, fun, horrifying, fantastical. And you get to live on the edge, which is living and not just existing.

Is there any particular book you wished you'd written?

Oh, too many to name. I'm in awe of other writers.

What was your take on Tim Burton's vision of Dark Shadows?

I liked it but didn't love it, but then I saw both *Dark Shadows* TV series and I'm kind of a traditionalist. I'm not much of a fan for modern (ok, the 70s in this movie) smart-ass characters being stupid and shallow and thinking they are witty because they are snarky. A lot of films go there. I'd rather have clever and droll, sophisticated crisp dialogue that isn't the predictable punch line. Sure, be cynical and sarcastic, but with style. I'm a fan of black humor. The movie was well done, and as I say, I liked it, though it got unnecessarily chaotic towards the end. I found the opening (set in the past and full of atmosphere) lovely. I generally adore Burton and also Depp, so I was hoping for more but got less.

Is the feminine approach to Horror much different than the masculine?

People argue about this all the time. In some ways no. But some women do tend to write about female characters differently. I write a lot of female characters. Well, I guess I write a lot of male characters too! (Laughs). Anyway, for example, my story "The Age of Sorrow", that's typically me. This story is a kind of the last woman on earth and pays homage to Richard Matheson's wonderful novel, and the three films: *The Last Man on Earth;*

Omega Man; I Am Legend. To my knowledge, no one had written the last woman on earth in the zombie/vampire (as you view them) plague. A woman has a whole set of different problems to contend with. That story was published by PS Publishing in the UK and reprinted in the US zombie reprint antho *The Living Dead,* edited by John Joseph Adams, which I believe is still in the stores.

That's just one example and I could give you several, from me, from others. Lucy Taylor writes some interesting stories with female characters from a woman-writer's perspective. Check out her clever and humorous story in *Danse Macabre.*

You've written for the VampErotica *Comics; how did that differ from the storytelling of prose?*

Lots less writing, for one thing! I had written 3 stories that formed a novella and *VampErotica* wanted to use them. I did the scripting, not the artwork, of course. It was an interesting project to try to find the essence of the stories so they could be presented in just a few words on a few pages. Brainstorm Comics, which publishes *VampErotica,* is doing a graphic novel called Nancy Kilpatrick's *Vampyre Theatre* that includes the 3 stories, the 3 comics, some interviews and other things, and a link for a free download of a song based on my stories, written and sung by the Vampire Beach Babes. It's been in the works for a while, so when it's finally out, I'll post it on my website and also my Facebook wall.

Did you have any favorite comics when you were younger? Any now?

I liked Classic Comics a lot, which were the stories of the Greek gods and goddesses and how they tortured and/or rescued us mere mortals. My cousin read romance comics which I saw when I visited her I always found them weird, those close-ups of The Faces just before The Kiss, or The Faces, Tear-Stained. I loved the Dracula comics and had #1 for many years. One of my favorites was the original Silver Surfer because I related to his alienation—also had the original #1 of that for a long time. And later, I liked Neil Gaiman's *Sandman* world. There are some lesser-knowns that I liked, goth comics mainly: *I Feel Sick; The Crow* (well, not lesser known); *Johnny the Homicidal Maniac; Gloomcookie; Lenore; Writhe and Shine.* These days I don't get to read comics much. I think the last one I read was *The Walking Dead*—love the comic, find the TV show infuriating as hell (but I watch anyway; only zombie show in town).

What kind of work can we expect from you in the future?

I've been working on a series of 7 novels, all at the same time—I told you I'm a maniac! They are in various stages of completion. Book 1 is done, books 2 and 3 and about 60,000 words in, and so on. I am also editing *Expiration Date*, out in 2013, more stories of death by various means. I always have short stories coming out. I have *Vampyric Variations* out, another collection of my vampire stories that includes 3 novellas, the longest an original work. Meanwhile, I'm also working on that unusual zombie novel I mentioned earlier. I do a lot of things and writing time is scarce and precious to me. For instance, I teach writing courses online for a college, and I do private editing for people as well. At the moment, I'm attending the FanTasia Film Festival n Montreal which is 3+ weeks so I'm seeing 2 to 3 movies a day and will review those for chizine.com (you can find reviews from previous FanTasias in the *chizine* archives). And I'll likely review some for *Doorways Magazine*, which has a new editor. All these things take a lot of time. And when I'm editing an anthology, that takes a mega amount of time. This is time that I cannot devote to writing. I need to win a lottery, find a patron or marry a millionaire (make that billionaire, just to be safe).

Thank you for the interview, Nancy. Anything you'd like to say to your fans?

Thank you so much to book buyers for reading and enjoying my work. I love hearing from people who read my books and stories so please, email me (email on my website). Or better yet, join me on Facebook!

MEGAN HART

DARK FANTASY AND THE like almost insist that the world of the erotic can compliment it quite nicely. Enter Megan Hart, who has exhibited the ability to write matters of both the arousing as well as the horrific and seamlessly blends the two in work of hers such as *Beg for It, Hold Me Close,* and *Vanilla* or the Order of Solace Series. Her more mainstream work (albeit with a tilt of the dark or spicy) like *Lovely Wild* or *Tear You Apart,* respectively, shows her voice is among the prominent and most versatile in the ever-changing world of Speculative Fiction.

Her website (perhaps predictably) is at meganhart.com.

You have a manner of being able to write in the sensual mind as well as in the darker aspects of the human psyche. How do you separate that?

In some ways, I don't. I've often thought that fear and love activate similar responses. Sweating. Pounding heart. (Sometimes screaming!)

I can't resist asking the clichéd question, what is the difference between erotica and pornography?

It's all in the eye of the beholder! But the way I look at it, pornography is most often visual, while erotica is more mental. Not always, of course, but that's a good place to start. Also, for me, erotica is meant to move you in more than simply physical ways, while porn is meant to arouse only the body. It can be a really subtle difference, though, and what's porn to one person is erotica to another and vice versa. I have written straight up porn, erotica, erotic fiction and erotic romance, and they all differ in the tone, content and word choices, but what makes them different is the intent behind the piece.

What goes into your preparation of writing a novel, and does it differ in it depending on what you're writing?

First, I avoid getting started as long as possible. Then I bully and chastise myself into getting to work. Then finally, once I get started, I pound away at the words until I finish the book! It doesn't differ much depending on what I'm writing. I almost always have to gear up before I can plunge in! But once I do, I can write fast and finish a project quickly.

What motivated your decision in posting playlists on your website in association with your work? It's a wonderful idea.

I write to music. I love music. Listening to a playlist while I'm writing can set the mood for me, so I have certain songs that fit a story and help me every day when I sit down to work. People seem to be interested in what goes into writing a book, and for me music is such a huge part of that, so I decided people might like to know what I was listening to! Also, I believe in spreading the love, so when I find music I love, I want to share it and let other people know about it.

How did you approach the writing of Every Part of You, *given that it was a serialized series?*

The same as anything else. Each piece had to end, for me, satisfactorily while at the same time leading into the next piece. I'd written a serial before, The Resurrected, which had a slightly different format, so it wasn't a completely new experience.

Why did you decide to use first-person view in a good amount of your work?

I'm not sure it was a conscious decision. Especially for erotic fiction, first person feels so intimate, it just fit. I like first person stories! Maybe I'm lazy, so I only need to write one point of view that way!

I have a horrible time writing dialogue. How do you come up with modern or entertaining dialogue without accidentally going into satire?

I try to write the way people talk, without the umms and likes and hmmms. I try to give each character a voice, too, distinct from the others, so if you read the dialogue without tags you can guess who's speaking. Real people have vocal tics or phrases they use a lot, and I think characters should too, but in way smaller amounts!

Do you keep anything special in mind when writing dialogue or the POV of a male character?

I do try to think how men speak differently than women. Never having been a dude, I can't say I always get it right, but I do try to make sure that in the POV of a male character or using his dialogue that I wouldn't have him speaking or thinking the way a woman would. Writing romance, too, there's a fantasy element to it. We want to read about a guy who talks and thinks in the way we'd love a guy to speak and think, maybe not necessarily how he would if he were real. So there's that, too.

Do you have a particular favorite work of your own?

Tempted is one of my favorites. *The Resurrected. Tear You Apart.*

When will we see a spinoff novel of Switch's *Eric?*

I'd love to write Eric's story! LOVE TO. And you know what? Maybe I will!

What's your opinion of "Mom Porn" like the Fifty Shades *wave?*

I don't care for the term, to be honest. I'm a mom, and my porn is certainly not gender specific! I think the phrase is a short cut to poke fun at the idea that women have sexual appetites. That's a hot button for me. I write sexy fiction for strong, sexy readers (of all genders and gender identities) and with no shame in the pleasure of it! I am happy the success of those books pushed people into reading, people who hadn't picked up a book for pleasure in years rediscovered the joys of a great read. Whether or not you think the books are good or not, they definitely turned mainstream attention toward erotic books, and that's been good for me!

What went into your signing on with Harlequin?

I'd been writing for small presses for a number of years. I'd never thought about being a Harlequin author because I didn't write category stories. At some point along the way, I'd already been writing sexier stories, leaning toward erotic romance (which was becoming more popular) and Harlequin Mira started their Spice line. I knew I had a story that would be a good fit, and I wrote it. That book was called *Dirty* and I just knew it was going to work for the line. It all happened from there.

What motivated you to write erotica, or any genre you've written in, published or not?

I write books I'd like to read. I like sexy stories about flawed people. I like scary stories about messed up people making bad choices. I like dense, character driven novels about tragedy and triumph. So, I write books I'd like to read!

What is it about Nietzsche that influences you?

To be honest, I don't know anything about Nietzsche. I just like the quote about chaos!

What do you do to unwind?

Watch movies. Read. Go to the ocean. Sleep!

Megan, thank you very much for taking the time to talk with me. What is to be expected from you in the future?

Right now, I've finished up two connected contemporary romances for Montlake Books. I'll have three paranormal erotic romance novellas out from Silhouette Nocturne. I'm writing a horror story for a project called Intersections, a Ouija themed anthology I'm putting together with my co-Captain Rob. E. Boley as well as some great authors, Douglas Clegg, Kerry Lipp, Sephera Giron, Brad C. Hodson and Chris Marrs. And I'll be starting a near future romance trilogy for St. Martin's very soon! Lots of irons in the fire!

BRUCE S. LARSON

OUT OF THE GREAT NORTHWEST comes author Bruce S. Larson, a storyteller continually gaining steam on the genres where weirdness and wonder can be found. From the short stories in the Grail series regarding a take on professional monster hunters to collections like *Nightmares and Other Vices Vols. 1* and *2, Zombie Domination* and his novel, *Beyond Apocalypse,* Bruce has proven a consistent imagination and a particular, unique voice in the field of speculative fiction.

Bruce's website can be found at thewritebruce.com.

Bruce, how has being from the Pacific Northwest effected your visions of the New Weird?

Epic scale. Trees towering overhead. Vast mountain ranges are visible east and west. Big animals like bears can roam outside even in the suburbs. Seriously. One was shot just a street over from where I live a few years ago. When I was a kid, we'd have to interrupt games of catch or Frisbee in the street so people on horses could ride through. Horses are big animals. As a small kid, they looked like living mountains on hooves walking on by. I even saw the ash plume of Mt. St. Helens eruption from 200 miles away. Friends and I would scale trees and look out across Puget Sound. So, things tower above as natural skyscrapers and it gives you a sense of a world greater in scale than what we humans typically live in. That, and we have some nice beaches.

Another thing is darkness. Not just the gloomy weather (that I love). I spent a lot of my childhood in the shade of evergreen forests. Some people equate darkness with evil. But if you push through darkness you can own the fear it might cause you. Thick forest was all around and even cloaked our local parks. Now, I can't image I'd want any child of mine to do what I did with my pals. I can hear my adult self yelling *Sonny! You could break your neck!* But alone, children are as adventurous as epic heroes. And yes our parents loved us, but the culture and perhaps locale granted us a lot of person freedom in childhood. So we children of the evergreens would brave spit bugs in tall grass, cross logs over swift streams, and snap spider webs across the darker, narrower trails to penetrate the shadows and maybe find a deep, black pond hidden in the woods.

And if there were older kids pounding stolen booze or smokes, we'd throw pine cones and run like hell! Off to the next adventure.

I think, later on as teens, some of us took bigger risks riding transit into downtown Seattle. The city. Now, there's a scary place. More people. Maybe more monsters. No ponds. Not natural ones, anyway.

I look back and feel fortunate to have lived where and when I did. It was a once rustic setting that slowly, sadly evolved into a full-on suburb. Now children of the smart phones push through glass doors and traverse crowds to ignore fountains in shopping malls as they stare at little, bright screens. And, thank you, Cris, for this opportunity to sound like a doddering 106 year old. (I AM NOT!)

But, you know, if they are reading a books of mine on those screens, it might be okay, after all.

What was the turning point for you to decide you wanted to pursue writing?

Like all artists, my creative interests are broad. But writing became the dominant outlet. Honestly, what made me focus on writing was a line from a TV mini-series. When I was a kid, perhaps in my teens, I saw reruns of *Roots: The Next Generations*. In it, James Earl Jones plays Alex Haley. He identifies himself on screen with the line: "Haley. Alex Haley. I'm a writer." I heard that and it just stuck in my head. My fate was decided. My creative energies were given a main focus. I was going to be a writer.

I wish I had started submitting much earlier than I did in the subsequent years. Experience is a form of success. There was the dream to submit. My Dad had seen his crime stories published in penny pulps of yore, many "yores" ago. (I was born late in my parents' life and my older siblings were already adults.) I wrote scripts and stories with an idea of sending them out that never left home. Eventually I wrote a short story I did submit. I guess I finally thought I had something that was good enough, even with smart friends, teachers, profs, and various professionals already thinking I had talent. Once I did that first submission—yep, rejected—I was off and have never stopped writing fiction. Of course, back then a few friends thought I was off my rocker for even trying. Yet here I am now being interviewed by a fellow writer after crafting several works for willing readers. So it hasn't all been rejections and frustration. Maybe mostly, but not all. (Laughs.)

Can you tell us about who influenced your writing?

There are those formative years when you are more sponge than spigot. I loved everything SF. I think I was drawn to SF by Surrealist art. My Dad was an influence, too, just by always being at his favored, old typewriter or scribbling on a legal pad. I graduated from staring at weird things to reading about the amazing. I think *Omni* magazine widened my experience of both and created a bridge between them. I was really into A.C. Clarke and Harlan Ellison. Later I found Philip K. Dick and still love finding a short story of his I have yet to read in some yellowed collection. It will be a sad day when that can no longer happen. I guess that's a reason to look forward to memory loss. Maybe.

Horror-wise, there were a lot of writers in the, I dare call it recent past, like yourself, who were getting short stories on magazine pages. I can think of Greg F. Gifune and Michael McCarty and wish I could name them all. You read a lot when you want to be part of the party. And there are the academic must reads that are also true impacts like when you read your first Poe, Bierce, and even the short works of that King dude. Heard of him? Right. Nathaniel Hawthorne, too. As a student I remember being captured by his atmosphere. Sometimes what they show you in school *is* worth reading, not just skimming for the test. Honest, kids.

In college I studied classic myth, along with biology, believe it or not. I'm still amazed at how many people have never heard of the *Epic of Gilgamesh*. But I'll evangelize on Utnapishtim or Atrahasis, later. I was taken by the continued influence of ancient writing on modern stories. I loved how Oliver Stone wrote his script for *Platoon*. It may be a grim and gripping war movie, but there is a lot in that script that's draws on Biblical characters such as Elijah and Ahab. So that style also had an impact on me.

I can never underestimate the influence of my parents who were always encouraging me to watch and read science related material. They bought me *Omni* and other magazines like *Discover*. Both of them were

SF fans. And my father's genes are certainly active in me. He was a writer, mostly for his military and pastoral professions, but always composing something for most of his life. He introduced me to SF through movies and books. Both my folks encouraged me to think, learn, and create.

Do your first influences still have an effect on your current writing?

They must, even if I don't think about it. You know, I once quit a Creative Writing class in ideological pique after the instructor said she would teach students to imitate their influences. *Bah! That is not creative!* I thought back then. But time and experience can make you reconsider your earlier, lofty scoffing. One reader commented to me that I reminded her of Harlan Ellison. She quoted from one of my short stories, and then Mr. Ellison to illustrate her point. I never set out to write like Mr. Ellison. (He would likely grumble if I did.) I simply try to write as Bruce S. Larson. Nevertheless, the influence is there. So, short answer: yes. Even if I'm consciously unaware of it. Here I thought I was channeling Aeschylus. *Ahem.*

You've also designed your own covers and exhibited some of your freehand work on your Facebook page. Who are some of your visual influences? Kirby certainly seems to be one. Is that accurate?

As far as the covers go, I have been privileged to have the expertise of graphics design pro Bonnie Hammond and the artistic skills of Erik England to make mere ideas become reality. I have endeavored to learn better technique on my own, but there is no substitute for an art professional's eye and skill with technology. Like any job, nothing ever materializes without work, submission, review, and finally approval. So I may have an idea, I may even throw together a mock-up, but it all goes through scrutiny. And changes. That said, I'm happy to be part of the process, and grateful for the artists and experts who make a book cover a thing to shine on the shelf, or beam off a reading screen.

As far as my personal influences, I suppose as a child who grew up reading comics it's fair to say there is an influence from them and from the greats like Kirby. As an adult, I find Kirby's output and imagination to be amazing. The comics I bought when young were done by subsequent artists and writers like Byrne, Simonson, among others. A lot of those were bought as back issues. Today, sites like "1970s Sci-Fi Art" post works by Kirby among fantastic vistas by Bob Eggleton and Rodney Matthews and many more. So you could almost call Kirby a new influence when

I doodle. When I was quite young I recall seeing some of Dali's work and trying to wrap my child's brain around it. Also as a kid, I found an old *World Book Encyclopedia, 1972 Year Book* in my Dad's office. It had a series of surrealistic "Inflation Monster" paintings by George Roth to illustrate an article. I was fascinated by the weirdness, and it stuck in the grey drive.

Is there a particular goal you have in mind regarding your artwork?

To have some fun with it and hopefully never be too embarrassed by it. What I post is usually solicited by friends. It's hobby. Writing is my refined field. I am ever aware I am not a trained pencil and pad artist. I know many people with visual arts training and talent. Hopefully they smile along with the rest of us looking at something I drew.

I actually might have more fun posting the odd link to my own site. There are fewer responses than to pretty pictures, but I see the clicks to my posts from "behind the curtain" in the meta-data. It's fun to see people actually take time to read a post. I can be a more free on the site with humor or diving into the surreal, as with the Spider Mercy stories. Perhaps cock an eyebrow with the parallel Earth bits. And it's all free folks!

You've written quite a bit regarding new takes on old monsters, such as the undead in Zombie Domination. *Do you have an affinity for any particular "classic" sort of monster like vampires, etc?*

Not for any single one. I like being an equal opportunity terrorizer. Sometimes a classic monster works well to support a theme. Sometimes you see a way to use classic beasties in new ways—or so you hope! Other times you just have a desire to dive into a sub-genre and do a cannon ball. Or, maybe just show you can swim. There is one story in that collection "Acid to Ashes" I dare to think is good. It takes a planet's zombie apocalypse and adds a dimension with another human-made monster. That monster is designed as something to make zombies run screaming. Most people know to run from zombies. But now what is that thing on the horizon? Don't just amp the gore. Expand the terror.

You've been able to use humor, or at least a cockeyed view of it, in some of your stories. How do you temper these stories so they're not too humorous (or not too scary) to take away from the thrust of the story?

Concise, dry wit. (Laughs.) Having a solid idea of the characters, helps. As in the Grail, or better known as Mr. Ice stories. That character has a grudging, yes, perhaps, cock-eyed view of the twisted world he hunts in. So I think he would leaven the sense of dread with dark humor. But ultimately he's there to kill something savage and at times that goes south, fast. So, it's not a part for Will Ferrell or Kevin Hart. To me, a sharp quip is better when unexpected. Especially from a person who seems dead serious. In a grim situation such as a dark, horrific future, the laugh comes as much from the surprise of the quip as the humor of the phrase. And, like jokes, it's timing. When describing gore and pain it's best to put the punch lines on hold. For a minute or two. A few of my family were career military and had interesting posts overseas. Having met a few "special operators" you get a sense they use humor, dark and otherwise, as a personal tactic. So I've incorporated that into some characters. It allows a person to acknowledge the danger, but helps them maintain a psychological grip. That, and I'm sort of deft, personally, with a witty phrase. No, really. Cris, why aren't you laughing?

Your novel, Beyond Apocolypse, *was sort of demons in SF Horror. What motivated your development in the story and will we be seeing more of that universe?*

I guess I'll answer the last part first. Is it a leak to say I already have maybe as much as a fourth of a sequel typed? I don't believe in staunching the creative flow if it starts. Just don't neglect your day job. No release date is set. I'm still waiting for J.J. at Disney and Guillermo del Toro and Legendary Pictures to call on the first book. (Pause.) See, there's that wit of mine. Or delusion. Any way. I sure as, well, hell, hope to drop another *Beyond Apocalypse* book. I think the first ends strong, and it ends big. But it's a universe we're talking about. A vast, fiery one. So there is potential lurking in the quantum entangled web of the Great Widow.

So, the second part. My motivation. Strap in. This could sound weird. Of course, you could say there is a rebellion theme through the book. In fact, it almost feels odd that rebellion is a theme within a lot of myth and religious tales where you might expect to read about obedience. (But I think all writers across time know how boring that would be.) The initial idea for *Beyond Apocalypse* was: if you lived in a universe where there was no doubt an almighty force was at work, and you in fact punch a time card for this demiurge, could you still be an agnostic? Odd question? Well, I have known many people who believe in a traditional or new age deity and practice a formal religion. Nevertheless, I see many ultimately form their own beliefs even if they don't reject their faith completely. The book's readers see an evolution in an important character who harbors a secret, personal faith that is ultimately based on something he never imagined. Apocalypse is a synonym for revelation. As individuals, we are always in discovery. I'm sure this is true if you are a thinking person born on Earth today, or a giant demon born in Hell in a far-future, dark age. Shocks to belief can get tricky if the fate of the universe is at stake. But this can happen to us all. So ultimately, no matter how powerful the forces are around you, as a thinking individual you will have personal apocalypses in life.

So, start with an odd concept and it develops into a theme. Then you add Hell, solar-scale machines of ancient origin, exploding planets, demons with guns, and epic battles that shape galactic history. Put them into a bag, then use the twist tie provided and shake. Stand back.

Beyond Apocalypse *struck me as having a strong Kirby New Gods/Starlin Thanos mythology influence?*

Well (laughs) I can see that. It was not the starting point. But I did like the Starlin-written Thanos when I was a teen after discovering old Adam Warlock back issues in a comics store. Mr. Warlock, or rather, Mr. Starlin, seemed influenced by Michael Moorcock. Kirby did a comics adaptation of Clarke's *2001: A Space Odyssey*, and I imagine was influenced by the cosmic scale of Clark and many SF and Fantasy writers. So I hope *Beyond Apocalypse* is in the epic tradition that influences a lot of Speculative Fiction.

Do you consider yourself to be an author of one genre over another?

I wanted to be a Science Fiction writer when I grew up. I still lean to it, but now I would say "no." And I think the concepts of branding may be changing as the market evolves. This can be beneficial to writers. A creative person is not constrained by one influence. I don't think any artist or writer is mentally bound to a single genre or style of expression. If you are a musician, you don't just play the saxophone. You might have a guitar in the corner at home. Singers also act, etc. I think genre constraints in writing mostly come from outside forces, those demiurges of publishing. But as long as I can, I hope to continue exploring possibilities in all fields. In the olden days, a writer used multiple pseudonyms for different genres. I see myself as a modern writer who combines aspects of the wide Speculative Fiction universe. I suppose that's my brand. Just don't try to fix it on me with searing metal. At least not without Tylenol.

What went into the creation of the character of Mr. Ice?

Oh, man. Here we go into weird again. It's like I'm an SF writer or something. Ultimately he is the redeemer on a fairly hellish Earth. He can't save everyone, but his temporary presence can destroy a monster and the situation it exploits and stop human predators as well. Then the survivors can build a better life. Sound thematically familiar? Perhaps even a bit messianic. Well, I wanted to use such a character theme in a future SF/Horror setting. I hope to fully illustrate the genesis of Joshua Grail, AKA the well-armed Mr. Ice, in his own novel down the road. Before then, a collection of all those stories with new ones is a certainty. And here is a note to others on persistence: rejection in one market is not doom for a character. Grail/Ice started as scripts for more adult-oriented comics. Yet he came to readers' attention in prose. Writing those scripts helped me master the short-short story. That skill has helped me in every other length and format of writing. But Mr. Ice also brought me some drinking silver when I wrote the scripts into prose and then sold the stories. Like any predator, a writer must adapt. And, crumbs! sometimes you even make a "kill." That being an acceptance letter.

Are there sub-genres in the SF and H fields that you prefer or would like to write in?

I feel a Western is in me somewhere, *pardner*. But that's not SF or H. It could be. With zombies. Or maybe a bar set in a trans-temporal nexus in the Old West. I may have done that one, already. But if I think I can see a dimension in something I'd like to explore, I'll go for it. The inspiration can pop for any genre or its subsets. You run with an idea and it may become a completed story. Some ideas sit as sort of "pet thoughts" for a while before even becoming written notes. Such as? Well, I see Shelley's Frankenstein's Monster as the first classic SF monster. Now he'is seen by many as part of the same family of much older monsters such as vampires. But ol' Frankie was created when science replaced magic as a means for conjuring. Now both exist in the collective myth of Horror. But what of real and natural terrors such as a rabid grizzly bear? Fear of that real monster is certainly older than fear of supernatural monsters, and so science created beasts as well. Each could fall within its own sub-genre. Can you imagine a story with all three? (Minus Abbott and Costello.) Vamp. Frank. And Smoky in a 'roid rage. I want to write that Horror story. Not only because it has classic creatures of different origins, but you can explore and compare the types of monsters. So keep a look out for that one, and other, um, recombinant stories. Writing is exploration.

How has your creative process changed from when you started?

Speed, mostly. I know there are faster writers. But I'm not slow. I've generated six books in five years and I hope to become more efficient and keep getting better as a writer. I think I'm better at layering multiple themes into my stories. I also know there are more eyes on my pages, so I feel a duty to keep making good stories, long or short. There are readers who know my work, and those who will discover it—whom I hope will be a very large number one day. Like tomorrow. *Ahem.* The speed allows me to create more content in less time and keep perfecting the craft. It allows me to tackle a plot I might have once considered something that needed more development time. But I do feel a responsibility to write well and keep people entertained, and perhaps even give them an idea to consider they didn't see coming.

What projects do you have in the works you can tell us about?

Well, if del Toro or Abrams do contact me—or now you're laughing!—I may have to delay these projects. But just in case, here goes: There will be a collection of the Joshua Grail/Mr. Ice stories coming soon. All the SF-Horror you love in compact stories and longer ones with no less punch. I want to follow that with a Grail/Ice novel that steps back to his first encounters with monsters in the Earth-spanning megalopolis. We'll learn what motivates a man to face death, or, perhaps worse, look to inflict it on savage predators of various origins.

In the future we will see a sequel to *Beyond Apocalypse*. There is a huge ax floating in space and a massive, black sword on its own trajectory, and there are hands and other appendages looking to wield them. Secrets lurk in Hell that threaten the hope of peace in the smoldering galaxy and the universe beyond. The giant arachnid mind of the Great Widow has more revelations to spin. And what lives on Hell's very surface seeking vengeance against creation? Hmm. I'm fairly sure we will all find out.

The one thing leading all projects out of the gate is the novel *Caught Dead*. In it I invert the zombie epic and add the dimension of a spy thriller. And, yes, maybe an undead horde, or two. The hero, Dr. Dean Cedars, has survived an assassination attempt. Mostly. He's dead, but is now a zombie on the run. The information on intelligent undead in his brain is wanted by governments and other powers. They'll do anything to get it, including slicing off Dean's head. Although technically dead, he'd like to avoid this. He hopes to complete his work and restore his life. But perhaps completing his work will bring apocalypse. He has an underfunded and outgunned ops team protecting him, and he may even be able to trust them. But then he learns who was really behind his research and why. Revelations keep popping up, and so do enemy agents with circular saws. Dean would pull his hair out, if he wasn't afraid his scalp might come with it.

And because *Zombie Domination* has done well, I may just whip up more hordes of the undead. I admit to being a bit like my Viking ancestors, so if the numbers are there, the words will follow. Readers are one of a writer's biggest influences.

JAY WILBURN

Speculative authors are people, too, and therefore, Jay Wilburn is a stay-at-home dad as well as a voice in contemporary Horror and Science Fiction. His works have appeared in anthologies like *Bleed* and *Zombies: More Recent Dead* as well as his twelve-book cycle, *Dead Song Legend Dodecology*. I was anxious to interview a fellow parent who specialized in some of the darker aspects of literature, and Jay did not disappoint!

His website is jaywilburn.com

Being a dad myself, I'm curious as to your opinions on child-rearing by a stay-at-home-dad who writes Horror?

My personal beliefs tend toward traditional Christian and politically libertarian. I give my kids pretty strict guidelines on right and wrong with the caveat that we don't tell people outside our house how to live their lives. Most of the time I just make an effort to not lose my cool every time I have to correct them and I count that as a victory. I don't get upset when they read or think for themselves. On politics and such, I just tell them people think different things and I try to articulate both sides of whatever they're asking about. I'll say I don't know as often as I can get away with it.

Dead Song Legend Dodecology is a rather unique twelve-book cycle. Could you give us an idea of what went into the initial concept and what goes into making them a reality?

It started as a weird short story that I gave to a charity anthology that asked for weird zombie stories. It was a nameless character in a sound booth doing a voice over about music collectors in the apocalypse. It shouldn't have worked as a story. It got picked up by Best Horror of the Year and then someone paid me to reprint it again. I decided to work it into a novel. I could tell it wouldn't fit, so I thought it would be a trilogy. When I realized it was bigger, I outlined the entire mythology and realized it would be twelve books. I decided to go for it and even hired a producer and musicians to help me record songs described in the story. Luke Spooner came on for the art including covers and interior illustrations and volunteered a song too.

Do you have a routine where you write at a certain time for a planned amount of work?

I ghostwrite too, so to get the work for hire done and my own work too, I have to produce volume. At one point, that was ten to twelve thousand words a day and meant writing from morning to night with short breaks every day. I've changed it up where I had a couple days each week dedicated to only my work. As I've dealt with health issues, I've needed more rest and don't hit those kind of numbers each day. I tend to look at deadlines and split projects over a number of days. I set times on each project. I'll stop on this at 10 AM. I'll stop on that at noon. I'll work on this until 2. I find that I get further than I expect and can take longer breaks or spend more time on a project, if I'm ahead. I am prone to long naps too.

Time Eaters *involves time-travel; did you approach the writing of it because of the SF/H combination?*

I was a sci fi reader before I was into horror. I tend to write more horror. I had an idea of doing a time travel novel where characters faced the natural consequences of discovering time travel. When I mapped out what those would be, it became a horror novel too. As I figured out the story, it even became extreme horror. I wrote several time travel short stories as practice to work out story, rules, and details. A number of those sold. Sci-Fi and Horror used to be more closely linked in film, television, and print than how they are viewed today. What I found with *Time Eaters* is that the typical sci fi time travel reader is not prepared for extreme horror. That is a polarizing book as a result. On the various review sites and blogs, it tends to bounce between one and five star reviews with very little between.

Given the opportunity, would you return to teaching?

No. I think I did good things as a teacher, but I was done. Public school is a system with some tragic, fatal flaws. It is a real disservice to students and our nation as a result. For teachers, it is ridiculously hard and overwhelming in ways that are difficult to compare to any other job anywhere. What teachers have to put up with is so far beyond what most people understand that it is a wonder they can hold on from year to year. On a personal level, after I made that leap to full-time writing, something changed in me. I can't go back. I let my certificate lapse and watched the bridge collapse behind me.

With ghostwriting, what are some of the upsides and downsides of writing on someone else's behalf?

I greatly expanded my toolbox. I took risks and learned things that I wouldn't have done for my own work. I created an immunity to writer's block. I now have the ability to take ideas that shouldn't work and then construct viable stories out of them. Ghostwriting money is considerably faster than money that comes from my own publishing, so it is a good supplement. Some people can be ridiculous and some are downright crazy. You can just walk away from them though. I went to a bookstore and found works that I ghostwrote on the shelves in biographies, self-help, nonfiction, romance, Fantasy, and Sci-Fi. I know I'm good enough to get works on the shelves, but those books made it where they did because of the names attached to what I wrote. I've worked for people I have to pretend not to know at conventions as others fawn over them and their work. It has taken some of the magic out of the industry for me, but I'm not intimidated by those people or those publishers. They may not want my name yet, but obviously they want the quality of work I can produce.

How did you get into ghostwriting? Is it something you'd recommend it?

I quit teaching to take care of my son who was sick. I was making some money from writing, but not consistently and not fast. I started small on the freelance websites and built my reputation up from there. I started getting middle range work and bigger off site name jobs and then was paying rent, groceries, bills, my own travel, and editing/ art/ formatting costs for my books with ghostwriting money and my own publishing. I would never tell someone they should do it and wouldn't tell them not to. It is a slow build and it is the Wild West out there. You compete against everyone and everything is unsure. Giving up the work forever is a huge leap that not everyone can do. Every scene, every story, and every character you create can never be used by you again. That terrifies some. I have no fear of running out of ideas, so I'll use a great idea for a ghostwritten work, knowing I can come up with something else for myself.

Do you write anything (ghostwritten or not, keeping in mind you may not be able to say much about the specifics of what you ghostwrite) outside the Horror genre?

I write sci fi and steampunk and will dabble in work other places. Ghostwriting I do everything. I write nonfiction, spiritual, romance, literary, genre work of all types, and more. Every style has its own rules and expectations.

You wrote The Enemy Held Near *with Armand Rosamilia. How do you approach working with another author?*

The collaboration dictates the style. Oftentimes you alternate chapters or write different characters. The more loosely you hold the story, the better the product will be. If you let the story develop itself beyond whatever outline you start with, you can make something amazing that is greater than what could have done on your own. *The Enemy Held Near* may be my greatest work to date as a result.

What made you decide to use a mute boy as the narrative voice in your novel, Loose Ends?

This is probably high minded for a zombie novel, but I was a big fan of Kurt Vonnegut's style of using a narrator that was technically in the story, but seemingly observing the characters and action from the outside. It was a first person novel, but being mute at the time of the experiences he is narrating, he relates events without steering the other characters directly all the time. Also the boy grew up largely after the zombie apocalypse, so he relates what the adult characters talk about, but his perspective and point of reference on their cultural references is outside the experience of the characters and the audience. I thought, ironically, the mute narrator provided a unique voice.

Would you say zombies are your favorite "classic" monsters?

Yes. I think they still have the most untapped story potential. More has not been done with them than has been done. They may be the most over-used, but under utilized monster available.

Who would you consider your contemporaries?

I lose my shit when people like Joe McKinney, Jonathan Mayberry, or Brian Keene know who I am or react to a story or say my name on a podcast. They are the guys I read before I was writing professionally. I am rereading all of Stephen King's work to learn everything I can from him and what he does. They are before me and above me. I am friends and peers with Armand Rosamilia, Mark Tufo, Jack Wallen, Max Booth III, Jessica McHugh and many more. These folks are all better than me in important ways and I strive to do the best I can because they show me what is possible.

You have a patreon.com page where you post readings of your work. What is your impression thus far on the impact fan-funding sites like that are having on writers?

I will give whatever sources that I can a try. Sometimes I have people jump on that one and sometimes I run dry. Everything is hit or miss and some people make it work. The market is always shifting and you get on board where you can, if you want to keep up.

What sort of entertainment not Horror-oriented do you enjoy?

I ride a bicycle. I read widely. I shoot a bow and arrow. I live near a beach and take my kids there. I'll binge watch TV shows on Hulu or Netflix.

What can you tell us about your future projects?

I'm about to release the first book of *The Great Interruption* that I wrote a long time ago. It's a different sort of apocalyptic story. I'm writing and will make a quick turn around on *My Racist Summer*. This is a political/ crime thriller satire about a progressive journalism student that is accidentally assigned to intern at a white supremacist newspaper during the summer of 2016 and they react to all political and social news of this summer. I'm tracking news stories as they unfold this summer and writing these characters' reactions to them and arguments about them. The story will reflect back our own social media dialogue to us in all its bare ugliness. Book 4 of the Dead Song Legend will come out some time this winter.

RICHARD CHIZMAR

IT'S NOT EASY WRITING AN INTRODUCTION for Richard, as what can you say when Stephen King himself interviewed the man when Richard's website went live? Richard is the founder and publisher of the premiere Horror magazine, *Cemetery Dance* as well as Cemetery Dance Publications, which offer premium editions of works penned by some of the most legendary names in the genre. The anthologies he's edited alone number over thirty, and the man's made his mark as an award-winning author, nabbing two World Fantasy Awards, four International Horror Guild Awards, as well as HWA's Board of Trustee's Award.

Richardchizmar.com is where he resides in cyberspace.

What do you feel is the motivating factor for the attraction to Horror as entertainment?

Escapism, thrill seeking, and many people just flat out enjoy being scared…as long as they can turn on the lights afterward and go upstairs to their warm and cozy and safe bed.

Given you are working with names such as Stephen King, how do you view the new wave of Horror authors?

I'm excited about what is happening in the genre today. There aren't as many quality mass market or independent publishers as there once was, but a handful are still alive and kicking, and the most talented authors are still finding their way. Sometimes through the more traditional path of publishing and sometimes via the self-publishing route. It's a wide open genre right now, and writers like Josh Malerman, Michael Wehunt, Sarah Pinborough, Rio Youers, and a whole bunch of others are leading the way.

Are there any authors out there that you enjoy reading who you would like to see get more exposure?

Too many to list here. But I believe the persistent ones will see their way into higher circulation print in time. Exposure has to be earned the old-fashioned way—hard work and dedication. There truly are no shortcuts.

Cemetery Dance became a kind of gold standard in the genre, growing as it did to establish itself. Do you think someone else could create another Cemetery Dance *now or in the future by a similar evolution?*

Sure, it could happen. All it would take is someone with a head full of dreams, a big heart, a refusal to fail, and an overwhelming love for scary stories. In fact, I hope it does happen. I really need another good magazine to read.

Was there a specific thing you looked for when choosing material for inclusion in the magazine's early days?

Story, plain and simple. Of course, I paid attention to writing style and characterization and theme, but my main focus was always in the story. Did it capture my imagination and take me to another place? Did the story frighten me, put me on the edge of my seat, did it make me think about the world around me?

Has there ever been a concern about your role as editor taking time or attention away from your own writing?

Oh, yeah. All the time. In fact, I didn't write much prose at all for about a ten-year period. Wrote some non-fiction and some screenplays, but mostly focused on the publishing business and raising my sons. In the earlier days, it was a constant struggle and juggling act, and the publishing business *always* took precedence. One of the nice things—and there are many—about having a great staff of co-workers is that I now have time to write every day. It's been a long time coming, and I'm really enjoying it.

What goes into the picking of a particular author's specific work for the limited editions?

First and foremost, if I publish you, it means I am a huge fan of your writing. That sounds awfully simple, but I know from almost 30 years of experience, that it's simply not always the case with every publisher. Sometimes, commercial considerations take priority. Publishing limited editions is an expensive and risky prospect, so we certainly include commercial viability in our decision-making, but it's not the first thing we look at. That philosophy has worked well for us for 28 years now.

What are some of your current projects in screenwriting?

Couple really exciting scripts that I can't talk about yet, sorry! I'm also about to start writing a good, old-fashioned slasher film for an indie company. Really excited about this one.

When adapting another author's work, how much communication is there between you and the writer?

It really depends on the particular project and author. Usually, there is very little communication with the writer unless he is involved with the film as a producer or director. Some authors get final approval of the script, but that is rare.

Is there a particular screen adaptation you'd like to write?

I would have loved to adapt the remake of Stephen King's *IT*. As for other dream projects, I'd have to give the nod to Robert McCammon's *Boy's Life* and Dan Simmons' *Summer of Night*.

Any particular one you'd like to avoid?

No specific titles come to mind, although it would be a difficult task to adapt a novel I didn't enjoy. Too many other good ones to play around with.

How has social media affected your writing and editing?

Social media has definitely helped me establish contact and communicate with many readers who enjoy my writing and the books I edit and publish. It's been a wonderful thing in that regard. It's also allowed many editors and publishers to reach out and invite me to contribute to their projects. That's always a nice thing. The best thing about social media is having the ability to instantly talk books and movies with a whole bunch of like-minded folks.

As not only an editor, but as a writer, do you see any ebb and flow regarding certain situations/monsters? In other words, vampires, haunted houses and other classic tropes? Any you'd like to see the end of?

Absolutely. Like any other entertainment field, there has always been a cyclic nature to the Horror genre—in both literature and film. Supernatural, psychological, vampires, zombies, evil little kid, haunted house, and many more—they all have had their time in the spotlight…and they all will again.

Given you're always doing what seems like ten projects (at least) at once, what do you do when you find time to unwind?

Most of my down time is spent reading for pleasure, watching movies, fishing, and watching my sons' sports team play several times each week. I'm very fortunate. It's a good life.

What can we expect to see from you in future?

The rest of 2016 is busy for me. My short story collection, *A Long December*, is due from Subterranean Press in early November. *Darkness Whispers*, a novella I co-wrote with Brian Freeman will be published later in November from Scarlet Galleon Publications. And, finally, *Heroes*, a chapbook featuring my short story and the script adaptation (co-written with John Schaech) and a comic adaptation, as well as a brand new introduction and afterword, will see print from SST Publications in December. I also have brand new short stories appearing in a variety of exciting anthologies and magazines including *Dark Hallows 2, Christmas Horrors, You, Human,* and *Ellery Queen's Mystery Magazine.*

ROB E. BOLEY

Rob E. Boley is a man who likes to keep busy. His engaging series, The Scary Tales, involving mash-ups with familiar fairy tales with classic Horror creatures is going into its sixth book with *That Crooked Mirror*. He's branched out into the world of coloring books with Amy Kollar, using a Kickstarter campaign for *That Naughty Pipe*. His passion for writing is contagious to his readers, and carries them along twisted carnival mirrors of imagination, and his shorter works like "All of the Above", "A Clown and a Dragon Walk Into a Bar" and "The Yard" only illustrate that further.

Robeboley.com is where the man resides online.

What goes on in your creative process when writing in the Horror gene?

The horror genre is a great fit for me because I've dealt a lot with anxiety over the years. When I was younger, I wasted countless hours worrying about horrible things happening to me. Now, as a horror writer, I can channel that energy into my stories. So, instead of dwelling on awful things happening to me, I conjure up terrifying things that will happen to my poor characters. It's a win-win. I get some relief from anxiousness and my readers get some tense tales.

So, my creative process is essentially productive worrying to the detriment of my characters. Don't get me wrong, I like my characters. I get to know them and I enjoy spending the time with them. But if it's them or me, they're going to get the axe any day of the week!

Would you consider the Scary Tales *Series being part of the mash-up approach we see with such things as* Pride and Prejudice and Zombies?

Sure, *The Scary Tales* would definitely appeal to readers of mash-up stories like *Pride and Prejudice and Zombies*. I didn't ever intend to write a mash-up series. What happened was, my daughter had a phase when she was in pre-school during which she wanted to watch Disney's *Snow White* movie several times a week. So, I'd watch it with her. But after seeing the same thing over and over again, the ending really got on my nerves.

It was too easy. I couldn't fathom why anyone as intelligent and merciless as the Queen would take the time to create a curse that could be so easily broken. So I had the thought that the Prince's kiss could actually be a catalyst for a second, more viral phase of the curse. And boom—Snow White wakes up as a zombie.

Originally, I'd envisioned it as a short story, but once I started writing it, the characters propelled the story into a full-blown novel. Except that novel became a planned trilogy. Once I started incorporating elements from *The Wolfman* and *Frankenstein*, I soon realized that I could mash-up all the other major monsters from the classic Universal Pictures films. And so, a series was born.

I think what sets *The Scary Tales* apart from other mash-up series is that I'm not mocking the original source material. I absolutely love fairy tales and the Universal Pictures films. Marrying them together has been an honor and a treat. Essentially, the series is my love letter to those films written in the margins of Grimm's Fairy Tales.

With the series now well underway, did you approach writing That Merciless Truth *any differently from the previous stories?*

Each of the books definitely has its own arc and mood. This novel starts with the band of would-be heroes completely wrecked and split apart. Some are dead. Some are prisoners. Some are stranded and injured.

It begins in a very dark place. This gives me some time to develop the characters as individuals apart from the group. Specifically, this books features a lot of Queen Adara (the somewhat-evil queen who conjured that wicked apple) struggling on her own. She's quickly become one of my favorite characters in the series, and this book really showcases how she's grown as a person since her curse backfired on her.

This book also introduces Goldenlocks, my mash-up of Goldilocks and *The Mummy*. Her character is several hundred years old, so her origin allows me to explore the ancient history of the Land, the medieval fairy tale world in which *The Scary Tales* series is set. Some of this history has been hinted at in previous books, but now the readers get to see it.

This book also sets the stage for an epic battle to come in the next book, *That Crooked Mirror: A Scary Tale of Cinderella & The Invisible Man*.

Have you considered a particular fairy tale character, but then set the idea aside to wait until it followed the release of another book?

Not really. Most of the main mash-ups used in the series have come along at the right time as the overall plot has advanced. I have come up with a few ideas that don't really fit with *The Scary Tales* main narrative, so I've considered doing a book of related short stories or novellas at some point.

I also recently had a successfully funded Kickstarter for a *Scary Tales* spin-off coloring book! It's called *That Naughty Pipe: A Scary Tale of the Pied Piper and Gremlins*. For this book, I'm partnering with an amazing artist and fellow Daytonian, Amy Kollar Anderson. I've been a huge fan of her art for years, and she loves my *Scary Tales* series. So, it's been a real pleasure working with her. The coloring book should be out in sometime this fall.

Has there been a twist in a story for the series that you decided against for being too dark?

Quite the contrary, actually! There's a big moment at the end of the forthcoming *That Crooked Mirror: A Scary Tale of Cinderella & The Invisible Man* that my editor tried to talk me out of. It's a harsh scene, for sure, and it's going to break some readers' hearts, but it was the right thing for the story.

This series has a lot of dark moments, but they're broken up with plenty of humor and lightness, too. And while I like readers to enjoy it and have fun, I still want to keep this *anything-can-happen* tone. I mean, it's a freakin' zombie apocalypse. No one is safe! Any post-apocalyptic tale starts to lose me when it seems like the characters are immune to mortal danger. That's not how life works, and it shouldn't be how stories work either.

In the original fairy tales, the villain's motivation isn't always made clearer than "well, they're evil." Do your antagonists see themselves as evil?

No, no, no! I'm a firm believer that everyone sees themselves as the hero in their own story. A villain who is evil for evil's sake is pretty damn boring. For that matter, I like my heroes to be pretty flawed. Hence, you get Grouchy the dwarf who struggles with anger and jealousy. Or Snow White who tries to drown her personal demons with alcohol. Or Red Riding Hood who acts super rude because she's insecure about losing control.

Since I alternate my chapters from different characters' points-of-view, it allows me to delve not just into the motivations of the heroes, but also the villains. When I started writing the background for Queen Adara (the evil queen), I wanted to give her a real tangible reason for creating that curse. I gave her a troubled past, an abusive father, and the loss of her sister—her best friend and Snow's mother. Adara's character arc in the series is pretty epic. She goes through a lot.

Do you see the series going on indefinitely?

Nope. *The Scary Tales* will end with Book 9. However, I haven't ruled out the possibility of creating more spin-off stories, such as the coloring book mentioned above. If enough of those happen, I'd love to see them collected in a book at some point.

Also, I love the idea of doing *A Scary Tales Holiday Special*. It would be a wintry tale featuring Yeti and a mash-up of several different holidays like Christmas, Hanukkah, and Kwanza.

As a parent, it interests me to know how you approach with what can be a rather unsavory genre as a parent yourself?

Interesting question. The thing is, my daughter has been integral to my evolution as a writer. Before becoming a dad, I wrote almost exclusively poetry. Something about becoming a parent grounded me, though. It made me take root and grow and delve into longer projects. I suddenly had stories to tell. Shortly after she was born, I started writing.

The first story I had published, a dark take on *The Cat in the Hat*, was inspired by reading that book to her. The first book I had published, *That Risen Snow*, came as a result of her, too.

But honestly, I don't think about her as I'm writing horror. Like, I don't think about what she'd think if she read the horrors I produce. I simply write the stories as they come to me. Sometimes, though, I think being a parent gives you a unique insight into real horror. Being a parent is a unique kind of love. And with that comes a unique kind of hurting. I'm sure I've tapped into that with some of my stories.

With your own writing, which form did it first take; screenplay, short story, etc?

Early on, I mostly wrote poetry, everything from sex to nature to everyday life. After becoming a parent, I started writing fiction. I think I cranked out a few short stories first, followed by some screenplays that I never did anything with. I then went on to write, hell, three books that are still sitting in a closet. I think each of them has some great moments and original notions, but I don't know if I'll ever get around to cleaning them up and making them publishable.

Eventually, I'd like to write a screenplay for the first book in *The Scary Tales* series. I'd love to see these books on the big screen, or even as a T.V. series. I've also recently delved back into poetry, except now I'm writing mostly horror poetry. I'll have a few poems published later this year.

Is there a story, regardless of medium or genre, you wish you could've written?

The first two that pop into my head aren't books. I'm not sure what that says about me as a writer . . .

The first is the comic book series *Locke and Key*, written by Joe Hill, illustrated by Gabriel Rodríguez, and published by IDW Publishing. I'm love Joe Hill's novels and short stories, but *Locke and Key* may be my favorite work of his. It has everything I love in a great story—imaginative fantasy, flawed yet likable characters, insightful flashbacks, solid character arcs, compelling darkness, and riveting tension. Add to that Rodríguez's gorgeous artwork and you've got a damn masterpiece!

The second is the *Serenity* movie written and directed by Joss Whedon in follow up to the *Firefly* T.V. series. A lot of folks aren't wild about the movie, but I think it's a tight piece of writing. He only had two hours to introduce viewers to these amazing characters and their world, to juggle multiple character arcs, and to provide a fitting conclusion that would've spanned over several seasons. And wow, the result is epic.

What do you keep in mind when writing material geared specifically to the Young Adult market?

This is something I struggle with. You ask a hundred writers what's appropriate for a young adult reader and you'll get a hundred different answers. I think the important thing when writing YA is to try to remember what it was like when you were a young adult—to get in touch with that stage of life.

It's such a fascinating point in a person's life, when you're balancing on this precipice. You suddenly have so many new powers and yet often so few real responsibilities. You have so many freedoms and yet you're not yet your own person. Like Alice Cooper said, "I'm in the middle without any plans, I'm a boy and I'm a man." It's a wonderful and horrible place to be, so it's no wonder that so many great stories come from it.

How much planning do you put into your stories?

For me, much of the creative process happens on a subliminal level. I don't actively plot or outline my stories. Rather, I start with characters and a problem, and then figure it out as I go. Most of the major swerves or revelations happen either spontaneously during the act of writing or while I'm doing something relatively mindless like driving to work or walking around the neighborhood.

When I studied under fantasy writer Jeffrey Ford at the Antioch Writers' Workshop, he said this amazing thing like, if you already know the story before you begin, then it's dead on arrival. I couldn't agree more. I love it when my characters surprise or shock me, because I know they'll definitely do the same to my readers.

When will we be seeing a collection of your work or novel outside of Scary Tales?

Hopefully, you'll be seeing a non-Scary Tales novel in the near future. I've written a post-apocalyptic zombie/ghost novel set in the near future and am currently shopping it around. Imagine *Night of the Living Dead* meets *Beetlejuice*, set in a three-story blanket fort. Boom! That's it in a nutshell.

I've already written Book 7 of *The Scary Tales*, and Book 6 is currently in production. So, since I'm near the end of the series and already one book ahead, I'm working to have other books in the pipeline. Aside from the one mentioned above, I've got early drafts and ideas for plenty of others. I'm even bouncing around ideas for a collaboration with an amazing fellow horror/fantasy author. As for a collection, that's something I'm considering. I have enough short stories that have been published over the years that I could put together a decent collection. I'm sure it's only a matter of time.

Is there a specific genre outside of Horror that you'd recommend to up-and-coming writers?

My advice to up-and-coming writers is to read as much and as often as they can. And definitely, don't limit yourself to one genre. Read everything. Young adult. Fantasy. Contemporary. Non-fiction. Romance. Science fiction. All of it will inform your writing in one way or another. I think the biggest thing is to not limit yourself to one or two genres. Branch out. Odds are, you'll be glad you did.

As well, read articles, especially science and history. Watch *Ted Talks*. The more fascinating notions you can feed your brain, the better! I can't tell you how many times I've read an article or watched a clip online, and it provided a perfect idea for the story I was writing at the time. The more interesting tidbits you can toss into your brain, the more likely you'll have one of these serendipitous moments.

What would you like to see more of in contemporary Horror?

Honestly, there's so much great horror out there right now and I've read only a fraction of it. So, I don't know that I can say with any authority what I'd like to see more of. Odds are, someone's already doing a hell of a job writing it.

But I'll tell you what I like. I like horror that's gritty and vicious and keeps me tensely turning pages, like Kealan Patrick Burke's *Kin* or anything by Jack Ketchum. I like horror that's immaculately written featuring surprising combinations of sensory detail, sex, and gore—such as Megan Hart's zombie serial, *The Resurrected*. I like horror that features brilliant spins on old tropes set in gorgeously described settings, such as *Those Across the River* by Christopher Buehlman.

Do you still have involvement in wolf sanctuaries?

I wish! Far too long ago, I made two volunteer visits to Mission: Wolf, an amazing wolf sanctuary in a desolate part of Colorado. The first visit in particular was a life-altering event for me. I spent about a month there building fences, caring for the wolves, and doing a variety of tasks. It showed me that I could do anything. Oddly, I didn't write a single sentence or stanza while there that was worth a damn, but it was a blissful experience all the same. I'd love to return sometime with my daughter, maybe when she's a bit older.

For now, she and I make at least two volunteer trips per year to help out a wilderness preserve here in Ohio called the Arc of Appalachia. I've served on their board of trustees and have been volunteering with them in some capacity for over fifteen years. People think of Ohio and they think of cornfields. But we have some amazing wilderness here, and the lovely folks at the Arc of Appalachia are protecting as much of it as they can.

What sort of genre stories do you enjoy now; Game of Thrones, Preacher…?

One of my favorite reads right now is the *Saga* sci-fi comic book series written by Brian K. Vaughan, illustrated by Fiona Staples, and published by Image Comics. I'm a huge fan of Vaughan's work, and *Saga* is him at the top of his game. Image is also publishing a great horror comic series called *Wytches,* written by Scott Snyder and illustrated by Jock. It's creepy as all hell. Oh, and I love *The Walking Dead* comic series by writer Robert Kirkman and artist Tony Moore. The show has its moments, but the comic is straight-up brilliant.

I'm a sucker for a good BBC crime drama, too. I'll binge watch shows like *Luther, Happy Valley,* or *The Fall* any day of the week. I love anthology-style shows like *The Twilight Zone,* too, and have found the British *Black Mirror* series created by Charlie Brooker to be wonderfully imaginative.

What things do you have planned for the future?

I'm currently working on a Ouija board-inspired horror anthology with author Megan Hart. It's called *Intersections: Seven Tales of Ouija Horror*, and it looks to be an eclectic collection. We've recruited an impressive line-up of authors for the book, including Douglas Clegg, Sephera Giron, Chris Marrs, Brad C. Hodson, and Kerry Lipp. It'll be released for a limited time on Friday, January 13, 2017.

Beyond that, I'll be finishing up *The Scary Tales* series. It'll be a relief to wrap that story up, but I will certainly miss those characters. Like I said, I wouldn't be surprised if I come back to them eventually. First, though, I have a whole array of other books that I need to finish. I have ideas for a serial killer book, a ghost story book, and even a paranormal romance. Lately, I've been writing a lot about ghosts, so don't be surprised if my next non-*Scary Tales* book features some spooks and spirits.

www.ingramcontent.com/pod-product-compliance
Lightning Source LLC
Chambersburg PA
CBHW060314230426
43663CB00009B/1698